FOREVER STRONG

FOREVER STRONG

THE STORY OF 75 SQUADRON RNZAF 1916-1990

Norman Franks

Foreword by Leonard Cheshire

Random Century

The author, publisher, and 75 Squadron Association would like to acknowledge the invaluable research undertaken by Robert Moore in the early stages of the preparation of the manuscript for this book.

Design and production by G. Leather

Random Century New Zealand Ltd
(An imprint of the Random Century Group)

18 Poland Road
Glenfield
Auckland 10
NEW ZEALAND

Associated companies, branches and representatives throughout the world.

First published 1991
© Norman Franks
ISBN 1 86941 102 1
Printed in Singapore

All rights reserved. No part of this publication may be reproduced or transmitted in any form or by any means, electronic or mechanical, including photocopying, recording, storage in any information retrieval system or otherwise, without the written permission of the publisher.

Contents

Foreword   **vii**

1	**From small beginnings**	1916 – February 1940	1
2	**First operations**	March – August 1940	10
3	**Barges and Berlin**	September – December 1940	19
4	**Italy; Cologne; Berlin**	January – May 1941	26
5	**Ward VC and recognition**	June – July 1941	36
6	**Wellington ways**	August 1941 – April 1942	45
7	**One thousand strong**	May – June 1942	53
8	**Wellington finale**	August – October 1942	62
9	**Newmarket**	November 1942 – February 1943	70
10	**The Battle of the Ruhr**	March – May 1943	78
11	**Keeping them in the air**		86
12	**Mepal**	June – September 1943	97
13	**Stirling swansong**	September 1943 – March 1944	106
14	**Lancasters and D-Day**	April – July 1944	114
15	**Night and day**	August – September 1944	125
16	**Back to Germany**	October – November 1944	132
17	**Back on the ground**		139
18	**The last winter**	December 1944 – February 1945	146
19	**Victory in Europe**	February – May 1945	155
20	**No. 75 Squadron RNZAF**	June 1945 – 1953	161
21	**Vampires and Canberras**	1954 – 1969	168
22	**Skyhawks**	1969 – 1990	181

Appendices

A — Commanding Officers 1916 – 1990   193
B — Awards to 75 Squadron in World War Two   195
C — Raids flown by 75 Squadron 1940 – 1945   200
D — German aircraft claimed by squadron air gunners 1940 – 1945   213
E — Squadron operational losses 1940 – 1945   216
F — Non-operational aircraft losses where casualties occurred 1940 – 1945   235
G — Operational aircraft which either crashed in the United Kingdom or returned with dead or injured aircrew aboard 1940 – 1945   237

Index   **246**

Foreword

The evil and horrors of war, even of a just and necessary war, cannot be denied. Yet it is often out of war that some of our greatest virtues are forged: not only individual courage and sacrifice, but also the loyalty and comradeship of whole nations. When war broke out in Europe in September 1939, and the life and death struggle against Hitler's Germany began, the response throughout the Commonwealth was spontaneous and single-minded. By the time it was all over more than four million men and women from the Dominions and Colonies had rallied to the cause. From start to finish the part they played was of immense importance, in terms not merely of manpower and material, but equally of the moral strength they engendered. New Zealand, some 12,000 miles distant with barely one and half million people living in peace and prosperity, chose to contribute in full measure to the Allied war effort in Europe and the Middle East, and later in the Pacific.

This book describes, with a wealth of detail from personal recollections, how a handful of New Zealand airmen, arriving in England early in 1939, became the nucleus of No. 75 (New Zealand) Squadron, the first Commonwealth squadron to be formed in Bomber Command; how the squadron gained great distinction throughout its prodigiously active operational service (achieving the fourth highest number of sorties in Bomber Command); and finally, how, in recognition of its outstanding record, the proud title of No. 75 Squadron was transferred from the Royal Air Force to the Royal New Zealand Air Force in 1946.

Each participating country, of course, had its particular strength and virtues, but the impression made on me by the New Zealand aircrew with whom I flew is one that I shall remember all my life: in particular, a total dedication to the completion of whatever task they were given combined with a unique sense of humour and a determination to see that we 'Poms' were kept in our place.

I am grateful for this opportunity to make my own tribute both to a great squadron, and to the very many New Zealanders with whom it was my privilege to serve. I wish this excellent book every success.

LEONARD CHESHIRE
(Group Captain, VC, OM, DSO and 2 bars, DFC)
July 1990

1

From Small Beginnings

1916–1940

The use of the aeroplane in warfare was something very new when the Great War burst over Europe in 1914. Still in its infancy, the flying machine was viewed with scepticism by the Generals and field commanders, but with enthusiasm by those men air minded enough to realise the potential of manned aircraft.

The Royal Flying Corps (RFC) had been formed in 1912 as a result of this enthusiasm and because the Generals thought they had better go along with the idea, rather than appear old-fashioned. If, in due course, the flying machine turned out to be no good, they had at least given it a chance. But it did not fail, and while the RFC and the Royal Naval Air Service (RNAS) were small compared to the vast armies on the Western Front over the years 1914–18, they made their contribution.

One part of this new service was bombing the enemy from the air, not only above the battle front but way behind the fighting, where the enemy's logistical heart could be attacked — lines of communication, dumps, rail transport and, later, even towns in Germany itself where the weapons of war were made. But swords are usually double-edged. What the RFC and RNAS (later the Royal Air Force (RAF) when these two services were merged on 1 April 1918) could do, the Germans could also do.

Germany's initial reaction to total war was to bomb England using airships; the huge, gas-filled dirigibles like the Zeppelin. These great 'monsters of the purple twilight' inflicted numerous casualties on the population of many English towns. Later, large German aeroplanes joined the war against England.

As both sides developed their air services, the immediate requirement was for aircraft for defence against air attack. Thus the requirement was for more squadrons, not only to go to France but to serve in England as defenders. The problem was very real by 1916 and among the squadrons due to be formed during that summer and autumn, some would have to be used for Home Defence (HD). Among them would be 75 Squadron.

No. 75 Squadron RFC was officially formed on 1 October 1916 at Goldington, Bedfordshire; its first Commanding Officer (CO) being Major H. A. Petre DSO MC. Henry Aloysius Petre had been one of the early airmen of Britain, holding Royal Aero Certificate Number 128, dated 12 September 1911 — before the formation of the RFC! Indeed, he had been interested in aviation two years earlier and had constructed his own Petre Monoplane. After becoming a pilot he helped design the Handley Page monoplane for military trials in 1912, and the following year, founded a military flying school for the Australian Government. He is regarded as the first flying Australian. During the early war years he served with the Australian Flying Corps in Iraq, and was decorated for actions against the Turks before returning to England.

The embryo squadron was equipped with BE2D and BE2E aeroplanes, a two-seater Corps observation machine, pressed into service as a Home Defence fighter and fitted with one or two Lewis guns. They were not very efficient as fighters (or scouts as they were called in those days) although not a bad aircraft to fly.

Early in 1917, the War Office considered disbanding 75 and 77 (HD) Squadrons during a lull in the airships activity over England, as the RFC in France urgently needed their pilots for the spring offensive. In the event another squadron was despatched to France and some pilots taken from other HD squadrons to equip it. However, in mid-1917 the air raids on England increased and on 28 August, the War Office approved the Upgrading of the Home Defence Group to a Brigade with three Wings — Southern, Eastern and Northern. No. 75 Squadron, along with 37, 39, 50 and 51 Squadrons, became part of the Southern Wing.

By this time, Major T. O'B. Hubbard had taken command (3 July 1917). However, Tom Hubbard left at the end of the month, taking command of 73 Squadron in France, and his place was taken by Major T. F. Rutledge MC. Even in these early days the squadron was beginning its association with the far side of the world. Not only had Henry Petre been part of the early Australian Flying Corps, but Thomas Forster Rutledge came from Victoria, learned to fly in 1914 (Aero Certificate No. 841, July 1914), and had commanded No. 1 Australian Squadron in the Middle East in 1916–17.

In the latter half of 1917, 75 Squadron took its place within the anti-Zeppelin pattern which extended Eastern England's defensive line from east of London into Suffolk and Norfolk. The squadron was split into three Flights to spread the defence line: A Flight was at Hadleigh, to the west of Ipswich; B Flight at Harling Road, northeast of Thetford; C Flight flew from Elmswell, to the east of Newmarket. The squadron's patrol line was a zig-zag from Southend to Stow Maries, to Goldhanger, to Warmingford, Hadleigh and onto Elmswell.

In truth, 75 had an undistinguished war, flying old BEs, and BE12s (a single-seater fighter version of the BE2, but again with little real power), and some Avro 504 training aircraft. It even boasted some Sopwith Camel scouts late in 1918, but none saw action. The squadron did fly operationally against both day and night raids upon England by airship and aircraft, but none of the pilots engaged the enemy. In late 1917, 75 became part of 50 Southern Wing.

Those records which do survive, indicate that 75 Squadron flew some 16 interception sorties between September 1917 and August 1918, but had nothing to show from it except a few crashes. Only once was an airship even seen, but it could not be engaged. Three of the squadron's flight commanders were Captain C. B. Cooke (A Flight), Captain C. W. Mackay and Captain F. G. B. Reynolds (C Flight). One of its pilots was Lieutenant C. F. Wolley-Dod, who later became a pilot with Instone Airline in the early 1920s. Another was Sergeant Pilot Thomas Stanley Sharpe whose son, Robert, would fly with 75 Squadron in World War Two.

The last two COs were Major C. S. Ross, who took over in October 1917 and Major C. A. Ridley, who took command just after the Armistice, till disbandment. Both Clifford Ross and Claude Ridley were other 'early birds', having learnt to fly in 1915.

The squadron was finally disbanded at North Weald, on 13 June 1919.

◇ ◇ ◇

BE12 single-seat Scout of the type which the squadron flew during World War One.
(RNZAF)

Sergeant Thomas Sharpe, Royal Flying Corps, who served in 75 Squadron in 1916. His son was to be a pilot in the squadron in World War Two. (MRS P. SHARPE)

Maurice Buckley MBE, commanded the New Zealand Flight in July 1939, then 75 (NZ) Squadron in 1940.

Line up of HP Harrows, used by 75 Squadron between 1937 and 1939. (HAL WATTS)

The Harrow which Hal Watts force landed at Leiston with engine failure, its port wing being torn off when it hit a tree. The code letters FO were allotted at the time of Munich (the 'F' is obscured by the lowered flap). (HAL WATTS)

Vickers Wellingtons of the original New Zealand Flight in 1939. The nearest is NZ302. (RNZAF)

No. 75 Squadron re-emerged nearly 18 years later as part of the RAF's expansion plan, when it was reformed from B Flight of 218 Squadron on 15 March 1937. Its role was that of a Heavy Bomber Squadron based, as 218 was, at RAF Driffield, Yorkshire. Pilot Officer G. I. L. Corder, two NCO pilots, and 47 NCOs and airmen came over from 218 Squadron. Other duties were filled with postings from other units. Its initial equipment consisted of four Vickers Virginia night bombers plus two Avro Ansons. The Virginia was a twin-engined biplane, looking very like the old Handley Page bombers of World War One vintage.

Command of the reformed squadron went to Squadron Leader Herbert Leonard Rough DFC, who had achieved his present rank in 1933. When more pilots arrived, A Flight was commanded by Flying Officer J. H. Lowe, while Corder commanded B Flight. By the following month, each flight had two Virginias and three Ansons, with a seventh Anson in reserve. Night flying began on 20 April.

Over the next weeks the squadron commenced its work-up period, and taking more Ansons from 215 Squadron, eventually had six in each Flight. Then in September, with the pilots now accustomed to twin-engined aircraft, new equipment began to arrive — the Handley Page Harrow heavy bomber.

The Harrow was one of those typical ungainly and not particularly attractive aircraft of the 1930s. It was, however, one of the early monoplane bombers in service with the RAF but never flew operationally. It was a high-wing aeroplane with a large, spatted fixed undercarriage, a crew of five and a bomb load of 3000 pounds. Its two Bristol Pegasus XX engines gave it a maximum speed of 200 mph, a cruising speed of 163, and a range of 1250 miles.

Over the winter of 1937–38, the squadron crews gradually converted to their Harrows and commenced the long training schedules. Shortly after midnight on 5 April 1938 came the first fatalities. Harrow K6995 crashed five miles west of the airfield, killing all five men on board. Death in training or in action are part and parcel of an operational squadron, and these were merely the first in a long line of men to die over the next seven years.

As 1938 progressed, the squadron became fully established with a total of six aircraft in each Flight, with four more in reserve. Towards the end of May, it took part in the Empire Air Day display at Blackpool. Then in July it left Driffield for Honington in Suffolk. By November, an increase in strength gave the squadron 19 officers and 16 NCO pilots, with 200 other ranks.

Another Harrow incident occurred in September and involved a young pilot with 75 Squadron, Pilot Officer Hal Watts. By this time the squadron had had the letters 'FO' painted on their aircraft in place of the number '75'. Hal recalls:

> *I* was solo night flying in driving rain. Trying to get back to Honington in appalling conditions and flying at a very low altitude in the Saxmundham district, one engine suddenly failed. I came in low over some houses, trying to find a place to land. I attempted to get down at Hill Farm, Leiston, but the port wing clipped the trees and I came down more quickly — but safely! The torn off wing blocked the Leiston-Kelsale road.
>
> Fortunately, there were no injuries sustained and I discovered I had actually landed at West House Farm — Messrs Tyrell Brothers. A farm labourer, Arthur Chambers, dashed from his cottage to help and both the St John's Ambulance and Doctor David Ryder Richardson came to our assistance and rescue.

Hal Watts, who later flew with 214 and 101 Squadrons, became a Wing Commander and finished up as Senior Air Staff Officer (SASO) with the Pathfinder Force, having won the DSO. Hal also had another interesting flying experience during his period with 75. He test flew (unofficially) a private aeroplane designed and built by an ex-naval gentleman, but fuel problems meant Hal ended up amidst the wreckage on the Bury St Edmunds golf course!

The usual peacetime training continued during the next months, with, of course, the scare at the time of Munich. Then at the beginning of March 1939 came a change of role. No. 75 Squadron became the Pool for No. 3 Group, Bomber Command, effectively assuming the role of what later became known as an Operational Training Unit (OTU). Inexperienced aircrew, from regular airforce entrants and from the newly established Royal Air Force Volunteer Reserve (RAFVR), began to pass through, having been trained to an operational standard.

◇ ◇ ◇

Meanwhile, events in far away New Zealand were put in motion which would have far-reaching effects for 75 Squadron. The New Zealand Government had elected to purchase 30 of the new Vickers Wellington bombers being built in England. This, of course, meant a number of men from the Royal New Zealand Air Force (RNZAF) going to England for some months in order to become familiar with the new aircraft and to eventually fly them back to New Zealand.

The Wellington was very new. It had made its maiden flight in June 1936 and the first production Mark 1 had flown in December 1937. It entered RAF service with 9 Squadron at RAF Stradishall in October 1938. The designer, Barnes Wallis, who had earlier designed the R.100 airship and the Vickers Wellesley bomber, incorporated the unique geodetic method of construction in the Wellington.

The Mark 1C had two Bristol Pegasus XVIII (Mark III) engines which gave it a maximum speed of 235 mph at 15,500 feet and a range of 1200 miles carrying 4500 lbs bomb load. With 1000 pounds its range increased to 2550 miles. Service ceiling was 19,000 feet.

The early Mark carried two .303 machine guns in nose and tail turrets, but later versions increased the tail gunner's armament to four guns. If required, it could also carry two .303 beam guns. Such was the popularity and sturdiness of the Wellington, that it became Bomber Command's main aircraft for the first years of the war. It also flew, in various roles, in all the major battle zones of World War Two.

◇ ◇ ◇

In July 1939, an enlarged No. 75 Squadron moved to RAF Stradishall. The previous month, at RAF Marham in Norfolk, the New Zealand airmen who had come for the new bombers, had established the New Zealand Flight. Its Commanding Officer was Squadron Leader M. W. Buckley MBE, a New Zealander from — coincidentally — Wellington! Maurice Buckley was coming up to his 44th birthday and had served in the RNAS in World War One. He had joined the RNZAF in 1926. When the call came for him to command the Flight, he was on an exchange posting as a flight commander with 38 Squadron, which was also at Marham and which also flew Wellingtons.

Other New Zealanders also serving with the RAF were then posted to the Flight to swell the number of those from New Zealand itself. The following men formed the New Zealand Flight by the end of July 1939:

Squadron Leader M. W. Buckley	Squadron Leader C. E. Kay
Flight Lieutenant C. C. Hunter	Flying Officer J. Adams
Flying Officer F. J. Lucas	Flying Officer A. A. N. Breckon

Flying Officer J. N. Collins
Pilot Officer W. H. Coleman
Pilot Officer W. M. Williams
Sergeant W. D. Steven
Leading Aircraftman (LAC)
  D. C. McGlashan
Leading Aircraftman (LAC)
  E. P. Williams

Flying Officer A. B. Greenaway
Pilot Officer T. O. Freeman
Pilot Officer N. Williams
Sergeant T. R. Read
Leading Aircraftman (LAC) J. T. White
Leading Aircraftman (LAC)
  R. A. J. Anderson

They were joined in August by Squadron Leader R. J. Cohen, who had been designated to command a second Flight, and Flight Lieutenant I. G. Morrison, who would be a member of that Flight. The intervention of war cancelled the formation of this second Flight.

Cyril ('Cyrus') Kay, was born in Auckland and joined the RAF in 1926. He was appointed to the RNZAF in 1935. As it turned out, the trip to England to collect Wellingtons, which should have lasted just a few months, lasted for nearly four years! Cyril recalls:

> *I* had previously been in the RAF on a short service commission and later I joined the RNZAF. Shortly before the war, the New Zealand Government decided to have Wellington bombers and so I led a group across to England to pick them up.
>
> I was the Squadron Leader, second in command to the CO, Maurice Buckley. We were to have flown the Flight of Wellingtons out to New Zealand but the war intervened, so our Government agreed to hand the whole Flight over to the RAF. Therefore, we re-equipped with British armament and after a few months we were ready for operations — which is really how it all started.
>
> Personally, this suited me quite well. Obviously I was aware it would take some time to get the Flight ready to fly back to New Zealand, so I'd brought my wife and daughter over with me. So with my wife in England, I readily agreed to stay on, but a number of the boys went back home. The nucleus formed the Flight.
>
> We moved from Marham to Stradishall, for just a brief period, then on to Feltwell which became our permanent base. Feltwell was in Norfolk, just a grass aerodrome but quite adequate for our purposes.

Leading Aircraftman Don McGlashan, later Squadron Leader, also recalls:

> *I*n December 1938, six signals airmen from the 1937 RNZAF entry were selected to travel to the UK as part of the crews to bring out the first Flight of Wellingtons ordered by the RNZAF. They were:
> Wireless Operator (WOP) — acting Corporal Colin Beresford Graham Knight
> Wireless Operator (WOP) — AC1 Ronald Alexander John Anderson
> Wireless Operator (WOP) — Edwin Peter Williams
> Wireless Operator Mechanic (WOM) — AC1 Jack Harry Langridge
> Wireless Operator Mechanic (WOM) — AC1 Donald Charles McGlashan
> Wireless Operator Mechanic (WOM) — AC1 Joseph Thomas White
> (Anderson and Langridge were later killed in action with 149 and 99 Squadrons respectively.)
>
> In February 1939, we six arrived at RAF Mildenhall and were posted to 99 Squadron (Wellington Mkls). Airmen's living quarters were rather primitive compared to Wigram where we had been trained and the food in the airmen's mess was incredible. We were all given permission to withhold 2/6d per day ration allowance and feed ourselves off station! We could do this because we were paid at New Zealand rates in sterling. We were a cause of wonder to the RAF airmen because we never attended pay parades but

received a salary cheque monthly from the NZ High Commissioner's Office in London; and also, we could afford cars!

About July 1939, White, Williams, Anderson and myself were posted to the New Zealand Flight at Marham. We joined two RNZAF airmen already there — Thomas Richard Read, airframe fitter, and William D. Steven, engine fitter. They were corporals then and had come 'ashore' from HMS *Achilles* to which they had been attached to service the Walrus amphibians.

Late in August 1939, the Flight's Wellingtons as well as the RAF squadron aircraft, were taxied out to dispersal points around the airfield. I sat in one of them while doing a DI [Daily Inspection] and tuned in the wireless receiver, type R1082, to the BBC, to hear Mr Chamberlain's announcement that war had begun. I remember it was a brilliantly warm morning. A few weeks later we were told that the Flight was shifting to RAF Harwell to carry out OTU training. This was somewhat cursory.

One Saturday morning I was told to rush into someone else's aircraft as a WOP to Squadron Leader Kay, who was doing a taxi service to deliver some assorted airmen for a few days leave in Eastern counties. We'd been working 7 days a week for ages.

When airborne, I called Harwell D/F because the weather was shocking. When Harwell faded, I called 3 Group Regional Control without success, then called everyone and his brother, also unsuccessfully. I then discovered that the calibration book with all the frequency settings, was not the one for the transmitter in that aircraft!

I confessed my shame to Kay who laughed in my face and made me sit in the second pilot's seat to help him spot the names of railway stations as we flew around Suffolk and Norfolk at zero feet in dense cloud. He found all four destinations and we returned to Harwell.

Early in 1940 we moved to Honington, then, after a few weeks, to Feltwell. It must have been early 1940 because there was still plenty of snow about. A little later we became 75 Squadron and prepared for operations, which was to be leaflet dropping.

Joe White and I were then called by the CO, who told us that as we were Group 1 WOMs, we were grounded and showed us the AMO [Air Ministry Order] he had just received. Apparently the chop rate among crews with WOMs had been staggering and the RAF was running out!

White then went to A Flight as WOM under an RAF sergeant, and I went to B Flight under Corporal Ryder, also RAF. At this stage, the squadron's wireless servicing team consisted of:

1 sergeant	1 corporal	1 civilian
1 NZ LAC (White)	1 NZ LAC (McGlashan)	1 WOP — (grounded as a half-wit)
2 RAF electricians		

Somehow we kept the W/T and electrical gear serviceable. Months later after an injection of RAF wireless mechanics and electricians, we found that there was a Wireless Fault Report and we began to appear on it!

D. R. 'Diz' Day was one of the early RAF arrivals at the Flight. He had completed his initial WOP training, remustered to Air Crew and sent to 214 Squadron, for Air Gunnery (AG) training. He remembers:

We received our 'Flying Bullet' denoting our status as WOP/AGs and on 15th November transferred to the Flight at Harwell. We commenced with three crews and three Wellingtons but told that eventually we were taking 30 Wimpys to New Zealand, but this never happened.

We had lots of practice flying, day and night, then on 31st January 1940, we went operational at Feltwell. On arrival we were told that just before Christmas, 37 Squadron had just lost a whole squadron of Wimpys on a daylight raid to Kiel. They had been met by an equal number of Me110s and Me109s and couldn't have stood a chance with just two fixed guns in front and back, with only elevation and depression.

With our three main crews of Kay, John Adams and John Collins, we started flying five-hour sweeps over the North Sea. These were for the benefit of shipping and watching out for any attempt of invasion. Apart from our pilots and navigators, we were all still AC1s, on 3/6d a day, plus ten shillings a week flying pay. We didn't become sergeants until later in the year.

It was then decided to fit an under-turret to the aircraft, against attacks from below. It was a bit cramped and very cold. It didn't last long as it knocked 50 mph (80 kph) off our airspeed, so in future, the pilots should get down to sea-level as soon as possible if attacked.

With the coming of World War Two, the New Zealand Government, as already stated, had immediately waived its claim to the Wellingtons, placing them and their personnel at the disposal of the RAF. At first it was thought that the Flight would be disbanded, its aircraft and men being dispersed among the various Wellington squadrons already in being. However, the Air Officer Commanding in Chief (AOC in C), Bomber Command, Air Chief Marshal Sir Edgar Ludlow-Hewitt, expressed a strong desire that the Flight retain its identity and become a separate unit within the Command. New Zealand agreed, although it could not send additional air or ground crews at that time.

These decisions took a while, so it was not until March 1940 that the New Zealand authorities finally sanctioned the formation of a New Zealand Squadron within the Royal Air Force. On 1 April 1940 — the 22nd anniversary of the formation of the RAF — Air Ministry issued instructions for the squadron to be formed around the existing New Zealand Flight. On 4 April, 75 Squadron, which had meantime been posted to No. 6 (Training) Group, had its number plate with the letters 'NZ' added, transferred to a Royal New Zealand Air Force heavy bomber flight based at Feltwell. New squadron identification letters — the famous 'AA' — also appeared. History had been made.

2

First Operations
MARCH — AUGUST 1940

The first operational sorties were flown on 27 March 1940, when the unit was still officially the New Zealand Flight. Three Wellingtons were to fly reconnaissance and leaflet dropping sorties over Germany. These leaflet sorties, called 'Nickel' raids, had been flown regularly since the beginning of the war, as the policy was to bomb only military targets. Since Bomber Command could not be sure their bombs would not fall on civilians, the only 'safe' military targets were naval bases or the ships themselves. At this stage of the war, nobody wanted to upset the other side by actually injuring non-combatants!

Germany must have been awash with leaflets over the winter of 1939–40 and many RAF crews failed to return from carrying out this thankless task. Whether the Germans laughed at them isn't recorded, but perhaps some had the sobering thought that if the RAF could drop leaflets without too much interference, then they could eventually drop bombs.

However, on 27 March, Kay, Collins and Adams, flew Wellingtons P9206, P9207 and P9212 to the Brunswick, Utzen and Luneberg areas respectively, and dropped their 'bumpf'. Freeman was second pilot to Cyrus Kay, Harkness was with Collins, and Pilot Officer Larney with Adams. Cyrus Kay makes the following comments on this first sortie:

> Once we were ready, we made our first operational flight. There were three aircraft on the first mission. This was still the period of the Phoney War and we weren't allowed to drop bombs, so we were dropping leaflets. It was a night flight and we proceeded up the North Sea, turned in towards Hamburg and hit it spot-on, so it was a good test of our ability. We then flew to our respective areas, dropped our leaflets and flew home without any mishaps at all.

Diz Day, flying as front gunner to John Adams, recalls:

> We did our first night raid over Germany on the 27th March, to Hamburg. It should have been bombs — we could have flattened it! But it wasn't to be; it was a leaflet raid. We flew round Hamburg at 2000 feet, with little flak and searchlights, but that was all. We were so low we could see people and parked cars it was such a moonlight night. Our journey back was to be more eventful because after leaving Hamburg, 10/10ths cloud built up and I think we drifted off course. At 500 feet there below us was a fully

illuminated city when we reached our Feltwell ETA. So Adams decided it would be best to go across Amsterdam, to land in France.

The airforce at Amsterdam had other ideas and sent up two fighters to chase us out over the North Sea. So down to sea-level came John with the Wimpy, heading for Feltwell. Unfortunately, violent electrical storms forced us south, so John informed me and Jack Gibbs, the rear gunner, to tidy up in case we had to land on the sea and be prepared to release the dinghy.

The engines were now getting red hot through lack of oil so Jack and I had to use the emergency oil pump. We were still in trouble and just about ready to pancake when John came over the intercom to say he could see the White Cliffs of Dover.

Once over land, he shot up every aerodrome from Dover to Feltwell and we were last back after a 9½ hour flight, and almost drained of fuel. We went straight to the mess for coffee, bacon and eggs. The press gave us a wonderful write-up, but then they didn't know the full story.

Four aircraft flew another 'valuable' Nickel raid on 6 April to the Nienburg. Petershagen and Minden areas. These were P9206, P9212, P9207 and P9210, piloted by Messers Breckon, Coleman, W. Williams and N. Williams. All returned safely, their duty carried out. Apparently, by this date, the RAF had dropped a total of 65 million leaflets over Germany!

The Phoney War took a dent at this time when the Germans began their assault upon Norway. On 9 April they overran Denmark and landed troops at Narvik, Trondheim, Bergen and Stavanger, as well as bombing Oslo and Kristiansand. During the first naval battle of Narvik the next day, 75 Squadron were ordered to prepare four aircraft to stand by, but then stood down. However, one crew did fly what at the time was quite an historic sortie, certainly one of the longest so far.

Flight Lieutenant Aubrey Breckon, who came from Ohakea, had joined the RAF in 1935, transferring to the RNZAF in June 1939. He and his crew of Pilot Officer D. J. Harkness*, Sergeant Hughes (Navigator), LAC E. P. Williams (WOP/AG), and AC Mumby as air gunner flew to Wick in Scotland. Here they found a Wellington (L4387), normally used for training, which had been fitted with extra fuel tanks to extend its range. It also had everything necessary for navigation and a full complement of machine-gun ammunition.

Breckon was then told that at dawn on 12 April he was to reconnoitre the Norwegian coast to the Lofoten Islands and the Vest Fjord to Narvik. They would also take with them, Lieutenant Commander F. O. Howie RN, who would assist in ship recognition. Breckon later wrote out a report of the sortie, which in part, states;

> **W**e took off in the early morning in a bee-line for Narvik. It was a bumpy day and we ran into extraordinary weather conditions with heavy rain squalls and, finally, near the Norwegian coast, a snow storm. Indeed, for a long time we had 27 degrees of frost.
>
> As we reached the Norwegian coast we got ready for anything. The wireless operator manned the front guns; the second pilot stood at the astro hatch, acting as a fire-control officer and the rear gunner took his place in his turret.
>
> Norway, covered in deep snow, was an awe-inspiring sight and at the time any land was very welcome to us. Our real work had now begun, though the weather was steadily deteriorating. There was a high wind, and we were flying in and out of snow and sleet about 300 feet above the sea. There was such terrific bumps that the gunners frequently banged their heads as they were flung upwards out of their seats.
>
> We met an enemy aircraft as we went towards the Vest Fjord, but he sheered off

---

* Harkness was killed on 14 December 1942 with another unit.

when he saw us. We flew up the fjord through driving snow at only 200 feet. The clouds and cliffs seemed to be closing in on us and when we got to the end, we swung round, made a sharp turn and continued the reconnaissance southward down the coast as far as Kristiansand. Then we turned for home.

The trip back was without incident apart from the weather. We saw British Naval units in the North Sea, circled round them and exchanged signals by Aldis lamp. We had seen a couple of British destroyers and a merchantman at the entrance to one of the fjords. We had a strong wind against us on the homeward trip, and we were very glad to see the Shetlands as we approached Scotland. We had covered well over 2000 miles and as soon as we landed we were given hot drinks before we made out our reports and our photographs were developed. The second pilot and I, having no automatic pilot, had shared 14½ hours at the controls.

Their report that the main fjord was clear of enemy ships enabled the Navy ships seen on the way back to sail to Narvik and attack German destroyers there. In all, they took 72 aerial photos of abandoned German aircraft and seaplanes, plus troopships in the harbour. With this intelligence, RAF Wellingtons carried out a successful raid a short time later. They had consumed 933 gallons of fuel, returning with just 37 left in their tanks, plus 21 gallons of oil. The actual distance they had covered was 2060 miles.

Also on 12 April, four of the squadron's bombers, in company with eight aircraft of 37 Squadron, took off to attack an enemy cruiser reported off Norway. But, as leader Cryus Kay remembers, extremely bad weather caused the strike to be abandoned:

We flew several search missions over the North Sea and off the coast of Norway, looking for German pocket battleships such as the *Scharnhorst*, *Gniesenau*, etc, but saw nothing.

We carried 'B' bombs, which was a device we would have had to drop in front of a battleship had we found one. They would sink down and then rise up under the ship and explode in its soft underbelly. At least, that was the principle but we never saw a battleship and more often than not the North Sea was covered in mist and fog.

With the Battle for Norway still in full swing, the RAF mounted a number of attacks on the airfield and seaplane base at Stavanger. Three Wellingtons — piloted by Adams, Collins and N. Williams — flew there on 17 April, although Adams had to return early with electrical trouble. Then four days later the target was Aalborg, Denmark. Three aircraft — piloted by Adams, Coleman and W. Williams — took off at ten-minute intervals from 6.30 that evening. Diz Day records:

John Adams and crew were first away and on our approach to the target we found Ack-Ack reaching the height we were going to bomb from — 8000 feet. This meant climbing another 2000 feet which took half an hour. By this time the other aircraft had gone so we were the last to go in. I had a very good view of the damage, being in the front turret, whilst we were diving from 10,000 feet with guns blazing at searchlights. Hangers were extensively damaged as well as the runways.

But Norway's days were numbered, and by the end of April, the battle had been lost. The war certainly seemed to have started at last. But what was to follow?

Squadron Leader C. E. Kay OBE DFC (wearing white overalls), senior flight commander and then CO of 75 Squadron 1940. Left to right: Carter, Sgt E. N. Albert, (unknown), (unknown), (unknown), F/O W. M. C. Williams, Charles, P/O E. V. Best, S/L Kay, F/O J. Adams, F/L N. Williams, W/C M. W. Buckley, F/O F. J. Lucas, (unknown), F/L A. A. Breckon. (RNZAF)

Breckon and his crew after the flight to Narvik. Left to right: LAC E. P. Williams, F/Lt A. A. Breckon, Lt Cdr F. O. Howie RN, P/O D. J. Harkness, Sgt R. H. Hughes and AC T. L. Mumby. (IMPERIAL WAR MUSEUM)

The Wellington flown by Aubrey Breckon, departing from Wick on his historic long range reconnaissance to Narvik, 12 April 1940. Coded LG (215 Squadron), L4387 was a training machine, but had been specially equipped for this flight. Hurricanes of 605 Squadron are in the foreground. (RNZAF)

After the flurry of excitement off and over Norway, the squadron got down to some serious training. New crews arrived, some coming in from 214 Squadron, others from Manby. There were also some new aircraft, transferred from 37, 115, 149 and 214 Squadrons.

There was another scare at the beginning of May when Intelligence thought that Holland was about to be invaded. Four Wellingtons were put on stand-by, but the danger passed. Collins, Coleman and N. Williams had another go at Stavanger on 7 May, but cloud caused them to abort.

If the Phoney War had been dented in Norway, it certainly collapsed at dawn on 10 May 1940. That morning the Germans finally launched their assault on the west by attacking Holland, Belgium and France. Part of the German plan was an airborne assault upon Amsterdam and the Hague, seizing the Dutch airfield of Waalhaven. The battle raged throughout the day and that evening 75 Squadron were assigned to attack German troops and transport aircraft at Waalhaven. John Collins and the two Williams were briefed, noting that some reports said the airfield was in German hands, others that the Dutch were still partly in control. There was no moon, the weather was fairly good, the searchlights were weak, and there was a little AA fire — but whether German or Dutch, who could tell? In any event, all three aircraft returned after bombing the target.

The situation was still unclear the next day, with many confused reports coming from France and Holland, but by 12 May it was confirmed that German troops and transport were pouring into Holland across the River Maas. The Battle and Blenheim squadrons in France and the Blenheims of 2 Group in England were pounding the advance but having little effect. Despite valiant efforts, these light aircraft were being shot out of the sky. On the night of 12 May, 75 Squadron sent out three Wellingtons to attack German supply areas and road junctions behind the battle front. The ban on attacking targets which might result in civilian casualties had at last been lifted — it was now total war.

Despite flak and searchlights, Kay, Breckon and Coleman bombed Krefeld-Verdingen in individual attacks, causing fires on either side of the Rhine. One enemy fighter was seen but it made no move against the squadron's aircraft. Following more confused reports, the squadron was again called for action on 15 May, putting up six aircraft out of a total of 99 by Bomber Command, to attack the Ruhr. The New Zealand Squadron was finally going to hit Germany itself. Indeed, this was the first really strategic target bombing of the war, and 75 was part of it. It did not turn out to be an auspicious start, though. Weather and poor visibility was against the bombers and, while none were lost, results were disappointing. Of 75's aircraft, four brought their bombs home, a fifth jettisoned over the sea and only one — John Collins — found his target.

Two nights later a further three Wellingtons again went for the Ruhr, with three more attacking troop communications in Belgium. What was thought to be a blast furnace was successfully bombed by one of the Ruhr force, and a road convoy bombed by one of the latter three, even though all aircraft had problems with searchlights. They all returned, although fog over the base forced the Wellington crews to divert — something which was to happen with boring rapidity during the war.

Troop concentrations were again on the menu for the night of the 19/20 May, seven aircraft bombing targets at Givat, Fumay, Seneff and Haybes. However, there was another first for 75 — the first battle casualty. Pilot Officer Freeman's aircraft, R3158, received a heavy burst of machine-gun fire, and a bullet struck his second pilot in the right shoulder. Four of the squadron's aircraft were damaged by ground fire, one having a three-inch shell pass through the port aileron without exploding. Two nights later came the squadron's first battle loss.

This time it was German railways which received Bomber Command's attention, with 124 aircraft hitting these targets in western Germany, bordering France and the Low Countries. No. 75 Squadron put up eight aircraft, most crews returning with some sort of success achieved. However, one dispersal point remained empty, its ground crew waiting expectantly for 'their' Wimpy to return. However, the night sky remained empty. On the flight board next to the chalked number — R3157 F/O Collins — was added the three poignant letters 'FTR' (Failed to return). In his crew was Stan Brooks:

> *O*ur target was the bridge at Dinant, Belgium. The Germans were pushing their troops over it and it was necessary to check their progress. Just east of Tournai we started to lose height in preparation for our bombing run and around 2–3000 feet we received a direct hit from flak in the starboard engine. I had vacated the wireless operator's desk on crossing the coast and was in the front turret in case of fighters. The extinguishers had little effect and Collins turned the aircraft round to port to try and blow out the flames; also to try and get back over Allied territory. By this time the wing was well alight so he ordered everyone to bale out.
>
> I heard him tell our second pilot, Pilot Officer De Labouchere-Sparling, who was on his first op, to open the bulkhead door before he and the observer, Bob Thorpe,

jumped. When I opened the turret doors I saw they had gone through the open hatch. The rear gunner, our recently arrived gunnery officer, had decided to see what operational flying was all about — Pilot Officer Hockey was finding out!

My parachute I had left on the bed in the fuselage, which by this time was one mass of blazing fabric, starkly showing up all the geodetic framework down to the rear turret. As I stepped over the open hatch I could see John was beginning to have difficulty with the controls. I also saw his 'chute in the rack alongside the bomb aimer's position. I grabbed it and hooked it on his chest hooks, but owing to him wrestling with the controls I think I only may have put it on one hook. He was shouting to me to get out quickly. As I had taken his 'chute from its rack I noticed the altimeter was at the 1000 feet position. I hurried along, over the main-spar and was relieved to see my parachute still intact despite the flames.

By this time we were in a steep dive and the Wimpy almost out of control, John fighting it to enable me to jump. It started to roll over as I dived head first through the hatch and felt its sides catch my ankles as it rolled. I pulled the 'chute ring immediately, realising I had not much height to play with — I would guess we had been at about 400 feet. Just as the 'chute opened the bomb load exploded, the blast blowing me up till I was level with the canopy and as I resumed normal position I hit the ground with the blazing wreckage, showering down a few hundred yards away. It all happened so quickly I still had the parachute ring in my hand. I concealed it from the Germans all the war and presented it to the '75' museum in 1980.

I owe my life to that gallant gentleman, John Collins, who retained control of the Wellington long enough for me to obtain my parachute and bale out.

I landed amidst the German lines and was picked up immediately, the only 75 Squadron member to be captured as an AC1 airman; but I returned to England as a Warrant Officer at the war's end.

Stan Brooks had been posted to the 75 (NZ) Flight in November 1939 and being crewed up with Collins, flew leaflet raids and patrols over the North Sea until this fateful 21 May. He became the Honorary Secretary of the 75 Squadron (UK) Association. Of the crew, both Collins and the second pilot were killed; the other three ended up as prisoners of war.

◇ ◇ ◇

Although the Flight's transformation had been approved in April, it was not until 21 May that the additional personnel began to arrive to bring the unit up to squadron strength. So it was from this date that they actually began to feel like a squadron, which was now divided into two specific Flights — A and B.

Meantime, the Battle of France was in full swing, with the French and the British Expeditionary Force (BEF) in retreat. Over the next week the 'new' squadron flew extensively in support of the land armies, bombing both German lines of communication and transport centres to the rear. With Dunkirk and the evacuation of the BEF from France over on 3 June, the squadron were directed to Dusseldorf that night. Bomber Command sent 142 aircraft in attacks on various centres that night, its largest effort so far. On their return, the eight squadron aircraft had to divert due to fog.

There was still a battle going on in France, the French and what remained of the British army still retreating towards Cherbourg, so Bomber Command continued to support them with attacks on bridges, roads and troop concentrations, even French airfields taken over by the German Luftwaffe. No. 75 Squadron's efforts varied from eight aircraft to just one, such as when Coleman went out with four from 37 Squadron to bomb targets east of Aachen on 14 June. Then on 21 June came the

Flight of 75's Wellingtons; the squadron code of AA clearly defined.
(IMPERIAL WAR MUSEUM)

Flying Officer John Collins, Stan Brooks' pilot on 21 May. They were the first squadron crew lost in action; Collins died staying at the controls of his Wellington so his crew could bale out.
(S. BROOKS)

Squadron F. J. Lucas DFC and bar, "Popeye" to everyone, pilot and flight commander. He completed two tours with 75. (N. D. GREENAWAY)

Three AC1 WOPs in the early days of 75 Squadron. Left to right: Harold Smith (DFM), Stan Brooks, Eric Albert (DFM). Stan Brooks was taken prisoner on 21 May 1940 and became the secretary of the United Kingdom branch of 75's Association. (S. BROOKS)

announcement of the first decoration for the squadron. Squadron Leader Kay was awarded the Distinguished Flying Cross (DFC).

Towards the end of July, 75 was attacking Germany — Cologne, Frankfurt, the Ruhr, the submarine yards at Bremen — as well as targets in Holland on a regular basis. One of the latter brought the second loss to the squadron. No. 75 went to the Eindhoven area to bomb the railway yards, and to Gelsenkirchen. Three single-seater fighters — Me109s — were seen in the moonlight over the German target. One Wellington was seen to fall in flames. R3165, piloted by Flying Officer S. S. M. Watson, and his crew failed to return, and were later all reported killed.

A few nights later, on 25 July, the veteran Flying Officer W. H. Coleman and his crew failed to return from Kassel in R3235. After such a run of good fortune, the enemy defences were starting to get their act together and Bomber Command's losses were on the increase. No. 75 Squadron's, too, for on 3 August, Squadron Leader W. J. Collett's Wimpy was damaged over the Ruhr. Bringing it back, he attempted a forced landing at Marham, but crashed and all were killed.

There was, however, some good news. At the end of July, Sergeants E. P. Williams (WOP) and J. W. Carter (Observer) received Distinguished Flying Medals. In early August, Neville Williams received the DFC and Sergeant L. A. White (AG) the DFM.

Meanwhile, as Fighter Command fought and won the Battle of Britain in the skies over southern England, 75 Squadron continued its nightly bombing of the Channel ports and targets in Germany. As the war progressed, 75 would go to many distant targets. On 13 August, for example, nine Wellingtons flew to Stettin Docks on the Baltic coast, eight to bomb and one to take photographs. Weather was a constant problem with night bombing all year round, and thick cloud prevented all the aircraft dropping their bombs. Pilot Officer Freeman's aircraft was attacked by a Messerschmitt 110 night-fighter south of Kiel, but he evaded it and dived into some clouds.

During August the squadron was managing to put up 10 aircraft, sometimes 11, on most nights. Night-fighters again interferred with one of the squadron aircraft on 26 August near Nivelles, when aircraft went to Duisberg, Arnhem and Flushing. Pilot Officer Harkness was attacked by a single-engined fighter, which his gunner claimed was shot down.

As August came to an end, the Flight and Squadron completed its first year of war. They had carried out each and every task assigned to them as best they could and, with only three crews lost, could be thankful that their casualties had not been greater. If there had been any thought or suggestion that the fighting 'would be over by Christmas', all knew now that it would be a very long war indeed. What would the second year bring?

3

Barges and Berlin

SEPTEMBER — DECEMBER 1940

September 1940 began with 11 aircraft going to Soest, Hanover, Leipzig and Kassel, for this was still the period where Bomber Command was spreading its attacking force to create the maximum coverage. Massed bombing of a specific target was still in the future. Two brought their bombs back; one, flown by Pilot Officer Peel, crashed on landing at East Wretham, the satellite of Honington. The crew received injuries but they all got out before the bombs exploded.

Sergeant L. A. Hayter, from Greymouth, had transferred from No. 20 Operational Conversion Unit to the squadron in August. He flew his first Op as WOP/AG to Pilot Officer F. H. Denton on 1 September:

> *T*he 1st September we joined the war — a nursery trip to Soesterberg — a quiet trip except for a fire in an engine over the target! It was put out by a steep dive without setting fire to the fabric on the wing, thank heavens. Our second trip, carried out on the 4th, was an intruder raid on Chartres aerodrome in France which was being used as a Luftwaffe base for raids on England. We were timed to attack as the enemy aircraft were returning, waiting until the flare path was lit, then nip in and drop the odd bomb to cause confusion. By the number of Verey cartridges being fired off from below, we achieved our aim that night, but we were to suffer the same fate later!

No. 75 Squadron was called upon to carry out a variety of sorties during this time. On 10 September, seven aircraft bombed the docks at Ostend and Flushing. Pilot Officer R. M. 'Dick' Curtis, who had joined 75 in December, was one of two which attacked Ostend:

> *I* was one of the first pilots from England to be posted to the Squadron to bring it up to strength. I joined on 9th December 1939 and left on 10th October 1940, when I was posted to 20 OCU as a flying instructor. Initially, I was second pilot to Popeye Lucas. Our sortie to Ostend on 10th September was to co-operate with the Navy. My crew and I were one of two detailed for this operation; the other I feel sure was Pilot Officer Larney. Our particular task was to drop flares for the Navy to carry out a naval bombardment and then to bomb shipping in the harbour.
>
> We had an emblem on our aircraft — 'Cuthbert' [a skeleton rolling two dice] with whom we diced! This was copied from a large black and white drawing which I still have, prepared by my second pilot, Sandy Sanderson's, girlfriend. We kept the Cuthbert for many trips but on a sortie to Berlin, the hydraulics packed up two-thirds of

the way there and we limped home with undercarriage and flaps immobile to do a belly landing at Feltwell on a rather misty morning.

Dick Curtis was to receive a letter of thanks from the Admiralty following this night's work, and later, the DFC, announced early in the new year.

Pilot Officer Denton had succesfully completed his third trip on 7 September, but five days later, as Len Hayter records:

> *O*ur third — lucky three — passed Okay. But our fourth trip, which won the DFC for our skipper, nearly concluded our part in the war. The target was the docks at Flushing where invasion barges were assembling. Following our briefing, the skipper gave us his ideas for attacking this target, position to the east at about 10,000 feet — we never went above this height because he always had the oxygen bottles removed from the aircraft before a raid, having seen a Wellington blown up on a daylight raid when attacked by fighters — and he would then throttle back and dive to level off over the target at 600 feet. Then, power on, bomb doors open, bombs away, dive towards the North Sea and away.
>
> All went well until we levelled off and the power went on, then all hell broke out. We were coned in every damned searchlight they had and every gun seemed to be aimed at us. Then, as the aircraft lurched earthwards, I heard the skipper yell, "Jettison Bombs!" and heard our Observer, Andy Orrock, reply "Gone". Then as if in a lift, we were blown back up to nearly 600 feet. As we now headed out to sea, I was ordered out of the front turret and to take up 'ditching' position in the astrodome, from where I could see we had been hit in both wings. We made it home at low level, with Jimmy Farquahar, our WOP, sending out SOS messages in case we ditched.

'Nose Art' was a feature of the early Wellington bombers. Dick Curtis DFC and his crew pose in front of their 'Cuthbert'. Left to right: Curtis, PO R. M. Sanderson (2P), Sgts Ritchie (WOP), McMaster (N), Beckett (FG) and Goodhue (RG). Sanderson was killed with his own crew in October 1940. (R. C. CURTIS)

Pilot Officer F. H. Denton (DFC) (with bombs) and his crew. Left to right: Sgts Jimmy Farquahar (WOPAG), Chalky White (2P), Sgt Andy Orrock (N), PO R. G. Jelly (RG) (killed 29 September 1941), and Sgt Len Hayter (WOPAG). (L. A. HAYTER)

'Achtung Anzac' with dripping blood and the word 'Tovarich'. Left to right: Sgt L. W. Kennedy (WOP), F/Sgt K. A. Crankshaw DFM (DFC) (AG), Sgt Frankie Curr DFM, P/O R. Hull (N), Sully Sullivan. (W. HARDY)

Pilot Officer Denton's Distinguished Flying Cross was an immediate award. The Wellington (P9212) returned with shell holes through both wings and machine-gun bullets through the front turret without Len knowing about them. It was estimated that they were down to 150 feet when blown back up to 600!

Le Havre was the target on 18/19 September, and several ports, including Hamburg, on 20/21. Pilot Officer M. R. Braun and his crew failed to return from Ostend that night. Then on the night of 23/24 September, the big one — Berlin!

For the first time, Bomber Command had decided to concentrate its main strength against just one German city and what better way to start than to hit the German capital. In all, 129 Hampdens, Whitleys and Wellingtons were sent to 18 separate targets within the Berlin area, including railway yards, power stations, gasworks and factories. Of these, 112 reported bombing the city over a three-hour period, for the loss of three aircraft — one of each type.

The New Zealand Squadron sent 10 aircraft and all returned despite meeting intense flak and 5/10th cloud. The 10 captains were, Flight Lieutenant Lucas, Pilot Officers Gow, Best, Denton, Curtis, Harkness, Larney, McArthur, Morton and Sergeant Noden. Again, 75 became a part of RAF history.

After their excitement over Flushing, Len Hayter recalls their Berlin trip passed 'without much ado'. But then came their fateful ninth operation — to Bitterfield, on 29 September:

> *R*eturning from a raid on Bitterfield we ran into intense flak and in taking repeated evasive action we digressed from our intended homeward route. Weather was also against us and with the radio breaking down we at last found a friendly pundit — Weston Zoyland in Somerset — miles and miles from Feltwell or even Norfolk!
>
> With little fuel left after 9½ hours flying, the skipper tried to find us a place to land, then through a brief break in the clouds we spot the Bristol Channel. Then one motor began to cough and we were advised that we would have to bale out. I was the first to go, leaving via the front hatch. I made a heavy landing and knocked myself out. When I came round it was pitch black and about 5am. I was lying on a grass surface of a steep field, unable to see any distance so I lay down and dozed off to sleep, re-awakening at first light. I made my way down the field and came to a cattle track and not being 100% certain I was in England, I hid my parachute and then strolled along till I found a farmhouse. After some questioning by the farmer from a bedroom window — pointing a shot gun at me — he came down and let me in and his wife made some tea.
>
> Eventually, help came in the shape of the police who collected me from a nearby house which had a telephone, and they took me to Exford where three of my crew had been sent. I was told the Wimpy had crashed across a road near Simmonsbath. I then met up with 'Chalky' White, the second pilot; Andy Orrock; Jimmy Farquahar, who told me that the skipper* had broken his ankle and was in Minehead hospital, and that Pilot Officer Jelly, our rear gunner, was dead.
>
> Upon our return to Feltwell, we were crewed up with another pilot — Pilot Officer Pownell RNZAF and a new NZ gunner. Together we flew on until he had completed his 30 trips, by which time Andy, Jimmy and I had done 21. When Pownell informed us that he had been given the option of a rest or getting a crew together to fly a Wellington to the Middle East, we elected to stay together, but our operations with 148 Squadron till August 1941 is another story.

In October, Cyrus Kay left the squadron on a posting to RAF Honington, on completion of his tour. He had flown numerous sorties as flight commander. The

---

* Denton later returned to 75 to become a flight commander. Later in the war he commanded 487 (NZ) Squadron, flying Mosquito aircraft.

other Flight was being commanded by Aubrey Breckon, who had also received a DFC, mainly for his Narvik reconnaissance mission. DFCs also went to Adams, Freeman and Coleman. Other pilots, too, would soon receive DFCs — McArthur Lucas, Bill Williams and Boffee. Several more awards went to members of aircrew, so that by the end of the year, the squadron had received 11 DFCs and 13 DFMs — a very creditable performance.

The squadron operated on 10 nights during October, flying again to a variety of targets in Germany, Holland and Belgium. Among the targets were Luftwaffe aerodromes at Brussels and Eindhoven, and the docks of Hamburg. Diz Day remembers 21 October, when the squadron went to Eindhoven, Hamburg and Dusseldorf. On this occasion he was not flying with his usual skipper, John Adams, but Flight Lieutenant Gilbert:

> *I* was on the radio with a new crew and we were on our way back from Dusseldorf in 10/10ths cloud when the radio went u/s. It took a while for me to get it going again, and as it happened, just as I did so we were at 200 feet, when all of a sudden we were all over the sky! I sent out an SOS — Mayday — and Manston answered and said that we were very close and would put on their landing lights.
>
> Going into land, flaps down, the pilot saw a high tension pylon looming up and tried to climb again but with flaps probably still down. We stalled from 200 feet and crashed on our port side.
>
> The aircraft caught fire but we were lucky and managed to push out of the starboard side, mid-way down the fuselage, then sprinted away as fast as we could from the exploding oxygen bottles, ammunition, etc. When the fire tender crew arrived, they thought we were all still inside.
>
> I had a piece of parachute which was recovered from the burnt out Wimpy — we all had a piece, on which we all signed our names. It turned out that we had hit a balloon cable at Dover, just as we crossed the coast!

Two nights later it was Berlin again, the squadron putting up five Wellingtons. But this was a small effort with only 79 aircraft, including some from OTUs, going for several targets. Just 11 RAF Wellingtons reached Berlin, the target for 75 being the station at Potsdam. They met heavy flak and cloud and, of the two Wimpys which failed to return, one was from 75. The pilot was R. M. Sanderson, who had been Dick Curtis' second pilot. He and his crew all perished.

The pace continued through November, the squadron putting up an average of eight aircraft on eight nights. Berlin was again part of the scene, when some of the 11 Wellingtons went to the 'Big City'. It was on one of these Berlin trips that Fred 'Popeye' Lucas completed his first tour, having flown 37 Ops. He 'celebrated' by landing at base with a tyre punctured by flak and describing three complete circles before the bomber came to a halt.

Popeye Lucas, one of the characters of 75, looked like his cartoon namesake, especially when he took out his false teeth! From South Otago, he had failed to gain entry to the RNZAF so travelled to England as a deck hand on a ship to try the RAF. Despite his poor academic background the RAF took a chance on him — provided he had his teeth fixed. He had them fixed all right; he had them all removed! Now at the end of his tour he left to become an instructor, but 75 had not seen the last of him.

They did, however, see the last of Maurice Buckley — at least as their Commanding Officer. Towards the end of November he was posted to 214 Reserve Flight at Stradishall. Under his guidance, the New Zealand Flight had grown into a full squadron, had started operations, and had begun to make a name for itself within the ranks of Bomber Command. His place was taken by an old friend, Cyrus Kay, who was promoted to Wing Commander:

> *A*t the beginning of October I had been posted to Honington as Operations Officer. It was while I was there that Maurice Buckley went sick, so the AOC appointed me to take over the squadron; which I did in November.
>
> The squadron, over that first year, had built up strength fairly quickly, always had over aircraft in first-class condition for Ops, had achieved a good record of reliability and serviceability, thanks to our ground crews. We had a letter from the AOC congratulating us on this record and we soon became up to squadron strength. We had good men, both air and ground crew, and with the Wellington, which could take the most amazing punishment, went from strength to strength.

Leaflets were still carried and dropped over Germany on these early raids, as Sergeant (later Squadron Leader) Arthur James remembers on these two November raids to Berlin:

> *I* think we were the first airfield equipped with a Bofors gun, manned by army personnel. We flew two raids to Berlin in quick succession without prior warning, and with little sleep. I overshot the runway on our return and hit the slit trench embankment at the end of the runway. We belly-flopped on top of the Bofors gun emplacement, much to the chagrin of the army lieutenant. My rear gunner rotated his turret to drop out without realising he was ten feet above ground! Result, one broken ankle.
>
> Leaflets were dropped en route and over target areas, pushed through the flare chute. They were in bundles held together by a single rubber band. I well recall one night when I was second pilot. A band broke on dropping the bundle into the chute and the inside of the Wimpy was plastered with leaflets; and there we were, over the target, killing ourselves with laughter. We finished up opening the astrodome and feeding them out on the palm of our hand, like feeding sugar to a horse. All the time the pilot was taking evasive action!

For Flight Sergeant R. G. 'Bob' Shepherd, the two Berlin trips ended, like Popeye Lucas, his first tour of Ops. As WOP/AG, Bob had flown 29 sorties between 8 July and 26 November — 21 with Pilot Officer Larney, six with Pilot Officer Saxelby, and two with Flying Officer Best. In all, Bob had flown to Berlin on four occasions. He later completed a second tour with 57 Squadron and won the DFC, ending his career as a Squadron Leader. He remembers an interesting item about the radio:

> *I*n my role as WOP/AG we had to help carry out the DI [Daily Inspection] on the aircraft each morning. In my case, check the radio, change the accumulators, check radio with base, check the R/T, check the front turret guns. Later on in the war, radio and R/T checks were limited, due to the Germans listening out on all frequencies, and it would indicate to them that preparations for a raid were in the offing, if they picked up our checking procedure.

A new record was achieved on the 6 December, with 13 aircraft being made available for Ops. These attacked various targets in France — St Omer, Villacoublay, Amiens Glisy, Dunkirk, and the Boulogne docks — mostly against airfields in the Command's anti-Luftwaffe operations now that the Germans were stepping up their night raids on England. Flak, cloud and searchlights hampered the raids and three aircraft failed to find their assigned target.

The main target for 15/16 December was Frankfurt, but a couple of the eight aircraft 75 put up, went for the Berlin railway yards. Little damage could have been achieved by these fairly isolated hit and run raids, but it kept the civilian population on their toes and out of their beds.

The last raid before Christmas was against Flushing on the night of 22/23 December. Bomber Command sent 59 bombers to Germany, France and Holland and lost just one aircraft — but it came from 75 Squadron. It was another maximum effort by the squadron — 12 aircraft — which went for Flushing and the aerodrome down at Rheims. Pilot Officer Morton's aircraft was engaged by a Me110, which his gunners hit, but they did not make a claim. Sergeant E. R. Chuter's target was Mannheim but he failed to return.

All the crew, with the exception of Sergeant A. H. Ritchie who was killed, were captured. Chuter himself was seriously injured, being repatriated in March 1944. Sergeant C. Falcon-Scott, the second pilot, escaped in 1941 and got back to England; as did the front gunner, Sergeant E. G. Willis, which must be some kind of record for a single crew. The navigator and WOP, Sergeants H. M. English and A. Donaldson were repatriated in July 1943 and February 1945 respectively.

With Christmas over, and having had a lull over the festive season, it was back to Germany on 29 December. This time two Wellingtons failed to return, and again one was from 75. Three aircraft took off for Hamm to make individual attacks and, while thick cloud didn't help, it did keep the searchlights out of action. Sergeant J. M. Garrett was the navigator in Pilot Officer H. D. Newman's crew, which was the crew that failed to get home. They were all taken prisoner. Jack recalls a Christmas rugby game that preceded the Op:

My stay on the squadron was brief, terminated by captivity in Germany. Our Flight Commander was one 'Basher' Bain, a very press-on character, both in the air and elsewhere, who, while an Englishman, qualified for real NZ status through his keenness on rugby alone!

Now rugby was officially 'out' for aircrew for the best of reasons, although there didn't seem to be much active policing of that edict. I can remember several games against neighbouring stations in which aircrew participated. The last game in which I played was against Norwich Grammar School. I forget the transport arrangements but I was one of eight or ten who crammed into Bain's Lagonda Sports for the ride.

The pre-game team talk dealt chiefly with the need for restraint in our dealings with 17 to 19-year-olds but at half time, while weight and experience had won us a reasonable lead, we had become somewhat thoughtful at the increasingly rigorous play by our opponents — as well as to our own fitness! Things got pretty rough in scrums and in one, Bain, head and shoulders thrusting out of the mass, yelled, 'Easy, easy you Feltwell Kiwis; remember these are only schoolboys.' With which, an arm reached up from below and pulled him onto a very brisk hook. The resulting black eye was a beauty, resplendent even under flying goggles for days afterwards!

Towards the end of the game I found myself alone in front of most of their main pack storming down on me — a real moment of truth; my only hope was that the ref might arrive in time. I had two ribs stove in and a deserved penalty awarded against me.

Back at Feltwell an after-hours visit to the MO [Medical Officer] got me triced up in yards of sticky plaster and a couple of days later our crew were off on what was to be our last Op. In the face of the official attitude to non-aircrew rugby, one couldn't 'go sick'. For me, the sequel came when, on being admitted to a Rotterdam hospital, the German doctor was stripping me and found me cocooned in plaster. In a perfect Oxford accent he said, 'I say, old chap, Churchill really is sending even his crocks now, isn't he?'

4

Italy; Cologne; Berlin
JANUARY — MAY 1941

The new year of 1941 stretched out ahead of the crews of 75 New Zealand Squadron. The severe winter, with snow and ice, didn't help matters, but the valiant ground crews kept the serviceability rate up, enabling the squadron to send seven Wellingtons out on that first night in January. Three nights later it was ten to Brest to attack major German naval units, with the squadron also sending aircraft to Duisberg. The next night it was seven to Wilhelmshaven.

Each day that operations were scheduled, the aircraft detailed had to make a NFT (Night Flying Test) during the day. Simple routine, but essential to ensure the aircraft was alright for the coming night raid. On 10 January, one NFT ended in disaster. T2550 'L', flown by Pilot Officer B. P. McNamara, completed his NFT then headed for Bassingbourne to drop off a pilot and pick up a replacement. Cloud base at Feltwell was down to 1500 feet and McNamara was warned that it could get lower so he headed back to base. Nearing Feltwell, he flew low and was trying to pinpoint his position when the Wellington hit some trees on a hilltop near Duxford, and crashed. Everyone on board was killed, except for the rear gunner who was seriously injured.

Wilhelmshaven was visited again on 11 January by six aircraft while two others headed for Turin, Italy. This was the first attack by the squadron on an Italian target, although one aircraft had to abort with engine trouble. Wilhelmshaven was hit again on 15 January but then bad weather restricted flying until late in January.

At the end of January, Pilot Officer Arthur Ashworth arrived on the squadron, a posting engineered he thought, by Aubrey Breckon. He was destined to become one of the most decorated pilots associated with 75. He says of his early days:

I joined the squadron having only once seen the inside of a Wellington and it wasn't till mid-way through February that I flew my first solo after two and a quarter hours dual. Shortly afterwards I was off, as a second pilot, on my first operational flight. I wasn't particularly apprehensive about this until I saw enemy flak coming up for the first time and suddenly realised that it was possibly intended for me! There were ten more trips before I was given my own crew. I had also spent a considerable time as OC [Officer Commanding] Night, out on the flarepath of that cold grass airfield.

I was very fortunate in being given the chance to learn something of the problems confronting the bomber crews before being sent off on my own. Many pilots were not given this chance, although most of them had been trained at Wellington OTUs which I had been denied. The most fortunate aspect of this period for me was being crewed up

Pilot Officer C. A. Pownell and crew. Left to right: Sgt Read (WOP), Sgt Emeny (FG), P/O Wilcox (RG), Pownell, Sgt A. P. Jones (2P), Sgt Scrivener (N). (A. P. JONES)

C. W. 'Pat' Scott back from 'Ops'. Printed above each bomb mark is the date of the raid.

Crew of 'F' for Freddie (X9634), summer 1941. Left to right: Sgt Les Gore (WOPAG), Sgt Syd Parrott (WOPAG), P/O Dave Florence (N), P/O Tim Williams (2P), Sgt 'Breck' Breckon (P), Sgt Henry Cotton (RG). (L. GORE)

with Pilot Officer Ron Simich, a New Zealander. Not only was he an extremely competent bomber pilot, calm but determined, patient and knowledgeable with a unique capacity for imparting that knowledge, but I learned more from him than from any other bomber source.

February began with further attacks on French ports. Then another pilot who was to make a name for himself arrived on 75 — Flying Officer David Prichard, from Dannevirke, who had just finished his OTU training onto Wellington, having previously been with a Battle squadron in France. He had applied earlier to join 75 but had first to complete his navigational training. Posted with him was Flying Officer T. F. Gill, whose elderly Morris car got them to Feltwell on 9 February:

> *I* well remember my arrival with Frank Gill on that foggy evening. As we drove round the airfield perimeter, an aircraft was attempting to make an emergency landing, came in more or less overhead and crashed on landing without injury to the crew but not so the aircraft.
> Frank and I were both Flying Officers by then, and were allotted what was known in pre-war days as a squadron leader's suite in the Officer's Mess block. It was a most comfortable unit, consisting of a bedroom, lounge (made up as a bedroom) and an 'en suite' bathroom and toilet. Real luxury for those days.
> We shared that room for the whole of our tour. I was posted to B Flight (Squadron Leader G. C. Bain, later Squadron Leader Widdowson) while Frank went to A Flight. By early July, I had completed my tour of Ops, which, like Frank Gill, I had come through unscathed.

Pilot Officer A. J. Falconer and his crew failed to return from Boulogne on the night of 21/22 February — all killed — again the only loss of the Command. Flying as second pilot was Squadron Leader E. V. G. Solbe. This was a piece-meal bombing arrangement, three Wellingtons going to Boulogne, the other four of 75 going to the German target, Wilhemshaven.

Clive Scott arrived on the squadron at this time and remembers:

> *O*n arrival, as was the procedure at that time, my crew was split up, I going as a second pilot to an experienced crew whose second pilot had just been made a Captain, and Jim Thompson, my second pilot, doing the same. I was to fly 12 operations with a New Zealand pilot before becoming a captain myself.
> I did my first Op on 21st March to the French port of Lorient, the target being the submarine pens. It was an uneventful trip except for the take-off, which was on the shortest length of grass available due to the unusual wind direction. We almost went through the trees beside the Officer's Mess rather than over them.

The squadron was now in an almost nightly routine, weather permitting, operating on 11 nights in March, including another to Berlin on the night of 23/24, six squadron aircraft being part of the 35 Wellingtons and 28 Whitleys sent there. A couple of days earlier, on 18 March, 11 aircraft had gone to Kiel and Rotterdam. One aircraft had run out of petrol on the return journey so the crew baled out over Yorkshire. Sergeant D. Gilmour (WOP) was the sole casualty, his parachute failing to open.

The squadron in fact was going through a period where losses were almost non-existent. In fact, following the loss of Falconer on 21/22 February, there were no more losses till early July, which is quite a statistic. The Germans tried, however. On the first raid in April, when Brest was the target, a Me110 had a go at one

Wellington, but it was shot down. The pilot, David Prichard, then ran into more trouble — a mid-air collision:

> *O*n the night of 3rd April we were returning from Brest when we were attacked by a Me110 night fighter which was promptly shot down by my rear gunner for the trip, Flying Officer Davenport-Brown, our Squadron gunnery leader from Wanganui.
>
> Whilst we were looking for Bridport, our south coast crossing point, we inadvertently flew over the naval base at Portland Bill and were treated to some pretty heavy RN light anti-aircraft fire. A few minutes later, flying west and still looking for Bridport, we collided with a Blenheim which was flying in the opposite direction. Shortly afterwards the Blenheim crashed on the mainland with fatal results.
>
> With the assistance of my co-pilot, Pilot Officer Jeff Rees, we managed to keep the aircraft more or less straight and level and, after a Mayday call, we were directed to land at Boscombe Down. I managed to put the Wellington down some 30 minutes later and on 'three wheels'! None of my crew were injured, but the aircraft looked decidedly the worse for wear!

The port wing of the Wimpy had been buckled, with the leading edge smashed in to a depth of 60 centimetres. Half the port elevator had been ripped away, with the other half pulled out of its bearings but still attached to the con rod. The underside of the rear turret was also damaged and Brown caught a knock on one knee. Flying Officer W. D. Brown, who had also forced a German fighter away from the bomber in which he was flying at the end of February, received an immediate DFC. Over Brest, he had seen the 110 flying 90 metres behind the Wellington and fired three bursts into it. It then went into a loop, plummeted down and hit the sea with a dull red glow — confirmed by the crew of another Wellington.

Brest was attacked by 75 three times in early April, after reports that the battleships *Scharnhorst* and *Gneisenau* were there. Berlin was also a target on 9 April. Clive Scott was on this Berlin show:

> *W*e saw lot of fighter, flak and searchlight activity and had an engine overheating. I was told to pump oil to what turned out to be the wrong engine. The Captain had told me the wrong engine which I had to point out to him when I went forward to the cockpit and read the temperature gauges!
>
> The navigation on the way home was hopelessly inaccurate and I had to tell the navigator where we were as I was map reading in the bright moonlight.

Berlin came round yet again on 17/18 April, as Arthur Ashworth remembers only too well:

> *T*he trip itself was comparatively uneventful but we were over a continuous cloud sheet for most of the return journey and unbeknown to us, the winds had changed during the flight. With very little navigational aids available to us at that time and not being able to see the ground, we went past our base. After descending below the cloud we called to 'Darky' [the 1941 version of Mayday] on the primitive TR9 set and were guided by searchlights to Ternhill, having now been in the air for almost nine hours.
>
> On landing, Simich overshot the flarepath and we finished up in a nasty tangle of barbed wire. A Polish crew who landed just after us were not so fortunate and their aircraft was extensively damaged. There had been a mix-up in laying the flarepath, which was only 300 yards long and was laid downwind, so that, there was little, if any, chance of making a successful landing.

◇ ◇ ◇

Life on a bomber station wasn't always one way — the Germans hit back on occasions, as Sergeant Gwyn Martin (Navigator) can testify. Just as he arrived on the squadron, a Dornier 217 intruder, flew over and round Feltwell, trying to find Wellingtons returning from Germany. When that excitement died down, he eventually got to his new billet and went to bed. The next morning he found his room cold and dirty; the reason, he soon discovered was that there was no glass in the window. It had been blown out in an air-raid on the station a few days earlier! Shortly afterwards, he and four other companions from OTU were assigned to be the crew of Pilot Officer George Curry, who had just completed his 15th Op:

> **G**eorge took us on a brief air test and we had the opportunity to see the countryside around Feltwell, before George pronounced the aircraft faulty and we landed for lunch. We were approaching the Mess, hungry after a long morning, when the air-raid sirens started up and we were engulfed by a stream of NCOs carrying dinner plates on their way to the air-raid shelters. We joined them, conspicuous in our newness — we were the only ones who didn't bring their lunch along!
>
> This apparently had been a regular feature of life on Feltwell in this spring of 1941, and this lunchtime, a solitary Dornier, using cloud cover, skilfully attacked aerodromes in 3 Group. While the raid was in progress, Group Captain Buckley, the Station Commander [and previous CO], gave a running commentary over the public address system, a blow by blow — or a bomb by bomb — account of what was happening. This he gave from the top of the exposed air control tower, but his voice never wavered even when the Dornier machine-gunned the 'drome.
>
> The Dornier dropped 20 or so small anti-personnel bombs to the accompaniment of random gunfire before the all-clear sounded. No one was killed or injured and it was the last time Feltwell was to be attacked by a lunchtime bomber.
>
> After our interrupted lunch, we were detailed to attend a demonstration of a new type of incendiary bomb, 20 pounds in weight, with a phosphorous-rubberoid base which was difficult to extinguish. It also had the ability to re-ignite. The smallest quantity of the filling had the ability to burst into strong burning flame, a quality unconsciously demonstrated by the Group Captain when he kicked at a small and apparently extinguished fragment and set his shoe ablaze!
>
> This ended the demo and we returned to our duties, only to hear Group Captain Buckley on the PA system warning all personnel who had attended the demo to disrobe in the open air and submit their clothing to inspection. Apparently, upon his return to his office, his trousers had caught fire!! The whole camp laughed at 'Bucko' telling the joke against himself. He was a natural leader and a father figure to us all.

George Curry*, Gwyn Martin and the rest of the crew flew their first two Ops together at the end of April, as Gwyn remembers:

> **W**e were to bomb the invasion barge fleet at Ostend, but only if we had a clear view of the aiming point. It took us about 1½ hours to reach Ostend, but I could see nothing of Belgium let alone Ostend harbour. So after being shot at for 15 minutes, we returned to base with our bomb load.
>
> A few days later we were ordered to bomb an oil farm near Rotterdam. The night was as black as a cow's belly. We found the mouth of the Scheldt — it was hard to miss — then flew eastwards for some minutes but failed to see the oil storage tanks. We came out westwards to the mouth of the river and then back towards Rotterdam but still no sign of the target. Each run was made at a lower altitude than the last until we were down to about 3000 feet — not a good height to fly a Wellington in a hostile

---

* George William Curry DFC later commanded 627 Squadron, and received the Distinguished Service order (DSO) in October 1944 and a bar to his DSO in February 1945.

environment. George and I decided to give it our best and we dropped our bombs on what we considered to be Schouwen airfield, set course for home and landed safely after five hours of acclimatisation in enemy airspace.

May 1941 saw the squadron hit Hamburg on four separate nights, as well as Brest and then Cologne. While the squadron got away without losses to enemy action during this period, they did lose an aircraft on 6/7 May. That night, 115 aircraft went to Hamburg and all had returned safely. However, Sergeant D. L. Nola hit a balloon cable at the mouth of the River Humber as he re-crossed the English coast and crashed. Sergeant Craven in the rear turret was the sole survivor.

Five days later, on another trip to Hamburg, Squadron Leader R. P. Widdowson, a Canadian, was attacked by a night fighter or intruder on the way out which killed his rear gunner, Sergeant E. G. Gannaway. The Wimpy was badly damaged but Reuben Widdowson brought the Wellington safely home. Sergeant L. A. 'Joe' Lawton was the navigator. He had been with 38 Squadron in 1940 but had been wounded in September. When he was fit his squadron had gone to the Middle East so when asked if he had a preference for another squadron, he asked for 75. He joined the crew of Squadron Leader Widdowson in B Flight and carried out his first raid on 2 May. Their second pilot was Sergeant Tony Saunders, later to become a highly decorated bomber pilot. On the night of 11/12 May Joe remembers:

> Our rear gunner, Peter Gannaway, from Hawkes Bay, was killed by a Ju88. Our aircraft was attacked from dead astern and the fighter must have seen us against the lighter sky. An armour piercing 20 mm cannon shell went through Peter; Tony Saunders and I going back to pull him from the turret. We gave him morphine to deaden the pain and then I tried to operate the turret but it was u/s. We aborted the mission and returned to Feltwell. Peter had not realised how badly injured he was and he died shortly after we landed. He was buried at Feltwell and the funeral took the usual format — a slow march to the cemetery and after the burial, the band would strike up Colonel Bogie as we marched away.

Arthur (Artie) Ashworth went to Hamburg on the night of 8/9 May, although he also had other things to think about at the time:

> The 3rd of May was my 21st birthday and it was also the wedding day of Sergeant Jimmy Blundell, the WOP in Ron Simich's crew. The whole crew were present at the wedding, the reception and certain jollifications which occurred during our one week's leave. Even I would be forced to admit that this was not the most sober period in our lives!
>
> On the 7th we departed from Southport where the wedding had been held and travelled overnight, via London, so that we could be back in time to rejoin the squadron on the 8th.
>
> After breakfast on the 8th, I was asked by Squadron Leader J. M. Southwell if I thought I was capable of taking a Wellington on operations that night. Being now 21, over confident and big-headed, I told him I thought I could and was promptly told to take his aircraft and crew that night.
>
> By this time I had flown 11 Ops with three different captains; had done 77 hour 45 minutes as second pilot; nearly 12 hours dual; and although I'd flown a further 11 hours in command, I had never landed a Wellington at night!
>
> By an amazing coincidence, the Navigator in Johnny Southwell's crew was Sergeant Ted McSherry, who had been the stroke of the youth's rowing four of the Wellington Rowing Club for two New Zealand Championship regattas. I was the bow in the same crew.

Our system of navigation in those early days was crude in the extreme. We used dead reckoning, supplemented by visual pin-points, bearings and drifts, using either the bomb sight or the tail turret. Although all navigators were trained in astro navigation, it was inaccurate and very rarely used. At briefing, only the suggested route and a time to bomb were given, plus bomb load, direction of approach and the height of attack.

On this night our target was the submarine yards at Hamburg and we duly arrived over the city at the appointed hour. We were at 11,000 feet and had approached from the north, having crossed the enemy coast just north of the western end of the Kiel Canal.

As frequently happened, the German defences decided to lie 'doggo' in the hope that if they didn't annoy us we wouldn't annoy them; or that we would be unable to find the target. However, on this raid, because it was a clear night and the amount of water pointing like an arrow to our target in Hamburg, we easily located it and dropped our load. As soon as our bombs were on their way down, the searchlights came on, although we were not coned, and both heavy and light flak guns started firing immediately.

We returned home the way we had gone in and reached base after six hours 25 minutes. The whole way I had this niggling doubt as to my ability to put the aircraft safely back on the ground. In the end I needn't have worried, as Wimpy proved again what a lady she was and the landing was almost perfect. The next night, we veterans bombed Mannheim.

Sergeant Leslie Gore, WOP/AG in the crew of Pilot Officer F. Andrews, RNZAF, remembers the Mannheim trip. They were mid-way through their tour:

*I*t was our 15th trip, and it gave us our biggest fright. We were making our bombing run over Mannheim at approximately 13,000 feet, when both engines failed. Frank, our skipper, calmly feathered the props and completed our run; bombs away from Dave Florence, our Canadian navigator, and we turned for home, steadily losing height as we glided away from the target area. After about 20 minutes and many attempts to restart the engines, they eventually came to life at 3000 feet and we reached base intact. They diagnosed the trouble as iced-up carburettor air intakes which thawed out on the loss of altitude.

I also recall the night when we were caught over Hamburg during a maximum effort of nearly 100 aircraft over the target in the shortest possible time during the full moon. I was in the front turret on this trip and Frank was throwing the Wimpy about like a fighter — I'll swear we were on our back once! Suddenly we almost collided with another Wimpy. It was so close we could read the squadron letters on it — they were AA-K from our own squadron. This near collision must have confused the searchlight crews as the cone split, not knowing which aircraft to follow. We escaped from there flying down the River Elbe to the coast at 2000 feet.

After a trip to Brest, Hamburg and Mannheim, then Cologne on 23 May, there was a different kind of sortie mounted on 27 May. It was the time of the sinking of the mighty *Bismarck*, and her partner, the *Prinz Eugen*, was being sought. David Prichard and his crew were one of the 12 aircraft from 75 that took part in the search:

*I*t was a daylight search southwest of Land's End and I flew as No. 2 in a vic [V-shaped formation] of three aircraft led by Frank Gill. Following a fruitless search we set off for base and whilst still some distance from the coast, the formation was attacked by two single-engined Arado sea-planes. They both fired at us from rather long range, so we made a more difficult target by the 'corkscrew' manoeuvre. We jettisoned the bomb

Ready to start their tour, left to right: P/O H. D. Newman (2P), P/O A. S. Anderson (N), P/O C. K. Saxelby, P/O N. D. Greenaway (RG), Sgt H. G. Campbell (WOPAG), and Sgt R. Brown (FG) (N. D. GREENAWAY)

Briefing for Berlin, 9 April 1941, with Wg Cdr Kay at desk. Left to right: front row P/O Struthers, F/O D. L. Prichard (DSO), P/O Evans, F/O T. F. Gill (DSO); Second row: F/L Fletcher, (unknown), F/O McKay — Nav Leader (in armchair), S/L R. P. Widdowson (DFC) (in greatcoat); Third row (extreme left): Sgt S. Parrott, Sgt L. Gore. (VIA L. GORE)

Pilot Officer Norman Greenaway, rear gunner, cleaning his .303 machine guns, RAF Feltwell, 1941. (TIMES)

load to make evasion that much easier to perform. We returned the fire but with no obvious results and, after a while, the enemy aircraft withdrew.

Next morning, I was informed that, following an airframe inspection, a small hole in the rear of the port engine nacelle revealed at least six holes in the stowed dinghy to make it useless. A fractured rum bottle, part of the emergency ration, had an incendiary bullet lodged in the neck. Fortunately for us, the ignited incendiary material must have been extinguished by the rum. I still have the bullet as a memento of the incident.

Gwyn Martin was in another vic of Wellingtons:

*O*ver the Scillies we were given a latitude and longitude reference point for interception about 300 miles to the southwest. Our aircraft kept formation on the left of our leader, Flight Lieutenant Fletcher. Our navigation leader was Sergeant Micky Minchin of whom it was said, 'He would get lost on the London Underground'. My lack of faith in Minchin's ability was shared by the third navigator in the formation, Pat Carling. He and I kept our own individual air plots and after an hour or so we had both spotted a decrease in wind strength, missed by Micky. There followed an argument between the three pilots, as to whose plots were to be followed. Minchin and Fletcher lost and the formation altered course.

At about 11am we heard that the *Bismarck* had been sunk, and to proceed towards Brest to contact a Hipper class cruiser believed to be the *Prinz Eugen*. We flew a square search on Fletcher's orders and reliant on Minchin's navigational genuis. After an hour or so my air plot looked like the scratchings of a demented hen! During this time we were drifting ever closer to the French coast, but we saw nothing of the ship.

It came as a surprise to find ourselves in a patch of clear sky, like dancers on a ballroom floor, and there behind us at about 600 yards was an Arado seaplane. It was firing at us and what is more it was hitting us with its 20 mm cannon and two machine guns. Our turret guns were harmonised at 300 yards for night operations and had not been changed, which enabled the Arado to come to within 400 yards with impunity. The engagement was over in about two minutes but we had all sustained damage. Then Fletcher led us off into a bank of cloud, leaving the Arado victorious and alone in his patch of sunshine. We had obviously come close to the *Eugen* as she carried a couple of Arados on her.

We then set course for the Scillies at 300 feet and just minutes later we saw a Ju88 approaching us at right-angles at wave top height. We could see the crew clearly as it traversed our path less than 100 yards beneath us and apparently oblivious to our presence. We considered briefly the possibility of dropping our bomb load on him or shooting at him, as any evasive action by him might have involved him putting a wing in, but they only lasted for as long as it took for him to pass us. This was the closest I had been to the enemy and had seen three German faces.

Clive Scott, still flying as second pilot, also doubled as a gunner on this day when the Arados attacked:

We dived to sea level to stop them getting a shot at us from underneath. I manned the 'K' machine guns which could fire through a very small arc to the rear quarters of the plane. The seaplanes kept coming at us, taking care to keep out of the arc of fire of the rear gunner. Once only did I get them in my sights but unfortunately in the very short time they were there I was too slow in releasing the safety catch.

Another Wellington had joined our formation, having become separated from the one it started out with. It flew in the 'box' position and so bore the brunt of the attacks, suffering damage to its hydraulics.

5

Ward VC and Recognition

JUNE — JULY 1941

June 1941 was to be an outstanding month for No. 75 Squadron. For the first half of the year it had constantly achieved good results and a high rate of serviceability, which must have pleased those who had helped bring the squadron into being. It undoubtedly encouraged, too, those back in far off New Zealand to know 'their' squadron was doing so well.

During this historic month, the serviceability rate was to increase further and it would see three records broken for Wellingtons available for night operations. The operations commenced with just three aircraft being sent to Dusseldorf on 2 June as part of a force of 150 to hit that city.

Popeye Lucas had completed his rest period and had returned to the squadron as A Flight Commander. Les Gore, remembers Dusseldorf:

> After our 18th trip with Frank Andrews as captain he had completed his tour and was posted to an OTU, and so we were to get a new second pilot, and Sergeant 'Breck' Breckon, our New Zealand one, became the new skipper. As our new second pilot hadn't arrived before our next trip, Squadron Leader Lucas DFC, CO of A Flight decided to take us in order to check-out Breck.
>
> This proved to be our worst trip, the target being Dusseldorf in the heart of the Ruhr, with a full moon. Popeye Lucas hadn't been on Ops for some time and took us in far too low, right in the thickest area of flak, and we got a mauling. Our hydraulics were shot away, starboard fuel tank holed, loosing 100 gallons of petrol, and many holes from shrapnel. Again, with good airmanship, we got back to England, crash landing at Newmarket.
>
> Afterwards, Breck became our skipper and we completed our remaining 11 trips without too many problems.

Gywn Martin records the fate of the second pilot and front gunner in his aircraft:

> Our pilot [George Curry] was nearing the end of his tour and his nervousness was transmitted to us by a new pitch to his voice. We were in the process of acquiring individual and collective twitches and each cancellation made it harder to hide or disguise our apprehensiveness. We flew to Hamm on the 12th June, flak and searchlights providing above average opposition.
>
> We arrived back in the early hours of the 13th and after a few hours sleep, without a thought for the significance of the date, made our preparations for a thrash in Norwich. Eddie Callender rode pillion on my Sunbeam and Smithie rode pillion on Tompsett's

Triumph Speed Twin. We had a good night out, beer in the 'Bell', dancing and female company in the 'Samson & Hercules Ballroom', a few hours sleep in the Temperence Hotel next door (!), leaving for Feltwell in the early morning.

Eddie and I left on the slower Sunbeam first and we were surprised to arrive back at base before the other two. I had expected Tompsett to pass me on his very fast Triumph. I went to my room, washed and shaved, then made my way to the ante room to be greeted with the news that Tompsett and Smithy and been involved in a serious accident. Tompsett was dead and Smithy was on his way to Norwich infirmary. They had met an army convoy on the crown of a road, hitting a Bedford half-track head-on.

Smithy went through the windscreen of it and killed two of the soldiers. He received horrific injuries: two broken legs, fractured pelvis, ribs, arms and head. How he survived, not only to live but to fly again, is beyond comprehension. He spent a year in hospital, then went to Moreton in the Marsh for a refresher course on Wellingtons. His father had been a First War pilot and was at Moreton as a flying control officer. Father and son enjoyed a few months with each other before learning of Smithy's posting to the Middle East.

The night before he was to ferry an aircraft to Malta, he and his crew were killed on take-off — the duty officer that night was his father!

On 16 June, 75 put up 15 aircraft — again to Dusseldorf — to create a new record. All reached the target, bombed and got home, although one aircraft was attacked and damaged by a Ju88. Two nights later it was another record — 17 Wellingtons on the line for Brest and those two ships again. A force of 57 Wellingtons and eight Stirlings took off, but smoke screens and haze made identification of the target near impossible.

On 24 June, the record for aircraft moved to 18; for Kiel and again to Dusseldorf. It had been a very special day for the squadron in any event, for His Royal Highness the Duke of Kent had visited Feltwell to meet them and No. 57 Squadron who shared the station. He watched as the squadron took off for Germany in the falling darkness.

More was to follow. A letter was received from the AOC 3 Group, Air Vice Marshal J. E. Baldwin, written to Maurice Buckley:

*W*ill you please congratulate the CO and maintenance personnel of 75 Squadron on their exceptional record of serviceability and operational effort during this month.

The following days must be a record for this unit:
    18 June, 16 aircraft out of a strength of 16
    21 June, 17 aircraft out of a strength of 17
    24 June, 18 aircraft out of a strength of 18

As is only to be expected, I note 75 Squadron tops the serviceability list of squadrons in the Group. Such an exceptional standard can only be achieved by the competence and enthusiastic effort of the ground staff, ably backed by good engine manipulation by pilots and captains, and also in no small degree by the operational skill of the crews who have carried out their missions without sustaining any major damage to their aircraft.

Very many congratulations,

Yours sincerely, J. E. Baldwin, AOC, No. 3 Group.

Despite stirring words, the individual is still human and open to human emotions. Each raid was faced with varying degrees of apprehension; that was natural and expected. But nearing the end of one's tour, things got worse. George Curry, Gwyn

Martin's skipper, whose second pilot and rear gunner had been killed and injured a few days earlier had still to finish his tour and, while it might have been the Duke of Kent who waved them off on 24 June, he had been in no mood to appreciate it, as Gwyn remembers:

> George became even edgier and showed no sign of interest in our selection of Sergeant Thompson as a new front gunner and made no move to replace Smithy. We drifted dangerously into our 16th Op and George's 30th — and last. The target was to be the naval dockyard at Kiel. Not the best of targets for your last — seven hours there and back, five over the sea silhouetted against the brilliance of the Aurora Borealis. This trip was a nightmare.
>
> It was a beautiful night with visibility seemingly unlimited. Our run in to Kiel took us along the well-defended Kiel Canal with its ample flak and searchlights clearly defined in the brilliance of the night. Approaching the target I could see my bombing run clearly, set my sights and gave George a course to steer. We had barely shed our bomb load when we were coned in searchlights and were at our most vulnerable; but George came good. He stall turned the Wimpy and lost the lights in the suddenness and wildness of the manoeuvre which took us down to about 6000 feet in seconds. It was a brilliant piece of flying.
>
> We reached home without further incident and in the morning we said goodbye to George, collected our leave passes, and went home for a week.

Artie Ashworth was caught in the Kiel searchlights and had to jettison his bombs:

> As we approached the German coast just south of Denmark, it seemed to me that it was still virtually daylight and, also, that we seemed to be alone. We flew over the peninsula towards Kiel. We were almost over the target when we were coned and all hell broke loose from German AA batteries. I used every trick I knew but could not escape from the glare. Finally, I dived the aircraft frantically towards the Baltic Sea and jettisoned the bombs, and eventually escaped the beams, then crept shamefacedly over Denmark at lower altitude to return home.
>
> I did not return to Kiel until an attack in 1945, but never again was I to jettison bombs in this way.

David Pritchard was in the 'wars' on the night of 30 June, the target being Cologne. For this night's work he was to receive the DSO — the first awarded to 75 Squadron:

> We had just passed through the searchlight belt and were still some distance from the target when we were attacked by a Heinkel 111 night fighter, which I clearly saw as it passed by on the starboard side. After bombing the target area, we set off for home. Our aircraft had sustained fairly heavy damage from cannon and machine-gun fire in the port engine and the undercarriage areas, in addition to which I was unable to close the bomb doors. As luck would have it no crew member was wounded.
>
> Upon arriving over Feltwell, I informed the Duty ATC [Air Traffic Control] that I had a badly vibrating engine and no hydraulic pressure, although by this time we had managed to get the wheels down and locked. I was given permission to land. About three-quarters of the way along the landing run the port under-carriage collapsed and we skidded along on the belly of the aircraft before coming to a grinding halt not too far from a concrete pill-box, part of the airfield defence system. With a strong smell of earth in our nostrils and a lot of dust, the crew left the Wimpy as quickly as possible, none the worse physically, for our latest experience.

The run of good luck ended on the night of 3/4 July. Sergeant I. L. Reid and his crew failed to return from Essen, one of 16 aircraft put up by 75. In total, 90 bombers had gone for the Krupps armaments works, four failing to get home. Clive Scott had finally become a captain in June and was on this Essen raid:

I saw little of the target as usual because of haze. We were held in searchlights for about 30 minutes and were subjected to intense flak. I was twisting, climbing and diving so much that I could not make a steady course towards the UK and back plotting of our route showed that we had been driven down the Ruhr before we broke out of the barrage. My crew, whom I had ordered to put on parachutes, cheered me on, shouting. 'Keep her going, Skipper!' We had a few holes in the fabric and next day the ground crew found a nasty piece of shrapnel stuck in a metal fairing.

Sergeant Jimmy Ward following the award of the Victoria Cross. Left to right: Sgts Gwyn Martin (DFM), Paddy Black, A. G. Windiate, Ray Curlewis, Jimmy Ward, Monty Partridge. (IMPERIAL WAR MUSEUM)

Pilot Officer H. A. Roberts being congratulated on his 'landing' of X9764 after returning from Hanover on 12 August 1941. His crew had all baled out.

Pilot Officer Oliver Matheson (front) and crew with their bomb-squirting soda cyphon. P/O Eric Fowler is directly behind Matheson. (FOX PHOTO)

But all the real excitement of early July came a couple of nights later. Ten Wellingtons from the squadron set course for Germany, part of a force of 49 Wellingtons going to Munster on the night of 7/8 July. Bomber Command's main effort this night was to Cologne and Osnabruck, but 75's ten aircraft went to Munster. Squadron Leader Widdowson crewed one of them and his second pilot was Sergeant J. A. Ward from Wanganui. James Ward had only arrived at Feltwell on 22 June, the day before his 22nd birthday, a birthday celebrated by flying on his first mission — to Dusseldorf. During the next five weeks, Ward flew on four more Ops, so that on 7 July, he was on his 6th trip.

For this raid, 'Ben' Widdowson had been allotted a new Wellington Ic, L7818, coded AA-R. The rest of the crew consisted of Sergeant L. A. Lawton, navigator; Sergeant A. J. R. Box, rear gunner; Sergeant W. Mason, WOP; and Sergeant T. Evans, front gunner. Ward, Lawton and Box were all Kiwis; Widdowson, Canadian; Mason and Evans an Englishman and Welshman respectively.

They took off at 11.10pm, arriving over the target without incident, bombed, and began the trip home. Soon the Dutch coast was ahead, but suddenly their dark world erupted in a hail of cannon shells ripping through the underside of the Wimpy. The hydraulics were ruptured, causing the bomb doors to drop open, Mason's TR9 wireless set was smashed and the R/T severed. Nineteen-year-old Alan Box in the rear turret was wounded in the foot, but then saw their attacker — a twin-engined Me110 night fighter — right in front of him as it banked away after its first pass. Without really thinking, Box opened fire on the 110 at pointblank range. His bullets smashed into the fighter, which fell away on its back, tugging a plume of smoke seen clearly in the moonlight. The 110 was seriously damaged and made an emergency landing at Texel.

However, the damage had been done. A petrol feed pipe in the starboard engine had been hit, and they were trailing a five-foot long tongue of flame back over the fabric-covered wing. Widdowson yelled to his second pilot to get everyone prepared for a bale out, adding, 'And see if you can put out that bloody fire!'

With the message passed to put on parachutes, Ward, Lawton and Mason started to rip away the fuselage fabric on the starboard side. Ward tried to use a hand-held extinguisher through the gap, but the slipstream was against all efforts. Ward then picked up one of the canvas covers used to cover the cockpit when on the ground and said without any fuss, 'Think I'll hop out with this.' He was going to climb out onto the wing and try to stuff the canvas cover into the burning hole to smother the flames!

Joe Lawton tried to dissuade him but Ward insisted on going out. He did agree though, to clip on his parachute chest-pack. Then, with a rope anchored around Lawton's chest, and tied about Ward's waist, the New Zealander went out through the astrodome and onto the top of the fuselage. He was met by the 100 mph howling slipstream, but gradually edged his way down onto the wing, kicking foot holds through the fabric as he went. All the way he was hindered by the chest parachute but he continued down, then along the wing, punching hand and footholds in the fabric, towards the gaping hole beside the engine. Flames were still belching back from it.

Then, holding on with just one hand and both feet, he stuffed the canvas cover into the flaming hole until sheer pain forced him to let go. The slipstream then began to tug the cover from the hole, Ward having again to force it in. After this attempt he let go again, and seconds later the cover was whipped away into the night.

But the flames had lessened and, being unable to do more, he began to make his way back, helped by Lawton on the end of the rope. He finally made it and Lawton pulled him back through into the relative quiet of the fuselage after the howling gale outside. Widdowson headed out across the sea towards England, the fire now much less. A brief flurry of flame shot out shortly afterwards, but most of the fabric had now been burnt or torn off. Finally, at 4.30am, Widdowson put the battered Wimpy down at Newmarket without flaps or brakes, being halted by a barbed wire fence at the end of the landing run.

The Bomber was a write-off, and the damage had to be seen to be believed, as Fred Howell, an airman with 214 Squadron at Newmarket, records:

> *It* is more than likely that I am the only person in New Zealand to see Jimmy Ward's aircraft land after the episode which earned him the Victoria Cross. As I recall, the aeroplane finished up in a barbed wire fence on the far side of the airfield. When my fellow airmen and I saw how badly shot up and burnt that aircraft was, we marvelled at its ability to have made it back to England. Half the rudder was shot away, much of the fabric covering had been burnt from the fuselage and wings, and the hydraulic system was in a sorry state.
>
> The following morning, Newmarket's Commanding Officer ordered all personnel to parade. We assembled in front of the aircraft, which by this time had been towed adjacent to the main grandstand. The CO explained, to all on parade, Sergeant Ward's actions of the previous night and then informed us that from now on the aircraft was strictly out of bounds. It was eventually removed and I understand, broken up and written off. A pity it was not preserved for posterity.

Joe Lawton was also amazed at the state of the Wellington:

> *I* was appalled by the damage to our aircraft and perhaps had we known of its full extent, we would have baled out after the fighter attack. It had become obvious to Ben that the controls had also been badly damaged. Both lateral control and maintaining altitude were problems. It was not until the approach to land at Newmarket Heath, we found the landing flaps would not extend and the brakes did not operate. I believe we survived the landing only because of the experience and skill of Ben Widdowson. Only after the crew left the aircraft did we see the large part of the vertical stabilizer was missing and damage to the elevators was also considerable.
>
> Later, Jimmy Ward received the VC; our pilot, Ben Widdowson the DFC; while Alan Box received the DFM. Our rear gunner had thought he'd shot down the attacking aircraft, but research has shown that he damaged it and it landed in a damaged condition at Texel in the Frisian Islands.

Widdowson and his crew returned to Feltwell and went straight to bed. As they slept, Cyrus Kay wrote up the official summary of the night's operations and, after giving it some thought, made recommendations for awards to some of the crew:

> *It* was part of my job to help de-brief the crews when they came back and this was an obvious act of much bravery. I considered it was up to VC standard, so I said so in my report. They must have agreed at HQ, and then all the way up the line.
>
> The Wellington, of course, was different to other aircraft with its lattice-work geodetic construction and fabric covering. Thus he had been able to dig his hands through the fabric and get a grip on the lattice work. The danger, of course, was that with the fuel fire spreading, that unless it was put out, the aircraft was doomed. If the fire reached the wing tanks, they would have exploded and that would have been that. When he was outside, the crew could do nothing for him as he inched his way along the wing, the slipstream being in the region of 180 mph, trying to blow him off, so it was an

extremely brave thing to do. The Wellington, of course, could take incredible punishment, but this was exceptional.

Kay's recommendation for Britain's highest award for bravery in action was approved and on 5 August 1941, the *London Gazette* officially announced the award. Shortly afterwards, Jimmy Ward was given his own crew and became aircraft captain. Widdowson's crew was split up after the Munster raid. Joe Lawton became a spare navigator, flying with any crew who was without one. Later, he became Navigation Leader on 115 Squadron at Marham. He received the Air Force Cross. Widdowson died of cancer long after the war, and Alan 'Shorty' Box died of a heart attack several years ago.

The third consecutive Munster raid came the next night, then Bremen on 13 July. On this raid Sergeant Minikin lost his starboard engine when climbing out at 6000 feet. He turned back to the coast but lost height and crashed next to the beach off Corton, near Lowestoft. Only he and his second pilot survived; the other four men were killed.

Two nights later it was Duisberg. Sergeant Bob Fotheringham and his crew failed to return and were all killed. Also, Pilot Officer W.J. Rees ran into trouble. First, they were caught by searchlights and hit by flak, and then attacked by a night fighter over the target area. Their Wellington was badly damaged when cannon shells exploded in the cockpit and blasted open the mid-under hatch.

The second pilot was killed; the navigator, Pilot Officer Hunter, fell from the aircraft as he went aft to see to the wounded. The Flight Engineer, Sergeant Conibear, and the rear gunner, Sergeant Gwyn-Williams, were wounded, Conibear later dying in hospital. Sergeant J.W. Lewis, at his radio, was shocked and deafened by exploding shells, but he recovered. He helped the wounded, repaired his radio, then collected maps and assisted Rees in setting a course for home. Both Rees and Lewis later received the DFC and DFM, respectively, for their skill and bravery.

Towards the end of the month, 24 July, came a daylight attack on Brest — the *Gneisenau* again! A major raid had been planned, with 150 bombers attacking in three waves. The first two drew up the fighters, and they caught the third wave of 79 Wellingtons from 1 and 3 Groups (including 75). The opposition was stronger than anticipated, and it cost the RAF ten Wellingtons and two Hampdens. The last wave did not have fighter escort!

Of the six squadron aircraft, Sergeant D.F. Streeter and crew were shot down and killed. Artie Ashworth was on that show and saw what happened:

> *O*ur briefing was from Wing Commander Trevor Freeman [tour expired from 75] who was by then a Staff Officer at 3 Group, and he also led the formation. Together with six Wellingtons from our sister squadron, 57, six of us took off to head for the Scilly Isles. From there we did a circuit of the Brest Peninsula to attack from the southwest. We were not bothered at all by the fighters on our way in, although we saw other aircraft in trouble.
>
> Over the target we were subjected to very severe AA fire, during which all the aircraft were hit. One of them, on the other side of the vic in which I was flying, lost an engine and proved easy prey for the fighters waiting to pounce as we left the flak. The rest of us high-tailed it for England.

Gwyn Martin was on the Brest show, and recalls:

> *T*he two all-NCO crews drew the short straws and occupied the rear stations — tail-

end Charlies. We were one, Don Sreeter the other. It was odd to find ourselves taking off in daylight when we'd be normally going to bed. The formation was led by Wing Commander 'Haystacks' Freeman. A solitary Spitfire appeared in our midst near the Scillies and in less than two minutes, vanished as suddenly as it appeared.

Then we were alone in the blue sky, 22 aircraft ahead of us, Don on our port side 50 yards away. With no navigation to do, I moved from astrodome to cockpit, watching for fighters. Then the French coast came up and things started to fall apart.

There was a slight turn to port and as we banked we caught the combined slipstreams of the 22 aircraft ahead; so did Don, and we nearly collided, but changed positions! We could see his instrument panel clearly as he slid underneath us. It was then that Jock reported five Me109s coming in line astern; Don's gunners seeing them, too.

The 109's line of attack took in Don Streeter first. The initial burst of fire from the 109 leader set Don on fire and he appeared to stop in mid-air, and the last view I had of Don was as his aircraft fell away beneath us. Half the 109 pack went with him for target practice while the 109 leader and two others regrouped above us then dived to finish us off. He hit us several times before he broke off his attack at 300 yards. I could see Jock's tracer framing him the whole time. My activities with my midships Vickers gun served only as a morale booster but in no way did I pose a threat to the 109s. My chief concern was to avoid shooting off our own wingtips and tail unit in the excitement!

Jock kept up his fire on the second 109, his tracer going below us. Then he lifted his nose and found himself too near us and committed the error of presenting enough of his underside to Jock's guns. He went off below us on fire. The third 109 broke away at 500 yards and dived.

We were now alone on the bombing run, and had lost power in the starboard engine. We were 1000 yards behind 57 and 75 Squadron. I came forward to the bombsight to guide Tony for this last, long two minutes to the target.

Looking down on Brest Harbour that day I felt like closing my eyes in order to avoid seeing the flak. The sky was full of bursting shells and lazy streams of tracer. The *Gneisenau* was covered in netting through which her flak barrage was being fired. I aimed my stick of six bombs to hit the ship on a long diagonal and then watched them fall in perfect flight to curve into the side netting. The flak left us on the outskirts of Brest and right on cue were two more Me109s.

They turned back from their engagement of the others to give us their undivided attention. Jock hit the leading 109 as he hit us. A German cannon shell went through the side of the front turret and finished up, spent, in Thompson's crutch! The second 109 fired briefly from 800 yards then dived after his leader, heading down towards their base at Morlaix.

Tony Saunders nursed his Wellington back to England and made a belly landing at Boscombe Down without injury to his crew. Thompson, of course, had been slightly wounded by the cannon shell and went off to hospital. They had had a tough mission, even being shot at by the Royal Navy as they headed over the Portsmouth area, but they had made it.

6

Wellington Ways

AUGUST 1941 — APRIL 1942

There was now increasing evidence that the German defences were beginning to stiffen considerably. Searchlights and flak gunners seemed to be working more in co-ordination than had earlier been the case and night fighter activity was on the increase. Raids to Mannheim, Frankfurt and Calais on 6/7 August cost the squadron one crew, that of Sergeant L. I. A. Millett. Both his gunners died but the rest were taken prisoner.

Yet, whatever the Germans put in their way, Bomber Command were getting through, even if the sophistication of finding, marking and bombing targets was still to come. What bomber crews in the early war years had to contend with only proved to those who followed what devotion to duty these men showed. Take for instance the ordeal of the Australian Pilot Officer H. A. Roberts and his men on the night of 12/13 August.

Hannover was the target for Roberts' trip, but on their return journey, Wellington X9764 was attacked by a night fighter over the Zuider Zee. The aircraft was hit by a long burst of fire before the rear gunner spotted the German and sent it down in a steep dive. However, the Wellington had been extensively damaged. The ASI (Air Speed Indicator) and main hydraulic pressure pipe was shot away, which allowed the bomb doors and wheels to drop. The wing dinghy was half released, aileron controls were hit, and the wireless damaged. The aircraft fell into a dive but Roberts struggled and eventually regained control and headed for Newmarket, the engineer warning him that fuel was leaking from three damaged tanks.

Nearing Newmarket, the engines suddenly fell silent as the fuel ran out. Roberts immediately ordered the crew to bale out, which they did. But by the time the five men were clear, he had no time to jump himself. Putting on his landing light he was lucky enough to spot a fire break in a forestry plantation and put the Wimpy down on that with remarkably little damage. As well as these sorts of difficulties when flying on Ops, there was also the problem of actually finding the target over a blacked-out Germany.

That same night saw the loss of one of the Command's trial 'Gee' sets in another Wellington, although the Germans did not get hold of it. Gee was the RAF's first major improvement to navigation, a device which enabled a bomber's navigator to fix the aircraft's position. The Gee Box received pulse signals from three separate stations in England, computed the difference, and produced a fix. Its range depended on the bomber's height and distance from England, but it worked for some 640 kilometres and to a height of 20,000 feet. In reality it only helped the navigator to get to the general vicinity of the target when forecast winds proved incorrect and might have blown the machine off-course. But it was a start.

An enemy innovation which occurred from time to time, and which should have been used much more often, was the use of intruders. Squadron aircraft returning from Hannover on the morning of 15 August came into contact with one such intruder, a Ju88, which attacked one bomber head-on over Feltwell, but it missed its intended victim.

In addition to recent awards — the VC to Ward, DSO to Prichard, and DFCs to Rees, Widdowson and Artie Ashworth — DFMs went to two rear gunners, Sergeants E. Callender and H. R. Corrin, and the DFM to Gwyn Martin. An additional DFC went to Pilot Officer C. Stokes, a rear gunner.

Gwyn Martin remembers a trick which the Germans used to try and confuse the RAF's attacks. The date was 6/7 September, the night Pilot Officer J. E. Johnson and crew failed to return:

> *H*uls, was my moment of greatest disillusionment. Before Huls I believed most newspaper reports of our activities and in the progress of the war. After Huls I believed in nothing. The target was a small factory situated near a frog-shaped lake, north of Essen. It was a most difficult place to approach without being sucked into the Ruhr valley defences. We searched the area thoroughly at ever decreasing heights until we were caught in searchlights and passed from gun to gun on the edge of the Ruhr, until we were in a desperate situation at 1500 feet over the centre of Essen. The bomb load was jettisoned over an urban complex and we dived at speed, benefitting from our lighter weight and headed north.
>
> Barely five minutes into our return flight, at 1000 feet, I looked out to starboard and there in the light of a pale waning moon, could be seen quite clearly the frog-shaped lake. Beyond was the target covered by camouflage netting which extended out into the lake, thereby altering part of its characteristic shape. There was no sign of activity, no fires, the only ones visible were to the northeast, 15 miles off.
>
> We returned home and were the last to land. At de-briefing, we tried to justify our dropping the bombs but there was the hint from the Group Captain that we were cowards. However, I stuck to my story and emphasized my view of the target on our exit which conflicted with the evidence from other returning 75 and 57 Squadron crews. Only one other navigator corroborated my story, a chap from 40 Squadron at Wyton. Later, a PRU Spitfire picture of the target confirmed our claims.
>
> Yet the headlines in the newspapers read, 'Bombers of Bomber Command criss-cross their way to destroy the German rubber industry at source . . . . etc'. It was absolute rubbish. The Huls factory was not hit until the Americans succeeded in doing so in 1944 — in daylight!

Gwyn's tour of 30 Ops ended with a trip to Brest on 13/14 September — two years to the day from when he had joined up. He was promoted to Pilot Officer after his return from a Bombing Leader's course, which he failed!

◇ ◇ ◇

September saw five crews fail to return: Johnson on the Huls raid, Sergeant K. Roe over Keil on the 11th, and Sergeant W. M. Smyth on the 17th. The other two were lost on a trip to Hamburg on 15/16 September — the squadrons's first double loss in one night. But more importantly, one of the crews was skippered by Jimmy Ward, on his 11th sortie and, his 5th as captain.

Of the 169 bombers that went to Hamburg, eight were lost. Ward's Wellington —

Air and ground crew of L7818 'R'. Left to right, standing: Sgt A. G. Windiate (AG), Sgt Gwyn Martin (DFM) (N), P/O George Curry (DSO DFC), Sgt Brian Smith (2P), Sgt E. Callender (AG), Sgt J. B. Tompsett (AG). In front are the radio mechanic, armourer, fitter and rigger. (G. MARTIN)

Cecil Ball's kite, AA-B 'Z1570', lost over Hamburg 28 July 1942, when captained by Flight Sergeant A. G. Jones. (F. W. J. CHUNN)

Pilot Officer Artie Ashworth, second from left, would win the DSO and DFC with 75. With him are Sgt Ted McSherry (N), Pilot Officer Wilson (2ndP) and Sgt Broad from his crew. (A. ASHWORTH)

X3205 — was hit repeatedly by the city's deadly flak and set on fire. Only the observer, Sergeant L. E. Peterson, and the WOP, Sergeant H. Watson, managed to escape by parachute. Ward and the other three sergeants were buried in Ohlsdorf Cemetery, Hamburg.

Joe Lawton, who had been with Ward on the night he won the VC, also came close to death on the night of 20/21 September; the target was Berlin and 12 aircraft had been assigned from 75. Joe recalls:

> *I* went to Berlin with Sergeant Matetich. The radio operator did not receive a recall signal from Group for all aircraft to return to their bases because of dense fog being forecast for our return. So we proceeded onto Berlin — alone. We wondered why we were subjected to a fair amount of opposition both en route and over the target!
>
> When we got back to Feltwell, we could not land and all the aerodromes were under heavy fog, so we were ordered to head the aircraft out to sea and bale out.
>
> We baled out over Horsham St Faith in pitch dark and fog, so it was impossible to see the ground before hitting it. I hit with a terrific jar and cracked two vertebrae which have given me trouble ever since. By some coincidence, it was exactly one year to the day since I'd been wounded — 20th September 1940 — and now this 20th September I'd baled out and hurt by back. However, I was operating again on the 28th — to Genoa.

As if to underline that the Germans were getting better at defence, 75 Squadron lost no less than six crews the next month, including another double loss over Cologne on 15/16 October. Sergeant Matetich was among those lost. Six more were lost in November, with three failing to return from a trip to Essen on the night of 8/9 November.

However, Wellington Mark IIs, with Merlin X engines, were beginning to arrive on the squadron. The Mark III, with two 1500 hp Bristol Hercules XI engines, would begin to arrive in the new year. Also arriving was the 4000 pound bomb — the famed 'cookie'.

As well as new aircraft and arms, the squadron now had a new Commanding Officer. Cyrus Kay left in September, his place being taken by Wing Commander Reginald Sawrey-Cookson DSO DFC, an Englishman who had joined the RAF in 1937. He was 26 years old and, despite his distinguished career so far, was not too well liked by the squadron. The fatherly figure of Cyrus Kay was always on hand to make sure everyone knew what was required, and was always there at the beginning and end of raids. But Sawrey-Cookson had a different way of doing things and, unhappily, the morale of the squadron suffered a little at this time.

With the coming of the winter weather, Operations tailed off a little. It was not until 12 December that the first month's sorties were flown, and Brest was again the target. In fact Brest became a feature of the month. *Scharnhorst* and *Gneisenau* were still in port and a potential menace. They had to be bottled up, watched and bombed whenever possible. As we know now, both ships, together with the *Prinz Eugen*, were to make their famous 'Channel Dash' to Norway the following February.

The Brest flak and fighters were never pleasant. Sergeant J. K. Climie had to land at Exeter after one raid to get medical attention to Pilot Officer Gunning, wounded by shrapnel. Then Sergeant L. L. Bentley died when his damaged Wimpy crashed at Berners Heath, Norfolk. All his crew were injured. On another day, Sergeant Machin got as far as Dartmoor on one engine before he and his crew baled out.

Sergeant P. L. 'Bill' Burridge saw Brest from the rear turret of a Wellington at this period:

> *O*n a raid on Brest, we were detailed to draw the flak from the heavies who would bomb from above us. We had one 4000 lb bomb. When there was no signal, we went in and flew round as briefed for as long as we could, then bombed a heavy flak battery prior to returning to base, full of holes. On landing, we were asked where we had been and we replied — Brest. We were then informed that there had been a recall, which we had missed. However, we had photos to prove where we had been. The aircraft had received a hit (amongst many others) and a piece of shrapnel had gone through the turret and cut my Irvine jacket across the back!

The squadron had a rest over Christmas 1941 but it was back to Brest on 27 December — resulting in Machin's loss on Dartmoor. Then suddenly it was 1942 and the first Mark III Wellingtons began to arrive. Weather and training on the new type curtailed operations for most of January, and by the end of the month there were 16 Mark IIIs on strength. This Mark gave an additional 32 kph on speed, extended the range by more than 480 kilometres, and gave an additional 1000 feet of service ceiling, now to 19,000 feet. In addition, the tail gunner now had four rather than two .303 machine guns with which to defend the machine.

The severe winter continued to hit Feltwell as February began, the aerodrome actually being out of action due to heavy snowfalls. The aircrew suffered additionally by having to attend lectures, while the pilots kept their hands in on the Link trainer, flying training sorties when weather allowed. Then came the 'Channel Dash'. No. 75 Squadron were able to put up just two bombers to attack the heavily defended convoy of German ships — in daylight, but in poor weather. It and fighters thwarted their efforts, but they got back safely.

By the end of February the total of Mark IIIs had risen to 21, but one — X3355

'W' — crashed at Lakenheath when the starboard and then the port engines cut out. The pilot and one airman were injured, while two other airman and an NCO co-pilot were killed. Bill Burridge remembers the incident:

> **S**ergeant Colville was carrying out an air test on a new Mark III. It was a foggy day and he had taken three ground crew with him. During the flight one engine failed and the plane was losing height when the other engine cut-out. The controls jammed and the aircraft just missed a farmhouse before hitting the ground and bursting into flames. Colville was badly injured and the second pilot, too, and died in hospital.

It was not unusual for ground crew personnel to be taken up on air tests. They liked it, liked flying and it gave them a boost to actually fly in the machine they spent many hours keeping serviceable. On this same night, LAC Bob Smith, a fitter, went up in Q-Queenie:

> **N**FTs [Night Flying Tests] were usually about a half hour in duration, but this night we were up for two. A new crew were in charge and I was in the bomb aimer's compartment. Above cloud base the weather was brilliant and we seemed to be flying around for a long time when we came through the clouds and to my surprise we were over the sea. I could see the coast about three miles ahead and as we neared, noticed gun flashes. We hastily climbed back above the cloud and although I initially thought we must have been off the Dutch coast, it was Norfolk. We then passed over the 'drome a few times and found the reason we didn't land was that the crew was still lost!
>
> There was a reception committee waiting when we did land. We had been reported missing and I was the only ground crewman on board — with no parachute!
>
> Y-Yorker crashed on this night. Owing to a mistake with the petrol cock behind the main spar, she got airborne and then stalled through lack of petrol. One of the ground crew killed was a pal of mine, Wilf Pawnell.

◊ ◊ ◊

The first real 1942 Op for 75 and for its new Mark IIIs came on 8 March, ten aircraft going to Essen; there was a follow-up raid the next night. Then it was Kiel — and disaster.

Eight aircraft were assigned and they found clear weather over the target — the U-boat yards — after 5/10ths cloud on the way in. They met searchlights and heavy flak, and three aircraft failed to return. As the total losses that night were just five, 75 took the brunt of the missing. The crews of Squadron Leader Kitchen, Flying Officer Sandys, and Sergeant Parnham were all killed.

Pilot Officer Alan Slater and crew failed to return from Essen on 25 March. Bill Burridge was the rear gunner, flying his 10th trip:

> **I** was detailed to fly with Sergeant Mclaughlan and his crew on their first operation — to Dunkirk — on 13th March, as their rear gunner had gone sick. We took quite a pounding over the target and forced landed at Martlesham Heath. Pilot Officer Climie came to collect me the next day as I was required to fly with my own crew.
>
> Then on the night of the 25th, we were sent on a raid to Essen. The starter motor on the port engine burned out and I assisted Bill Beardmore to start it with the starting handle which made us late for take off. We flew direct to Essen and on the run in took a pounding from ground fire.
>
> We received a direct hit in the bomb bay which was full of flares. As the flares were to be used as a marker for the main stream, it was not possible for us to jettison them. We were unable to put the fire out, so the aircraft was eventually abandoned and I landed

in Duisberg where I was given a hostile reception by the natives until taken prisoner by some Ack-Ack gunners.

Slater and his crew were all captured with the exception of the second pilot, Sergeant John Addis. In fact, Addis had just been given his own crew but said he would fly this one last Op with Slater. Bill continues:

> Our second pilot and WOP — Ted Wainwright — had worked out a plan whereby if they ever had to abandon the aircraft and were a parachute short, they would clip the remaining parachute on one hook of each of their respective harnesses and jump together. So on this night, when it happened, they both jumped together, but with his arm through Ted's harness while Ted held him with one arm. Tragically, when the chute opened, the second pilot was thrown off.

Two more squadron aircraft were lost on a raid to Cologne on 5 April, one captained by the CO, Sawrey-Cookson. Four Wellingtons were lost that night, so 75 again took a high percentage loss. It is recorded that one Wellington bomber, with a Canadian crew, fell into the centre of the city and onto a crowd of people watching the raid. Its bomb load exploded, killing 16 and injuring 30 of the spectators!

The squadron's new 'boss' was Wing Commander E. G. Olson. Ted Olson came from New Plymouth and had joined the RAF in 1926 before being appointed to the RNZAF in 1935. He was 36 years old and, after service in Egypt and India in the 1920s, had returned to New Zealand as an instructor. After the start of the war, he was chief instructor at Wigram and Hobsonville.

He joined 75 when its morale was a little low due to the recent losses, but he quickly brought stability to the squadron and was to lead it through one of its most successful periods. Indeed, for three months during the summer of 1942, the squadron held the 3 Group record for sending out more aircraft than any other squadron. His two Flight Commanders, were Frank Denton, who had returned for a second tour, and Squadron Leader R. J. Newton, from Christchurch, who would eventually command the squadron.

But success didn't come instantly and, when the squadron returned to Cologne on the night of 22/23 April, it met heavy opposition. In total, 64 Wellingtons and five four-engined Stirlings went for Cologne; all carrying Gee, with which 75 had been training. It was an experimental raid, the crews being ordered to use Gee as a bombing aid. Some crews bombed accurately but others were anything up to 16 kilometres from their supposed aiming point.

Two Wellingtons were lost, one being from 75, and the squadron had two others badly shot up. Flight Sergeant T. S. Mahood and his crew were all killed, while Pilot Officer Jarman, attacked by a night fighter, returned with two dead and two wounded aboard. Jarman was hit on the way out by a Ju88 which made one pass, killing the second pilot and the rear gunner. The navigator and wireless operator were both wounded, Jarman having to make a crash landing at Feltwell. Flight Sergeant I. J. McLaughlan was also attacked by a night fighter, killing the second pilot out-right and wounding the rear gunner. This Wellington, too, made a successful crash landing.

Warrant Officer A. G. E. 'Butch' Pugh, a New Zealand WOP/AG, was in McLaughlan's crew. He remembers this sortie:

> The raid on Cologne was on the eve of my 21st birthday. The raid had been uneventful, the target bombed and course set for home. We were about 150 miles from

the European coast and I was in the front turret. At midnight, a cheery greeting from the skipper on my arriving at the magic age of 21, was followed three minutes later by a shower of tracer from the rear of the aircraft, which passed under my feet, and the aircraft commenced a descent.

My immediate reaction was — 'well you are 21, will you make 22?' A quick check on the intercom showed the pilot, navigator and WOP, were OK, but no response from the second pilot or rear gunner. Our hydraulics were useless and the trim tabs had been shot away, so Mac had the whole weight of the aircraft on the control column. As my front turret was inoperative, I extricated myself and went back to the cockpit and was asked to go to check on the second pilot and rear gunner.

The second pilot was slumped over the interior mounted oil tank and had been killed instantly. The catwalk to the back of the Wimpy was a shambles but I managed to rouse the gunner who had been hit in the foot, get him out of the turret and back on the bed so I could apply a field dressing and give him a shot of morphia.

On return to the cockpit we had a crew conference. The aircraft was losing height but the engines were still OK, but our chances of making base seemed remote. We agreed to keep going to get to the French coast or even the Channel and possibly ditch and hope to be picked up by the rescue boys.

We made it to the coast and decided to go for broke and make for base. Mac had a sore back from holding the aircraft up so I stood alongside him and helped to take the strain off his back. We made Feltwell, landed wheels up with the aircraft looking like a pepper-pot, with only four of us to celebrate my birthday. Mac was awarded an immediate DFM, and the rear gunner eventually recovered from his wounds and was repatriated home.

April ended with raids to Rostock and Cologne, and mine-laying sorties on the 27/28th. This was the first mention in the squadron records of mine-laying, which like most squadrons, was to become a regular feature of night Ops. Code named 'Gardening', aircraft would fly out to drop mines outside German harbours or in known shipping lanes and channels. Often these 'Gardening' sorties were flown by crews flying their first operational sorties, to give them experience in night flying to the enemy coast. It was safe enough, but the number of crews who failed to return from these sort of missions did show that it was not always a 'piece of cake'.

7

One Thousand Strong

MAY — JULY 1942

May 1942 saw the squadron undergoing intensive training in all aspects, including Gee. Operations to Stuttgart, Essen and Mannheim were interspersed with mining sorties to Kiel Bay, which cost the squadron the crew of Flight Sergeant M. F. G. Fraser on 15 May. Other crews reported AA opposition from flak-ships, which probably accounted for the lost Wellington. Training cost 75 another aircraft on 21 May, Pilot Officer Smith flying into a hill in bad visibility at Leek, in Staffordshire. Only the rear gunner survived, with injuries.

The main event of the month, however, was the Command's Maximum Effort on the night of 30 May. The target was Cologne, but what was significant was that for the first time during the war, the attacking force would top 1000 aircraft.

Air Chief Marshal Sir Arthur Harris, Commander in Charge of Bomber Command since 22 February 1942, wanted to hit Germany with a large force, and a magic number of 1000 aircraft was good publicity value. He had inherited a force of only 470 night and 78 day bombers in February but, despite losses to enemy action and to other Commands — Coastal and Middle East — he had been able to increase his force. True, he had to 'borrow' crews and aircraft from OTUs to reach the grand total of 1047, but he made it.

The majority of this force still consisted of twin-engined bombers such as the Wellington, Whitley and Hampden types, but the new four-engined bombers were fast coming off the production lines. While the Wellington was well represented with a total of 602 going out on this night, there were also 131 Halifaxes, 73 Lancasters and 88 Stirlings. It was a massive assault, and it is thought that nearly 900 bombed the target. Two other figures that night reached new heights — losses totalled 41, and 75 Squadron's own 'Maximum Effort' reached 23 Wellingtons!

The squadron recorded a successful raid, seeing many fires started from their bombing, the bomb loads including a goodly number of the very effective four pound incendiaries. They lost just one aircraft, that of Pilot Officer D. M. Johnson, whose rear gunner was the sole survivor.

Sergeant R. S. D. Kearns, from Reefton, who would win the DFM with 75, the DFC with 156, and the DSO with 617 Squadrons, flew on this first 1000 bomber raid just prior to coming to 75. He recalls:

> This was my first operation which I carried out from OTU whilst awaiting a posting to an operational squadron and to be detailed to go un-accompanied by an experienced pilot was a singular honour! At take-off my crew and I were extremely nervous and

when we tried to sing our favourite song to boost our morale — 'Tumbling Tumble-Weeds' — it was so flat as to be unbelievable.

The spectacle was the fire of the burning city. It was visible for over 100 miles away and to us an awe-inspiring sight both on the way to and from the target.

Sergeant Neville Hockaday had just arrived on 75 Squadron, but did not fly on this night. However, he recorded his recollections in his, as yet, unpublished manuscript:

> My new room-mate, John, had completed 18 Ops in nearly five months and some of the crew had begun to develop the 'jitters'. This was highly dangerous, as they began to feed off one another, breeding even more nerves. From what I could see John (a navigator) was in a bad state.
>
> Before each raid, John had a simple routine to cover the pre-raid hours. First, he sat down on his bed and wrote a letter to his wife. When he had done that, he would put it in an envelope, which he left unsealed. On his return he would add a figure at the bottom of the letter before sealing it. That figure represented the number of the trip he had just completed. It was a simple way of indicating to her that he had safely returned from another raid and the progress he was making towards the completion of his tour. Having written his letter, John lay down on the bed, shut his eyes and relaxed until it was time to go down to the Crew Room. When he went, I walked down with him.
>
> The grass outside the hangars this night had disappeared under the bodies of the crews of 47 Wellingtons — 20 from 57 Squadron, 23 from our 75 Squadron, and four from Flying Training Command. That amounted to almost 250 aircrew.
>
> It was still broad daylight as the crew coaches arrived, open top lorries, and the camp bus, to take the men to their aircraft. There was a great deal of noise and bustle as they embarked and within 15 minutes all had been driven off to the various aircraft dispersals around the perimeter.
>
> Later the peace of the evening was shattered by the spitting sound of the first aircraft engines to be started up. As each engine was tested the noise rose to a crescendo, then fell away as the throttle was closed again. We then watched as the aircraft moved along the perimeter track on the far side of the airfield, which reminded me of an army of soldier ants making their orderly but relentless way forward.
>
> After take-off, the evening sky above Feltwell was alive with aircraft but in less than half an hour after the first Wellington had rolled down the flarepath, we could see the tail light of the last aircraft disappearing in the direction of the Suffolk coast. We began to drift away, some, like us adjourned to the bar, but there was no point in staying up, for the first aircraft would not be due back until 4am.
>
> John woke me up upon his return. 'How was it?' I asked. He said he was sorry for waking me, then added, 'It was fine, but I'll tell you about it later. Now I must get some sleep. Goodnight.' It was 5am. I rose at 7, trying to be as quiet as possible. Over breakfast talk was of last night's raid. Then at 9am we went into the ante-room to listen to the radio. The announcer was saying: 'Last night our bombers were over Germany. One thousand bombers raided the old town of Cologne. Forty-one of our aircraft are missing.'

Two nights later came the second 1000 raid, this time going for Essen. In the event, only 956 bombers could be mustered, although a further 48 Blenheims did make intruder sorties against German airfields, so 1000 aircraft did take off for Germany. No. 75 Squadron sent off 20 aircraft and all came home. However, the RAF lost 31.

By comparison, the next raid on Essen, the following night, was made by just 195 aircraft, 16 from the squadron. This night, Pilot Officer C. W. P. Carter and crew were all taken prisoner.

◇ ◇ ◇

Crew of 'P' Peter, Feltwell, August 1942. Left to right: F/O F. W.J. Chunn (RG), F/Sgt Fern, F/O E. G. D. 'Riki' Jarman DFC, P/O Jock Taylor (N), P/O Ron Davey (AG).

(F. W. J. CHUNN)

Flight Sergeant C. W. B. Kelly (Navigator), later Squadron Leader DSO DFC, inspects the damage to his Wellington, RAF Feltwell, after a fighter inflicted damage to 'M' Mother over Emden, 6/7 June 1942.

(C. W. B. KELLY)

LAC Gray repairing the rear turret of W5663, damaged over Duisberg, 15 July 1941.

(D. MORRIS)

After the big publicity raids came the nightly slog. Essen and Emden were the main targets for June, and then Bremen three times at the end of the month. Neville Hockaday flew his first raid, to Essen, on 5 June and wrote:

>Some of our fellow pilots were very experienced: Squadron Leader Frank Denton, Ball, Pete Gunning, Ricky Jarman DFC, Ian McLachlan DFM, and J. C. Wilmshurst. One night in April, both Jarman and Mac had been attacked by night fighters and by a bizarre coincidence, both aircraft were attacked from underneath and in each case they had lost their second pilots; Nicol with Jarman, Fountain with McLachlan.
>
>On the morning of the 5th I was told I would be flying as second pilot to McLachlan that night. The 'Jeremiahs' were quick to remind me that the last second pilot Mac had carried had died at his look-out post at the astrodome. I countered this with the comment that lightning was reputed not to strike in the same place twice. When I found the target was Essen, I felt that I could not have asked for a greater baptism of fire.
>
>The operational duties of a second pilot in a Wimpy were somewhat restricted by lack of space. He sat beside the pilot for take-off and landing, assisting in such things as raising and lowering the undercarriage and flaps; switching on and off the various fuel pumps, and generally making himself useful. During flight he took up his station at the astrodome, acting as an extra pair of eyes scanning the sky for enemy night fighters.
>
>Over the target some of the flak came close as we approached and I got a whiff of cordite as the aircraft flew into puffs of smoke left by the exploded shells. The ground over the target area resembled an active volcano, with the frequent eruptions caused by the bombs exploding on the ground.
>
>McLachlan let me take control as we recrossed the North Sea. He stretched his legs and disappeared into the cabin, only to reappear a short while later, carrying two cups of syrupy coffee, one of which he passed to me, the second he carried down to the front turret for Walters. Then he went back to have his own coffee. As we crossed the English coast just north of Great Yarmouth, he reappeared, took back the controls and flew back to base. After lunch the next day I made the following entry in my Flying Log Book: WAR OPS 1 — ESSEN, 3 hours, 40 minutes.

The newly arrived crew of Jack Wright made their first trip when they went to Emden at this time. It was a memorable first Op, as Charles Kelly, the navigator, remembers:

>When we arrived on the squadron the aircraft had just been fitted with the new navigational fixing system, code-named GEE, so we were training every spare moment. The system was basically simple to use but training in speed and accuracy was necessary.
>
>At this stage, our pilot was required to do a couple of trips as a second pilot to an experienced crew to get the feel of things. Also I managed to get in an 'Op' as a replacement navigator with another crew and I think that some of the others managed to get one in, to keep up with our pilot.
>
>As a new crew we were expected to take any available aircraft but later on with a few Ops behind us, we could anticipate the allocation of a permanent machine together with its ground crew, and this eventually turned out to be D-Donald. On this we put our Donald Duck mascot, painted by one of the ground crew, a chap named Prince; a Londoner, I believe.
>
>Our first Op as a crew turned out to be one of the luckiest of the whole tour. We were caught by a Ju88 on the return from Emden. It was especially lucky for Nick Carter, our WOP. He was standing with his head in the astrodome (an extra pair of eyes to look out for fighters), and he spotted the Junkers at the same time as our rear gunner. Now just aft of the astrodome were two narrow steel doors or panels, hinged together in the centre which could be opened up across the aircraft and thus provide some protection

from the rear both for the occupant and the crew members further forward. I don't know whether even he is sure when he ducked down behind the doors, before or after the fighter opened fire, but in any event he left a fraction of his rear anatomy sticking out. As a result, he lost a piece of his trousers!

This naturally provided a lot of hilarity afterwards but, more importantly, it provided us with a salutary lesson that all available eyes were needed to cover the sky to the rear, both to port and to starboard, above and below — especially below.

The aircraft became very difficult to control on the way home as some of the control cables had been damaged. We also got in a spot of bother when we finally reached base. Unbeknown to us some damage had accrued to the wiring relating to the control of the VHF radio equipment, which caused it to be in the transmit mode, and for it to transmit all conversation made over the aircraft intercom.

Nearing base there was a bit of chit-chat about the attack, with a few choice epithets to describe the night fighter pilot, and all of this was heard by aerodrome control and the CO, who was in the Control Tower at the time. This resulted in Jack being summoned to get a 'strip torn off'!

Essen on 8/9 June cost the squadron the lives of two crews, those of Pilot Officers R. J. Smith and G. E. Murdoch. The second trip to Emden, on 20 June, cost 75 another crew and then it was the third 1000 raid — to Bremen on the night of 25/26 June. Again, the main force fell short, just 960 aircraft, although 56 more 2 Group aircraft hit German airfields. Coastal Command were also allowed to participate, and they listed 102 Hudsons and Wellingtons as going to Bremen. Never before or afterwards were so many varied aircraft types used against Germany in one raid: Wellingtons, Halifaxes, Lancs, Stirlings, Blenheims, Hampdens, Whitleys, Bostons, Manchesters, Hudsons and Mosquitoes. Forty-eight failed to return, including 23 from OTUs and five of the Coastal aircraft.

All 20 aircraft sent by 75 returned, among them Neville Hockaday flying on his fifth 'freshman' trip. He could now take his own crew on Ops, but later on it was not usual for a new pilot to fly so many 'second dickie' trips. As the war progressed, second pilots became a luxury Bomber Command could ill afford to risk, so the 'for experience' trips were restricted to just one or two. In any event, the second pilot position in Wellingtons, except for experience flights, had now come to an end. To lose one pilot and crew was bad enough; to lose two pilots in one aircraft was expensive.

So Neville Hockaday went to St Nazaire on 28 June, dropping mines. The next night it was back to Bremen, with the force of 18 aircraft put up by the squadron. But the night did not get off to a good start.

There is no more vulnerable time for an aircraft than on take-off. The fuel tanks are full, the bomb bay loaded to capacity, and the crew, especially the pilot, are anxious and apprehensive. Fortunately, accidents were few but if the slightest problem arose at the critical stage of lift-off or when climbing away from the airfield, chances of survival were not good. On this night, Sergeant R. Bertram and his crew crashed on take-off and blew up. There were no survivors.

Another crew, that of Pilot Officer W. J. Monk, failed to return and Neville Hockaday and his crew came close to joining them, as his rear gunner Bruce Philip, from Christchurch, explains:

> *T*hat is one night I will never forget. We had been on the squadron for about three weeks and had done about three Ops, each with different crews and aircraft, but tonight was different. We were on our own, with our new aircraft 'F' for Freddy, with a 4000 pounder slung underneath, something we hadn't experienced before. The night

was perfect — a full moon to the south and the Northern Lights to the north, while due west was the dark strip between the two skies.

We crossed the Dutch coast with a small amount of flak, then set course for the target. The skipper said he was going to climb to a thin layer of cloud above us at about 13,000 feet but at 11,000 my microphone started to freeze up and as I tried to thaw it out, I saw this night fighter swing out of the north sky into the dark band to the west, then zig-zag towards us at high speed.

The crew up front realised what was wrong. I heard the wireless operator say he would take his station at the astrodome as this is the procedure under these circumstances, so that he could be the skipper's rear-facing eyes and instruct him which evasive action to take if necessary.

The fighter, which was a Ju88, came in for his attack, dead astern and slightly above us. I opened fire at just over 200 yards to get the advantage and could see some of my tracers ricochet off the nose of the aircraft. He then opened fire with two cannon and four machine guns, but his attack was a dismal failure. His firing was continual and when he started, it was below us to starboard. He then swung across to port below us, then lifted, over compensated and fired over us, moving over to starboard.

By this time he found he was going to overshoot so pulled away to port, showing his undefended belly to me. I was just going to give him a final burst right there, which is every gunner's dream, when the wireless operator told the skipper to dive to starboard, taking the fighter out of my sights, but not before I saw that his starboard engine was belching lots of flames and black smoke. I did not see it again.

We continued on and bombed our target and returned to base unscathed, one helluva happy crew. At de-briefing interrogation, I claimed a possible kill, but we learned later that an Australian pilot from our squadron, was only about a mile away and saw the whole engagement and even saw the fighter crash.

June ended with yet another commendation from the Air Officer Commanding 3 Group, Air Vice Marshal John Baldwin, who wrote of:

*T*he very fine work which has been carried out, not only by the operational crews, but by the maintenance personnel. It is one of the most successful squadrons within a Group which prides itself on maintaining an operational record unsurpassed by any other Group in Bomber Command. During the last four months, No. 75 Squadron has three times headed the monthly total of operational sorties within the Group — in other words, during these three months they sent out on more raids, more aircraft than any other squadron. In the fourth month they were second, their total of sorties being only two behind the top squadron.

The squadron naturally felt pleased again for recognition from on high for the work they had been doing. The squadron would continue in this vein for the rest of the war, but it was about to enter one of its most costly phases.

◇ ◇ ◇

Two crews were lost in early July — Pilot Officer T. M. Smith's over Wilhelmshaven on the 8th, and the veteran Sergeant Wilmshurst on a daylight to Dusseldorf on the 10th. The latter consisted of just eight Wellingtons, four from 75, using cloudy conditions to hit Dusseldorf and Duisburg. The bombers were recalled before they reached their targets, and 75's was the only loss.

Daylight sorties were quite a novelty for night bomber crews and six more aircraft went to Bremen on 20 July. None were lost although one squadron aircraft was attacked by four German fighters but it escaped. Duisberg drew the attention of Bomber Command in the latter half of the month. Then it was Hamburg on 26 July when two aircraft were lost. Sergeant C. V. Macpherson and all his crew died while Pilot Officer I. J. Shepherd and all but his rear gunner, Sergeant John Dixon RAF, died. Dixon, who later emigrated to New Zealand, relates:

> We were coned over the target area but managed to drop our bombs. Sudden evasive action was taken by our pilot by making a stall-turn and diving down the searchlight cone. Soon we were at roof top height and flying through a murderous barrage of light flak. We were finally shot down near the village of Dose, about ten miles west of Wilhelmshaven. I proved to be the sole survivor and was taken to Wilhelmshaven Naval Hospital. From there I was taken by train, via Hannover, to Dulag Luft and eventually to Stalag 8B at Lamsdorf, near Breslau.

There was a second Hamburg raid two nights later, and because of bad weather over England, only the 3 Group airfields were able to operate. It turned out to be a major disaster for the squadron, with six Wellingtons not returning.

Sergeant R. S. D. 'Terry' Kearns, now on the squadron after his baptism on the first 1000 bomber raid, was on both these Hamburg trips. On the first his gunners silenced a machine-gun post, so he must have been flying rather low! Of the second, Terry recalls:

> The second Hamburg raid was known to many of us as the 3 Group raid on Hamburg. This was intended to be another 1000 bomber raid but as we approached the target it was obvious that all was not well.
>
> Aircraft were being coned in searchlights and blasted with heavy and light flak and quite a few were going down in flames. On our run in we managed to get in without too much difficulty and had just released our bombs when we were coned and the 'fun' started! Despite all my efforts we could not get out of the searchlights and I decided to dive down at maximum speed away from the target. As we got low down, the searchlights could not follow us but we were still in the defensive area, so the only thing to do was to stay low.
>
> This was effective for a short while but then the Germans layed their searchlight beams along the ground in an endeavour to blind us. This resulted in a cat and mouse chase at ground level, round woods and under power cables, etc. Luckily, we managed to survive but the memory of it remains.

In all, 3 Group lost 16 Wellingtons and nine Stirlings, while the OTUs lost five. An intruder Blenheim was also missing.

Flight Sergeant John Gilbertson, from Hawkes Bay, was 22 years old. With the exception of his rear gunner, he had an all-NZ crew. Most of 75 were carrying incendiaries and were part of the second wave of bombers to hit the city. Flight Sergeant Martin Byrne, from Auckland and ten years older than his skipper, was manning 'Gee', their new navigational device and, as they could not see the ground because of the severe weather, Byrne was able to confirm they were over the target. Then flak and searchlights also confirmed their correct position and Byrne went forward to the bomb aimer's spot. After bombs-gone, Gilbertson headed for Soltau, their turning point, west, towards Holland and Egmond, their next route mark.

This route took them over the Zuider Zee where, without warning, they were hit by a night fighter whose fire racked through the underside of the Wimpy. It was 3.05am, and the German pilot was Lieutenant Wolfgang Kuthe with his gunner, Unteroffizier Helmut Bonk.*

---

* Kuthe and Bonk were killed in a flying accident in April 1943, having gained eight night victories.

Gilbertson fought to control his stricken craft, while his rear gunner, Bill Titcomb, seeing the fighter, began to fire at it. But the bomber was badly hit. Ron Callaghan, the WOP, went forward, finding Byrne on the floor, wounded in the back, and also saw that Gilbertson had blood on his temple. Alan Rutherford, the front gunner, had moved out of his turret, but then the Wellington hit the water and broke in two.

Only Callaghan and Rutherford survived, although both were injured. They must have floated through the opening of the fuselage and their Mae Wests kept them above water until they were rescued two hours later. When the Germans later lifted the wrecked forward part of the bomber from the water, Gilbertson's body was still in its seat, Byrne beside him. Titcomb's body was washed ashore a couple of days later, by which time Callaghan and Rutherford were on their way to a POW camp.

◇ ◇ ◇

Terry Kearns was out again the next night, 29/30 July, when the squadron sent ten aircraft to Saarbrucken. He was attacked by a Ju88 but managed to evade it. Butch Pugh, whose pilot (McLachlan) had become tour-expired and left, had a new pilot, Sergeant Brady, from New Plymouth, and, of course, a new gunner, Sergeant Alan Lewis, of Hamilton. They were the only aircraft of A Flight available for the Saarbrucken raid. Butch, who was having to cope with a revised number of trips to complete a tour — it had at that time risen from 30 to 35 — recalls:

> The last five trips were hell and we all felt we had been cheated. But on 31st July, I was definitely on my last trip — No. 35. The target was Dusseldorf and everything was normal until we actually got to the aiming point. The skipper called, 'Bale out, I can't control the aircraft, it keeps turning to port.' I had little intention of being a guest of the Germans on this my last trip, and suggested we keep turning until we cleared the target area. We then heard a ghastly moan on the intercom and a quick check evoked no reply from the rear turret. I asked the skipper to hold on until I checked the rear turret.
>
> I stumbled down the catwalk and found the turret turned to port. In the darkness and probably panic, I could not find the exterior turret release to centralise the turret. I grabbed the axe and chopped the doors open and saw Alan slumped over his controls. I reached for the left-hand control but it wasn't there, but eventually found the right-hand control and moved the turret round. I managed to get Alan out — no easy feat as he was six foot tall — and struggling up the catwalk I eventually got him onto the bed.
>
> For some unknown reason the aircraft had stopped turning and we were heading for home. I found Alan had a torn left ear and the centre of his left hand was completely gone as if cut with a pastry knife. I then took over the rear turret.
>
> We landed at Box and only later did we discover why we had kept turning. Alan had seen a Stirling above us open its bomb doors but couldn't remember anything else. The Stirling had dropped its bomb load and one four pound incendiary bomb had gone through the turret copula, hit Alan's ear, broke off the left turret control and come to rest on the ammunition belts. An armourer later found the bomb and showed us. The hole it made set up an air eddy which forced the rudder into a port turn. When I centralised the turret, the hole had come under the coaming and the problem disappeared. Alan lost all the fingers of his hand but the thumb was saved, enabling him to manipulate a mechanical hand.

Butch Pugh rose to become a Wing Commander, receiving the OBE in 1970 when he retired from the RNZAF.

Charles Kelly recalls this intense period:

> After our memorable trip to Emden, we got in about 10 trips over the next few weeks,

but apart from a few flak holes and getting into some unlikely attitudes trying to get out of searchlights and away from fighters, and putting on our parachutes at least when we got coned and didn't think we were going to get out of it, things went relatively smoothly for us.

Squadron losses were average as far as we could judge, but worse was to come. We lost eight over Hamburg! By this stage we were becoming almost an experienced crew, relatively speaking, but the losses over those two nights pushed us well up the squadron rankings. I will always remember the Sergeant's Mess being like a morgue. The rooms of the missing aircrew being sealed off until the Adjusting Officer had time to sort out personal effects etc to return to the next of kin.

From memory we had only about six operational crews of any real experience, plus some fresh replacement crews when we went back to Hamburg, Saarbrucken and then Dusseldorf.

Artie Ashworth was also on the Dusseldorf raid. Having finished his first tour with the squadron, he had gone to Malta and Egypt to fly Wellingtons and later Bristol Bombays, but had been recalled to England in May, mainly to support the 1000 bomber raids. He arrived back on 75 for another tour, going to Duisberg four times in a row. Ted Olsen had arranged for his posting back to 75, and Artie was soon promoted to Acting Squadron Leader. He finally left at the end of August to join the HQ of the new Pathfinder Force.

8

Wellington Finale

AUGUST — OCTOBER 1942

Some VIPs visited Feltwell at the beginning of August 1942 — the New Zealand High Commissioner, Bill Jordan, accompanied by Air Commodore L. Isitt and one of 75's previous pilots, Wing Commander Trevor Freeman DSO DFC. It was a chance for Bill Jordan to meet the squadron's new Commanding Officer, for Ted Olson had left in late July.

Ted Olson had been a popular CO, and now went to command RAF Station Oakington, just up the road. He was to receive the DSO for his command of the squadron. One of Olsen's wishes was for the squadron to become totally manned by New Zealand aircrew. This was never achieved during the war, but later the command positions were taken by RNZAF officers. Ted Olsen died in May 1945.

The new CO was Wing Commander Victor Mitchell DFC, who had joined the RAF in 1936. A Scot, he was 27 years of age. It did not take him long to establish himself and, under his command, 75 continued to maintain its high reputation within Bomber Command.

There were several press photographs taken during the visit, including one showing Mitchell, Jordan and the Feltwell Station Commander, Group Captain J. A. Powell DSO OBE, with some 80 to 90 men, mostly aircrew, all cheering. Looking at that photo one wonders how many of them were among the three crews who did not get back from Mainz on 11 August. There were 68 Wellingtons out of the total force of 154 that night. Of the six which failed to return, three were Wellingtons and all came from 75. Of the 15 men, just four survived as prisoners.

Sergeant Neville Hockaday had a close call that night, but got home. The target was an intriguing one for him, as his maternal grandfather had been born in Mainz and for all he knew members of the family might still be living there.

◇ ◇ ◇

There now came a major event for the squadron — moving base. RAF Feltwell had been home since April 1940 but on 15 August the whole lot moved to Mildenhall, Suffolk, halfway between Newmarket and Thetford. Initially, 75 shared the new base with 419 Canadian Squadron, but a few days later the Canadians left for Yorkshire.

Each NCO crew was allocated a semi-detached house — former married quarters — adjacent to the Sergeant's Mess. NCOs of mixed crews shared a house. One of their locals became the 'Bird in Hand'. Shortly afterwards, Group Captain Powell arrived from Feltwell to command Mildenhall.

Two nights after their arrival, the squadron were operating again, albeit on a very reduced scale. But by 27 August when they went to Kassel, 12 aircraft were operating. It was not a good night for Sergeant Burrill, who met a Ju88 when 50 kilometres from the target. The Wimpy was badly damaged in the encounter, with the port engine being knocked out. The rear gunner, Sergeant Gorman, claimed the 88 shot down. Even though the bomb load was jettisoned height was gradually lost, so that by the Channel they were down to 700 feet. Some light flak gunners had a go at them over the Dutch coast, but Burrill struggled with the crippled bomber and made a successful belly landing at Wattisham.

On the same night, Flight Lieutenant A. F. A. Osborn and crew failed to return. All were killed. The next night, two crews were missing from a raid on Nuremburg — those of Sergeants Davis and Perks — while Neville Hockaday nearly ran out of petrol following some persistent attention from a FW190.

Neville Hockaday's encounter with the Focke Wulf 190 — normally a single-seated day fighter — was a recent innovation by the Luftwaffe to increase night fighter defences against the increasingly strong Bomber Command night raids. Conventional twin-engined night fighters — Me110s, Ju88s, and even Do217s — were, like Fighter Command, controlled from the ground. Sent into the bomber stream, these night fighters — called Tame Boar ('Zahme Sau') — would pick up individual bombers on their airborne radar. The first excursions by free-ranging day fighters would, in 1943, become better organised under the name of Wild Boar ('Wilde Sau'), operating mainly over the targets where attacking bombers could be more easily picked up against the burning target or in searchlight beams.

However, it was a Tame Boar which shot down the crew of Flight Sergeant Bill Parkes on 6/7 September during their 18th trip. They were returning from Duisburg when they were picked up on the radar set in the Me110 of II/NJG 1 from St Trond in Belgium. The pilot, Major Walter Ehle, already had 31 kills, 28 of them at night. His fire set the Wellington's starboard engine on fire, and after another attack it fell vertically to crash into a railway embankment near Alphen. Ehle, holder of the Knights Cross, was killed in a flying accident in November 1943 after bringing his score to 38.

◇ ◇ ◇

The squadron operated on 19 nights during September 1942, putting up an average of 6.6 aircraft on each. The largest number — 15 — went to Duisburg on 6 September, but lost two. September was to see eight crews lost with others shot up. Three were lost over Dusseldorf on the 10/11 September.

During the raid on Essen on 16 September, Sergeant K. Blincoe's aircraft was hit by flak in the starboard wing shortly before bombing. A large hole was blasted between the motor and the fuselage, which made it impossible for the pilot to turn to port. Struggling back, they were attacked by a night fighter near the Dutch coast, which hit them several times from underneath, wounding the WOP, Pilot Officer H. Lowe. With their hydraulics shot out, they had to make a belly landing at base. Another night fighter, a Ju88, attacked Jack Wright's Wellington on the return journey, but it was shot down by his front gunner, Flight Sergeant R. C. Reynolds, and seen to explode.

In fact, Neville Hockaday's rear gunner, Bruce Philip, had spotted the Junkers, warning Hock that it was approaching. But it went by them, trailing another Wimpy up ahead. Bill Gordon, in the front turret, then kept him covered, ready to fire if the German attacked the other RAF plane. Then the 88 went by the other Wimpy to attack a third Wellington, but the luckless night fighter pilot had unknowlingly put himself right in front of Bob Reynolds, who nailed him.

Jack Wright completed his tour — 33 Ops — towards the end of the month and received the DFC, as did Charles Kelly. The crew later went to 156 Squadron, Path Finder Force (PFF), and Jack and Charles won DSOs. Jack also took Alf Drew from Hockaday's crew, and Ken Crankshaw, another WOP/AG who completed a tour with 75. By the end of their second tour, Drew, Nick Carter and Bob Reynolds had received DFCs; Crankshaw the DFC to add to his 75 DFM. Charles Kelly:

*O*n one occasion we had attacked Essen and met radar predicted flak. We had just dropped our bomb load when a salvo from a flak battery burst exactly at our altitude but, fortunately, slightly ahead and to one side. Jack instinctively turned towards the burst. A few seconds later came the second burst, the same distance ahead and on the opposite side, so that Jack repeated the manoeuvre of turning into the burst. This continued for some minutes as we weaved right and left, and finally got clear. But it seemed like an eternity and the inside of the fuselage stank of cordite fumes.

We had moved to Mildenhall in August and had settled down with our own aircraft — D-Donald — and in addition, our aircraft had the bomb doors removed so that we could carry one 4000 pound blast bomb. These bombs protruded below the aircraft, hence the removal of the doors. We quite liked carrying the 4000 pounders, and you didn't have to check for any hang-ups as the old Wellington jumped for joy when you let one go! The highlight of our last sorties was certainly the shooting down of a Ju88 which sneaked into the path of our bombers. After that we reckoned that we had more than evened the score. Jack completed his 30 trips and so we were delighted when the CO, Wing Commander Victor Mitchell, asked us if we minded him taking over as Captain for one more Op to bring the rest of us up to the required 30. It turned out to be a relatively uneventful trip to Krefeld — and that saw us out.

Riki Jarman's 'P' Peter (X3751). (F. W. J. CHUNN)

Bomb train. 500 pounders heading for the bomb bays.

Sgt Derek Morris, squadron armourer, RAF Feltwell. (D. MORRIS)

In early October, two more experienced crews completed their tours: Frankie Curr, his 56th Op (although not all with 75); and Neville Hockaday, who chalked up his 33rd. Hock had decided to fly more than the necessary 30 trips in order that his crew complete their tours with him rather than having to be split up and complete the required 30 as spare bods with other crews. Frank Curr received an immediate DFM and Hock also received the DFM. Their crew was in fact the last Wimpy crew to complete a tour with 75. Curr later also flew Ops with 156 Squadron.

As crews with completed Ops departed, others began arriving. One new member of 75 to arrive at this time was Earl Belford:

> *I* arrived at Mildenhall in September 1942 and remember so well the little railway station at nearby Shipea Hill. The previous day, we graduating flyers had a choice of Marham or 75 at Mildenhall. I must say, 75 had a reputation for having more than its share of casualties. 'They' said that they went in too low and got shot down as a result! Well, believing that it is best not to tempt fate, I said I'd go where I was needed most. So I survived 13 months of varied duties and life with a truly dedicated squadron and some fine people.

Most of the next month was taken up with mine-laying sorties. Three crews were lost during the first half of the month: Sergeant G.W. Rhodes and crew over Osnabruck on 6 October; Sergeant Shalfoon on a 'Gardening' trip on 11 August; and

Sergeant Walters on a raid to Kiel on 13/14 October. Sergeant Davey ran out of fuel returning from Kiel and crash landed at Lakenheath, four of the crew being injured.

However, things came to a temporary standstill on 15 October as the squadron was changing bases once again; this time going to Oakington, just outside Cambridge. The squadron was about to lose its Wellingtons which had served them, and RAF Bomber Command, so well. At Oakington was a Conversion Unit, commanded by Squadron Leader Crompton. Here the squadron would gradually convert to the Short Stirling bomber. 'B' Flight went first.

The Stirling had four engines and needed seven crew members. Thus the existing crews would have to double up on engines and take on two extra men per crew — a Flight Engineer and a Bomb Aimer. Until now, the navigator/observer had aimed the bombs. The Short Stirling was the first four-engined monoplane bomber to enter service with the Royal Air Force, and, unlike the Halifax and Lancaster, was specifically designed as a four-engined bomber rather than a progression from a twin-engined design. The Lancaster, for instance, had emerged from the Manchester.

Having been first thought of as far back as 1936, the Stirling design had to cope with some problems; one supposedly being the size of aircraft hangars. Because it had to be taken into hangars, the wing-span was restricted so it was designed with a very low aspect ratio wing. (Oddly, the wing-span was only 30 metres, yet hangars could take aircraft with a wing-span of 36 metres. The Lancaster, for instance, had a span of 31 metres so this argument appears false!) Also the bomber weighed some 31 tonne all up, limiting its service ceiling and presenting bomber crews with an additional challenge on Ops. Finally, as the Short Company built the Sunderland, the same general wing configuration needed to be maintained to employ the same Gouge trailing edge flaps. This made the choice of a shoulder-wing layout essential, resulting in a very high and complicated undercarriage arrangement, giving the Stirling a very steep ground angle. On the ground, therefore, the pilot sat six metres above the tarmac!

Unlike the Wellington, with its fabric coverings, the Stirling had an all-metal stressed skin and was powered by four Bristol Hercules engines. Maximum speed at 10,000 feet was around 370 kph, with the range around 3200 kilometres, depending on bomb load. Ceiling was in the region of 17,000 feet. The aircraft also had an additional gun turret — the mid-upper — which meant air gunners tended now to man the rear and mid-upper guns full time, and the front guns only at specific times.

The Stirling prototype made its first flight in May 1939, although it crashed on landing. Despite this inglorious start, Stirlings began to equip No.7 Squadron by August 1940, going into action the following February. By August 1942, the Mark III Stirling was arriving on 7 Squadron, but 75 Squadron operated with the Mark I until Mark IIIs began to arrive in February 1943.

No. 75 Squadron began to equip with Stirlings in October 1942, becoming the sixth RAF squadron to fly them (after 7, 15, 149, 214 and 218 Squadrons). Initially, the crew consisted of pilot, navigator, bomb aimer, flight engineer, wireless operator, mid-upper gunner and rear gunner.

One of the recently arrived crews who were now well into their tour was that of Flight Lieutenant L. G. Trott, from Auckland. His crew was W. J. R. Scollay (navigator) from Wellington, D. L. Popperwell of Gore, and Sergeants M. Manawaiti from Timaru and Harold Hamerton from New Plymouth. 'Pop' Popperwell and Bill Scollay would later become Bombing and Navigational Leaders on 75. They were also one of the few crews to be decorated 'en masse' at their tour end. Bill Scollay later became the main founder of the 75 Squadron Association. He died in January 1990. Harold Hamerton says of this transition period:

> **W**hen we moved onto Stirlings, we gained two extra crew members, one French Canadian as flight engineer and a mid-upper gunner, an Englishman.
> My log book has Kiel, in Wellington 'Y' BK724, as being our last Op from Mildenhall, on 13th October and our first air test at Oakington was on 18th October, in 'V'. In the event we didn't stay at Oakington long, and our first flight at Newmarket was on the 31st October. Both 'A' and 'B' Flights converted at Oakington, but in single Flights.

Earl Belford also recalls:

> **W**e had flown just four missions from Mildenhall in Wellingtons and then we went to Oakington to convert to Stirlings. I well remember my first thoughts when I saw a Stirling, looking out of one end of a hangar. 'No way will that thing ever get off the ground!' But they did, and one of the finest aircraft for crew comfort and reliability ever built was the Stirling.
> It was at Oakington during our conversion that I experienced my first 'near miss'. We had to do a number of solo circuits and landings to complete our course. Because I was an Observer, I was the pilot's assistant in take-offs and landings. I left the brake 'on' at this instance and after we hit three times and was about to nose over, I quickly let it off and so completed our course. Needless to say, thereafter, the words 'brake off' were included in my landing patter!

One of the conversion pilots at Oakington was George Sanders of 7 Squadron, who relates:

> **A**lthough I was seconded to 75 Squadron and acting as CFI [Chief Flying Instructor], I was also serving on 7 Squadron, flying Ops. We set up a nucleus within 7 Squadron and used two new Stirlings, with appropriate 75 markings correctly affixed. These were kept well away from the others on the far side of the airfield.
> I remember one incident when one of these aircraft returned to the airfield with parts of trees, branches, etc, poking out of engine cowlings and leading edges. The crew's faces were white and hands trembling like alcohol remorse!
> It appeared that, being a fine sunny day, they decided to stooge along the river Cam, spotting for any nude beauties on the banks thereon. Stirlings were not the best as a river boat, nor when altimeters start reading fathoms and they found the aircraft awfully sluggish to pull up when they did spot what they were looking for, hence the clumps of willows, elms and oaks which got in their way! It was a hell of a laugh at the time, but Oh, what a blistering they got from the ground crew and of course from their CO and from the Station Commander, 75's old CO, Ted Olson!

Meantime, 'A' Flight, still at Mildenhall, flew the last of the squadron Wellington sorties, which included Cologne on 15 October, then daylight raids on the infamous Dortmund-Emms canal at Lingen. Twelve aircraft and three more Wimpies went to Essen on 22 October. These were limited raids in cloudy weather, but the following day, the Air Officer Commanding 3 Group — now Air Vice Marshal the Hon. R. A. Cochrane CBE AFC — paid the squadron a visit to congratulate the crews who had flown the previous day on successful raids. Ralph Cochrane, later commanded 5 Group.

The next night came another long trip to Milan on a follow-up to a daylight raid on the same city during the day! Of the eight crews sent, two failed to return. From one, Sergeant H. J. Hugill's crew, he and his navigator were killed and the front gunner taken prisoner. But the WOP, Sergeant E. Worsdale evaded capture and the rear gunner, Sergeant L. Newbold, was also later reported safe in Switzerland. The other crew of Sergeant McConnel were all killed.

These were the last Wellingtons lost by 75, and the last Wellington sorties were flown on 25/26 October — mining sorties off the Frisian Islands (two) and Brest (two).

Then, following 'A' Flight's departure to Oakington on 29 October, the squadron's headquarters finally moved from Mildenhall to its new home at Newmarket — Rowley Mile. A new era for 75 Squadron was about to begin.

9

Newmarket

NOVEMBER 1942 — FEBRUARY 1943

Earl Belford recalls the move to Newmarket, where the landing field was the actual racecourse:

> *W*intry weather set in and we only did one trip from Mildenhall to Turin before the time came to shift airfields. We were, in fact, the first crew to land at the grass field, Rowley Mile, Newmarket Heath. I re-visited Newmarket in 1978 and felt this was my home 'drome; this is were it all happened for me, this is the place 75 Squadron made its mark. If my log book entry is correct, our landing there was on 8th November, 1942.
>
> Eventually we were assigned Stirling BK778 'U' and flew her until our last operation to Modane on 16th September 1943. She was lost to enemy action in the Baltic on 4th November 1943.
>
> We had one Stirling on the squadron which did noble duty. That was BK619 'O' — she flew 42 missions, fourth highest among all Stirlings.

George Sanders was still helping to convert crews from Wellingtons to the new Stirlings:

> *T*here was a period of general turmoil of all personnel attempting to gain or possess admission to this fine Olde English Racecourse and accommodation within the grandstand and other buildings. They came in waves — aircraft, bus, truck, car, motorbike and cycle; not forgetting feet! We watched from vantage points and believed it to be a rabbit warren infested with ferrets.
>
> A few days later we made an inspection and I was pleasantly surprised how well organised the grandstand barracks had become. It also appeared spacious, cosy and agreeable. Goodness knows what would have happened if a few bombs had straddled it. This organised move was well carried out by ground crew and deserves mention.
>
> We now had about six aircraft by then and had been practising circuits and bumps for sometime, as it was not a particularly nice 'drome for the heavies. The main runway ended at a most formidable dyke. Having already experienced one bad landing at another airfield some years previously, I took special care to avoid this one.

Sergeant Norman Bartlett (flight engineer), who was to arrive on 75 the following spring, flying two tours with 75, remembered an incident concerning the 'famous' dyke:

> *O*ne morning, returning from an Operation, we saw that a Stirling was spread-eagled

The Short Stirling. AA-C for Charlie, en route. It carries 25 bomb/sortie markings on its nose. (VIA J. GRUBB)

Sergeant R. W. 'Bob' Sharpe, whose father flew with 75 in 1916. Bob was shot down 2 December 1942 and taken prisoner. (MRS P. SHARPE)

LACs R. Bartlett and J. Murray inspecting and packing boxes of four pound incendiary bombs. (C. C. SHEPHERD)

on the racecourse, and the Duke of Norfolk, who was the racecourse steward, was going up the wall, creating about clearing it in time for racing. [Racing continued at Newmarket in the war, if nowhere else.] The aircraft had failed to clear Devil's Dyke, which runs across the racecourse. However, the wreck was cleared in time, and the racing programme fulfilled.

Newmarket was a great posting. We were in billets right opposite the 'White Hart Inn' and the town's open air swimming pool, so there was plenty to occupy our minds.

The squadron was declared operational by 20 November and that night four Stirlings were put on Ops. The target was Turin. Two nights later two aircraft set out for Stuttgart but one had to abort with its rear turret u/s. On 28 November, four aircraft went back to Turin, but one lost an engine and could not maintain height. It had to jettison its load and abort. Earlier that day, the squadron had its first fatalities with the new aircraft. Sergeant Broady crashed while converting at Oakington, and he and his crew all died. The month ended with two more aircraft assigned for Turin but both had to abort. Things had not got off to a very good start.

Things didn't improve the next month. On 2 December, only two of the five Stirlings assigned to attack Frankfurt actually got off, due to a variety of problems. Of these, Sergeant A. Scott failed to return; the squadron's first Stirling loss on Ops. Later, it was reported that Scott and his mid-upper gunner had been killed; the six others of the crew (he had been carrying a second pilot) had been captured. The rear gunner, Sergeant R. E. Preston, was to die in captivity in April 1945. The only one to bomb the target and return was Leo Trott, who off loaded his bombs from 10,000 feet.

Another newcomer to the squadron at this time was Sergeant R. W. Sharpe. He actually asked to be sent to 75, as his father, as mentioned earlier, had flown with it in 1916. However, as the squadron had been in the midst of converting, he and his crew were seconded to 115 Squadron who shared Mildenhall. He flew several Ops with them before finally getting to 75 in September. His first trip in a Stirling proved to be his last:

On 2nd December I was told to fly as second pilot on BK618. In retrospect this decision seems incredible in view of the fact that I had never been inside a Stirling in my life! In the event I went, without comment, with Sergeant Scott and his crew. Prior to take-off the Wing Commander said, 'This will be something to write to the old man about, Sharpy!' How right he was!

After a successful attack we headed southwest, away from the target. After ten minutes we were attacked by night fighters from below and the starboard outer engine caught fire. After a second attack the fuel balance lines across the wing roots fired and the aircraft was like a blow torch from the cockpit aft. Sergeant Scott nodded to me to try my controls after he discovered no response to his. My stick, too, was absolutely dead.

Scott then yelled to abandon and showed me the hatch in the nose. By this time the bomb aimer and flight engineer had gone. I waited on the edge of the hatch for Scott but the last I saw of him, he walked into the flames towards the navigator's section. He had obviously no chance of survival in those flames and his motive still remains a mystery. It may be that he went to do what he could for the rest of his crew.

I then jumped and as the aircraft's tail passed over me I pulled the ripcord. Three things happened at once. The canopy opened, the aircraft exploded, and I smashed through a very mature pine forest. When I regained my composure I found that I was sitting on a sapling with the canopy caught up in an enormous pine tree. After a struggle I freed myself and got out of the forest and started to walk but I had a very stiff neck, so walking was uncomfortable. Many years later it was found that it had been fractured.

After a few miles I sat down to rest and must have fallen asleep, for I was roused by a cockney voice, saying, 'Wotcher, mate — are you English?' It transpired that my captor was a local miller who had spent many years as a baker in Knightsbridge!

Bob Sharpe died in October 1989.

Four Stirlings flew 'Gardening' sorties on 4/5 December, but this was made possible only by great efforts on the part of the armoury personnel, as the raid was changed from land to sea late in the day. For this effort, the AOC sent the ground crews a message of appreciation.

Then A Flight returned from Oakington, so the squadron was one again and now fully back on the job. Training still took up a good part of the flying activity, with some 'Gardening' sorties plus a long haul to Turin for five crews on 9 December thrown in. Nine aircraft were to drop more mines on the 16th, but the third aircraft off, swung on take-off. The pilot, Sergeant B. A. Franklin, straightened and became airborne, only to crash two kilometres away from the aerodrome. Two mines on board exploded and all seven men aboard were killed. It was later established that the starboard undercarriage had hit Devil's Dyke, ripping off the oil tank to the starboard inner engine. That engine then seized, causing the Stirling to spin into the ground. The following six aircraft did not take off.

If the squadron had thought that a change of aircraft might improve its luck on Ops, they were wrong. On the night of 17/18 December five Stirlings were assigned as part of a small force of bombers (16 Stirlings and six Wellingtons) going for the Opel works at Fallersleben, in the Ruhr. The bombers were to head in at low level, then climb to 5000 feet in order to bomb. Wing Commander Mitchell decided to fly on this one, going with a new crew captained by Warrant Officer T. H. Bagnell. Of the five, four failed to return, including that of the CO. The only one to get home had failed to locate the target so bombed an alternative — an aerodrome. They were twice attacked by fighters which put four holes in the Stirling. In all, six Stirlings and two Wimpies were lost on this show.

Three of the crews all died, but the fourth, piloted by Flight Sergeant K. J. Dunmall, came down on a lake by Kudelstaart, near Aalsmeer, Holland. The rear gunner of this Stirling — BK620 — was Sergeant J. S. Voice, who was celebrating his 21st birthday and had taken a large slice of cake with him. Due to some navigational difficulties they drifted across Hannover where the flak gunners gave them a bad time, and other aircraft could be seen falling in flames. After bombing, Dunmall found one engine had been damaged and a second beginning to malfunction. As if this was not enough, a night fighter attacked them three or four times, putting a number of holes into the bomber which was now losing height rapidly.

Dunmall ordered the crew out, Voice taking his piece of cake with him as he went. He landed in a tree and moments later met up with the Bomb Aimer, Pilot Officer E. E. Williams. That night they shared the cake and the next morning made tracks for the Dutch/German border, but were quickly captured. Eric Williams, of course, became famous as an escaper through his book *The Wooden Horse*, tunnelling from Stalag Luft III to return to England, where he was awarded the Military Cross.

Dunmall crash landed on the lake and was rescued by a villager who came out in a boat. The Stirling sank but was brought up and recovered nearly 40 years later by a team of Dutch aircraft recovery enthusiasts led by J. D. M. Graas.

The loss of Vic Mitchell and four crews was naturally a blow to the squadron just as they were getting started. But everyone rallied round, and Squadron Leader

Fowler took temporary charge. Training continued, although sadly depleted of aircraft. On 20 December, only two aircraft could be sent to Duisberg and one of those went u/s. With Christmas coming up the squadron was stood down for the rest of the month. Training was maintained as much as possible, but snow on 30 December didn't help.

As January began, it was back to 'Gardening' — a good stand-by when full Ops were not possible. Indeed, except for a couple of raids upon Lorient, the trips that month were all mine-laying. The Lorient trip on 23 January took Sergeant R. M. Kidd and his crew from the squadron — the first loss of 1943. Kidd in fact managed to evade, but the rest of his crew died.

Even on 'Gardening' trips, enemy reception could be rough. Over the Gironde Estuary on 18 January, Sergeant Bennett, on his first trip, met with a hot reception. But successful evasive action after combats with three enemy aircraft enabled Bennett to bring his crew home safely.

February saw no improvement. Nine Stirlings went to Hamburg on the night of 3/4, and two didn't get back, coming down over Holland. Worse, both were piloted by senior captains, McCullough and Blincoe, and both were carrying second pilots on 'second dickie' experience trips. This, therefore, left two new crews without pilots. Could it get worse? Yes it could.

Five aircraft went to Turin the next night, bombing markers laid down by Pathfinder aircraft, but only three got through. One returned with turret and intercom problems, while the other failed to gain enough height to clear the Alps and returned. Then the very next night, another aircraft failed to get home from mining off the Frisians. It had crashed off Cromer on the way out when a fire broke out in the Stirling. Nobody survived.

On 13 February — unlucky for some — 11 aircraft went back to Lorient. The cost was Sergeant R. A. Williams and crew; two dead, including the pilot, four taken prisoner, and one evader.

Fortunately, this was the last loss of February, but further sorties were dogged by serviceability problems, with aircraft going u/s prior to take-off, or returning with a myriad of technical failures. The only bright spots were the arrival of a couple of new Mark III Stirlings towards the end of the month, and Leo Trott and crew flying onto Nuremburg, after their aircraft was damaged by Ruhr flak and they had had to jettison their bomb load. Upon their return they were able to make out a target report, despite 8/10ths cloud above the city.

During February, Geoff Rothwell DFC arrived on the squadron as a Flight Commander. He had already completed one bomber tour with 99 Squadron and had recently returned from America, where he had done some liaison work with the US Air Corps:

*T*he American experience soon seemed like a dream as I quickly became immersed in the gloom of wartime Britain with the blackout and many shortages and restrictions. However, it was good to be home and, after a spell of leave, I was posted back to 3 Group to convert onto four-engined Stirlings. It was not a popular aircraft as it was unable to gain altitude at which the Halifaxes and Lancasters operated. AA fire, of course, was more accurate at the 10–12,000 feet where we flew than at 20,000 or more where they operated, so the casualty rate for Stirlings was high. However, I enjoyed flying them and found they were very manoeuvrable and had reliable Bristol engines. It was unfortunate that they had a complex electrical system which gave endless trouble and the serviceability record was poor.

I was given a crew and posted to take over a Flight in 75 Squadron at Newmarket. My navigator, wireless operator and bomb aimer were New Zealanders, and my experience of instructing many New Zealanders at the OTU at Moreton-in-the-Marsh enabled us to fit into the squadron in a harmonious manner, and we soon developed into a happy crew.

It was, of course, a coincidence that I should be returning to the airfield where I had completed my first tour of operations. It was like a home-coming for me and I received a warm welcome from the kind and hospitable Newmarket civilian population who remembered me from my time with 99 Squadron, three years earlier.

Just two years three months after my final operation of my first tour I began my second. Being relatively experienced I did not have the customary familiarisation trip with another captain as new pilots had, but went straight into my 38th operation, planting six 'vegetables' in a 'garden' north of the Frisian Island of Terschelling. The fifth vegetable exploded on contact.

This code language meant that we dropped parachute mines in an area in the vicinity of Terschelling. We carried out a similar operation the following night and were shadowed by a night fighter but were not attacked.

We were now working well together as a crew and no further 'freshman' trips were necessary, so we were in the main force two nights later when the target was Berlin. [1 March 1943] We bombed with incendiaries in the heaviest attack yet on the German capital. We could still see the glow of the fires when we were 200 miles away on our journey home.

We met intense flak when we strayed over Osnabruck on our way back and were attacked five times by night fighters. One fighter was claimed as a probable by my gunners. [Sergeants Negus and Howat] We did not escape unscathed as there were numerous holes in the aircraft, the aerial was shot away, and the windscreen was shattered by flak. After my longest flight ever, we landed at RAF Stradishall, logging 8½ hours.

Over 300 RAF bombers, 60 of them Stirlings, had gone to Berlin on 1 March. Eight Stirlings came from 75, but two yet again had to return early. Bomber Command was now using 'Oboe' and H2S as navigation and bombing aids, and H2S had been used on this night.

'Oboe' was a blind bombing device which had been developed in 1942 and was given to the Command late that year. Two stations in England transmitted pulses which could be picked up by an aircraft and retransmitted to the ground stations. By receiving these pulses, the aircraft could keep itself on track to pass over the assigned target. In turn, the stations measured the time it took to receive back the pulses and were then able to calculate the bomber's position. The stations sent a short signal at the moment the aircraft should release its bombs. 'Oboe' could be quite accurate but, as the curvature of the earth could upset the pulse line, it could only be used effectively on targets nearer to England. Another drawback was that the station could control only six aircraft per hour, and with just three stations this meant only 18 aircraft — which were, of course, Pathfinders.

H2S, which also became available at the end of 1942, was in fact a forerunner of a simple airborne ground-scanning radar set. It did not give a very good picture in the early years, although coastlines, wide rivers and lakes, and even the outlines of large cities could usually be distinguished. It was, however, more of an asset than a hindrance, and an improvement on dead-reckoning calculations. 'Gee' had been regularly jammed by the Germans.

H2S was not as accurate as Oboe for bombing, but its range was better as it was carried in the aircraft and could, therefore, be used on long range targets. Again it was the Pathfinders who were first given H2S, in order to mark targets more accurately. Main Force squadrons, like 75, were naturally relying on the Pathfinders to locate and mark the aiming points. One severe drawback of H2S, not immediately apparent or certainly not admitted, was that German night fighters were able to home in on H2S emissions with their airborne radar!

Sergeant Norman Bartlett with his crew had now arrived on the squadron and they immediately went into the 'freshman routine' of 'Gardening' Ops to get them operational:

> After a couple of NFTs and a minelaying Op in the Frisians at night we were on our way. In those days, the photo-flare had to be pushed out, as well as the mines, at 500 feet. On this trip, nothing happened, no gunfire, no searchlights, so I thought to myself, what a doddle. But it was only my first. Four nights later we were detailed for another minelaying trip in the Gironde Estuary. We descended to 1000 feet, 900, 800, 700 . . . . and I heard the bomb aimer say, 'Mines away'. I pushed the flare out, jumped to a window and took a look at the river, which was all lit up with searchlights, which seemed to be shining on top of the water, and the light flak and incendiary shells were criss-crossing all over the place! The skipper was weaving and the rear gunner screaming that we were going into the sea. But Dicky French got us home safely.

A successful attack on Essen was carried out on 5/6 March, heralding the commencement of what has now been called the Battle of the Ruhr. Sir Arthur Harris — 'Bomber' Harris to some, 'Butcher' Harris to others — had been waiting for the winter weather to pass before beginning what he was to call his 'main offensive'. He wanted to smash Germany's industrial heartland, thereby denying Hitler's forces from receiving the weapons with which to wage war.

Bomber Command, with its recent innovations of target marking, pathfinding aircraft, Gee, Oboe and H2S, could now concentrate on attacking one main target with a large force of bombers. Gone were the days when attacks on targets were mounted by individuals or a handful of aircraft. There were always other minor operations on each night, in order to hopefully confuse the defences. And there were also 'spoof' raids — whereby a force would form up and head for a locality, only to turn back to their bases once German radar had picked it up and the Germans had begun to organise their night fighters.

German night fighters were becoming increasingly successful. Their 'aces' were starting to emerge. Pilots and crews with 20, 30, 50, even 100 night kills, would eventually shine bright in the Luftwaffe's galaxy. They became expert at finding and shooting down RAF bombers — they got plenty of practice! So, too, did the fighter controllers who guided the fighters into the bomber streams.

Already bomber crews, who had been attacked but returned, were reporting increasing attacks from underneath. The reality of what was actually happening, naturally escaped them, but the Germans were no fools. To attack from dead astern or from behind and slightly above put them and their aircraft in danger of the deadly fire from six .303 machine guns. Rear and mid-upper gunners commanded a large area of sky in the direction of the expected attack. Thus the Germans had developed their upward firing cannon, which they called 'Schraege Musik' (literally, 'Oblique Music'). This cannon fired upwards at angles of 10 to 20 degrees from the cockpit areas of Me110s.

Once a German fighter had found the bomber, either by airborne radar or by eyesight, he would merely slip underneath where the sky appeared darkest to the RAF rear gunners, position himself below the bomber, and let fly with his 20 mm guns. Not, of course, into the fuselage and bomb bay — that could bring a mass of exploding debris down on him — but into the wings, where engines and fuel tanks would just as easily knock down the British 'terrorfliegers'. It gave the RAF crews little warning of attack, but, of course, gave them a chance to get out of a bomber with a blazing wing, rather than having their fuselage, and themselves, raked with gunfire. But they had to be quick. A bomber with a serious wing fire didn't last long!

On the Essen trip, one aircraft crashed on take-off but the crew escaped serious injury, while another was forced to abort. But the seven others of No. 75 Squadron bombed, and reported fires seen from as far as the Dutch coast. The AOC in C sent his congratulations.

Harris was now able to concentrate his force upon the Ruhr, as well as hitting the German U-boat bases from time to time (the Battle of the Atlantic was raging). No. 75 Squadron would have its share of both in the coming months.

10

The Battle of the Ruhr

MARCH — MAY 1943

Nuremburg wasn't in the Ruhr, but 75 went for this seat of Nazi Germany on 8/9 March, eight of the nine despatched bombing it successfully. One aircraft had to abort with engine trouble and one failed to return — Sergeant C. R. Davey. Pilot Officer Douglas Lowe's Stirling was attacked by a night fighter near Saarbrucken on the way home, cannon and tracer shells slashing through the cockpit, wounding the second pilot, Flying Officer C. Eddy. Lowe (later Air Chief Marshal Sir Douglas) also received cuts to his face, but put the bomber into a corkscrew and lost their attacker. The next night it was Munich with five aircraft, while two others put mines into the Gironde.

Then came Stuttgart followed by another trip to Essen. A raid on Augsberg for 15 March was cancelled. In fact several mid-March Ops were called off, some at the last minute, much to the annoyance of the ground crews but perhaps relief of the aircrews. Nine aircraft sent to St Nazaire were even recalled when just 20 minutes from the target. Then it was Berlin again, and yet again, on 27 and 29 March. Sergeant Bartlett made both trips:

> On the first raid it took us 7 hours 40 minutes — quite a quiet trip; straight in, no trouble with the bomb run, bombs gone, and straight out, left hard circuit and away home. Nothing wrong with their defences, they were all there. I don't know what made us so immune, which is more than can be said for the 29th!
>
> It took us 8½ hours to get home — on three engines. After the Lord Mayor's Show, we floated up to the target. Then the rear gunner screamed: 'Fighter on the port quarter!' An attack started and I looked down the rear of the aircraft and saw a line of incendiary shells going through the fuselage. Then the mid-upper cried that it was coming in again from the port for a second attack. We heard both gunners cry out they'd got it — both claimed it. Then a searchlight caught us, passing us from cone to cone, trying to get us out of the target area, to blow us to pieces.
>
> Then the port outer engine caught fire with a long trail of flame from it. I told the skipper to try a steep dive and he went down from 14,000 to about 9 to 10,000 feet, and we got away with it and got home despite another two fighter attacks — nobody hurt — our mid-upper claiming a second kill.
>
> I recall our WOP, Rupert Moss, seeing a couple of swans over Berlin at about 14,000 feet and reported it to the Intelligence Officer when we got back — which he duly noted!

Geoff Rothwell had been with the squadron just long enough to get his feet under the table when the bombshell came:

*W*e had flown some seven trips in 12 days, all near to the limit of our range and endurance. Then, returning from a spot of leave towards the end of March, I arrived in time for a visit from our Base Commander, a New Zealander serving in the RAF, Air Commodore 'Square' McKee*. When the flight commanders were introduced to him, he asked them where they came from. I, of course, had to admit to being English, whereupon he said that although there was nothing personal, I would have to be posted to another squadron as it was now his policy for the senior posts in the New Zealand Squadron to be staffed by New Zealanders. Naturally I was disappointed but I could appreciate his reasoning. He promised, however, that I could keep my crew wherever I went. When the posting came through it was to 218 (Gold Coast) Squadron at Downham Market. I felt I would be reasonably secure as a flight commander there, as I was pretty certain there were no African natives serving in Bomber Command!

I finished my 'tour' with 75 with a couple of trips to Berlin. On the first we were heavily engaged by flak at 9500 feet over the target and returned to find many holes in the fuselage. The second flight was more spectacular as we experienced severe icing over the Danish coast and dropped 4000 feet out of control due to the ice accretion on the wings. The trip was aborted and we returned to base, to fight another day.

My flight was taken over by Dick Broadbent, who received promotion to squadron leader and who was to greet me when I arrived in Kerikeri some 25 years later. We finished up in a partnership, owning a motel and bookshop after I retired from planting in Malaysia.

Geoff Rothwell went on to complete his second tour with 218 Squadron and received a bar to his DFC. He then began a third tour with 138 Special Duties Squadron which ended with a crash on Texel after dropping two Dutch agents to the resistance. After the war he received the Belgium Croix de Guerre and was made a Chevalier of the Order of Leopold.

◇ ◇ ◇

After the heavy losses suffered by the squadron in the early weeks of 1943, there had been a welcome lull in casualties. But this run ended after a raid on Duisberg on 8 April. Warrant Officer J. A. Walsh crashed at Bressingham, Norfolk, shortly after radioing that he was lost. All seven men died.

Two nights later, Sergeant J. Webb and crew didn't get back from Frankfurt, while Flight Sergeant C. Rothschild, a Canadian skipper, had his Stirling shot up over Frankfurt. With leaking fuel tanks, he failed to make the English coast before running out of height, so ditched off Portslade. All the crew were rescued by an RAF Walrus amphibian of the Air Sea Rescue service.

In Rothschild's crew were two Canadian twins — Robert and Richard Tod, WOP and AG respectively. They had consecutive service numbers, having joined up together, trained together, were crewed together and posted to 75 together. Robert received the DFM for his part in this night's episode, helping to get them back and calling on the distress frequency. Sadly, both boys were also to die together, with another pilot, on 23 June. They were buried together in Medemblick Cemetery.

The flight engineer on Rothschild's crew, Sergeant Eric Grainger RAF, and the bomb aimer, Sergeant J. L. Richards (NZ) were also killed along with the Tods on the night of 23 June, while the navigator, Flight Sergeant George Sampson (NZ), was killed on the very same night, with yet another pilot.

---

* Andrew McKee DSO DFC AFC, formally with 99 and later CO of 9 Squadron, before commanding Marham and Mildenhall, in addition to commands at 3 Group. Air Marshal Sir Andrew McKee KCB CBE DSO DFC AFC retired from the RAF in 1959, returned to NZ, and became chairman of National Airways. He died in 1988, aged 87.

Visit by NZ High Commissioner, W. J. 'Bill' Jordan, 7 August 1942. The CO, Wing Commander V. Mitchell DFC, leads the cheers. Behind Mr Jordan is Mildenhall's Station Commander, Group Captain Wasse. (SPORT & GENERAL)

Sergeant W. A. M. 'Bill' Hardy, rear gunner, (right) with Sgt M. T. T. Manawaiti, a Maori WOPAG who was to win the DFM. (W. A. M. HARDY)

Wing Commander Michael Wyatt (DFC), commanding officer of 75 Squadron May to August 1943, following his 'holiday' in Spain. (M. WYATT)

Wing Commander E. P. 'Hawkeye' Wells DSO DFC, the famous New Zealand fighter pilot visiting 75 Squadron: (left to right) unknown, F/Lt Ness (Adj), F/L Bill Scollay (DFC), Wells, S/Ldr R. Broadbent (DFC), F/O P. J. O. Buck (DFC), S/L G. Allcock DFC.
(SPORT & GENERAL)

Squadron Leader Dick Broadbest and Hawkeye Wells inspect the damage to the rear end of Peter Buck's Stirling (BF517) after his crash landing at Newmarket, 27 April 1943. The rear gunner was killed and two others wounded in the night-fighter attack.
(SPORT & GENERAL)

Geoff Rothwell and crew after leaving 75 Squadron for 218. Known as 'Rothwell's Ruffians', they are (left to right): Ginger Negus (MU), Mac McGrevy (FE), Jock Howat (RG), Jacky Drawbridge (N), Rothwell, 'Whistle' Entwhistle (WOP) and Wal Fielding (AB). Drawbridge, Entwhistle, Negus and Hewat did not survive the war.

(G. M. ROTHWELL)

The squadron had now hit another wave of losses. A raid to Stuttgart on 14/15 April claimed Pilot Officer D. G. McCaskill, while Pilot Officer A. G. Tolley went missing after an attack on Rostock on 20 April. On this same raid, Sergeant H. J. Dalzell, from North Canterbury, collided with a Lancaster after leaving the target. Luckily, there was only slight damage to the rudder and fin, and he returned to make a perfect landing. But the Stirling had lost most of its height before Dalzell had regained control, and he then faced a difficult flight home. He later received the DFM. Dalzell was having a charmed life, for the previous month he had a miraculous escape when a 2½ inch shell splinter tore through the side of his cockpit, ripped his tunic and was deflected by a cigarette case in his breast pocket.

Luck was also with Douglas Lowe on the 16/17 April raid on Ludwigshaven. He met heavy and accurate flak over the target and on landing found his throttle had jammed. He got the Stirling down alright, but crashed into a partly built hangar. The aircraft was wrecked and, although some injuries were sustained, the crew survived. Luck was, however, not with Pilot Officer K. H. G. Groves and Flight Sergeant K. F. Debenham, neither of whom got back; only one crewman survived as a prisoner.

The following day, 17 April 1943, Richard Broadbent, of Wanganui, arrived on 75, to take command of 'C' Flight. Not all heavy bomber squadrons could boast three Flights, but 75 was no ordinary squadron, as Richard recalls:

>**B**y the time I arrived on 75, I had completed one tour of 34 Ops, with 40 Squadron, flying Wellingtons, followed by about 19 months as an Instructor. I was delighted to find myself going back on a squadron and somewhat surprised to find myself being advanced to the rank of squadron leader so quickly. I had always served on mixed units prior to this and looked forward very much to getting onto a squadron manned predominantly by New Zealanders.
>
>No. 75 Squadron by this time was a very large outfit. Each Flight had, from memory,

12 aircraft and around 14 complete crews, which later was increased to 16 or 18 aircraft and 19 to 20 crews. So as a Flight Commander, I had to look after the day-to-day problems associated with about 100 aircrew members, the ground crews who serviced the aircraft, and to try generally to ensure that the Flight could put on a maximum operational effort when required. Such duties as OC [Officer Commanding] Night Flying, Briefing Officer, representing the squadron at conferences, etc, came along as well.

Newmarket airfield was a very ad-hoc set up. We flew off what had been the Rowley Mile racetrack — grass — and there were very few concrete hard-standings for the aircraft. Racecourse buildings — grandstand, stables etc — were used for various functions, while we lived partly at Sefton Lodge on the other side of Newmarket Town. Some were billeted in the centre of the township in the Jockey Club headquarters. With such a spread-out arrangement, it sometimes seemed impossible to get any cohesion. But on the whole, everybody enjoyed living, as it were, on top of and being part of, Newmarket township.

The CO was now Wing Commander Gerald Arthur Lane DFC, who despite Square McKee's hopes, was an Englishman, from London. He had previously been CFI [Chief Flying Instructor] at No. 22 Operational Training Unit. Until recently the flight commanders had been Squadron Leaders G. M. Allcock DFC, from Wellington, and G. E. Fowler DFC, from Derbyshire, England, who had already served a tour with 75. At about the time Dick Broadbent arrived to command the new third Flight — initially with eight aircraft — the other flight commanders were Squadron Leaders F. A. Andrews and R. H. Laud, both of Auckland.

The Ruhr — Duisberg — was hit again on 26 April, but of the ten squadron aircraft detailed, one failed to take off (pilot taken ill) and two aborted. Stirling BF517, piloted by Pilot Officer P. J. O. Buck (NZ), carrying a second pilot for experience, was severely mauled. They were attacked by an unseen night fighter, mortally wounding the rear gunner and slightly injuring two others. Buck began to lose height, having lost an engine, so ordered everything that could be jettisoned to be so. He was thus able to retain sufficient height to get them home for a crash landing at Newmarket. The famous photograph taken of the tail of this Stirling clearly shows the damage inflicted. Peter Buck was awarded the DFC and his navigator, Pilot Officer John Symons RCAF, one of the wounded, also won the DFC for staying at his post to navigate them home, despite his injuries.

At the end of the month, came a return to mining, first to the Frisian Islands, then to Kiel Bay and yet another disaster. Eight crews were assigned to go to Kiel on the night of 28/29 April, part of a mammoth force of 207 aircraft to mine the seas off Heligoland, in the River Elbe, and in the Great and Little Belts. An estimated 593 mines were sent into the water but the aircraft met much flak both from the shore and flak-ships strategically located by the Germans. Although it was a huge operation, the losses were unexpectedly high, no fewer than 22 aircraft — 7 Lancasters, 7 Stirlings, 6 Wellingtons and two Halifaxes — failing to return. Four of the Stirlings were from 75 Squadron — 28 men killed!

This made 11 aircraft and ten crews lost during April; other aircraft had been damaged, other crewmen had been killed or wounded. One didn't have to have a degree in mathematics to calculate the odds of a crew completing a tour of 30 or 35 trips. The squadron's morale, already badly shaken, took a further dive when yet another crew failed to return from mining in the Frisians on 5/6 May. There seemed to be a slight increase in crews not taking off due to illness or mechanical faults, while others came back early with more problems. The squadron was facing a possible crisis.

A new Commanding Officer arrived — Wing Commander Mike Wyatt, another Englishman, who had been flying with 15 Squadron. He had run into trouble during a raid on Turin, and rather than bale out into captivity over southern France, the crew elected to let Mike Wyatt crash land their Stirling in Spain. This he succeeded in doing and eventually he managed to organise his crew's release. They returned to England and their squadron via Gibraltar. Wing Commander Wyatt remembers:

I took over 75 Squadron on 3rd May 1943. I'd been flying with 15 Squadron, originally from Bourne, a satellite of Oakington. I'd been missing from a raid on Turin and had crash landed in Spain, but eventually re-joined the squadron just as it was about to move to Mildenhall. I hadn't been there many weeks when I was sent for by Group HQ and was told about the state of 75 Squadron and was asked if I'd like the job as CO, but was told it was going to be a very tough one.

The morale of 75 at the time was very low. Their operational success rate was absolutely appalling and was one of the worst in Bomber Command. There were various reasons for it though.

The airfield at Newmarket was so close to the town — the Messes were virtually in the town — and there was far too much hospitality. All these New Zealanders rather fascinated the horse racing fraternity and Newmarket was the only place where horse racing continued during the war. They would not, of course, allow the racecourse to be turned into a proper airfield, with proper runways and so on. We used the Jockey Club which is where I had my sleeping quarters and the Officer's Mess was just on the corner of the road south of the Club, on the main street.

The chaps were being entertained far too much and I think there was a terrible number of sore heads on a lot of mornings. It seemed to me they were enjoying life rather more in Newmarket and had begun to lose sight of the main reason for being there. The AOC outlined all this to me and said it was up to me to sort them out and get them back to being an operational squadron.

In fact this didn't take very long and by June they were back to sending out maximum aircraft each night, and were then as good as any other squadron. They just needed a bit of stirring up really and someone to get them out of the rut.

They had had some heavy casualties, of course, and now, when the least little thing went wrong with their aircraft, they were turning back. Aborted sorties were one of the problems. But when it was explained to them that some small electrical fault didn't mean one had to stop the operation, and they could certainly carry on and complete it, they gradually got the idea.

I could also see it was bad to have them at Newmarket — there were far too many distractions — and the AOC had mentioned to me there was the possibility of moving, and then the new airfield at Mepal came up. I was told there was a chance we could have it and I jumped at the chance.

Our Station Commander then was Michael Wasse and he agreed with my sentiments, and so we moved to Mepal on 28th June. It was right out in the 'sticks' and when the squadron arrived there, they were horrified. They couldn't believe they could be sent to such an out of the way place — everything new — nissen huts instead of the rather better accommodation they had had at Newmarket. But then, after the usual binding, etc, they gradually settled down and I think they eventually became one of the better squadrons in the Group and in Bomber Command. They had a really good rate of operations and frequently put 18 aircraft into the air. Their loss rate wasn't as bad as some, having then a certain amount of luck in that respect.

I had some good chaps to help me, of course — Andrews, Broadbent, Bill Scollay, and Joll. I realised I had made myself fairly unpopular at first but in a short time the standard of operational flying improved out of all recognition.

This is not to say that life became all work and no play with my arrival as CO. On 'stand-down' nights we had some very memorable parties with the Station Commander always in the thick of it. At this time my private means of transport was a 500cc Fiat Topolino and with monotonous regularity this little car disappeared whenever we had a party. It always turned up again, either on top of an air raid shelter or on top of one of the many huts in the camp. Goodness knows how the lads got it up there, because we always had the devil of a job to get it down again, and on one occasion even had to use one of the cranes from the MT [Motor Transport] Section. It's amazing what strength a skin-full of beer induces into people!

Meanwhile, operations continued from Newmarket during May and June with raids on the Ruhr and mining sorties taking priority. One early result of Wing Commander Wyatt's arrival came on 23 May — the squadron put up 15 Stirlings, the largest number so far, against Dortmund. They lost one, but only one returned early — with engine trouble. Another aircraft, captained by Flight Sergeant W. D. Whitehead, of Papakura, was hit by flak just as it released its bombs. The port outer engine caught fire and the searchlights quickly picked out the flaming Stirling. They dropped 500 feet, the propellor flew off and the engine stopped, putting out the fire. But they got home.

The crew of Flight Sergeant H. C. 'Speed' Williams were engaged by two Ju88 night fighters, and with no hits scored by them, his two gunners — Flight Sergeant W. A. C. 'Bill' Hemsley in the mid-upper turret, Flight Sergeant Ivan Kaye in the rear — claimed both fighters damaged.

The missing crew was that of Sergeant S. M. Tietjens. There was only one survivor, Sergeant Les Vale, the rear gunner:

*T*he 24th of May was Empire Day, as it used to be known, and will live with me always. We had bombed the target and dropped our bombs so were on our way back when the sky seemed full of fighters. I seem to recall an explosion and the next thing I can remember was that I was on the ground with several people standing around me. I found it impossible to get up owing to a leg injury. It was only a very short while before uniformed German soldiers arrived on the scene and my term as a prisoner of war had started. I found I was always being interrogated about my collegues, and as time progressed I realised that the explosion was probably the answer and by some miracle I had been blown clear.

Steve Tietjens was a New Zealander, as was John Turnbull, the navigator, whose brother Bryan was flying a successful tour of duty with RAF Coastal Command, sinking one U-boat and damaging others, to win the DFC. Les Vale came from Worcester, England.

Then came 29 May, a year after the start of the 1000 bomber raids. On this night, 75 Squadron put up another maximum number of Stirling — a record 23 — to Wuppertal. The total force was 719 bombers and the raid was one of the outstanding successes of the Ruhr Battle. The Pathfinders marked well and Main Force squadron's bombing was hugely successful and accurate, with large fires in the centre of the old town so severe that it was almost a firestorm (a term later used with increasing regularity). It was estimated that 80 per cent of the Barmen district was demolished, with five of the six largest factories being destroyed along with over 200 other industrial premises and around 4000 houses.

However, 33 aircraft, representing 4.6% of the raiding force, were lost. Of these, eight were Stirlings, with four coming from the long suffering New Zealand Squadron! It was still going to be a very long, hard road.

11

Keeping Them in the Air

Whatever the crews did over Germany, it was the men on the ground who kept them flying. No squadron can operate without the dedication, hard work and professionalism of the ground crews and supporting administrative personnel. This chapter will record some of the work the ground echelons carried out. After all, they were the backbone of the squadron. Where a bomber crew might be on the squadron some months, the ground crew personnel could be around for years.

Corporal J. H. 'Ted' Leck served with 75 Squadron for four and a half years — from 1940 till just before Lancasters arrived in 1944 — as a fitter:

> *I* was posted to 75 at Feltwell as a very moderate AC2 flight mechanic in 'B' Flight. Flight Sergeant Tim Healey was in charge of the Flight maintenance, a Regular RAF rigger by trade. On his promotion to Warrant Officer, our new 'Chiefy' was Flight Sergeant 'Spud' Murphy OBE, another Regular. He was in charge for the rest of my time on 75. I mention both as they 'Kept them Flying' and were a credit to 75.
>
> I began my job by refuelling etc. Then one day I had to change a complete set of plugs. I was so careful in case I made a mistake that the corporal came to see if I was still awake! In a few weeks I was as good as the next man, and was given my own kite to look after, together with a rigger who attended to the airframe.
>
> Feltwell in those days had no runways, just all grass with a dip in the middle which, on take-off, nearly stopped your heart. The flare path consisted of a single row of lights — no perimeter lights. All of us had to do the flare path duty in turn, which sometimes made one's hair stand on end. Five of us stood at the first light with the Duty Officer and the black and white chequered Ops trailer. Night take-offs were not so bad as it was usually still light, but when they returned it was a different story.
>
> Thirty-five Squadron also began to operate from Feltwell and when they all returned, all circling the drome together, all tired men and wanting to be down, it made the Duty Officer's job a hard one. The idea was, that one of us had an Aldis Lamp and the DO told you to flash a 'green' light to a kite he had picked out and that Wimpy could land. The trouble was that sometimes two aircraft picked up the signal and tried to get down together, or someone in trouble had to get down without delay.
>
> We always had trouble with air raids at Feltwell and the flare path had to be put out at once. On good nights this only meant switching off the current, but on thick misty nights when we used gooseneck parafin flares, it was a case of us all running along the line, putting them out by hand, and sometimes, a Wimpy skipper, anxious to get down, came in and nearly parted one's hair! Still, the system worked and serious accidents were very rare.
>
> Aircraft coming off the flare path were met by a small pick-up truck with a board lit

up on the back, saying 'Follow Me', and was led around the perimeter to its dispersal point. This was okay for 35 Squadron and 'A' Flight of 75, as they were dispersed around the flying field, but 'B' Flight was a different matter. We were dispersed up a small hill in what had been a cornfield and had a gap in a large hedge which the aircraft had to go through and dispersal was then another quarter of a mile.

The routine was that the truck brought the aircraft to the gap and left it. There was then a line of ground crew at intervals, each with two torches. The Wimpy stood there at the gap, flashing its aircraft letter, so we knew where it had to go. The first airman made a circular movement with his torches to say follow me, then with the torches over his shoulders, he ran in front of the aircraft until he was in range of the next man, and with the whirling props of a Wimpy at your backside, one certainly ran! The last man put the aircraft in its bay and turned it round. In winter time, all this took place in pitch dark and with very tired pilots.

One night I got a rare fright. I was last man and was seeing in 'R-Robert', my own kite. The bay was last on dispersal and down a small incline. The pilot followed me to the bay and I gave him the signal to stop, so I could get him to turn round, but with no response. He kept on coming and I knew behind me was rolls of barbed wire which protected the edge of the field. I was now frantic, so I dived onto the ground and let the Wimpy come on. The props whirled over me and the next thing was barbed wire being whipped up into the engines. The aircraft stopped and a very white-faced pilot got out and told a whiter-faced mechanic he was sorry but he had run out of brake pressure!

I never got over the feeling one got when the aircraft and crew you had seen off just a few hours earlier didn't return. Sometimes we waited out on that dark dispersal point for hours after the rest were back, because at odd times there was the sound of engines. The flare path would light up again and there was its nav lights and an 'ident' letter flashing. Somebody would exclaim, 'About bloody time too!', but more in relief than anger. On other nights, after waiting anxiously, the dispersal telephone would ring and the duty sergeant would say, 'Pack in, lads. R-Robert has gone down.' How cheap life seemed.

In the early days the bombs carried were 250 and 500 pounders, with the occasional 1000 pound. They also carried leaflets, fake German ration cards, and once, on the Dutch Queen's birthday, tiny packets of tea to drop over Holland. Once we changed the 'Peggy' engines for the more powerful Hercules, with their fixed two speed props, the bomb loads got bigger — up to a 4000 pounder.

I got the first Wimpy to carry a 4000 bomb and a lot of top 'brass' came out to dispersal to see this massive thing loaded up. The target that night was one of the Channel ports. The aircraft never came back! We ground crews rarely knew the targets and never asked, but by the fuel load we could make a good guess.

I remember, too, when three Wimpies took just four 250 pound bombs to Turin, quite a feat for the old girl on Peggy engines and with no de-icing system. I think it was just to remind the Italians that they were not out of range.

The first 1000 bomber raid was something to remember. We all had a pep-talk by the Chiefy, maximum effort, no slip-ups or mistakes, plus a load of rubbish flown in to make up the numbers, but they all came back.

It is funny how things happen. When Sergeant Ward won the VC, I was the mechanic that helped to see the aircraft off. It was not my aircraft, but as the pilot ran up the engines he called me into the cockpit to adjust his seat. All I could do was to make a 'parcel' of an old engine cover so the pilot could raise himself. The pilot gave me a 'thumbs up' and away they went. It was this cover that Ward used to push into the burning hole on the wing. The rope Ward used was that which usually hung down by the astrodome to help men get out in a ditching. Credit must be given to the man who held the rope and helped get Ward back in [Joe Lawton].

Lou Raven was an electrician, joining 75 in March 1940, one of the first skilled technicians to join it. He remembers first, the arrival of the Wellingtons:

*E*ventually, the great day came when the first Wellington was delivered. We all swarmed round it, from CO down to Orderley Room clerk — it was magic! Gradually the number grew and we worked like mad to get them operational. Then came the first operation, a leaflet raid over Germany.

Two good friends of mine then were Corporals Paddy Campion and Fairfax who eventually became Warrant Officers — both Regulars and they did much to get the squadron ready.

During 1940, when there was a scare that German parachutists might drop on RAF aerodromes, we were issued with pick-axe handles to help defend the place! A few pistols were issued to officers and we had a few RAF Regiment personnel on the far edges of the drome with old anti-aircraft guns.

We did have some attacks. On one night, German aircraft followed one of our Wellingtons to the runway and badly damaged it with gun fire. Likewise, another German used to lurk above the clouds and swoop out and give us a hard time with gun fire out at dispersal. As I could run pretty fast I escaped being shot up. As we ran for a nearby shelter I arrived first, but others following were injured with bullets in the legs, etc. On another occasion a German came swooping down, gunning and killing a poor old boy and his horse who were carting along the road edging the airfield.

We had a tragedy during an exercise in 1941. I had fitted up an experimental kite with some special lighting from Air Ministry, and the bomb aimer was to wear special dark glasses to simulate night flying. This day we took up five navigators to train and I sat by the pilot. Suddenly there was a sudden rush of air into the kite. It turned out that one of the navs, who was on the small side, had approached the front to take up his bombing position and somehow the front hatch became undone and he fell straight through. We were flying near Ely at the time, the Cathedral was in view on our left. A farmer found his body, eventually, in some undergrowth.

There was also the time when a Wimpy returned from a raid and it was reported that the rear gunner was out of action. On learning that it was one of my own pals, I

Squadron armourer, with the look that says it all! The bombs are 500 pounders.

Ops are on! Re-fuel and re-arm 'em boys! 250 pounders being rolled out.

No. 75 Squadron armourers. Back row, left to right: Styles, Morris, unknown, Gubbins, Kane, Bert Simmonds (rep from Parnell Aircraft), Nesbitt, Sgt Jones (i/c), Trott. Middle row, left to right, McClure, Jackson, Hart, Taylor, Longstaff. Front row, left to right: unknown, Dyson, unknown, Priestley, Pennington(?).

(D. MORRIS)

ventured out to the kite to help. The MO turned away in horror and it was me who eventually managed to free him and get him out. His head had almost been severed by a piece of shrapnel.

There were other frights, like the day I was in a kite with the pilot, checking a mag-drop fault, about two hours before take-off. Suddenly a huge shout went up as one of the bombs fell off and hit the ground!

George Lax arrived at Feltwell in January 1940 as Aircraft Hand, General Duties (ACH (GD)) but spent much of his early days on guard duty in case the invasion came. He later took a fitter's course and returned to Feltwell and 75 Squadron:

I recall the night a bomb went off whilst it was being loaded into a Wimpy outside a hangar and destroyed the aircraft, but I do not think there were any serious casualties.

When we moved to Mildenhall I went into 'B' Flight with Flight Sergeant Murphy and stayed there when 75 moved to Rowley Mile. We and a squad of fitters remained in order to get all the u/s Wimpies serviceable and whilst there I was made up to Sergeant.

Then came Newmarket and the Stirlings, and had aircraft 'T-Tommy' with Flight Lieutenant Des Thompson and his crew. They finally left to join a Pathfinder squadron and were lost. I remember painting a coat of arms of his old school on the nose of 'Tommy', having been a sign writer in civvy street.

We had good times at Newmarket but I recall the night a Stirling caught the Devil's Dyke on take-off and blew up, which caused that year's St Leger to be postponed. Then we went to Mepal and I was one of the last to leave Newmarket in the Stirling of Squadron Leader Andrews. Shortly afterwards I was posted to the Far East.

Derek Morris was a former Halton apprentice, and after a period with 74 Fighter Squadron, moved up one number in March 1940. At 75, he became the resident gun turret expert:

*T*hat was my main job on the squadron apart from the sweat shed on Ops days when bombing up was in fashion! I was a Corporal in August 1940 and a Sergeant the following August.

A pump on the port engine passed oil under pressure to all turrets by a system of pipes throughout the aircraft. One thing which springs to mind: we initially had Vickers turrets but within weeks we received the Mark 1A aircraft which had Fraser-Nash, nose, tail, and mid-under turrets. They were fantastic to fly in, for lowering the turret in flight gave the impression that the aircraft was going up, leaving you suspended in mid-air.

This mid-under turret weighed about 1000 pounds and it was considered that the weight penalty and slight speed loss when lowered was not worth the defence it offered. Consequently, we were instructed to remove them all! Now this turret was fitted just to the rear of the bomb beam, the ground clearance below it was about 14 inches. In fact, for landing, the footwell in which the gunner's feet normally resided was wound up by a cable and retracted level with the fuselage. One gunner in 1940 lost his boots when landing — he should not have been in the turret for landing and should certainly not have been daft enough to leave his footwell down with his feet still in it!

As the turret was about four feet high and it also had four feet of lowering gear and framework above it, it presented a problem in its removal. With the first one, I and a mate, disconnected all the supplies and holding nuts and once the thing was loose, the problem was to lift the tail sufficiently to remove the turret. We used the hand operated crane in the hangar, connected to the tail lift point, under the strict supervision of the flight sergeant airframe fitter. We got it up to flying position and still the clearance was only about three feet. After consultation with the engineer officer, the airframe NCO permitted us to go a little higher, then positively stopped as the C of G [centre of gravity] was so far forward, the Wellington was in danger of tipping onto its nose.

We were still about a foot short; the turret was on the hangar floor but still in the aircraft. While arguments continued, lunch-time arrived. Instead of going to the cookhouse, we armourers returned five minutes later with a heavy sling which we slung over the air-craft's tail and with a dozen well-fed armourers hanging on, we carefully hoisted the fuselage up and released the turret.

In the following two weeks all 16 mid-under turrets were removed; in every case the final hoist before the turret fell on the floor was done at a mealtime! I don't think the airframe 'chiefy' ever fully realised how it was done.

Another long service NCO was Stan Sharpe, who joined 75 in November 1940, staying till early 1944, and rising from AC1 fitter to sergeant:

*T*he first plane I worked on was a Wellington and on the side was painted a head of a Maori Chief with the inscription 'Ake Ake Kia Kaha' — For Ever and Ever be Strong — beneath. I was with 75 when the losses were heaviest. Just before Christmas '42 we lost four aircraft one night. I think Flight Sergeant Rousseau went down in 'W' Willie, whilst his regular mid-upper gunner, was doing a three month's sentence in Brighton for tipping some WAAFS [Women's Auxiliary Air Force] out of bed, and missed the trip.

I remember being in a hangar on the Heath when Squadron Leader Laud gave everyone a pep-talk, urging all to greater efforts, in the spring of '43. He was shot down shortly afterwards.

The Station Warrant Officer at Newmarket was Warrant Officer Spencer who was 69 years old! We called him 'Snowy' because of his white hair. He had been in the Engineers in WW1, having joined them in 1912, and transferred to the RFC [Royal Flying Corps] in 1916. He did a great job in improving conditions for us.

At Feltwell we had a Corporal Alcock, a married man who was senior to me. He volunteered for aircrew, then one of our sergeants was posted so I was made up to sergeant, which wouldn't have happened if Frank Alcock had not gone. He was posted back to 75 and lost on his fifth Op. If a crew got in 12 Ops, it was a lot at that period of the war.

Just before Christmas 1943, Johnny Grubb and his crew invited some of us ground staff NCOs out for a drink. When the drink ran out, we all decided to head for the Sergeant's Mess. Johnny, who was about my build, got fed up returning airmen's salutes, so on the way back he suggested we exchange great coats and hats and that I would do the saluting. It is amazing what one will do when you've had a few!

Fred Ball joined the squadron around Christmas 1940 after training on aircraft electrical equipment, coming under Sergeant Paddy Campion and Pilot Officer Thompson, who was in charge of the whole section. He was still with 75 on VE day! He remembers several incidents at Feltwell and later:

*O*ne day a Wellington came in fitted with an extra large bomb, and the aircrew and ground staff gathered round to inspect. One of the aircrew came into the plane and we pointed out to him the manual release. He then bent down and before we could stop him he operated it. The bomb fell on the tarmac and everyone scattered. But looking back I think it was a bit too late to run.

Some aircraft were dispersed on the other side of the public road leading to the railway station. A Wellington crossing this point one day was in collision with a three-ton truck which had gone out to dispersal. The truck was knocked onto its side and the Wimpy had a damaged wing.

Then there was the occasion one aircraft was found to have a flat battery just before take-off. I rushed to get a replacement and seeing a small Standard van, I flagged it down. We had travelled a short way when the officer in the front said he hadn't seen me at teatime and told him I'd been too busy. As he turned I saw all this 'scrambled egg' on his hat. It was the Station Commander and I was worried I'd said the wrong thing. Having got the battery back, he asked me how long it would take to fit and I replied, 5–10 minutes. He then waited and when I'd done, he drove me to the airman's mess, ordering the NCO in charge to give me a good tea!

Most aircraft movements are done with hydraulics but on the Stirling it was done by electricity. We had 32 motors, alternators and generators on each aircraft! All had to be removed after a certain number of hours and inspected. Some of this would be done at dispersal — in the dark, in snow — and refitted next day. At Mepal, I remember the time when an aircraft was left with some delayed action bombs aboard which exploded about two in the morning! The Lancaster was destroyed, of course, with debris flying up to half a mile away, some landing in Sutton village. A couple of houses were damaged which then had to be demolished and rebuilt. It was some bang!

LAC Ernie Brook joined 75 in 1941 and recalls the occasion when four crews were lost over the Baltic in April 1943:

*T*he following day I was ordered by the CO at 2pm, to have 11 football players at the sports ground at 3, to play an aircrew team. It was hoped that it would help to take thoughts away from the previous night's disaster. The result was of no consequence and as we all came off the field at the end of the game, arms all around one another, it had done the trick. It was a very moving occasion and there were a few wet eyes amongst us. That night we all went down to the 'White Lion' and no one under the rank of sergeant was allowed to buy drinks at the bar. It was the first and only time I've known aircrew having to take ground crew back to the billets.

We always had a good football team on 75, but at Mepal in 1943–44 was our finest season. We cleared the deck in everything we played for, winning the RAF Challenge Cup, RAF League, Ely and District League, and Ely and District Cup.

One of the oldest men on the squadron must have been Len Weeks, who had joined the RAF in 1919 and who had left the service as a corporal in 1927. He was recalled in 1939 and became a sergeant in 1941, taking charge of ground staff of 'A' Flight at Mildenhall, Oakington and Rowley Mile, Newmarket, then Mepal. When he joined 75 he was 39 years old:

I remember the pilot of a Wellington who returned from a 'voluntary' daylight raid — suicidals, we called them! All the fabric had gone down one side and all the geodetics were exposed. I watched a few yards away as the medical staff removed the body of the dead rear gunner from his perspex turret. The pilot was Flight Lieutenant Cookson.

I also remember my last Flight Commander, Squadron Leader Joll, when as the 'Chiefy' of 'A' Flight, we had our morning chats re bomb loads, distribution of petrol in various wing tanks, etc, according to the distance to the target.

Security was very important and one night we were told we would have a mock attack by the army, who would make a white chalk mark on any aircraft they could get to undetected. I was detailed to take charge of about 16 mechanics to spread around our dispersed Wellingtons to prevent any marking being done. It was a dark night, and regrettably, at daylight, ALL our aircraft were found to be marked! This was very understandable — the lads were unable to work all day and then keep a 100 per cent watch on their aircraft. I think this exercise helped lead to the formation of the RAF Regiment.

Winching the bombs into the bomb-bay was exacting work. (RNZAF)

I also recall the WAAF who 'lugged' a box of incendiaries from under a Wellington when one of the 30 had dropped off and was on fire!

In contrast to Len Weeks, Arthur Harris (a great name to have in Bomber Command!) was just 18 when he arrived at Newmarket in the spring of 1943. He became an assistant armourer at the Station Armoury:

*T*he bomb store — dump — was situated across the other side of the airfield, a remote and isolated place, which at times was very cold. We were transported there at daybreak and remained there until midday dinner and evening tea meals. In the afternoons we had a snack van round.

The hours were long and mostly for seven days a week, for there was much to be done. We prepared, for Ops, canisters which were about six feet long by eighteen inches wide, and had to be loaded with four pound incendiary bombs. The canisters had several sections and the bombs were held in place by a drop-bar, and we tested the

Danger — engine fitters carrying out a 30-hour inspection. Their skill kept the Wimpies flying. (RNZAF)

release mechanism by applying a 12-volt current from a truck battery. The larger type bombs were loaded on to trolleys, which were then taken to the fusing shed, before being taken out to the aircraft. We also had to fit parachutes to the sea mines, working outside in all weathers, and not being able to use gloves.

Many times this work was in vain, when Ops were scrubbed at the last minute and all the bombs had to be unloaded, returned and defused.

We also spent time down at the village railway station, off-loading bombs and explosives for transfer to the dump.

One sad recollection was when the squadron was going from Stirlings to Lancasters. One ground crew chap working on a Lanc had his head chopped off by the prop. Previously, of course, one could walk beneath the Stirling's props as they were much higher off the ground.

One of the arrivals in the winter of 1942–43 who had to report to Len Weeks was LAC Jack Richards. He was then assigned to aircraft 'C' for Charlie, under Sergeant Mitchell and Corporal Pearson:

The Stirling was a very high aeroplane and one of my jobs was to climb up onto the top of the cockpit to clean the windows — a job I was always shit scared of, as it almost called for a parachute! Flying was in my blood and I flew on every possible air test which I am certain helped me understand the aircraft and its mechanics far more than just doing daily inspections.

Life for the aircrews seemed very cheap in those days. We should just get used to a crew and get to know them, then they would go missing, and I recall the deep shock of neither plane nor crew the next morning. But by 10 or 11am, a new aircraft would arrive to be lettered and then a new set of faces would appear. Flying Officer Shorty Wilson was one of the best crews I ever became attached to. They completed over 20 Ops in 'our' plane until they were one of the three who did not get back from a mine laying trip on the night of 3/4th November 1943.

Wilson was very strict and never allowed his crew to write slogans or anything on the aircraft, but on that last night, the bomb aimer, Flying Officer Dance, wrote in the dew on the tail flap, 'Dance man Dance.' This caused a few sharp words with Wilson who requested me to wipe it off. This seemed to break the happy atmosphere which this crew seemed to have. For years afterwards I had their picture on my wall, and there has never been a 4th November that they have not been in my thoughts.

Syd Gittings was in charge of the Modification Section at Mepal and his wife was also on the squadron, in Signals. He joined 75 when they had Wellingtons, so saw them right through to Lancasters:

> *O*nce, when working on a Wellington, one of the chaps was detailed to top-up the hydraulic header tank, the filler point of which was situated in the top of the fuselage, next to the opening for firing the Verey pistol through. This 'erk' promptly proceeded with a large can of fluid, climbed up on the aircraft, opened the Verey pistol aperture and poured in the total contents of the can! He had completely missed the filler point so one can imagine the state inside the aircraft. It was impossible to negotiate the cat-walk, the stuff was all over the place. It took days to clean it up.
>
> Another 'expert' had been detailed to carry out a DI [Daily Inspection] on a Stirling. After he had been inside the aircraft for some time, all of a sudden the poor old machine started to shudder and gradually made a very graceful belly flop onto the ground. Everyone, of course, started to do their 'nuts'! Our man had broken the geodetic lock and of course, a few tons of aircraft landed on the deck with an almighty thump. I think he got posted.

Corporal H. C. 'Bill' Wilkins was a 'B' Flight armourer, who was posted to 75 late in the war, having been on Coastal Command at Gibraltar for three years. He replaced a New Zealand corporal who had been repatriated home:

> *I* remember that during the six months before VE day we were bombing up almost every night in a most intensive final assault against the Germans. Our efforts were fortified by a special supper in the mess beforehand and a rum ration was delivered to dispersal points by a marvellous armament WO. I also remember bearing in mind the strict instructions given us on our armourer's course concerning the care needed in fitting fuses to delayed action bombs. I was rather perturbed on my first spell of duty to see a sergeant from the Station Armoury hammering the bomb tail unit into place with great gusto!

Another of the squadron's armourers at Mepal was Harry Osborne, who also recalls the rum ration:

> *M*any of the armourer NCOs were New Zealanders. My memory of them is a very

happy one, especially of Mick Ongar, Toby Connors, Jack Walsh and the late Ben Benson. Our officer was Jack Lewis, whose interest in his boys (sober or drunk as they might be) was great.

Ours was a hard job and I believe in 1944 we broke Bomber Command's record for the number of sorties in a month, in spite of very few Ops for the first two weeks. The rum ration which was brought to us on the Flights was always very welcome!

I have memories of the night one of our aircraft blew up with a full load of bombs. No loss of life but several aircraft written off. Another night a Jerry intruder scattered a load of anti-personnel bombs over the drome. All armourers volunteered to search the field for these bombs which had failed to go off, having been dropped from too low a height for them to become armed.

Friday and Saturday nights were mainly spent at the 'Palace' in Chatteris — after the pubs closed — dancing to the squadron's dance band. Their opening number was 'The World is Waiting for the Sunrise' and the last number was the greatly loved, 'Now is the Hour.' This still brings tears to my eyes when I hear it.

Many of the lads used to spend the night in the police station cells through the kindness of Inspector Bush.

I married a girl from Chatteris which I think was the last wartime Chatteris wedding. My best man was fellow armourer Percy Newman. I remember the bed springs where we stayed had been undone and, in the early hours of the morning, I was trying to fix them. It was worse than bombing-up!

12

Mepal
JUNE — SEPTEMBER 1943

Royal Air Force Station Mepal was situated outside the villages of Mepal and Sutton, just to the north of Cambridge. As the crow flies it was only some 30 kilometres from Newmarket, so the Cathedral at Ely would continue to be a familiar landmark to the aircrews. Mepal was a brand new airfield which nobody had used yet, so 75 would be the first. And in many ways it would be the base mostly associated with both the squadron and the New Zealanders who flew from there.

June 1943 still found the squadron at Newmarket, the move to Mepal not happening till the 26th. What Bomber Command and Sir Arthur Harris were pleased to call the Battle of the Ruhr was still very much in progress and had two more months to run. No. 75 Squadron, along with nearly 800 other aircraft, contributed to the Battle in an attack on Dusseldorf on 11/12 June, while a futher 72 went for Munster. Wing Commander Wyatt flew with Flying Officer Eddy's crew on this night, but the Squadron's 'A' Flight Commander, Squadron Leader R. H. Laud, failed to return. Also on the Dusseldorf raid was 'C' Flight Commander, Dick Broadbent, who had to dive away from searchlights and fighters so fast his WOP, Flight Sergeant McIvor, burst an eardrum.

Three nights later Flying Officer J. L. Edwards and crew did not get back from a mining sortie over the Gironde. The Engineer was Sergeant J. G. F. Sansoucy, from Canada, who relates:

> *I* was assigned to replace another engineer in another crew and I believe they had only been on one trip, whereas this was my 14th. The trip was a mining sortie off Bordeaux but we had twice to cross the French coast and it was a clear moonlit night. As we approached the coast from inland we were hit by ground fire which damaged one engine and aileron on the starboard side. The pilot was having some difficulty with the controls when a Me109 night fighter attacked us. His first attack did us little harm but the next came from below and hit the pilot and navigator's compartment. The pilot himself may have been hit for he yelled 'Get out!' — which we did.
>
> Going down in my 'chute I saw the aircraft crash and then saw the 109 circling me and I became alarmed. But then I hit the ground and the fighter dropped a marker flare, so I knew he had seen me.

Sansoucy hid his parachute, cut off his insignia with a razor blade, and headed southeast. He was determined to evade and this he eventually did, aided in part by being able to speak French. This got him past German soldiers and helped him communicate with the French people who gave him assistance. He later crossed the

Pyrenees into Spain, then with the help of the British Consulate was on his way to Gibraltar and England.

The next raid was to Le Cruesot on 19 June. The targets here were the Schneider armaments factory and the Breuil steelworks. The Pathfinders located the target by dropping flares so that the Main Force bomb aimers could pin-point their aiming points. Only two Halifaxes were lost this night, but 75 had some damage from flak. Pilot Officer A. Sedunary lost his starboard outer propeller just before bombing, but continued his run. Flight Lieutenant French's Stirling was badly hit in the fuselage, main-plane and mid-upper turret, and petrol controls. The Flight Engineer, Sergeant Bartlett, put up a stout effort by hacking through the fuselage into the port wing root to access the petrol tank controls which he then operated by hand. Richard French received the DFC.

Fifteen Stirlings went back to Krefeld on the Ruhr on 21 June, the crews reporting the whole town a mass of seething flames which could be seen as far as the Dutch coast. On this night, with fighters active, 44 RAF bombers did not get home, but all of 75's contingent did. The next night it was Mulheim, and 35 RAF bombers were lost. Again fighters were active, three indecisive combats being recorded by the squadron's gunners. But fighters plus flak and searchlights scored heavily on 75, four Stirlings failing to get back to the Racecourse. Three of the crews were all killed, while five of the fourth aircraft were taken into captivity.

Two more crews were to be lost before the move to Mepal came — Pilot Officer Bluck against Wuppertal on 24 June, and Flying Officer Perrott on Gelsenkirchen the next night. All fourteen men died.

Then came the move to Mepal, as Dick Broadbent remembers:

*W*hen we moved to Mepal the squadron certainly appreciated the brand-new runways, taxiways and dispersal areas. I daresay the aircraft serviceability improved, too, because there were several hangars available for inside work on the aircraft.

Living and messing accommodation was still dispersed, but not so widely, and I have a feeling that on the whole, the squadron's morale and sense of togetherness was lifted enormously by the move. Casualties were very high during the whole period I was on 75 — the Stirling proving a delightful aircraft to fly, once airborne with the unwieldy undercarriage tucked up, but not such a good bombing or fighting machine because of its limitations of speed and height. It was also difficult to keep serviceable. Along with the other two flight commanders of my time, Frank Andrews and Jack Joll, I had one of the busiest periods I can remember. But there was no sense of despondency or overwork — we all felt we were really getting on with a necessary task and playing a pretty important part in the general war effort.

'A' and 'B' Flight aircraft were lettered 'AA' but 'C' Flight had the letters 'JN' before the individual aircraft letter. Mostly the aircraft situation was so plentiful by 1943 that we were able to allocate an aircraft to each crew and of course each crew took great pride in their own plane. Each plane had its own ground crew as well and it was the rule for ground and aircrew to share the servicing load as much as possible. My own Stirling Mark III was BK778 with the letters JN-U and over the eight months I was on the squadron, I flew all my operational sorties in old U for Uncle, and largely with the same crew. Our last flight in it was on the 20th October, to take a [now well-known] photograph of Mepal airfield. I then handed it over to another aircrew. Sadly, it failed to return from a mining trip in the Baltic Sea on 5th November.

Mike Wyatt also remembers the Stirling's shortcomings:

*T*he Stirlings were often used for mining operations. Mining was carried out at low level and one of the snags of the aircraft was that it couldn't fly as high as the Lancaster, so over the targets we were under the Lancasters — and the Halifaxes — and in danger of them bombing you. It was an uncomfortable feeling.

It was a very nice aeroplane to fly although inexperienced pilots found it difficult to take off because it had a tendency to swing to the right. It had a very tall undercarriage and this was very liable to collapse if you got into a right-hand swing, when the forward momentum caused a terrific strain on it. What one had to do was to put on loads of rudder and juggle with the throttles. Once airborne, of course, it flew very nicely.

Norman Bartlett recalled the time a Lancaster was found right above them over the target:

We were on the bombing run and I was watching for other aircraft when we heard a cry. Looking round, Jack Brewster, our navigator, was pointing upwards, open mouthed, his face all twisted with fright. I looked up and directly above, about 200 feet, was a Lancaster, with bomb doors open, ready to drop a 4000 pound 'cookie'. It was too late to do anything before the cookie dropped and as it passed us, it turned over and went by in a vertical position rather than horizontal, which probably saved us. Jack heaved a huge sigh of relief — and so did I!

Thirteen aircraft took off from Mepal on 3 July for Cologne — the station's first war operation — while four more flew a mining Op. Two days later came Mepal's first loss — Stirling ES436; Sergeant R. Thomas and crew failing to get home from mining in the Frisians. Then came Aachen on the night of 13/14 July. Nine Stirlings were part of a force of 374 bombers, and found a strong tail wind put them over the target rather earlier than planned. The town was left in flames, but flak and fighters brought down 20 RAF aircraft. No. 75 Squadron all returned, but they had some close moments.

Pilot Officer Cliff Logan's aircraft was hit by flak, which set his starboard outer on fire and damaged the elevator, but he made a good landing at Ford in Sussex. Pilot Officer A. Rankin's rear gunner, Sergeant Ogden, shot down a Ju88 night fighter; Pilot Officer Alexander's front gunner, Sergeant Scott, probably destroyed a Me210; while Sergeant Nicol's rear man, Flight Sergeant Cooksley, claimed another twin-engined fighter damaged.

Flying Officer Eddy's aircraft was damaged but he got back to make a crash landing at Oakington. However, as he touched down the undercarriage collapsed, and the bomber turned over and caught fire. Sergeant E. C. Viccars, the mid-upper, was killed in the crash, while Eddy, the navigator, engineer and WOP were all seriously injured; a second pilot was also injured. Charles Eddy tried to rescue his MU gunner, receiving the MBE for his efforts.

Then came a battle within a battle. Sir Arthur Harris had already decided to hit the important city of Hamburg during his Ruhr Battle, and had warned his Group Commanders that this target, Germany's largest port and second largest city, was on his hit list. Hamburg was no stranger to bomber crews, but it had not been seriously damaged. Harris now wanted Hamburg. Although beyond the effective range of Oboe, its docks and waterways were a good target for H2S, with the mighty River Elbe pointing the way like a finger.

The first blow of this Battle of Hamburg was made on the night of 24/25 July, having been postponed due to weather the previous night. No. 75 Squadron put up a maximum effort — 23 Stirlings — and because of the distance and the slow-climbing aspects of the Stirling, these aircraft were scheduled to be first off. In point of fact, Sergeant P. Moseley of the squadron, in Stirling BF443, was first of all aircraft to take off for Hamburg on this night, his wheels leaving the ground at 9.45pm.

Following him were a further 790 heavy bombers, and for the first time a new defensive 'device' was to be used — 'Window'. Window, was the code name for strips of coarse black paper, measuring 2 × 27 cms, each having a thin strip of aluminium foil stuck to one side. Released in bundles over Germany, the paper would create havoc on the German radar screens, as each piece of foil became a blip upon them. And not only on the screens of the German Wurzburg ground radar apparatus, but also on the smaller Lichtenstein airborne radar sets fitted to the twin-engined night fighters, such as the Me110, Ju88s and Do217s. As a matter of interest, Window was not new — it had been invented well over a year earlier. But as there was at this stage no defence against it, and could therefore be used by the Germans against Britain, it was not used before this time. It was now, however, thought that its use against Britain would not be a major problem, and its use in helping to reduce Bomber Command's night casualties, far outweighed the fear of successful use by the Luftwaffe.

On this night, two of the squadron's aircraft returned early with defects, but the remainder bombed successfully. Night fighters — probably confused night fighters, whose radar screens were almost blanked out with something looking like a mini-snowstorm — were in evidence. Flying Officer G. Turner, whilst trying to avoid a searchlight cone, struck a Ju88 with his starboard wing, the Junkers diving into the ground. The Stirling's wing was badly damaged, with about four feet being sliced off and the aileron and controls being smashed. Turner found great difficulty in keeping the Stirling on a straight course, but helped by his Bomb Aimer, brought the cripple home to make a perfect landing.

Dick Broadbent was on this and the next raid to Hamburg:

> *I* think the outstanding sorties during my second tour were those concerned with the raids on Hamburg on the nights of 24th and 29th July, when 'window' was dropped for the first time. The concentration of bombing on the town centre on both nights caused a holocaust — the so-called 'fire storm'. It was a revelation to see how such a simple device as strips of metallic foil could confuse and fox the highly sophisticated, radar-controlled defence forces.

Losses for the first Hamburg raid were light — just 12 aircraft — but 75 lost one, that of Sergeant H. Nicol and crew. The next night, they lost another — Sergeant Ashdown over Essen. But honours were evened when the gunners of Flight Sergeant H. C. Williams' crew destroyed a FW190. One of the gunners was Sergeant W. A. C. 'Bill' Hemsley:

> *O*ur pilot, 'Speed' Williams, was the best. He was slightly older than the average pilot and therefore was almost a father figure to us. He was a first-class pilot who relied on knowledge and experience, and he flew to the rules and never took chances. This no doubt was why, given the usual amount of luck, that he survived two tours of Ops and won the DFC. On our way to Essen on this night Flight Sergeant Ivan Kaye claimed a fighter shot down and we were attacked again when leaving the target, but were not hit.

Twenty-two Stirlings went back to Hamburg on 27/28 July with no losses, while 17 returned two days later. Night fighters were again much in evidence, two Ju88s being damaged by 75's gunners, with three other crews reporting engagements; but there were no losses. On the first of these two nights, the Stirling captained by Flight Sergeant E. J. Roberts was attacked by a Ju88. One bomb door was blown off and a petrol pipe line pierced, but Roberts got it home.

Losses were sustained on 30 July when 13 aircraft were part of the raiding force to Remscheid on the southern edge of the Ruhr. Oboe marking proved good and bombing results were excellent. Post-war evidence confirmed that 83 per cent of the town was devastated in this raid, with 107 industrial buildings being destroyed. Production levels never again reached pre-raid proportions. This is what Bomber Harris was striving for. However, it cost 75 two crews lost, although Flight Sergeant O. H. White's gunners claimed one night fighter destroyed and another damaged.

It was back to Hamburg on 2 August, but of the 17 aircraft which took off, six returned due to icing problems and electrical storms while two failed to return at all. Another was lost on 6 August during a mining sortie to the Frisians, but 19 aircraft attacked Nuremburg two nights later without loss. Pilot Officer Cliff Logan lost his navigational aids which caused problems on the way home. Running short of petrol, he had even told his crew to prepare to bale out when finally they found an airfield and landed. They had been airborne an incredible 9 hours 10 minutes!

Pilot Officer A. W. Burley had an equally anxious time during a trip to Turin on 12 August, having one of the port engines knocked out by a night fighter attack. But he continued to fly the remaining 600 kilometres to the target, bomb and return to make a perfect landing. For this feat, Arthur Burley received the DSO. This complimented several recent awards of DFCs to Douglas Lowe, Dick Broadbent, Frank Andrews and Richard French; with DFMs for Alex Brown, and to Alf Ames. Ames, a Fight Engineer, had been jolted and fell on take-off during another raid to Turin back in November. He sustained internal injuries, but kept this from his pilot, carrying on with the long trip. Only after they land did he report his problem.

Turin was again on the menu for 16/17 August, Wing Commander Mike Wyatt deciding to fly this trip for two reasons. First, it was to be his last with 75; and, secondly, because the last time he went to Turin, when with 15 Squadron, he had ended up a guest of the Spanish Government:

> *J*ust before I left the squadron, we had a raid on Turin and having had some trouble on my previous trip there, I decided I'd go on that one. We went down there alright but on the way back we were warned that the whole of England was getting blanketed out with fog and we'd have to be diverted. I personally landed at Ford in Sussex and the rest were dotted around all over the place. I'd hardly got into the bed I'd been allotted when I was woken by the Duty Officer and told we had to get back to Mepal at the first opportunity the next morning. So, much to their horror, I rounded up all the chaps and took off as soon as it was clear and found that, that night the squadron had to go on the Peenemunde Raid, which was rather an important one.
>
> Despite being dispersed the previous night, we got 12 aircraft up and didn't lose any on that particular raid. I also remember we had good results, confirmed by the bombing photographs. All this proved to me that, as I left, the squadron had really got back to full working order again.

The raid upon the experimental rocket establishment at Peenemunde on the Baltic coast was, of course, of immense importance as is now known. But then it was just a target, with perhaps a strong hint of it being emphasised that a good and successful attack was desired!

A different view of a Stirling.

Leaders, left to right: S/Ldr R. J. Watson DFC, OC A Flight; S/Ldr D. S. Gibb DFC, OC B Flight; W/Cdr R. D. Max (DSO) DFC, CO; S/Ldr J. K. Climie DFC, OC C Flight. Roy Max commanded the squadron from August 1943 to May 1944. Watson was killed in action 5 March 1944. (SPORT & GENERAL)

The crew of Jack Wright DFC. Back row, left to right: Charles Kelly, R. C. Reynolds, M. A. Carter. Front row, left to right: Jack Wright, K. Westerman, B. Neal. Westerman went to another crew upon joining 75 and was killed over Hamburg 28 July 1942.

(C. W. B. KELLY)

Shortly after this raid, Mike Wyatt was posted to 3 Group HQ as Group Training Inspector. He had done what he'd been asked to do — put 75 Squadron back on its feet — but now it was thought that 75 should once again be commanded by a New Zealander. Wyatt later went on to command 514 Squadron, flying Lancasters at Waterbeach, and to receive the DFC. The new 'Boss' of 75 was Wing Commander R. D. Max DFC.

Roy Douglas Max hailed from Brightwater, Nelson, and was the first New Zealander to command 75 for over a year. He had joined the RAF in 1938, having trained in New Zealand alongside Len Trent, who was to win the VC with 487 NZ Squadron in May 1943. Max had flown Fairey Battles during the Battle of France with 103 Squadron and, having survived that, continued to fly with 103 after they'd converted to Wellingtons. He then flew on the Atlantic Ferry Service, making three trips to England in Hudsons, before being given command of 75. His flight commanders were Frank Andrews, Jackie Joll and Dick Broadbent.

◇ ◇ ◇

Berlin was about to be back in the news with the ending of the Ruhr Battles. Advantage was still with Bomber Command, with the German's being very much on the defensive with Window blinding their radars, and Arthur Harris was anxious to knock out Germany by smashing its capital city. Although the major onslaught would come later in the year, when the longer nights would enable the RAF bombers to reach Berlin and return in darkness, August was to see two raids.

The first came on the night of 23/24 August, a total force of 727 aircraft being despatched. No. 75 Squadron was again down for a maximum effort, putting 23 Stirlings on the line. Only 20 were destined to return to Mepal and, of the 21 men lost, only one mid-upper gunner was to survive. And he was seriously wounded and in captivity.

Night fighters were very active and several encounters took place — the squadron's gunners destroyed one Me109, one Me110 and probably another, and damaged a Ju88. The night, however, belonged to Flight Sergeant Osric Hartnell White from Christchurch. He and his crew were flying their 12th operation, having recently flown on all the three Hamburg raids.

Approaching the target, White's Stirling was coned by searchlights and repeatedly hit by AA fire, but he continued on until the flak suddenly stopped. This usually heralded fighters and, sure enough, just moments later a Ju88 attacked, its fire killing Sergeant J. Poole in the rear turret. The aircraft went into an uncontrolled dive, White calling to warn the crew that they might have to bale out. The intercom then failed and in the confusion, the navigator, WOP and bomb aimer did take to their parachutes.

Meanwhile, White jettisoned the bombs and regained control at 6000 feet, then headed out of the danger zone. He found the Stirling, despite all the damage, still responded to the controls but without a navigator he would have to get himself and his two surviving crew men back. White, fortunately, had been a keen yachtsman back in New Zealand which helped him to return via Denmark. Once over base, he discovered that his flaps control had gone, that he could not get the wheels down and, without a radio, could not contact the ground. However, he made a successful belly landing before skidding to a halt. Two days later he was recommended for the Conspicuous Gallantry Medal.

Raids to Nuremburg on 27 August and Munchen-Gladbach on 30 August cost the squadron one crew on each night. Then it was back to Berlin on the last evening of August. This time 622 aircraft flew out, with 47 failing to return. No. 75 Squadron had assigned 18 Stirlings to this raid; two failed to take off and four failed to return. Sergeant Lew Parsons, Flight Engineer in Flight Sergeant Doug Henley's crew, recalls:

> **M**y experience with the squadron was brief but action packed. With my crew we joined on Saturday the 22nd August 1943 and were shot down on the Monday the 31st, having completed five and a half Ops! Our first trip was to Berlin, then two mining sorties, followed by trips to Nuremburg and Munchen-Gladbach.
>
> We were hit by a Ju88 night fighter over Berlin on the 31st, losing the port engine, and the port tail-plane and elevator were badly damaged. Jimmy Grant our rear gunner was wounded and trapped in his turret, the mid-upper concussed, and the Stirling lost height rapidly while the skipper tried to evade. He then pulled it out and held it in level flight while we assessed the damage. I instructed him to feather the port-inner engine and I closed the petrol cocks on No. 2 main tank. We could not maintain level flight due to the damaged tail and loss of one engine so decided to jettison all excess weight. Before doing this the WOP and I got the tail gunner out of his turret and sat him on the floor, then sat the dazed mid-upper gunner with him.
>
> I jettisoned the fuel from No. 2 tank and then the wireless operator, Bob Quelch, and I, began to remove guns and ammo, pitching them out through the rear escape hatch. The skipper, navigator and bomb aimer, set a course for home along the main stream route and endeavoured to keep the aircraft in the air. After about an hour, the skipper suddenly called, 'Bale out, bale out — you must bale out!' The WOP went through the rear hatch and I followed, expecting the gunner to follow.
>
> We had very little time or height. The WOP opened his 'chute and almost immediately

hit the ground, damaging his ankle. My 'chute opened and I at once was caught in a tree, which saved me from any serious injury, then the aircraft crashed into a hill and burst into flames.

Later I learned that the navigator and bomb aimer had baled out of the front hatch but both were killed when their 'chutes failed to deploy. It was our bomb aimer's — Ian Smith — 21st birthday on 1st September! Doug Henley was also killed. He was a rock-steady New Zealand pilot, and very capable. He had held the Stirling till the last moment so that we could get out and was killed as a result, when the aircraft crashed.

Jimmy Grant from Balclutha, meantime, wounded in the right arm and shoulder and having had his face peppered with shrapnel, had found his parachute shot to pieces as the others baled out. He was extremely lucky to survive the crash, scrambled out of the burning wreckage, crawled away, and went to sleep. Six hours later he was awoken by a German search party. The aircraft had come down in the valley of Ahr, west of the Rhine. Grant, Parsons, Quelch and Duggie Box, the mid-upper, were soon on their way to a POW camp.

Berlin had cost the squadron seven aircraft and crews on these two raids, with another having crash landed at base. This made the total losses for the last eight days to nine, perhaps ten. Because of the high losses among Stirling and Halifax crews, only Lancasters were sent out when Berlin was hit again on 3/4 September.

Nevertheless, the squadron still operated, flying more mining Ops as September began, then losing one of 19 Stirlings which went to Mannheim on the 5th. Three nights later, came a more unusual target — a German long-range gun battery, situated at Boulogne. No. 75 Squadron put up 17 of the 257 aircraft assigned, but the Oboe marking by Mosquito aircraft — who were experimenting with a new technique — failed and so did the raid.

The night, however, was marred and remembered because of a crash at take-off time. Many people remember this night, but George Stokes, Sergeant and mid-upper gunner in Sergeant Don Whitehead's crew, records:

At this stage aircrew had six days leave every six weeks, a block of six crews taking it in turn. If a crew got shot down, the other crews stepped up a week, so you would get leave after five weeks. I had arranged to get married on 14th September which was when we were due leave,but unfortunately a crew went missing, so leave came a week early.

We had only got a couple of Ops to do to complete our tour, so I elected to stay and fly as a spare gunner if required. Peter Dobson, our navigator, said he would take his leave, but would stay on the camp and help on the local farms with the harvest, saying we would be on end of tour leave in a fortnight.

On the night of the 8th September, he left our hut to go to the farm and the squadron was operating that night. As one of the Stirlings was taking off it swung and crashed into a small housing estate in Sutton village and, later, the bombs exploded.

The following lunch-time, Peter's body was found in the rubble of the houses, along with a WAAF officer. He had earlier borrowed a bike and this had been found, but the owner, of course, was on leave. It was only then I knew it had to be Dobbie who'd been killed. It was typical of him to have gone to help. They had both gone to ensure there was no one alive and trapped in the houses when the bombs went off.

Two civilians were also killed, with others injured. The pilot of the Stirling, Flying Officer I. R. Menzies, also died and so did two of his crew. The WAAF was Section Officer J. M. Easton.

13

Stirling Swansong

SEPTEMBER 1943 — MARCH 1944

Bomber Command were being increasingly engaged by night fighters in the dark skies over Germany and Holland. The Luftwaffe had quickly recovered from the effects of 'Window' and, while the RAF continued to use it till the war's end, it was never as effective as when used in the summer of 1943. As the more experienced night fighter crews discovered, the falling aluminium strips remained relatively stationary while the aircraft plot moved across their screens. Also, bombers ahead of or around the edges of the main stream were less protected and could be picked up on airborne radar.

The Germans had also begun to receive new equipment which could operate despite the effects of Window — 'Naxos' and 'Korfu' receivers which gave bearings on aircraft using and thus radiating H2S signals. With H2S sets being used almost entirely by the Pathfinder crews, the head of the bomber stream could be monitored and fighters could then be guided to the following bomber stream. RAF aircraft used for diversions did not carry H2S, so could be largely ignored.

As losses in Bomber Command continued to rise, the scores of the night fighter pilots began to increase. The nightly air battles became a bitter struggle, and more often than not the advantage lay with the defending fighters than the attacking bombers.

Two raids at the end of September cost 75 Squadron five crews — three over Mannheim on the 23/24th, and two more against Hannover on the 27th. One of the crews lost over Mannheim was Pilot Officer Cliff Logan and his crew, whose gunners, Crowther and Knox, had been successful so far by claiming one night fighter destroyed, one probable and another damaged. Only the rear gunner Knox survived this night, as a prisoner.

Des Horgan and his crew were successful against a night fighter on the Hannover raid, as he remembers:

> **B**omber Command losses between October and March 1944 were to be excessive to say the least. The German night-fighter pilot was a brave and worthy opponent, and they demonstrated this remarkable resilience during this period. This round of the war was definitely won by the Luftwaffe.
>
> The disappearance of the correlation between experience and loss rate should have been recognised by our Command as a warning signal, telling them that we were up against something new. That something new, was the upward firing guns. Conven-

tionally armed fighters would not have been able to approach the bomber from underneath and shoot it down without being seen, but increasing numbers of the German fighter force were not conventionally armed. They had cannon pointing almost vertically upwards with a single periscope gunsight arranged so that the pilot could take careful aim as he flew quietly below the bomber.

My first combat with this particular type of night fighter — a Ju88 — is something which I shall never forget. The target was Hannover. We had no problems on the outward journey and approached the target at the appointed time. The welcome can of orange juice had been downed, and my toilet tin had been handed up and used for the usual nervous de-watering ritual. A couple of minutes to go and as usual, right on time to the very second, the target indicators started to fall.

We were flying at around 13,000 feet and as we prepared for the run over the target, the reception from the local defence system started, and true to form put on the usual good show. Lots of flak and plenty of searchlights; the climax to our night's entertainment was to come sooner than expected.

With our bomb doors open, my bomb aimer was giving me a true heading to run in onto the target indicators. Approximately two seconds before bombs away, the rear gunner informed me that a night fighter was approaching from below and dead astern. Our normal fighter affiliation intercom patter followed and we knew that as soon as he saw our bombs go, he would come forward and give us a fatal burst of cannon before we could even close the bomb doors. This is not exactly what happened.

When the rear gunner informed me that the night fighter had disappeared from sight under his turret, I sat back on the stick and the rear gunner had a sitting shot at the Ju88, directly below, and he made no mistake. Unfortunately for me, in the heat of the moment I miscalculated a manoeuvre which I had practised on numerous occasions over England, and instead of slipping away to port or starboard as intended, my aircraft came over on to its back and literally fell out of the sky.

As I mentioned before, I will never forget what happened in the next couple of minutes. What actually happened when 20 tons of aircraft goes into a vertical dive, I know! I also know that I eventually regained control approximately 200 feet over Hannover, low enough for me to see three people standing on a street corner. We made it back to base and on inspection in the morning, R-Roger was a hopeless write-off, never to be flown again. Everything in the aircraft that was breakable was broken — a truly remarkable aircraft to fly reasonably well after such a hammering and to get us home in such a devastated condition.

Some weeks later, my wireless operator, over a drink in the Mess, asked me what street I had been looking for that night over Hannover

Des Horgan's rear gunner, was Sergeant I. Teaika, a Maori, who was credited with the destruction of the Ju88. A second Ju88 was also claimed as destroyed by the rear and mid-upper gunners in Flight Sergeant R. Burton's crew. In fact R-Roger (EF148) did fly again after repairs but was lost in November over Berlin.

Perhaps mention should be made here, that there were several Maori who served operationally with 75 Squadron. Two of them, Inia (Mac) Maaka and Mita Pinka, list the following who were certainly on the unit: Ted Grey from Otaki (WOPAG); Iwi Teaika from Christchurch (AG); Tommy Waerea, Rotorua (AG); John Parone, Taumarunui (AB); Guy Tomlins, Pakipaki (AB); Tap Heperi, Okaihau (WOPAG); Stan Higgins, Murupara (AB); Max Spooner, Taihape (AG); Bill Kereama, Marton (WOPAG); Phil Baker, Palmerston North (AG); Tom Wehi, Takapau (pilot); two Aucklanders, Rahui and Erlich; then there was a pilot named V. J. Zinzan, and also W. Rangiuaia, Amohanga and Tom Parata. Mita Pinka, from Matata, was a navigator while Mac Maaka was an air bomber from Taradale.

◇ ◇ ◇

The month of October 1943 saw 75 Squadron mainly engaged on minelaying operations of the Frisians and the Gironde. Two early Main Force raids were against Kassel on the 3rd and Frankfurt on the 4th. Flight Sergeant N. Parker's rear gunner, Sergeant S. W. Riddler, was killed after the bomber was hit by flak over Kassel. The rear turret was damaged and it was thought he may have baled out as the rear escape hatch was later found open, but otherwise his death remains a mystery. Sergeant H. J. Middleton and crew were lost over Frankfurt.

Then began a period of minelaying which was to last till mid-November. There was the odd trip that was different, such as 12 aircraft which flew as a diversion raid to Bremen on the night of 8/9 October, when the main target was Hannover. Sergeant Chris Dickinson was the Flight Engineer on 'Speed' Williams' crew, in which Bill Hemsley was mid-upper. They finished their tour on this Bremen show:

> **A**s our Ops total began to get into double figures, we looked at all the new faces and remembered the ones that were no longer around. We became rather hard and formed no really close friendships — that way we didn't get hurt.
>
> At first we became friendly with other crews but we were made aware that the chances of surviving a tour of Ops were very slim. When empty places at the mess table occurred quite frequently, the most upsetting thing was to see those seven empty spaces in your own hut, especially when the adjutant came along to collect their personal belongings.
>
> The crew to whom we had been most attached was that of Johnny Thomas with my chum Tubby Gale as flight engineer. When they failed to turn up after a raid [30 July 1943] which we had also been on, our morale was very low. We had seen an aircraft over the target with flames pouring out of both wings and we were certain it was a Stirling.
>
> During our tour I remember one very clear night, no moon, just stars against a dark blue velvet sky. I was in the astrodome keeping my eyes open for night fighters. We were not a very religious crowd I am sorry to say but, as I looked up at this beautiful sky, I couldn't help thinking that if the Creator of all this beauty was looking down on us, what must he think. There were these stupid human beings killing one another by the thousands, destroying not just factories but beautiful cities and buildings. When I looked down at a burning town with the sky crimson with flames and just below me an aircraft going down in flames with flak bursting all over the place, two words came to mind — Dante's Inferno.
>
> Towards the end of our tour our aircraft was fitted with 'Tinsel', a technique by which our wireless operator could feed the amplified sound of one of our engines on to German night fighter controller's frequencies, completely blotting out any speech between the fighter and the controller. This could only be used over short periods as our transmissions could be picked up by direction finders.
>
> Our skipper was awarded the DFC after our trip against the Modane Tunnel on 16/17th September, when our port inner engine caught fire crossing the Alps after an electrical fault. We jettisoned one of our 1000 bombs but took the other three on and dropped them on the target.
>
> On our last Op we were part of a Spoof Force opening the attack on Bremen four minutes before the Main Force turned off to attack the main target at Hannover. Fighters were dropping flares about us and a fighter attacked us on the bombing run, which we claimed as damaged.

Just two aircraft went to the Frisians on 24 October, but one had to return with engine trouble. The second one successfully dropped its mines but crashed 2½ kilometres southwest of Mepal, bursting into flames and burning out. The pilot, Flight Sergeant J. R. Randle, navigator, bomb aimer and WOP were all killed; the

Ready for the off. 4th from left is Sgt I. W. I. Teaika (RG), 5th F/L Slim Ormerod DFC (N), 6th Sgt Len Wright (FE), 7th Sgt D. Chatty Chatfield (MU), 8th F/O Johnnie Grubb DFC (P), 9th F/Sgt Des Horgan (P), 11th F/O Les Stickbury (N). (SPORT & GENERAL)

A 4000 pound 'cookie' ready for lifting.
(W. HARDY)

First Stirling crew to complete a tour on 75, and all were decorated. Left to right: Sgt (PO) Harold Hamerton (RG), P/O D. L. Popperwell (AB), Sgt M. T. T. Manawaiti (WOPAG), P/O Leo Trott (P), and P/O W. J. R. Scollay (N).

engineer and rear gunner were injured and taken to Ely hospital. Only the mid-upper got away without injury.

There was another disaster on the night of 4 November. Thirty-six aircraft dropped mines at various places, but of the four from 75 who went into the Baltic, one returned with a dead rear gunner after being shot up by a night fighter, while the other three were all lost! Despite this, mining continued on and off until the New Year, with occasional chances to hit Germany with the Main Force squadrons. But even these remained costly. The experienced Flight Sergeant N. Parker and crew didn't get back from Leverkusen. Of the 86 Stirlings which went out on that raid, 75's was the only one lost.

Bomber Harris had now turned his attention to the major effort against Berlin. The first of 16 raids which were to be mounted over this winter period, November 1943 to March 1944, had begun on 18/19 November. No. 75 Squadron got in on the Berlin show on 22/23 November, but with only four aircraft, one of which returned early with oxygen failure. Of the others, two failed to return. The squadron returned to mining.

Nelson Hugh Bawden, known as 'Jack', from Hastings was 29 when war began, so was too old for military service until the age limit was raised in 1941. Although married and with a son, he volunteered for aircrew as a navigator, and joined 75 Squadron with the crew of S. A. 'Fred' Clark of Christchurch. They flew their first Op on 2 October. Jack recalls the trip to the Bay of Biscay on 25 November:

> *T*his was a long trip to La Rochelle on the Bay of Biscay. We went down to Land's End, then around Brest to make landfall at San Sebastian. Then a timed run up the coast to drop our mines in the harbour of La Rochelle River mouth. We also took photos which later showed a large ship, larger than was thought to use this harbour. Later still we heard that Churchill himself looked at the print. We continued north, satisfied with our night's work.
>
> On the way home across the Brest Peninsula I was doing well on one of my first long navigational trips. Our bomb aimer, Tom Bradley — an Australian — spoke up and said there was a light on our starboard which seemed to be stationary. I told him he was seeing things but some of the others saw it and said we must be going round in circles. This had me worried, so I checked everything but could find no faults. The light could still be seen, so I looked myself and discovered they had been looking at the morning star! The pilot said thanks, but not a peep came from the others!

December 1943 began with a series of crashes. Three aircraft took off to lay mines off the east coast of Denmark on the 1st and the returning Stirling flown by Flight Sergeant G. J. Kerr crashed while attempting to land at RAF Acklington. The bomber hit a house killing all the crew, except the mid-upper, and five young children in an upstairs bedroom. Their parents and two friends sitting downstairs all survived.

The term 'special target' began to appear on the operational orders on 16 December. These were in fact the strange constructional sites that were starting to spring up along the coast of northern France — rocket launching sites for Hitler's V1 rocket bombs. While nearly 500 bombers went for Berlin, yet again, 47 aircraft went for a V1 site at Tilley-le-Haut. No. 75 Squadron sent eight aircraft, but two crashed on take-off and one aborted. Four other aircraft went to the Frisians, but Flight Sergeant C. J. Kinross crashed on his return, and once again it was only the mid-upper who survived, although injured. Over the next few weeks, the squadron would mine and attack V1 sites with boring regularity.

There was a lull at Christmas, although for Ronald 'Joe' Hunt, who had recently arrived with his crew to start operations, Christmas Eve gave him a few anxious moments:

I joined the squadron at Mepal in October, a few weeks after being married. My crew were half English and half New Zealanders which was the norm. We carried out a few Ops, then came Christmas. In previous years, Bomber Command had usually been fairly inactive over the festive season so I thought it would be safe to have my new wife down and accordingly booked us in at 'The Lamb' in Ely for two or three days.

Having arranged to meet at Ely Station on Christmas Eve afternoon, it was to my horror that I found my name at the top of the Battle Order for that night. My crew and I didn't worry too much as the weather didn't look very good and we felt confident that the Op would be scrubbed. As the afternoon wore on, we became increasingly anxious, particularly when at briefing the Met Officer said there was no chance that we would be able to return to Mepal due to fog and our diversion area was Tangmere on the south coast!

For security reasons I could not phone my wife, but at take-off time I was still hopeful of a cancellation, even whilst taxi-ing around the perimeter, but no luck. I was first off and as I flashed my aircraft letter and got a 'green', took off. Immediately my wheels were up, my rear gunner — Johnny Manns — reported a Red Verey signal from the control tower, signifying a recall.

Nobody else took off, so there I was airborne over East Anglia with a new bride in Ely. Standing instructions were not to jettison fuel or bombs, but to cruise around for a few hours, using up petrol whilst practising instrument flying etc.

I decided — to hell with that — so flew over to the Wash, jettisoned as much fuel as possible then returned to Mepal. When I landed I was still tons above the all-up safety landing weight. I raced down to Ely, obtaining a lift from a colleague and arrived at 'The Lamb' just in time to find my wife being chatted up by a couple of Americans.

The new year of 1944 began as 1943 had ended — mining, plus some bomb attacks on V1 sites, with bad weather thrown in for good measure. On 28 January Pilot Officer C. Baker was attacked and shot up by a Me110 night fighter whilst mining in Kiel Bay, but returned to crash land at Coltishall with two wounded crew members.

Mining sorties took up the whole of February, but at least the casualty jinx seemed to have been avoided, for only one Stirling was lost during the month, short as it was. W. J. 'Bill' Old, an Englishman, had done his navigational training in South Africa, and upon joining 75, his new crew were wondering if they had the right man:

*A*fter flying Ansons in Scotland, then leave, I was posted to RAF Stradishall to convert onto Stirlings. I had one day on a Stirling, one day on H2S and Gee, then off to 75 to join a crew that had lost three navigators through illness and had yet to go on Ops.

My skipper was Sergeant Des Daws, and he and the crew were extremely perturbed when they learned that my only experience of navigating, apart from training, was one trip in an Anson in Scotland, one circuit and bump on a Stirling at Stradishall, plus one day training on navigational aids!

So we all went along to see Wing Commander Max, who assured everyone concerned that I would have a thorough training on Bullseyes before going on Ops. As was usual with the RAF, one Bullseye and next night on Ops!

One laughable experience I remember: we had been on a trip to Kiel and on the way home the headwind was 120 knots and freezing cold. At a ground speed of 40–50 knots we were easy meat for the German Ack-Ack and fighters. Over Flensburg, North Germany, we met a terrific barrage from the ground, the Germans throwing up everything at us. The mid-upper, Johnny Walker, suddenly shouted, 'Oh, God!' I asked him several times over the R/T if he was alright, thinking he'd been hit, and eventually he replied, 'No, I'm not. I have dropped my bloody Mars bar!'

The ceiling for a Stirling was around 16,000 feet, at 170 knots, whereas the Lancasters could operate up to 27,000. Some bright guy at Command thought it would be a great idea to confuse the German Radar by sending in first, a wave of Lancs, and then Stirlings alternatively. This sounds a good idea in theory but with the problem of variable winds and attacks by fighters, the inevitable happened. We arrived over the target at the same time, the Stirling aircraft being in the sandwich, Ack-Ack going up through us, Lanc bombs falling past us from above. Lovely!

Sergeant Max Harris, Flight Engineer to Frank Scott's crew, arrived on 75 in early 1944:

*S*ometime about February or March 1944, we had what was to be a memorable flight when we took along a New Zealand army officer on an air test from Mepal. An hour or so later, during a 'beat-up', the aircraft struck the top of a large tree, severely damaging the starboard inner prop and removing most of the starboard tail-plane and elevator. A couple of more inches and the results would no doubt have been fatal.

A few weeks later when we had reason to visit the local police station to make enquiries, the police sergeant complained bitterly that our tail-plane was a nuisance parked in the hall of his home and that as we were the crew responsible, we could at least arrange to get the damn thing out of his way!

◊ ◊ ◊

In March 1944, the squadron was involved in another low-level job, listed merely as 'Special Operations'. Everyone was now aware of the build up to a possible invasion of Europe, and although Bomber Harris was still trying to smash Germany's industrial heartland, he had also to divert some of his effort into the pre-invasion tasks. This included hitting railway systems, road bridges and other lines of communication vital to the Germans on the Continent.

Meantime, the active Resistance movements in France needed to be supplied now more than ever with the tools to help with the demolition of rail and road traffic. For the last couple of years there had been a couple of squadrons devoted to just doing this vital job, as well as dropping agents over occupied countries. Now 75 Squadron was asked to assist in dropping supplies of explosives and weapons to these various Resistance groups — hence, Special Operations.

Johnnie Kempthorne (Major J. P. Kempthorne, Royal Scots Fusiliers) was with SOE (Special Operations Executive) and was an Air Liaison Officer with the RAF at Tempsford:

I was sent to 75 Squadron at Mepal to help organise drops during February and March 1944, and left them just as they were changing from Stirlings to Lancasters.

My job was to supervise the loading of aircraft and brief the crews on the operations, from the point of view of dropping areas, etc. It was quite a memorable time for me and a new type of operation for the squadron crews. I worked with the Navigation Officer, who was Slim Ormerod, and I recall one of the flight commanders was a chap by the name of Watson, who was shot down on one of the first sorties.

Squadron Leader R. Watson was indeed shot down, on the night of 4/5 March. The pin-point was Lake De Chancelade; 16 containers being dropped from 480 feet on receipt of a flashing lamp signal. It was called 'Operation Trainer 174'. Other similar operations had various codenames — all part of the 'cloak and dagger' image:

'Director 60', 'Author 17', 'Newsagent 5', 'Mongrel 6', 'Wheelwright 72'. Flight Lieutenant C. F. 'Slim' Ormerod arrived to take up the duties of Navigation Officer on 6 March.

It was back to mining on the night of 13 March, 16 Stirlings from the squadron going to St Nazaire, Lorient, La Rochelle and Brest. One returned early, crashed at Castle Combe and was burnt out, but none of the crew were injured. Flight Sergeant G. Rowberry failed to return from St Nazaire.

Another new Section Leader on 75 at this time was Flight Lieutenant L. O. Sims, who arrived from a Heavy Conversion Unit. He had completed one tour as Flight Engineer on 218 Squadron (26 ops) during 1942–43, and upon his arrival, Roy Max quickly made him Engineer Leader. As with all Section Leaders, Lyndon Sims often had to fly with any odd crew who were without a Flight Engineer, or to encourage a new engineer within a new crew. In this way he was to fly 22 Ops on this his second tour:

> *A*s Flight Engineer Leader one had to attempt to be something of a father figure and look after the general interests of the 30 plus Flight Engineers on the squadron. Quite easy really, as I was an 'old man' of some 26/27 years and most of them were not more than 20 to 22, as were most aircrew. Essentially, I felt the job was to watch over, guide and instruct them to ever better performance, and to pass on the lessons learned in my first tour. Very important was the task of checking every man's Log after operations and comparing his estimates of fuel used and remaining, with those obtained by the actual dipping of the tanks and giving advice etc, whenever discrepencies arose.
>
> Signals were frequently being received from Group HQ as to the importance of fuel economy and so I initiated Fuel Results Lists after every operation, thus inviting care and competition. By dint of much instruction to Flight Engineers and advice to pilots at briefings, 75 Squadron were consistently near the top of the League for the whole of No. 3 Group.

For some time now, the squadron had been relegated to the 'second eleven' as had most Stirling squadrons. With their limitations of operating heights, their casualty rate had grown. They flew at an ideal height for German flak and fighters. The danger of being bombed from above by Lancasters was also great. However, all this was about to change. On 13 March 1944, the first Avro Lancaster arrived at RAF Mepal to start the change of equipment. Another new era was about to begin.

14

Lancasters and D-Day

APRIL — JULY 1944

The arrival of the Lancasters was great news. After having the Stirlings for so long, it was pleasing to have the one aircraft which, more than any other, was to be synonymous with wartime Bomber Command.

Developed from the twin-engined Avro Manchester, the Lancaster was powered by four Rolls Royce Merlin engines, had a maximum speed of nearly 480 kph, a ceiling of around 25,000 feet and could carry 14,000 pounds of bombs over 2700 kilometres or 22,000 lbs over 1600 kilometres. Its defensive armament was eight .303 machine guns; four in the tail, two in each of the mid-upper and front turrets. It had been in RAF squadrons since 1942 and, by the war's end, almost 60 front-line squadrons had used it on operations. It had an impressive record.

The crews began to convert to the new bomber at 75's old stamping ground at RAF Feltwell, at No. 3 Lancaster Finishing School (LFS). But the squadron did not stop operations. As crews moved to Feltwell to convert, others continued to fly Stirlings on mining and supply drops to the Resistance. By April there were sufficient crews and Lancasters to begin sorties with them, and the first raid was flown on the night of 9/10 April. Eleven Lancs went to bomb the railway yards at Villeneuve-St-Georges, which proved a success for the force of 225 aircraft which took part — with no losses.

For the record, the first 75 Squadron Lancaster to take off on this night was ND747 piloted by Pilot Officer T. Buckley. Meanwhile, on the same night, four Stirlings, led off by John Grubb, bombed Lille.

It was railway yards again the next night, this time at Laon, with eight Lancs bombing. Five Stirlings also mined La Rochelle. Then came Aachen in Germany on 11/12 April but with just three Lancs from 75.

A Stirling was lost mining Kiel on 18 April, while ten Lancs went for the Rouen marshalling yards. A German intruder dropped three bombs on Mepal while they were away and the returning aircraft had to be diverted after the first three had landed.

Flight Sergeant (later Squadron Leader) C. A. Megson was a pilot on 75 at this time and remembers this raid — and one of the new Lancs:

> Lancaster Mark III JN-A arrived at Mepal in early March 1944. Having been checked and accepted, it was bombed up and made ready for an operation but prior to take off the airfield was attacked by a fighter and JN-A was damaged to such an extent it had to

be withdrawn for repairs. It was then considered as an unlucky aircraft and was offered to me which I accepted, as they had re-lettered it JN-X. As a crew we considered it to be lucky — and it was.

Our conversion was good, although there were only limited hours available. We converted whilst on the squadron, from Stirlings to Lancasters in one day, doing both day and night conversions in a total of just seven hours! Would hate to do it now.

A few days prior to our posting to 75, my wireless operator broke his ankle due to our skylarking in the billet. I was informed we would have to go without him and we would get a spare WOP, but we refused to go without him so he was posted with us and started his operations with his foot and leg in plaster. It was a damned nuisance in the aircraft as we kept falling over his foot which he had to stick out.

Kiel claimed another Stirling on 23 April, Flight Sergeant M. Lammas and crew all being killed. But it was the last Stirling lost by the squadron.

Then suddenly the squadron was back on Main Force raids, with Karlsruhe, Essen and Friedrichshafen. It was on the latter raid that the first Lancaster of 75 was shot down.

Friedrichshafen was way down to the south, almost on the Swiss border by Lake Constance. On the fringe of the German night fighter belt, the force of 322 Lancasters bombed in moonlight without interception, but the fighters arrived during the attack and 18 bombers were shot down. Flying Officer R. Herron and crew (ND796) were one of them. They were all killed.

Another Lancaster went down over the marshalling yards at Chambly on 1/2 May, which was nevertheless a highly successful raid and the yards were out of action for ten days.

But now came another change of command. Wing Commander Roy Max had finished his tour of Ops and command and was due to hand over in mid-May. Acting Squadron Leader R. J. A. Leslie AFC arrived from No. 311 Flying Training Command (FTC), and upon the departure of Max, was promoted to Wing Commander. Roy Max was to receive the DSO for his example and leadership of 75 Squadron during his tenure of office. He went to 3 Group HQ.

Wing Commander Leslie came from Inglewood, and was 25 years old. He had joined the RNZAF in 1939, transferred to the RAF in 1940, flying with Bomber Command in the early part of the war before going to the Middle East. Lyndon Sims recalls:

> *B*y May 1944, the squadron was almost fully equipped with Lancasters and the remaining Stirlings had been withdrawn. Also at this time our popular CO, Wing Commander Roy Max, had completed his tour of duty, and we were indeed sorry to lose him. Command of the squadron was taken over by Wing Commander R. J. A. Leslie, very different in his approach and manner, but equally dedicated to the task ahead.
>
> He immediately called me and announced we were going up together to test out these new Lancs. We took off, made some height, and he thought perhaps he would dive over the airfield with one engined feathered. I suggested — why not two, so we did just that! An amazed squadron was treated to the sight of a Lancaster diving steeply at high speed with two engines feathered, which I then unfeathered and brought to full power as we zoomed upwards from the dive. The Wingco was highly pleased and had impressed his style on the squadron. We got on well and made many air tests together after this.

With the invasion coming up, marshalling yards in France kept the squadron busy over the mid-May period, and on the 11th, it was able to put up 24 bombers, although one was lost. The target was the yards at Louvain, and Jack Bawden was in one of the Lancasters:

> We were shot-up on the way back from Louvain by a fighter at about 1am. The first I knew of it was when I was about to say to the pilot that he could start letting down, as we were about to cross the French coast. There were several thumps on the aircraft — cannon shells — and then we were on fire. I would not be telling this story if it had not been for our rear gunner, the late Pilot Officer James Trott DFC, for he shot down the fighter — I heard him say that he'd got the bastard just as the intercom cut out!
>
> The fire was caused by a small hole in the hydraulic pipe which worked a turret. A fire extinguisher would not put it out, so I took off my life-jacket and with other crew assistance, covered the fire and using the extinguisher again, out it went.
>
> We managed to get back to base with no trouble but next day, when we saw the holes about the rear gunner's position, Jimmy Trott went white! One hole under one arm next to his body, opposite to holes between arm and body; one hole near his neck and another between his legs, but just low enough to miss.
>
> Jimmy suffered from asthma and around 1984 had an attack on his farm just outside Otorohanga. He died on his way to hospital.

The fighter was a Ju88 and was the first night fighter claimed destroyed by 75 since it had converted to Lancasters. On 19 May, 75 hit the yards at Le Mans; and on 21 May, Duisberg with 25 Lancs. Lyndon Sims remembers:

> There was a shortage of engineers towards the end of May, so I filled in with Pilot Officer Gibson to Le Mans, Pilot Officer Buckley to Duisberg on the 21st, then Flight Lieutenant Clark to Aachen on the 27th.
>
> One hundred and twelve Lancasters of 3 Group took part in the Le Mans raid and we carried a load of ten 1000 pound and five 500 pound HE bombs. The complete rail system, marshalling yards, locomotive shed and an ammunition train were completely destroyed, but there was a most tragic accident. The Master Bomber and his deputy collided over the target and both crews were killed. The Master Bomber was the famous New Zealand Wing Commander J. F. Barron DSO and bar, DFC, DFM, and the Deputy was Squadron Leader J. M. Dennis DSO DFC, both from 7 Squadron. [On board Barron's aircraft was Flying Officer Jack Walters DFC, who had been a Flight Sergeant with 75 Squadron earlier in the war.]
>
> On the Duisberg raid we carried one 4000 pound and 16 containers each of twelve 30 pound incendiaries. 75 was part of a Main Force of over 500 Lancasters, of which 29 were lost. We lost one.

In between Duisberg and Aachen, there was Dortmund on 22/23 May, Bomber Command's first raid on this target for over a year. Three of the 23 aircraft sent out by the squadron returned early, while two others did not return. One of these was piloted by Pilot Officer Edgar Burke from New Zealand. They were on their way back after bombing when they were caught by a Ju88 night fighter and shot down, crashing near Overpelt in Belgium. All seven of the crew were killed as was the crew of the other missing aircraft, flown by Pilot Officer C. Armstrong. The squadron also lost two crews on the Aachen raid, as Max Harris recalls:

> When the squadron converted to Lancasters our crew were the lucky ones selected to test and accept all the new Lancasters. Being temporarily based at Waterbeach, we checked out each aircraft prior to delivery. Our own particular Lanc, ND802 JN-D for Dog, proudly bore the name 'The Flying Scottsmen' after our skipper, Warrant Officer

Frank Scott, and this was the aircraft in which we were shot down on the approach to Aachen on the night of 27/28th May. Our Navigator, Flight Sergeant 'Red' Hill from Christchurch survived and returned home in mid-1945. Frank and our Bomb Aimer and WOP were all killed. The rest of us, including a second pilot we had with us on this trip, were all taken prisoner.

The other crew lost on 27 May, captained by Flight Lieutenant S. F. Fauvel, was nearing the end of its tour. Just before their last trip, Joe Murphy had been playing snooker with one of the crew, who remarked, 'If the bastards are half decent, this'll be our last trip.' Unhappily it was — they were all killed.

◇ ◇ ◇

Suddenly it was June — not flaming June, but a wet and miserable June. This was giving problems for the planners of the invasion, which, unknown to all but a few, had been pencilled in for the first week of this fateful month. The Supreme Allied Commander, General Dwight D. Eisenhower, was faced with the difficult decision of whether to 'Go' or postpone. The trouble was, with everyone ready and the tides right for a landing in this first week, to postpone would give enormous logistic problems. At almost the last moment, the Met people promised a break in the weather, hopefully long enough to get the Allied armies ashore in Normandy. Einsenhower made his decision. The 'Go' would be the night of 5/6 June 1944. The greatest invasion in history was about to begin. No. 75 Squadron was part of it, as Jack Bawden remembers:

> *A*fter a dummy run the night before — cancelled — we at last took off for Caen in force, our target being a gun battery at Lisieux, each aircraft carrying 18×500 pound bombs. Each battery in the invasion area had 200 heavy bombers targeted on it. Our Zero hour was 5am and we were over the target 5 minutes after this H-hour.
>
> Most of us did not know it was D-Day. Weather over the sea was cloudy, so we could not see much — certainly not the 5000 ships which took part — but I think most of us guessed it might be the invasion.
>
> The first official news I myself had was on the 8am radio news, just as I was going to bed. The announcement said that the German High Command had announced that the Allies had landed in Normandy! On the morning of D-Day, all our aircraft had white and black stripes painted on the wings.

John Cowell:

> *O*ur Lancaster 'P' bombed Ouisterham half an hour before the Allied landings. The weather was wet and dismal, with visibility poor. There was little flak and no enemy fighters. We saw plenty of Allied fighters around at very low level. That same evening we bombed Lisieux which was uneventful.

Flying Officer Colin McKenzie, of Gore:

> *F*or a few days there was a feeling that a landing in France was imminent. On the 5th June some unusual events were happening. We were called for a flying meal at 2300 hours, followed by Briefing at 2345. Take off was at 0330 hours. We bombed on the French coast just on daybreak and were back at base by 0715.
>
> On D-Day morning, cloud covered the sea so we did not see any of the invasion craft. We had our interrogation and a meal and went to bed. We had no knowledge of

events until the news at 1300. We had another flying meal at 2100 and took off at 0030 to bomb Lisieux, ahead of the invasion troops.

On the morning of the 7th June, as we crossed the sea, there was much flak, as it seemed that our Navy types were firing at all and sundry. Crossing the coast to Lisieux, our rear gunner called out that the flak was close, but I calmed him down by assuring him that all was okay and the crisis past. However, when we got home we found that our W/T aerial had been cut away about a foot from Don's rear turret, so he was right — the flak had been close!

The squadron had put up 26 aircraft on D-Day morning, another maximum effort, followed by 24 the next night. For the next few days more than 20 Lancasters were out attacking targets in support of the invasion forces. Marshalling yards at Dreux on 10/11 June claimed two crews.

Despite the urgency to support the land armies in Normandy, it was equally important to continue to hit Germany's line of supply. Thus on the night of 11/12 June, 329 bombers headed for various railway targets, 75 heading south for Nantes, near St Nazaire. Over the target, the Lancaster captained by Pilot Officer C. McCardle was hit by ground fire. One shell exploded in the cockpit, wounding McCardle badly and injuring the Flight Engineer, Sergeant Benfold. Warrant Officer A. W. Hurse, the Australian bomb aimer, who was flying his 29th Op, grabbed the controls and helped by the navigator, Pilot Officer A. H. R. Zillwood, of Carterton, headed the bomber back towards England.

Several times, the wounded McCardle urged the crew to bale out, knowing he would not be able to land the Lancaster, but Alexander Hurse, whose pilot experience was just a little dual control, managed not only to get them home, but to land the bomber safely. He received the Conspicuous Gallantry Medal, the second awarded to 75, while Albert Zillwood received the DFC. By an odd coincidence, the third member of 75 to win the CGM — David Moriarty from Wanganui — arrived on the squadron the next morning. But more of that story later.

The marshalling yards at Valenciennes claimed the crew of Flight Sergeant R. Betley on 15/16 June, then it was back to the old V1 sites for most of the rest of June, until the last day when the squadron flew a daylight sortie. The target was enemy troop concentrations in and around Villers-Bocage, with its important road junction. Two Panzer Division were planning to pass through this town to attack the Normandy troops, but the bombing was so effective that the attack never took place.

Another first of the squadron occurred on this mission, when Squadron Leader N. A. Williamson from Gisborne had his aircraft damaged by flak fire and his engineer, Sergeant P. W. McDevitt, wounded. In order to get him medical aid quickly, Williamson headed for the bridgehead and landed on one of the many landing strips being bull-dozed behind the front lines. This was the first time a heavy bomber had landed in France since the invasion began.

The attack on Villers-Bocage also saw the first mission of Squadron Leader G. Gunn and his crew. His bomb aimer was Pilot Officer Angus M. Millar of Christchurch, who vividly recalls his feelings during his first Ops with the squadron:

*O*ur first Op was a daylight do to Villers-Bocage on a Panzer-choke point, on a glorious evening. It was peaceful everywhere and my feelings were anything but warlike, yet there I was, in an aircraft carrying 13,000 pounds of bombs and about to drop them on people who may, even at that time, be going to church, it being a Sunday.

As I recall it, there were over 250 bombers over the target. It wasn't accurate bombing at all but pattern bombing, used to give maximum effect of destruction over a limited area. With so many Lancasters milling around all on the same target, God knows how many civilians were killed or how many children — all of which was going through my mind as we returned.

At de-briefing I didn't want to speak to anyone and my remarks to the SIO [Squadron Intelligence Officer] were monosyllabic and very curt. Even my friends and fellow crew members were left out. I became withdrawn and morose and wanted nothing of them. God knows how they put up with me, as I was certainly unbearable.

It wasn't until July, when we made out first night Op that things took a turn for the better. We had suffered some losses, among them had been some great friends of mine. I can recall the run-in to the target on that night, remembering our recent losses, and even before I signalled 'bomb doors closed' I said in a scream into the intercom: 'Take that you bastards! Let's get the hell out of here.' And we did.

One never knows how one will react under stress, but from being a peace-loving person it became almost pleasurable to dish out to the enemy what they'd been doing to us. From a mediocre navigator/bomb aimer, I became a well co-ordinated member of a superb crew. Later our skipper took me aside, commenting on my remarks over the target, saying that since out first Op he and the rest of the crew had been worried about my behaviour and would have demanded a replacement had I not 'pulled my finger out' and become more warlike. A weak link like me could have meant their death under strain. I know I'll never forget the experience.

Yet another first came on 15 July, after two weeks of bombing V1 sites. Now that the rocket bombs were being launched against Britain in a full-scale attack, some of the raids were even made in daylight. But on the 15th, the squadron broke its record for the number of aircraft despatched — 30! Unfortunately the raid was then called off because of poor weather conditions.

Twenty-eight aircraft took off in the gloom of 18 July for a dawn attack on Cagny, part of a force of 942 aircraft that headed for the Normandy battle area. This was the day the Allied forces in France were going to break out of the bridgehead and start their advance. Operation 'Goodwood' was the code name for the British Second Army's armoured assault from Caen, the RAF starting the ball rolling with attacks upon five fortified villages to the east of the town. It was a total success, and has been recorded as being perhaps the most useful raid by Bomber Command in direct support of Allied armies in the war. No. 75 Squadron remembers the raid because of the actions of one of its pilots — Dave Moriarty.

Flight Sergeant Moriarty had taken off with the others at 4.30am and bombed Cagny amidst flak fire. Dave relates:

We were at 7500 feet when we were hit, which in daylight is not very high. When I came to my senses we were at 8000, so I must have fallen backwards with the stick in my tummy. There was a hole in the windscreen, not big, but big enough to do a fair bit of damage to the guy sitting in front of it — me! I had quite a bit of gunk and stuff all over my parachute harness and I realised when I put my hand over what turned out to be my good eye, there was nothing of the other one at all. Scotty, my Engineer, put a field dressing across the top of my helmet and I could feel warm blood inside the helmet which didn't please me a great deal. None of the boys could fly and as the aircraft seemed alright, decided to head for base with its familiar circuit.

It took us an hour and a half, and by this time my good eye was watering so badly I could hardly see the instruments, so gave the boys the choice of baling out, but they all agreed to stay. Scotty read out the heights as I came in and when we eventually got over the runway I levelled out and kind of fell in a heap but did no damage. Once I'd got off the runway the ambulancemen took over and the first thing I asked for was a cigarette — and I didn't even smoke.

Warrant Officer Frank Scott and crew, shot down 27 May 1944. Rear, left to right: Scott, F/Sgt Alan Mantle (MU); Middle, left to right: F/Sgt 'Red' Hill (N), Sgt Reg Dale (RG), F/Sgt Steve Cook (AB), Sgt Max Harris (FE); Front: F/Sgt Ron Howson (WOP). Scott, Howson and Cook all died; the others were taken prisoner. (F. M. HARRIS)

F/O H. J. Murray's crew, Mepal 1944. Extreme right: F/Sgt J. L. McFarland (N); second right: Flying Officer Murray. They were shot down on 18 April 1944, four being killed, three taken prisoner. (J. L. McFARLAND)

Navigation Leader, Squadron Leader Fray Ormerod DFC (centre) with P/O C. R. Tubby Baker DFC and F/O Eric Parsons. (VIA F. ORMEROD)

His Flight Engineer, Sergeant A. Scott, and Bomb Aimer, Ian Ward, got the bandage round Moriarty's injured eye, Ward thinking that if they didn't work fast, he was going to bleed to death.

Dave had lost his eye but he'd got his crew and Lancaster back. His well earned CGM was announced in the London Gazette on 15 September, the same date that the award of the Military Cross was announced to Flight Lieutenant Eric Williams, who, as mentioned earlier, had been shot down and taken prisoner back in December 1942, and escaped via his famous 'Wooden Horse'.

On the night of 18 July, 28 Lancasters from the squadron took off to bomb the aircraft factory and railway junction at Aulnoye. Night fighters were in evidence and the crew of Flying Officer G. Kennedy claimed to have hit two fighters. Acting Flight Lieutenant J. W. A. Myers from Invercargill failed to return, but although he was killed, the rest of the crew survived. Three became POWs, but three — Flying Officer W. Cunningham, the bomb aimer; Joe Murphy, the WOP, and Sergeant W. Mason, the rear gunner — all managed to evade, were captured, then escaped and got themselves back.

They had been attacked by a night fighter, but Myers had gallantly kept the crippled Lancaster steady as he told the crew to get out. Flight Sergeant J. W. Murphy, WOP/AG, was the last to leave and said later that he and the others owed their lives to their pilot. Joe recalls:

> We had flown on the daylight raid and had scarcely been asleep two hours when Snow Myers woke me in order for us to do a NFT on our Lancaster, 'G' for George. As it turned out, 'G' had to go in for a major inspection so we were allocated Eddy Howell's Lanc for that night. Both Snow and I agreed that nothing on it worked as smoothly as our own 'G'.
>
> After bombing Aulnoye we set off on our course for home. The H2S screen in front of me was not working properly so I called up the skipper and told him it appeared to be u/s so told me to switch it off. I then switched off from intercom, back onto my radio set but had hardly done this when the plane suffered a most terrible jolt which threw me from my seat and I banged my head on the roof. We appeared to drop as I got back to my seat and switched on the intercom once more. All I could hear was our mid-upper yelling to the skipper that our starboard outer was on fire.
>
> I later learned that the night fighter which shot us down came straight up underneath us. Cunningham told me that the bullets actually came through the cabin floor between himself and Myers and he had the feeling Myers was hit, as when the fire could not be put out, he yelled into the side of Cunningham's helmet that he should give the order to abandon the aircraft. Cunningham himself was a good pilot and was usually at Myers' side. The people on the ground in Belgium reckon the two planes collided, the German fighter crashing on the other side of the village, killing the pilot. This would account for the violent jolt which I felt and the severe damage to our starboard wing.
>
> On leaving my seat and picking up my parachute I went aft. Our mid-upper was out of his turret and fumbling to clip on his 'chute. I proceeded to the rear door and opened it but as flames started to be sucked in I closed it until I'd put on my 'chute, and checked on the rear gunner. He had gone and after telling the skipper, I then left the aircraft. The Lanc went out of control almost immediately and crashed, followed by two explosions whilst I was still in the air. I seemed to hang there in silence for only a few moments then I could hear what I thought was the wind in the trees and almost immediately landed on a barbed wire fence!

Bill Cunningham remembers:

> After releasing the bombs we made a slow turn to port and I continued to man the

front turret. On returning to the main cabin I managed to catch the handle of the compressed air bottle on my Mae West and inflated it, much to the amusement of the forward crew members.

Just as I'd settled down to carry our by duties at the H2S set, we were hit. The shells came through the floor between Snowy and myself. The starboard outer engine was on fire and by the time the engineer feathered it, the starboard inner was blazing, so Snowy ordered us to abandon. I can't say why Snowy didn't manage to get out, but by remaining at the controls the rest of us survived.

Joe and Bill were later helped by friendly Belgians, but some days later fell into the hands of a family who led them into a trap and they were captured. They then met up with Bill Mason and, when being shipped off by train, managed to escape during a raid. They eventually reached the Allied lines.

◇ ◇ ◇

Squadron losses had been fairly light over May and June, but this all stopped on the night of 20/21 July. The squadron scheduled 26 aircraft for this operation, part of a force of 147 Lancasters and 11 Mosquitoes to hit the oil plant at Homberg. The plant was severely damaged and oil production was cut, but night fighters caught the raiders, shooting down 20 Lancasters. Of these, seven came from 75! Colin Megson has memories of night fighters and other things that went bump in the night:

> *I*t was very nerve-racking at times seeing other aircraft shot down or going down in flames, especially over the target when you were usually on a straight run-in to bomb. On return, crews were usually very quiet if some had not returned. One particular night when we went to Homberg, seven aircraft failed to return.
>
> I remember running in; there were five Lancasters line abreast with me in the middle, when out of the corner of my eye I saw a fighter heading in from the port side with guns blazing. He got the two aircraft on my left but missed me, as I dived down and under the one on my right, and I actually saw him get one of the ones on the right. Three out of five was good shooting!
>
> Night operations caused many incidents where large numbers of aircraft were operating and unseen. You frequently flew through the slipstream of other aircraft which meant you must have been close to them!
>
> Weather reports en route were not always very accurate and occasionally led to heavy icing in cloud when you had to maintain strict heights. Flak could be very rough at times, especially at the lower levels Stirlings flew at, when you could actually see the stuff coming up at you.
>
> Night fighters not much of a problem as long as a good look out was kept at all times and no one could relax until you were home on the ground, as it was not unknown for aircraft to be shot down in the circuit waiting to land.
>
> Searchlights were only a problem if you were caught in the Master Beam and unless you did something quick you were soon coned by the others and heavy flak directed at you. Usually the Master was identified as it had a bluish tinge to it, rather than just white.

At the end of July, the squadron flew three times to Stuttgart, losing two aircraft on the first raid (24/25) and two more on the third (28/29). Intense AA fire had been met and night fighters got into the bomber stream, which probably accounted for most of the losses. During the air battles, 75 gunners claimed one FW190 and another unidentified fighter destroyed, and one Ju88 damaged. One Lancaster also had to fly home on three engines when hit by a night fighter over the target.

'Snow' Myers and crew, shot down 19 July 1944. Left to right: Sgt W. Mason (RG), F/O W. Cormack (N), F/L Myers, W. Cunningham (AB), F/Sgt J. W. Murphy (WOP). Myers died staying at the controls. Cormack (with two other crew members) was captured while Cunningham, Murphy and Mason evaded. (J. W. MURPHY)

Ian Blance and crew, shot down 28/29 July 1944. Back row, left to right: F/Sgts O. Spencer (AB), W. Hyde (FE), C. Grieg (N), F. Jenkins (MU); Front row left to right: A. Kirk (RG), P/O Blance, F. Climo (WOP). Greig was captured, and Hyde and Jimmy Kirk evaded, Kirk fighting with the French Resistance. The rest were killed. (A. C. KIRK)

Flight Commanders 1944: Squadron Leaders Bob Rogers DFC DFM, Jack Wright DSO DFC, Jack Bailey DFC and bar. (VIA F. ORMEROD)

One of the Lancs lost on 28/29 July was flown by Flight Lieutenant N. A. D. Stokes, whose mid-upper was Flight Sergeant M. K. P. Drummond:

> We had just crossed the lower Rhine and the first of the TI's were beginning to show. I had just said to the rear gunner to watch out for fighters and was just moving my guns to cover the front, when a fighter came straight through an area of ball cloud and cut us open like a plow along our port wing. A shell went straight through my turret cutting my helmet off at the ear, burning a line across my head and blowing off the whole of the turret perspex. I could see the port inner was on fire and later learned our rear gunner was killed in the first moment of the attack.
>
> The skipper had made an immediate 180 degree turn and jettisoned the bombs, but the engine was still blazing and we only had a few minutes to get out, so he ordered us to bale out.
>
> On opening the door I was sucked out and hit my head on the tail-plane, fell to earth, and regained consciousness on a tree top. I pulled my ripcord which took my weight the same moment as I hit the ground, breaking several bones and knocking me out again.
>
> I lay where I fell for two days before being found by French slave workers and taken towards Paris.

In excruciating pain, Drummond was taken by horse and cart to a farm and hidden in a hay loft and left for several days, then taken on to another place which seemed to be a closed brick factory. Here he was cared for until liberated by advancing Allied troops. The rest of the crew, except for the pilot, also got back. Like so many pilots, Stokes died keeping the Lanc steady for his men to get out.

The last July raid came on the 30th, an early morning daylight mission of 692 Lancs, Halibags and Mossies to attack German troops and armour in the battle zone. No. 75 Squadron's target was near Amaye-sur-Selles. It was a low-level attack in front of American troops who were waiting to advance. Cloud made it difficult and only about half the bombers were able to bomb. Four Lancasters were lost, Flight Sergeant C. Nairne of 75 Squadron being one of them.

One not insignificant story, told by Bomb Aimer Max Ruane who had arrived on the squadron with his crew, can be included here. Ruane recalls:

> After being assigned our billets and having been issued with our various bits and pieces, we were advised to go down to the cycle store and have bicycles issued — Mepal was a large place! At the store the airman laughed at our request as all the bikes had been issued long since. 'But don't worry', he had said. 'Just do down to the Flight Hut the morning after an Op — there will be plenty of spare bikes then!' Quite a sobering greeting for us.

15

Night and Day

AUGUST — SEPTEMBER 1944

Bomber Command were increasing their daylight raids on targets in Northern France now that the invasion had been successful and the troops were moving inland. Certainly the Allied air forces had almost total air superiority over Northern France, and in the main the sorties were of short duration. But initially it had not been all that easy.

Bomber crews experienced in night raids had to switch to daylight attacks with no training or practice in daylight formation techniques. In the first such raids, the bombers tended to spread all over the sky, making the Spitfire fighter pilot's job of protection very difficult. On one famous occasion, Fighter Command actually reported an RAF daylight bomber formation having spread themselves over an area 30 kilometres miles wide and 130 kilometres long!

These early raids were more spectacular than successful, bomber crews for the first time seeing both their target clearly and their bombs actually exploding. Also for the first time, crews actually realised just how dangerous night sorties were with so many aircraft in the bomber stream. How more did not collide had to be a miracle!

The V1 rocket launching sites were still appearing on the squadron's 'shopping list' of targets as August began. Then an oil storage depot for V1s at Bec D'Ambes, near Bordeaux, was the daylight target on 4 August, as John Aitken remembers:

> We flew at low level right down the length of England to Land's End. One aircraft was so low that it brought back some branches. Then down to the Bay of Biscay, also at low level. The weather was perfect; blue sky, no wind, the sea as smooth as glass — in fact so smooth that we saw an aircraft wipe its H2S blister off, on the top of a swell, but it recovered and carried on!
>
> Nearing the French coast we climbed quickly to 7000 feet and ran over the long sweeping beach to cross over the Gironde Estuary, taking the defences by surprise. In brilliant sunshine we could see the target of oil tanks and installations with a ship of some sort tied up at a dock. I saw no opposition, and there were massive fires and black smoke soon reaching our altitude. We then flew over the western part of France and were met by a fighter escort. There was some opposition from a heavy flak battery and it was interesting to see some of the fighter escort roll over and drop down into the murk below; and that was the last we saw of the heavy flak from that area.
>
> We passed fairly close to the Channel Islands on our way back to the south coast of England, and landed at base after a total flying time of 7 hours 55 minutes.

Seventeen of the squadron's Lancasters were part of a force of over a thousand bombers to attack tactical targets in the Normandy battle area on the night of 7/8 August, 75's target being in the Mare de Magne area. The Lancaster of Flying Officer G. Brunton did not return, but five of the crew survived, four of them evading and getting back to the Allied lines.

The next few days saw a variety of targets attacked in daylight — petrol dumps, marshalling yards, troop concentrations, and an aerodrome. A night raid on 12/13 August cost 75 one Lancaster. Six aircraft went to Brunswick; ten to Russelsheim. Lyndon Sims recalls the operations during this period:

> *A*ugust 1944 was exceptionally busy and I took part in six operations during the first two weeks. These were mainly against Flying Bomb sites and stores, and in the Normandy battle area. On the night of 7th August, the squadron was part of a huge force of Lancasters and Halifaxes sent to attack various enemy strong points confronting the Allied forces. I flew with Flying Officer Stott and we took off at 22.05. The enemy positions were completely ravaged and devastated, yet after the war, this attack evoked some criticism of Bomber Command for having so messed up the battle-ground that it slowed up the progress of our troops!
>
> On 14th August, at a morning briefing, there was a buzz of excitement. A large enemy force was concentrated at Falaise, holding up our armies and threatening to break out. An attack by the US 8th Air Force has resulted in casualties to our own troops and so No. 3 Group, including our own squadron, had been selected to make a further attack on this Falaise Bulge. Absolute precision was needed as our own troops were surrounding three sides of the area. I flew with Flying Officer Fleming, taking off at 2pm, on a clear afternoon. Over the Channel we were met by a massive Spitfire escort, high above and weaving their con trails in the sky. Aided by Oboe and a Master Bomber, the attack was pressed home and we were later told it had been very successful, with Group and Squadron congratulated on its precision.

The airfield attacked on 15 August (daylight) was St Trond in Belgium. This was the famous base of Nachtjagdgeschwader 1 (Night Fighter Wing) — NJG/1 — which had been a constant thorn in the side of Bomber Command. Among its most successful night-fighter pilots was Major Heinz-Wolfgang Schnaufer, who was to end the war with 121 night 'kills', Colonel Werner Streib with 66, and Captain Manfred Meurer with 65. The attack on this and other night-fighter bases in mid-August was a prelude to a renewed night offensive against Germany.

This new offensive began on the night of 16/17 August, the target being Stettin. With the land battles going well, and the invasion force now well established on French soil, Bomber Harris was about to be released from supporting the Allied ground forces, and he was once again, under Air Ministry control.

On 18/19 August it was Bremen, with 75 suffering three of its 25 aircraft damaged. There was then a break in the offensive until the night of 25/26, when it was back to Russelsheim. But this time the cost was higher. Two Lancasters from 75 failed to return, while that of Flight Sergeant O'Callaghan struggled home after losing both its ailerons during violent evasive action. O'Callaghan received the DFM for this. Flying Officer R. D. Mayhill was John Aitken's Bomb Aimer on this raid:

> *A* brilliant orange flash lit the sky ahead, revealing several aircraft on the same course and height. The ball of fire hanging, seemingly motionless, before plunging down to spread its flames over the ground. Our 'second dickie' had watched his first bomber shot down and his awed remark recalled the lasting impression it had made on us.
>
> We threaded our way between Nancy and Luneville and into Germany, keeping well

John Aitken and crew. Left to right: Henry Monk (MU), Gordon Grindley (WOP), Duncan Hodgson (N), Aitken, Taffy Taylor (FE), Ron Mayhill (AB), William Monk (RG).
(VIA D. W. HODGSON)

Lancaster AA-A 'Seven Sinners', RAF Mepal, 1944, flown by F/O Doug Fairbairn.
(E. WISE VIA TONY FAIRBAIRN)

Terry Ford and his crew completed their tour 6/7 December 1944. Left to right: Sgt Muller, F/O Weedon, F/O Chapman, F/O Ford, Sgt Glover and Sgt Fitzwater. (T. FORD)

clear of Saarbrucken ablaze with lights, the gunners reporting an aerial combat and a plane going down. A few minutes later I took a fix on the oil refining town of Homberg.

There was no mistaking the clustered searchlights over Karlsruhe and Mannheim, places to be avoided, as we continued east. I took running fixes on Mannheim before clambering down below the second pilot seat into the bombing hatch where the engineer was pushing out bundles of Window. I had almost 10 minutes, about 40 miles, with the tail wind I had set on the bomb-sight, to recheck my bomb load and camera switches and guide us over the target.

The perspex nose blister with lateral and downwards windows gave me a panoramic view and there was plenty to see. We were flying through parallel lines of parachute flares, turning night into a ghastly yellow glow that suffused over the clouds. On either side were clusters of groping searchlights, while ahead, across our track, was the illuminated main highway between Frankfurt and Mainz. In there, somewhere, was Russelsheim.

I could count up to 20 bombers keeping station, the fighters way above still dropping flares. An unmistakeable FW190 flashed at us, the mid-upper calling as I leapt up to snap the safety switches on the Brownings, but the fighter had chosen somebody else.

Suddenly a shower of bright green Pathfinder markers floated down over the myriad of twinkling lights that studded the target area. I lined up but down went vivid reds, the Master Bomber breaking into our headphones with new instructions.

My eyes were glued to the TI's coming up, while we were rocking and thumping in the slipstreams. Scatterred ack-ack gun flashes twinkled through the growing smoke. 'Bombs going!' The aircraft lurched upwards as the 4000 pounder tore free followed in quick succession by the eleven canisters of indendiaries. Then the skipper reported a fighter up ahead, in a searchlight. I was in the front turret now, debating whether to fire, but it was too far away as yet. The skipper urged me to fire but it was not worth giving away our position with such a long shot. Then the light went out and so we made for home.

We reached base three hours later. There was a brief delay over base, someone getting a priority landing, and at de-briefing we learned it was Eldrid O'Callaghan whose evasive corkscrewing was so violent he had ripped off both ailerons which left his aircraft with broken wings and quite a few handling problems. Allan Fleming in 'Round Again Nan', who like us was on his 24th Op, didn't come back. Nor did 'Snow' Barker in the famous 'S' for Sugar, the veteran Lanc with 54 trips. Snow had done 25 Ops, and also carried a second dickie on his first OP, which showed it could happen anytime, even to the most experienced crews.

We had landed at 0438 in the half light of dawn but it was after six before we were de-briefed, had breakfast and got to bed. We were woken at mid-day and told we were again on the Battle Order and needed for a DI [Daily Inspection] before flying meal and briefing.

Ron Mayhill was wounded before the month was out.

Twenty out of 21 aircraft despatched to Kiel on 26 August bombed the target. The aircraft flown by Flight Lieutenant Andrews was damaged by flak and his mid-upper gunner wounded. A. L. 'Tiny' Humphries was on this trip:

> One of the most frightening Ops was one flown early in our tour to the Kiel Canal — our second Op. Our mid-upper gunner, Scotty, swore a bomb fell between the wing and the tailplane. We were probably more easily frightened at that stage, than later!

Then it was back to Stettin on 29/30 August, part of a force of 402 Avro Lancasters, of which 23 failed to return. Enemy night fighters were up in strength, 75 reporting three combats, with one Ju88 claimed as probably destroyed by Pilot Officer J.

Scott's gunners. But not all 75's crews were going for Stettin — John Aitken dropped mines off Danzig:

> This was the longest flight we made, and was also the night on which we were fired at by a ship just a few miles off the coast of Norfolk.
>
> We crossed over Denmark and flew across the southern part of Sweden in violation of their neutrality. It was quite a change to see cities all lit-up after the blackout in the rest of Europe. After crossing the east coast of Sweden we flew southeast over the Baltic to Gdynia. The same night there were also raids on Stettin and Konigsberg, so we could see some of the action in the distance. We were dropping mines — known as vegetables — and our target area was inside a long spit called Hel. At the time a large part of the German Navy was in Gdynia; together with the shore defences they put on quite a show for us!
>
> We were quickly coned by 15 or more searchlights and subjected to a fair bit of flak. I wanted to get right out of it and make another run but the navigator said we were coming up on the dropping zone as he could see it on the H2S, so I straightened out for a final run in. We let the mines go and I know for a fact that their parachutes opened as I could see them all in the searchlights. On the way in we had someone else getting the same treatment but what happened to him I don't know. Most of the others dropping mines the same night were given targets some 10 to 15 miles out to sea, presumably in the channels leading to the port, and it was always seemed to me that we were given the job of holding the attention of the defences while the others did their work.
>
> Anyway, after we had got clear of the target we set course again for Sweden, and expecting to have sustained a bit of damage, we wondered what to do if we ran short of fuel. The engineer checked the contents of the tanks over a period and all seemed okay, but to be sure we cruised back at +1 boost and 1800 rpms, which gave the greatest range unloaded, but was not good for the motors.
>
> We crossed over Sweden again and then Denmark, just north of Copenhagen, over the North Sea, and arrived over base almost an hour after the others with a total flying time of 10 hours 15 minutes. It was a long time to be sitting at the controls and for the navigator to be concentrating on his charts, but it was good to be back before they scrubbed our name off the board!

Two days later came a daylight raid on a flying bomb dump at Point Remy in which John Aitken's crew were again involved. This was bomb aimer Ron Mayhill's 27th trip, and it was to be his last. On the bomb run, he was hit by flak and temporarily blinded in one eye. Blood streamed down his face, but he insisted on staying at his post and told Aitken to make a second run. This the pilot did and they bombed successfully. For this, Ron Mayhill received an immediate DFC; John Aitken also received the DFC, completing his tour in mid-September. John had an exceptional navigator in Duncan Hodgson as well as a set of twins as gunners, Henry and William Monk, from England.

◇ ◇ ◇

The Allied troops in France were now making their way along the northern coast of France, bypassing, in some instances, the heavily defended coastal towns. Le Havre was one. But on 5 September, Bomber Command sent nearly 350 aircraft to bomb the town, in which it was believed a large concentration of German troops had been stationed. No. 75 Squadron sent 25 aircraft but, as is now known, there were very few troops in the actual town. Most of the civilian population had been herded into the old part of the town by the occupying forces, and it was this section upon which the bombs fell, with the loss of some 3000 French men, women and children. One of the more tragic events of the war, with liberation so near.

Le Havre was again to be the target a few days later. But bad weather on 8 September restricted the assault with indifferent results, while the raid planned for the following night had to be abandoned. Philip McElligott, known as Paddy, was the tail gunner in Flying Officer Gordon Cuming's crew. Cuming hailed from Fielding. Paddy, who came from Cork, Ireland, recalls the 8 September raid:

> We were briefed to bomb from 3000 feet! When we got to the target we found the cloud base below 3000 and some aircraft were orbiting the target area but none were bombing. Accompanied by three other aircraft we went in below cloud and my recollection is that we were as low as 900 feet when we bombed. We were the third aircraft on the run-in, by which time the bombs from the earlier aircraft were exploding — our aircraft behaving like a bucking bronco and feeling as if it would shake itself and us to pieces.
>
> Being so low I was clearly able to see the German troops on the ground and, in particular, the crews manning the light anti-aircraft guns which seemed to abound and from the 300 yards that separated us from them, I felt I would recognise them if I ever encountered them again!
>
> At this extraordinarily low altitude I was able to fire my guns at the German gun-crews. Returning their fire, modest though it was from four .303 guns, compensated for the very uncomfortable position we were in bombing at such a low level, which really made us sitting ducks. The German gunners seemed to throw everything at us and it seemed miraculous to me that none of the four or so aircraft that bombed were hit.
>
> Because of the bad weather the Master Bomber eventually called off the raid. We flew almost at sea-level over the Channel until we reached Beachy Head and climbed to height for base at Mepal. I recall remarking jokingly as the English coast came into view: 'I never thought, as an Irishman, I would be so glad to see England.'

On the night of 11 September, the squadron lost an aircraft on a mining sortie in the Baltic. Frankfurt came next, but them came the Arnhem operation — 'Operation Market Garden'. No. 75 Squadron was involved on the night of 16/17th, as Paddy McElligott relates:

> The squadron diary records that this evening 10 aircraft took off to attack Emmerich, with much light flak and all aircraft returned safely. This is a totally inaccurate entry — nothing of the sort took place. No bombs were used! This was an operation in support of the parachute drop at Arnhem. Only ten aircraft, all from 75 Squadron took part.
>
> The briefing took place late in the afternoon amidst great security. More RAF police than usual were on duty at the entrance to the Briefing Room and we were not told what our bomb load was; and all bomb doors had been sealed before we got to our aircraft.
>
> Briefing stipulated we were to fly at 2500 feet — map read our way up the Neder Rijn, passing Rotterdam, Arnhem and on to a spot outside Emmerich. We were briefed that we had to drop our 'load' accurately and on a signal from the ground. A successful drop would be indicated by a green Verey light fired from the ground. It was emphasised that we must maintain the briefing height of 2500 feet. As I recall our return route from Emmerich was down the Waal, still map reading, and out into the North Sea via the Dutch island of Overflakkee.
>
> On the legs in and out, light flak and searchlights were intense and far too close for comfort. Our H2S scanner cover on the underside of the fuselage was shot off!
>
> We were not aware of any parachute operation at Arnhem at this stage but were rather curious as to why so many flak barges were on both the Waal and Nedir Rijn rivers. We assumed from the briefing and subsequent operation that we were helping some German equivalent of the French Maquis.
>
> When we got to Emmerich we orbited the DZ where the flak was just a trifle less

intense and duly dropped our load. Green Verey lights were seen and we set off home.

At a special briefing next morning, we learned of the big drop at Arnhem and our operation had been to divert German attention away from the town, and create an impression that airborne forces had been dropped on German soil. It seemed our 'sealed' loads consisted of miniature dummy parachutists, which when caught in searchlights, appeared to be real men coming down. On reaching the ground some mechanism fired green flares and set off the sound of gunfire!!

A daylight raid to Boulogne followed on 17 September, bombing German positions prior to an attack by Allied soldiers. It was Battle of Britain Sunday as the squadron sent out 14 Lancasters. Squadron Leader Garth Gunn from Masterton was commander of 'B' Flight. To ensure accurate bombing, as Allied troops were in the vicinity, Gunn came in at 3000 feet, a range at which he was extremely vulnerable to flak. The aircraft was severely damaged by ground fire but he managed to get back over the Channel with both starboard engines feathered. Attempting to land at RAF Hawkinge, he overshot, hit an obstruction and crashed. Gunn and his Bomb Aimer were both severely injured, and the Engineer killed. Gunn died four days later. Bomb Aimer Angus Millar was badly injured, with burns to both legs, fractured ankle, fractured skull, and facial injuries including having his nose almost torn off. He was to spend three years in various RAF hospitals. He later received the Croix de Guerre.

September trailed off somewhat, with one raid on Calais on the 20th, a raid on Neuss marshalling yards on the 23rd, then Calais again on the 25th, the 27th and again on the 28th. Most aircraft brought their bombs back from the last raid. The final Op of September was a mining trip to the Baltic.

The momentous summer of 1944 was nearly spent. None new it for certain, but the final winter of the war was now approaching.

16

Back to Germany

OCTOBER — NOVEMBER 1944

Another famous event in which 75 Squadron participated was the attack upon the island of Walcheren on 3 October. German coastal gun batteries dominated the approaches to the great port of Antwerp and in order to expedite the German's withdrawal from this part of the world, a plan was laid to breach the sea-walls, thereby flooding the low lying island.

Some 250 bombers made the initial assault, heading in in waves of 30, being marked by Oboe and controlled by a Master Bomber. Bombs of 500, 1000 and 4000 pounds rained down. By the fifth of eight waves, the wall at Westkapelle was breached, and widened by the following waves.

Two nights later the Saarbrucken railway system was the target for 530 bombers, 31 from 75 Squadron. The American 3rd Army was making its advance towards this town and wanted enemy communications disrupted. The raid was causing severe damage, but the Master Bomber called a halt after 14 of the squadron's aircraft had bombed. Flak clawed down three Lancasters, one belonging to 75; Flight Sergeant A. Galletly and his crew were killed. Paddy McElligott was on this raid:

> *I* recall we flew in formation low over France in a vic [V-shaped formation] of four aircraft before climbing in darkness to our bombing height of 14,000 feet. One of the four aircraft was flown by Alan Galletly, whose two gunners had trained with me. En route over France I saw one of the aircraft just behind ours dip and hit the ground in a ball of flame and smoke. From its position I was convinced it was Galletly. He was known as 'Pop' because he was much older than most of us — he seemed to be aged about 32 to 35 which seemed ancient to our 19 to 23 bracket. I believe records show that they collided with a Lancaster from 115 Squadron.
>
> This operation had other personal connotations for me, for over the target we were attacked by a Junkers 88. To find an enemy fighter amongst the flak in the target area was unusual. I returned its fire and felt sure I had hit the fighter from the impression given by the tracer. The mid-upper gunner opened fire after me but soon his guns automatically cut out when his turret was rotated towards our twin tail fins. Thinking it was a stoppage he operated the manual over-ride. I then became aware of tracer shooting over my turret.
>
> As I continued to fire, I called for the skipper to corkscrew port, which he did, and the Ju88 went down to our starboard. I asked the mid-upper where the second fighter came from that was firing over my head. He calmly said it was him!

Fighters were again in evidence on 6/7 October against Dortmund. Flight Sergeant

Farr and crew had a number of combats and his gunners claimed a fighter shot down. Flying Officer K. Southward was shot down and killed, but all his crew escaped to become prisoners. Then on 7 October it was back to Emmerich in daylight, and for real, not with Dummies!

Flying Officer Terry Ford was on this raid, but not with his usual rear gunner:

> **W**ing Commander Leslie AFC, our CO, had a very 'press on' spirit, which later won him the DSO. He was very keen to get maximum efforts. On 7th October, 1944, Harry Fitzwater, my rear gunner, fell sick, and rather than be an aircraft short, Wing Commander Leslie flew as my rear gunner!
>
> It was a daylight trip to bomb German troops encamped in the woods there. Leslie threw out all his ammunition over the target. 'In the hope that it would fall on some of the bastards!' He was like that. During briefings, when we were carrying incendiaries, he would end the chat by saying, 'Go in and burn the bastards.'

Another daylight raid on a German town occurred on 14 October; this time it was Duisberg. This was part of Operation 'Hurricane', laid on by Sir Arthur Harris to demonstrate to the enemy the overwhelming air superiority of the RAF and the United States Army Air Force by attacking the Ruhr in daylight. Bomber Command had husbanded its aircraft for the previous 48 hours so was able to send out 1013 bombers with fighter escort. Fourteen Lancasters were shot down before the defenders were overwhelmed. Tiny Humphries went to Duisberg:

> **T**he flak was rather heavy over the target. From memory it was so close you could feel the bumps and smell the cordite. The bombs had just been released when the nose dome was either shot off or disintegrated by a near miss or shell fragment. With the nose now open to the elements, the pressure of the air coming in pushed out all the perspex on the side of the Lancaster and also created a wind-tunnel effect right down through the aircraft. We immediately dropped from our bombing height of 21,500 feet, down to as low as possible. On the way down I think most of us thought 'this was it'. I remember shaking hands with the WOP as if this was definitely the last way out.
>
> However, Jack levelled off at about 1500 feet and we came back at that level. Although my navigation aids had gone, including all my maps and charts, we tried to look for any stuff down in the back of the aircraft, but nothing was of any use. We had general direction, so headed east and I happened to remember the co-ordinates on the Gee for Mepal, and set them on the instruments and once we came within range of Gee it was just a matter of positioning ourselves on a co-ordinate and flying until we managed to visually pick up the Station.
>
> The trouble then was that Jack Plummer couldn't shift. He couldn't even sit on his hands or put them in his pockets, and he wasn't really equipped for sub-zero temperatures. We found what gloves we could and put them on him but not being in a heated suit or anything, he took the full brunt of the cold air, which was well below freezing.
>
> By the time we got home, his hands were just about frozen solid. We had to assist him to get his hands off the control column and he had to go and spend some time in Ely Hospital.

Nelson Bright, a future CO of 75, was flying his tour at this time and remembers seeing Plummer being taken out of the aeroplane still 'holding' the control column which had had to be cut off below the hand grips! Jack Plummer received the DFC for this day's work.

Stuttgart was next (19/20 October) then a daylight attack on Flushing on the island of Walcheron. Seventy-five 3 Group Lancasters carried out this raid on a gun battery, and lost one aircraft — from 75 Squadron! Norman Bartlett had just returned

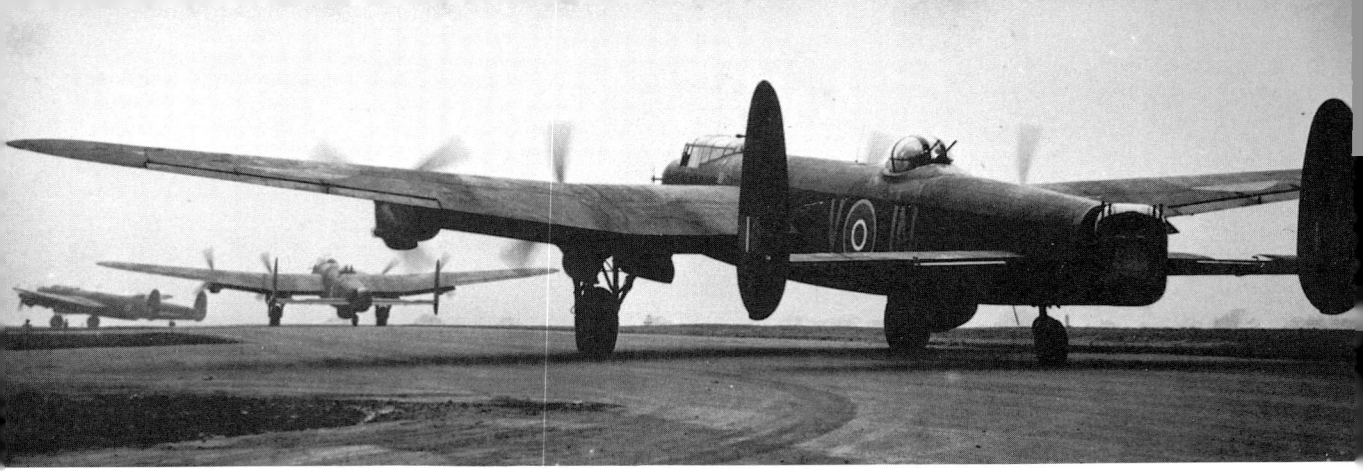

Lancasters of 'C' Flight taxi out for take-off.

Crew of F/O Gordon Cuming. Rear, left to right: Sgt Paddy McElligott (RG), F/Sgt Jack Christie (WOP), Sgt Bill Scott (MU); Front, left to right: Sgt Jack Scott (N), Cuming, Sgt Syd Sewell (AB).

(D. P. McELLIGOTT)

Crew of Jack Plummer DFC, shot down on their 32nd OP, 21 March 1945. Left to right: Jack Plummer, F/O R. J. Scott (MU), Sgt 'Tiny' Humphries (DFM) (N), F/Sgt A. McDonald (RG), Sgt M. Fell (FE), F/O J. Holladay (AB). Plummer, Hollaway and Scott were killed; the rest became POWs. Behind them is the Lanc in which they were shot down — NG449 AA-T. (A. L. HUMPHRIES)

to the squadron to start his second tour. He had been instructing at a Conversion Unit when, at a pub one evening, he ran into Squadron Leader Jack Bailey who was looking for an engineer and two gunners. Bartlett agreed to be his engineer and so after converting to Lancasters, Bailey and his crew arrived at Mepal:

> *I* still hadn't done any more Ops on my second tour, then on the 21st October a signal came through, not from Bomber Command but from the Canadian Army Command, asking if our squadron would go to Flushing and put a heavy gun out of action, which was preventing the Canadian Army from moving forward. It seemed a very interesting Op, low level, daylight, good clear weather — I really wanted to go on it, but the crew weren't down to go. I looked in the Flight Engineer's office and couldn't believe it; an engineer had lost his nerve, saying he couldn't go on. I was assistant Engineer Leader now, so I didn't ask any questions, except the letter of the aircraft in which he was to fly, then told the adjutant to put my name down in the authorisation book.
>
> Over the target I saw one Lancaster go down; the pilot seemed to have control but suddenly it went into a vertical position and then straight in. He seemed to bounce about eight feet, going into the deck tail first. I thought for a moment he was going straight for the gun. I saw the Jerries scarper for their shelter, and the Lanc missed the gun by about two feet. Jack later called me into his office and put a stop to me flying trips with just any squadron pilot. We eventually finished our tour together; Jack getting a bar to his DFC, while three of us received DFCs.

The squadron made a raid on Essen on 23/24 October, followed by what it called an unexceptional raid on the same target — in daylight — on 25 October. One man recalls these raids and that the second one was not unexceptional to start with. Flying Officer S. H. Richmond was bomb aimer in Flying Officer Eddie Robertson's crew. They were well into their tour of Ops, usually flying Lancaster 'W' Willie, named 'The Paper Doll', which, by the time they'd done their 32 trips, had itself completed over 90 sorties. Richmond remembers:

135

*A*s we were taking off from Mepal, just as we were airborne and heading over the bomb dump, our kite began to shudder and the tail felt to be getting lower as the plane began to relax its flight attitude. The skipper made a rapid check and discovered that the Engineer had operated the control to retract the undercarriage and had then, instead of returning the control to neutral, pushed it so that the undercart went out again. Only Robbie's speed of pulling the wheels up again enabled us to creep marginally over a row of oak trees in our path and thus be able to continue our trip in one piece instead of being blasted to smithereens, as we were carrying one 8000 pound 'cookie' and six 1000 pound bombs. I can tell you the Engineer never made that mistake again.

As we approached Essen we were caught in searchlights over the area and the kite behind us was shot down. Try as we might we could not shake off the group of lights which seemed to lock onto us. As a last resort, Robbie dived down through the beams of the lights and at terrific speed, pulled out to the side, and this did the trick. We were free from the lights and able to concentrate on the pounding of our heart beats as we set off in a beeline for home base.

A few days later, towards evening, we all cimbed aboard 'W' Willie. Robbie started up the motors in turn as always, then the ground crew waved us off and wished us luck. The engines revved and we began to ease forward when all of a sudden all our 1000 pound bombs fell off their hooks and landed on the ground. Panic stations, believe me!! Luckily the 8000 pounder remained hanging in place. To top it all, one of the ground crew had locked the rear door and taken the handle for re-opening it. There we were like cornered rabbits trying to claw our way out. Fortunately, the bombs were not armed and so fell safe.

Then it was Cologne's turn, Bomber Command making three attacks upon this much-bombed city at the end of October. Over 700 bombers hit the city in daylight on 28 October causing enormous damage, followed by night raids on 30/31st and 31st/1st November. Paddy McElligott recalls the third raid:

*T*his was the second time we visited Cologne within 24 hours. Group Captain A. P. Campbell, our Station Commander at Mepal, flew with us as bomb aimer. Our bomb aimer, Flight Sergeant Syd Sewell of Timaru, assessed the Group Captain's bomb aiming ability on this operation as 'shows promise!' I gather the Group Captain had already completed the requisite operational flying hours allocated to him for October and, by going as a bomb aimer, no doubt hoped his transgression would not be detected when the appropriate returns were submitted to Group.

Alex Simpson almost didn't get to Cologne on this last night of October 1944:

*A*t the last minute, my aircraft went u/s on start up and the stand-by aircraft, AA-K, was right across the other side of the airfield. By the time we could organise transport the rest of the squadron had gone.

We roared around to 'A' Flight dispersal, clambered into AA-K, fired her up, taxied out to the 'Christmas Tree', were given the green light by the ACP, and took off. As we proceeded down the runway, my impressions of AA-K were not very complimentary! We were taking all the runway to get airborne, so thank God it was the main runway, one mile long.

We crossed the fence, gear up, flaps up, reached 300 feet, called for climb power 2650 rpm, plus four boost and AA-K fell out of the sky! Back to full power, once again checked all the 'clocks' — everything immaculate. What was wrong? Called for climb power again and immediately we started to lose altitude, so I said to myself, 'Steady-on skipper, start again!' So I went back to the pre-take off check, put my hand down the left side of my seat to the bomb door lever — . . . . .!!! The bomb doors were open!

As they closed, the aircraft gave a wriggle and produced the performance I expected from a Lancaster. How the APC had not seen that our bomb doors were open I don't know, nor could he later explain it. There was little light offered by the Christmas Tree but he did shine an Aldis Lamp with the green shutter on us, which provided a fair amount of illumination.

Thank God again for the long runway as we had been told clearly in training that a loaded Lancaster could not be taken off with bomb doors open!! It had been my practice to put the bomb door control lever in the closed position as soon as I was settled in my seat, as part of the pre-start up routine. Having already done this in my own aircraft, I guess I subconsciously thought I had done it in the spare. Needless to say, it did not happen again.

No. 3 Group carried out a G-H attack on Homberg on 2 November. Twenty of the squadron's Lancasters took part, the total force being 184. This was the second daylight raid on this target in two days, 5 Group having attacked it on the previous day. G-H was a device for blind-bombing which had been tested operationally in the summer of 1943, but its use was delayed until 1944 when more sets had been manufactured. Tiny Humphries flew on this raid, but with Jack Plummer still on the sick-list, the CO took the crew:

I think some of the short raids just over the coast of France each had their own particular hazards about them. We often collected the odd hole or two because the bombs were dropped from quite low levels and that in itself was a hazard. You were prey to everybody who could fire a gun at you.

All the trips to the 'Happy Valley' were not to be looked forward to. One that does stand out was a trip that we did just after we'd had our nose shot off and Jack was still in hospital with frost bite. The CO, Jack Leslie, took us to Homberg on 2nd November, 1944, and we had the misfortune to have one bomb hang-up. Leslie announced he was going round again but the bomb aimer couldn't release it manually on this second run.

Well, if anything was calculated to be fool-hardy, going round again to drop one bomb over a place which had just been done over, that was! I would say that Jack Leslie was not the most popular skipper in that aircraft that day. None of us wanted to fly with him again! But we got back, although somewhat late. But that was Jack Leslie.

Two days later the squadron lost a crew over Solinger, Flying Officer J. Scott and his six men all being killed. Then Homberg came on the Battle Order again for 8 November — another 3 Group effort, with 136 Lancasters attacking the Meerbeck oil plant. The weather in early November was bad, and a couple of operations were cancelled. But then came Homberg — again!

When 75 Squadron had visited this target on 20 July 1944, it had lost no fewer than seven crews. Now, on 20 November — four months to the day — it lost three more; those of Flying Officer R. Gordon, Flying Officer H. Rees and Flying Officer P. L. McCartin. Of the 21 men, eight survived as prisoners of war. This was a daylight attack using G-H, and consisting of 183 of 3 Group's Lancasters. They bombed through cloud; in fact, the route to and from the target was flown in cloud. Their bombs were recorded as 'scattered'.

S. H. Richmond recollects how at least one of the Lancasters failed to get back:

*W*e had successive daylight trips to the oil refinery at Homberg, across the Rhine from Dusseldorf and Duisberg. We were operating on one trip with some Halifaxes which had about 1000 feet ceiling on us as we moved in to drop our bombs. The Halifaxes, using instruments, converged above us and as I was giving the pilot my instructions to head up to the target, all hell was suddenly let loose over the intercom. The mid-upper was shouting at the top of his voice. Later it was ascertained that a Halifax had moved in above us and had dropped its bombs, so that an 8000 pound 'cookie' just missed the mid-upper gunner and our fuselage, falling between the wing and the tailplane. In the same raid, one of our Lancasters had its tailplane knocked off in the same way!

As if trying to lay the jinx, 75 went back to Homberg on the following day.

Minelaying off Oslo Fiord on the night of 21/22 November cost the squadron the crew of Flight Lieutenant L. Martyn. This was followed two days later by a raid on an oil plant near Gelsenkirchen; again in daylight, using G-H, and again a solo 3 Group effort. Then a two-day break before hitting the marshalling yards at Cologne — again with G-H and just 3 Group Lancasters — with good results.

The following night (28/29 November), 21 Lancasters from the squadron flew to bomb Neuss, one of the aircraft being captained by Wing Commander Leslie. However, Leslie bombed Essen, which was also a target that night for 1, 4 and 8 Groups. Paddy McElligott remembers these raids:

> On the Cologne show, our instructions were to RV [rendevous] with a certain G-H equipped aircraft over Woodbridge and keep formation with it, and some three or four aircraft did so. The G-H Leader seemed to go off track so frequently that our Navigator, Flight Sergeant Jack Scott of Auckland, was beside himself with frustration. The G-H Leader took us, in our small formation, over some of the most heavily defended areas of the Ruhr. He seemed to be drawn to Munchen-Gladbach, which was 14 miles off track! — hence the log-book entry I subsequently made — 'Intense Heavy Flak'!
>
> Meanwhile, we could see the main bomber force in the distance and occasionally we would join up with them, only to find our 'Leader' wandering off again. Having eventually rejoined the bomber stream we dropped our bombs on G-H instructions as briefed and turned in formation of four aircraft for home. Our Leader started to wander up the Ruhr again which prompted our skipper to change course and rejoin the main stream. As we were doing so we saw our G-H Leader, now on his own, receive a direct hit. Smoke poured from the aircraft and it went into a spiral descent which seemed to tighten and soon he was lost from view in the smoke and haze below us. No one seemed to get out. [Only one Lancaster was lost on this raid.]
>
> For our crew, the attack on Neuss was fairly uneventful, but I have seen two entries in 3 Group Intelligence summaries and those in the squadron's diary, in respect of the CO. They read:
>
> 'One aircraft, captained by Wing Commander R. J. A. Leslie DSO AFC, carrying the 12,000 pound bomb, got in the wrong stream of bombers and bombed Essen.'
>
> 'Wing Commander R. J. A. Leslie, caught up in a Halifax stream — rather than cut across three streams, he bombed Essen instead.'
>
> I recall Wing Commander Leslie was noted for his final remarks at briefings, which invariably were, 'Off you go, and all the best'.

It will be noted in reading the above entry that Jack Leslie had received the DSO. This appeared in the London Gazette in December 1944. His tour was coming to an end, leaving the squadron in early December and being replaced by Wing Commander R. J. Newton DFC. Newton had been a Flight Commander on 75 Squadron in 1942.

On the last day of November, there was another 3 Group G-H raid on an oil plant, this time at Osterfeld. Just 60 Lancasters took part, 18 of these coming from 75. Terry Ford was on this raid and his bomb aimer, Neill Chapman, took a photograph of a Lancaster falling in flames near the target. Two Lancasters failed to return from this attack, one being that of Flying Officer J. A. McIntosh. Only his rear gunner survived — wounded — but he died in a German hospital on 28 December.

17

Back on the Ground

In Chapter 11 we saw some of the work of the squadron's ground personnel — the men who kept them flying. Recorded in this chapter, in a little more detail, is the work of three important sections of the ground echelons — the men who bombed up the aircraft, those who serviced the engines, and the men of the radar section.

Derek Morris gave us some insights into his work in the earlier chapter. He continues:

> The most physically demanding job we armourers had to do was, of course, 'Bombing Up' — not to forget, de-bombing!
>
> From the formation of 75 Squadron in early 1940, the bombing effort was small. Targets were sparse and in April and May 1940, leaflet raids were in fashion. By the time I left the squadron in early 1942, we were loading an ever increasing weight of bombs which needed a bit of planning and organisation to get all the aircraft bombed-up in the time available.
>
> It seemed to me that one of the reasons that the Wimpy was in use throughout the war was the fact that Barnes Wallis appeared to have designed a good, large (for 1938/9) bomb beam and then built his aircraft around it. There were 18 bomb stations arranged in six rows of three. Each bomb was held by its big hook to the bomb release slip, steadied by front and rear crutches and with fusing links (wires) from bomb pistols into the fusing units. At the bomb end the firing links were attached to a spring clip with a peg, preventing the vanes of the bomb pistol spinning, which was pulled off as the bomb left the aircraft. The bombs were quite safe until these vanes had spun off when the bomb was well clear of the bomb bay.
>
> With the usual bombs — 250 and 500 pound GP (general purpose), the Wellington could carry 18×250, or 9×500s. The use of the 1000 pound GP and the 2000 pound AP (armour piercing — used against ships in Brest, etc) necessitated the use of a special beam in the bomb bay, which also carried a smoke curtain installation. The lugs (4) on the aircraft to which the beam was attached, also could be used to carry a fuel overload tank.
>
> This special 1000 pound beam incorporated its own winch and the bomb, complete with its carrier, was winched up and held rigidly in position. A maximum of two 1000 pounders could be carried, one on each side of the bomb bay. (The centre section being far too narrow.)
>
> Another load much used was the four pound incendiary bomb. They were packed in a box, close together, holding in one another's safety plungers. It would, however, need to drop about 12–15 feet onto concrete to set them off, so they were pretty safe.

Two large portable winches operated from inside the fuselage. Once the bomb was winched up, four crutches were screwed down to steady the bomb, which were located inside the outer bomb doors — and there hangs a tale!

About July/August 1941, one of our aircraft taking off with a 4000 pounder on board, struck an airfield gun position and damaged a main wheel. The pilot was instructed to head out to sea, jettison the bomb and come back and attempt to land at our diversion airfield at Methwold. This he did and made a wheels-up landing. It wasn't till the next morning when the aircraft was jacked up that we found the bomb still aboard, as it projected about two inches below the aircraft, into the airflow. The Wimpy had in fact landed on the bomb! Luckily it was a grass airfield.

What had happened was this. On all of the normal Wellingtons, the bomb circuitry was not energised until the Master switch was operated. This was at the pilot's position and the switch was connected to the bomb door operating lever. On the 4000 pound aircraft, there was no need to open the bomb doors before dropping the bomb so the connecting link between bomb door lever and bomb master switch was removed, so the Master switch alone needed to be operated. The pilot had flown over the sea, opened his bomb doors, pulled the jettison toggle, and not realising that nothing had happened due to the electrical circuit still being switched off, closed the bomb doors and came home!

◇ ◇ ◇

During my two years at Feltwell, I was usually out on the airfield meeting the returning aircraft. An armament type (I was it!) had to be at the aircraft first to check that no explosives were where they shouldn't be. Second, to be on hand if the crew needed it.

The first casualty to come back was about June 1940. A tail gunner was struck by a 20 mm cannon shell which passed through the rear turret armour plate, the gunner's body, killed him instantly, and then exited at the front of the fuselage. That was the only strike on the aircraft and none saw the attacker.

On another occasion an aircraft returning from Duisberg [15 July 1941], unusually, taxied up to the control tower. After checking the bomb bay, I went down to the front hatch, to see blood dripping from the bomb aimer's glass panel. I helped out the crew. They had been attacked by a night fighter. The second pilot was dead, and the front gunner had a bad leg wound, losing a lot of blood, but he survived. The rear gunner was in a state of shock and deafened by a shell which had burst on his turret very close to his head, and the navigator had fallen through the panel fitted to cover the mid-under turret hole. The pilot and WOP alone had brought that one back.

◇ ◇ ◇

The Germans seemed to know where we were and had a go at Feltwell occasionally. A couple of times I remember trying to dig a slit trench with my fingernails in less than one second!!

One night, while out on the dispersal waiting for our returning aircraft which had already begun to land, a rather noisy aircraft with its nav lights on, landed, turned close to me and switched on a powerful yellow beam searchlight. It illuminated the control tower and the words Duty Pilot painted across it in three foot letters. The aircraft then turned, opened up and took off across the airfield — it was a Ju88! From then on a manned mobile AA gun was placed near the end of the runway when night flying was in operation.

In 1940, our Station Commander, Group Captain C. O. F. Modin, had a whistle installed near the MT [Motor Transport] yard, operated by compressed air and switched on from his office. We had the usual air raid warning sirens as well. When a raid was in the offing, the usual siren went but nobody took much notice and carried on working. When anyone sighted a raider near the airfield, they rang the Group Captain's office

Two 1500 pound mines being lifted into a Stirling's bomb bay.

No. 75 Squadron armourers at Feltwell. Back row, left to right: 'Pop' Fairbrother, 'Mac' McGibbin, Ron Price, K. K. Moore, 'Batch' Bunting; Front row, left to right: Mick Organ, Jack Walsh, C. Shepherd. (C. C. SHEPHERD)

Sgt Bert James RCAF (Radar) and Sgt (later P/O) Jerry Campbell, air gunner.

(BERT JAMES)

and he sounded his steam whistle alarm. We all knew when we heard that, we had only seconds to take cover! Very effective and it saved a lot of work interruptions.

◇ ◇ ◇

I had a good friend in the radio section, Syd Holmes, who had rebuilt rather well an aircraft TR9 radio set. We set in up in 75's crew room and used to listen out for returning aircraft. This set was more powerful than the one on the tower and sometimes we would re-transmit messages between the tower and returning aircraft. One night we heard one of our aircraft being diverted away as we were being fogged in at Feltwell. He was sent to another local base but a few minutes later he came on the air with a stream of bad language. Approaching this diversion airfield he had been attacked by a German night fighter. 'Why the . . . . can't you send me to a safe airfield!?' And a lot more in similar vein. We could understand his feelings.

Frederick Woolterton was at Mepal, serving on 75 Squadron as a flight mechanic. He gives a graphic account of a flight mechanics life at that time:

A typical day for a flight mechanic would begin around 0600 hours when the noise of the night duty crews returning to the billet would wake every one sleeping in the Nissen hut. A quick trip to the wash house for a cold water (no hot) wash and shave, then back to the billet to make beds, before cycling off to the cookhouse for breakfast. The food was, in the main, good but spoilt by bulk cooking and careless serving.

After breakfast, we would cycle to the flight hut around 0815 to read the Daily Orders and check if any snags had been reported on your aircraft. Then over to dispersal, overalls on — engine, cockpit and turret covers off, pull the trestle off its hard stand over to the first engine, to commence Daily Inspection [DI].

It could be quite pleasant working on the aircraft in the summer time but doing DIs in the winter was something different. Come rain or snow the DI had to be done, and it was no fun sitting on the trestle with the rain teeming down and as one removed the oil filter to check it, the oil would be whipped by the wind all over the place. It always seemed to be blown over your trousers, up your sleeves, or around your hands and face. With frozen fingers it was then a case of washing them off in a can of high octane, hands in pockets to feel a tingling warmth come to the fingers, then back to the DI.

When the aircraft was ready the crew would take it on a NFT and upon its return, armourers would commence bombing up and we would top up the petrol to the amount required for the trip — another miserable job if wet, sitting on the wing with water running down it and trying to keep the dip-stick dry long enough for a reading to be taken.

At 1530 the Night Duty Crew would go for early tea, returning at 1730 when the others would go for a meal, some to return to assist at take-off time, the rest going off duty till next day.

As the aircrew arrived, we would have cleared the area, the trolley accs [Trolley Accumulators — large battery trolleys used for starting engines] would be in place, and once they had stowed their gear we would chat till take-off time. Then came two duties that FMEs [Flight Mechanic Engineers] did not like. The first was to climb up into the undercarriage well to operate the priming pump for starting the engines. There was always a fear that, due to human error or mechanical failure, the undercart would fold up on you and there would be no possible way to escape being crushed!

The second unpleasant job was seeing the aircraft off the dispersal point, for this meant running backwards whilst in front of this lumbering monster, some 22 feet high, with four engines revving away, coming towards you. There was always the thought that if you tripped over there was a chance of being flattened by one of the wheels, or the thought that the Lanc might surge forward and a whirling prop chop you. This job became more unpleasant when the aircraft returned, with a tired pilot, anxious to get to dispersal, whilst you were equally anxious to get all the engines over the hard stand and not have one over the grass and mud.

When the aircraft did return, it would be checked for flak or fighter damage. The Duty Mechanic would put chocks in position, go into the cockpit to put locking bars on controls — perhaps find some chocolate or coffee left behind — have a quiet five minutes sitting in the warm oily/leather atmosphere, listening to the crackle of cooling engines. Then came another unpleasant job, to climb out onto the roof to unfold and drape the covers over the cockpit — a tricky job if a wind blowing or if raining. Then a climb onto the wing to cover over the engines, with engines and exhausts still warm.

This pattern of life changed when daylight raids started to take place after D-Day. Then it was reporting to the flights between 0400 and 0700, depending on the operations and doing the DIs when aircraft returned, ready for the next day.

We had other duties, too, especially on stand-downs. We could also be part of the Crash Crew. One night in November 1943 I was on this duty when an aircraft was reporting coming in to make a belly landing. As the aircraft made its approach, the ambulance and we on the crash wagon were to proceed down the runway, which had been flood-lit, to arrive alongside the aircraft as it crash landed on the grass. Away we went, tearing down the runway, hanging on for grim death and looking back, saw the aircraft making a fast approach right behind us! I thought it must be a cock-up, nobody had told him to land on the grass and what a mess he would make of us. But then the pilot slipped to starboard and pancaked onto the earth. As we leapt from the wagon with our hoses, the aircrew popped out of the hatches like jack rabbits.

On 17th November 1943 I was moved from 'A' to 'C' Flight and allocated to aircraft JN-F, which went missing two nights later. I spent many moments wondering if there was something I'd done or not done to the engines, but later learnt it had been shot down by flak and fighters.

The first Lancaster on our dispersal, JN-N, did not last long and our second one, JN-M, was received on 22nd April 1944. By the 26th May it had 11 Ops to its credit. Then on 27th May it was the stand-by aircraft. A kite on 'B' Flight had troubles so the crew, on their 29th OP, came over and took off in 'M'. On that trip JN-M and JN-D, with a crew on their 26th OP, both went missing. Next day a new 'M' arrived. 'C' Flight

Commander finished his tour on it on 1st June then a sprog crew took it over and completed their tour by 21st August. Then various crews came and went and JN-M made its 94th Op on 1st January 1945. By the end of the war, she had flown 101 Ops, a few food drops over Holland and a couple of trips to Italy to pick up POWs.

On Night Crew Duty there was a feeling of satisfaction on seeing your aircraft back on dispersal, though some returns were not so. For instance, I recall climbing into one aircraft as the engines shut down to be met by a stench of drying blood. The mid-upper had been hit by a piece of flak and was lying on the floor, wrapped in his parachute that his colleagues had put round him. Everything was splattered with blood, but we helped to lift him out to the ambulance. Another night I was met by an even greater stench. This crew had run into trouble and in some desperate evasion, the Elsan toilet had been dislodged, splashing the contents all over the fuselage. It took weeks to remove the stains and get rid of the smell!

Some incidents on dispersals I recall. One day I was working on my engine and enjoying the sunshine when I noticed everyone running. As Erks usually only run when the tea-wagon arrives, I prepared to climb down but then noticed they were scattering in all directions. I joined the race, not stopping to ask questions until later. It was then I learnt that a 'cookie' had fallen off as armourers were bombing up. Luckily, it did not go off. On another day same incendiary bombs were dropped, resulting in the lads 'playing football' with them, trying to kick them away from under the kite.

Radar had become an integral part of the the air war, and it took on even more important facets as the war progressed. The following extracts, taken from the VE Edition of 3 Group's 'Radar News', record the work of 75's radar personnel:

*T*he Section originated at Feltwell in December 1941 and consisted of a handful of men, namely, AC1 Philips, LACs Clarke, Turnbull and Robertson, who set about the job of fitting Gee Mark 1 to 25 Wellingtons. They were joined later on by LACs Moore, Dick Davies and Len Edwards. In July 1942 a trickle of sprog RDF Mechs [Radio Direction Finding Mechanics] began to arrive and 75 were more fortunate than the other stations by having Ken Holdsworth and Jim Williams as their sprogs.

Soon after their arrival the squadron moved to Mildenhall where lots of hard work was done, taking Gee units out of aircraft on bicycles — up till then, Radar Section had no transport. We only stayed at Mildenhall four months. From there we moved to Oakington to convert to Stirlings. We didn't stay there very long and we were destined to operate with Stirlings from Newmarket. When we arrived there we were met by eight new Radar Mechanics, Sid Selley, Algy Skinner, Morris Demirs, Jules Lattellier, Paul Rovira, Jock Wilson, Bill Young and Clyde Wyman.

By this time, Johnnie Philips had become a sergeant, AC Turnbull a corporal; AC Turnbull and LAC Robertson were despatched on a secret course [believed to be Mandrel, for jamming German radar] at TRE [Telecommunications Research Establishment]. Clare Clarke then became a corporal. At this period we were well off for men; Mark II Gee was fitted, and also 'Boozer'. Our first radar officer arrived, Lt. Renskers of the American Army Air Force. He stayed about two months, then P/O Bird (now F/Lt) replaced him. Johnnie Philips obtained his crown and Len Edwards and Ken Holdsworth became corporals.

When we arrived at Mepal we had a good crowd of lads: P/O Mit Riddle was our new radar officer. At this time we had three flights of Stirlings all fitted with Gee Mark II and Boozer. The old Section gradually broke up during our first few months at Mepal; F/Sgt Philips went to 514 Squadron to start G-H in the Group; Cpl Clarke left on his commission course and P/O Mit Riddle was repatriated. Bert James arrived here as Sergeant i/c and P/O Anthony (now F/Lt) as radar officer. We had another new intake of men including Cpl Wood, ex-balloon operator, (the man with the lowest demob number in the group), Cpl Wiffen, ex-accounts, LAC Chapman, Cox and the late LAC Bachard.

Later Algy Skinner left us for base and Sid Selley and Jules Lettallier went to 513 Squadron.

It was in March 1944 when new trouble started again. We were honoured by having the first Lancasters fitted with H2S. To help us out, Sid Selley and Jules Lettallier returned as corporals. Bert James became F/Sgt and Ken Holdsworth, Sgt. We soon got over the teething stages and all the Squadron on top line as far as H2S, Gee and Fishpond goes.

The Radar Section will always remember our Kiwi Radar Mech, LAC Bill Farmer. He became known to all of the Group as a 'Transformer Winder'.

At the end of 1944 we had a try at amalgamation with Signals, which didn't go too well. F/O Anthony left us and F/O Chalklin came in his place. The year 1944 was the hardest time for Radar Mechs, because operations were practically reaching their peak. However, at the beginning of 1945 another effort was made to try amalgamation; this time it proved a little more successful and Bomber Command were quite satisfied with our effort. During this period, we fitted all aircraft with G-H and so once more a Radar Mech's work was never done. Operations night and day and all this slogging led up to Victory in Europe Day in May. In the meantime, we had lost F/Sgt James to Waterbeach and had a few more Radar Mechs from Training School.

The Flight Sergeant Bert James mentioned above initially served with 115 Squadron at Marham, going to 75 in the summer of 1943. He was Royal Canadian Air Force and came to England in November 1941. His elder brother died with Coastal Command in 1943. Bert recalls:

*O*ur role as Radar Mechanics was to give all Radar equipment in the aircraft — we had 35 Lancasters at one time — a Daily Inspection. Faulty equipment was replaced by serviced equipment from the Radar workshop. Air Tests were frequent. One or two of our members attended de-briefings to find out if equipment on all the aircraft had operated satisfactorily. If not, it was replaced or repaired before the next operation. As ground crew, we performed some guard duties too.

Stirlings were easily serviced as far as Radar was concerned. Later at Mepal, the morale of personnel was great but living conditions left much to be desired.

After VE day, Commonwealth personnel began to be repatriated. As there was such a large percentage of Radar Mechanics who were RCAF, special permission was given to the RAF to keep many of them on the squadrons even though they had to miss their normal repatriation dates.

Canadian uniforms were considered to be superior to RAF uniforms and if a Canadian member of aircrew went missing on Ops, his kit was examined and anything serviceable was cleaned and put into the stores for re-issue. If a member of the RAF received a Canadian uniform, he had to replace the RCAF buttons with RAF ones. Sometime after VE day, I was on a parade, dressed in a Canadian uniform when the inspecting officer said, 'Why is this man wearing Canadian buttons on his uniform?' I spoke up and said, 'Because I am a Canadian!' Nothing more was said but I suspect he felt somewhat foolish.

At the wars end, the Squadron Radar Section personnel comprised:

FO Guy Chalken	Cpl Leonard Edwards	Cpl Sidney Selley
Sgt Ken Holdsworth	Cpl William Wiffin	LAC Larry Webb
Cpl Ronald Wood	LAC Peter Williamson	LAC Cyril Chapman
LAC Paul Rovira	LAC Richard Penrose	LAC Leslie Cross
LAC Allan Birch	LAC Frank Reynolds	LAC Alfred Aldis
LAC Frank Pomfret	AC1 William Scott	ACl Harry McKenna
LAC William Halsall	ACW1 Audrey Perkins	ACW1 Joyce Thorne
ACl Reginald Mansell		

18

The Last Winter

DECEMBER 1944 — FEBRUARY 1945

Railways, oil and mining were the principal targets and activities of 75 Squadron in December 1944. Marshalling yards at Hamm, Grenburg and Coblenz were all attacked during daylight raids, while the oil plants at Oberhausen and Leuna were visited at night and in daylight respectively. Between times, sea mines were laid in the Kattegat, Baltic and Heligoland Bight.

Twenty-one Lancasters were part of the raiding force of 94 bombers from 3 Group against Hamm on 5 December, all returning without loss. The next night Leuna was the target for 475 Lancasters from 1, 3 and 8 Groups. This was in Eastern Germany, near the town of Merseburg, to the west of Leipzig — a trip of 800 kilometres. It was the first major raid on an oil plant in this part of Germany; 75 being a part of it, with 12 aircraft. Alex Simpson recalls:

> Our briefing was to dive flat out after bombing to 12,000 feet, fly west to the Ruhr, climb to 16,000, cross the Ruhr at that altitude and then dive to 4000 feet and head home.
>
> After our bombing run I made a rapid descent, accompanied by a slithering noise that came from the rear and culminated in a thump under my seat — raised eyebrows all round! On commencing the climb at the Ruhr, the same noise repeated itself in a rearward direction ending in a thump down the rear-end. Obviously something was running free on our bomb doors. As it was not practice to inspect the bomb bay (by shining the Aldis lamp through a hatch on the steps leading to the bomb aimer's compartment) until we were out of enemy territory, I denied the request to do this, for whatever it was, was harmless (???) at this stage.
>
> The rapid descent from the Ruhr brought us to a layer of stratus at around 4000 feet, so I decided to stay on top of it, around 4600. I then gave the OK to my bomb aimer, Jack Hemingway, to check the bomb bay. Needless to say it was a very quiet aircraft!
>
> Hemingway reported that there was a 150 × four pound crate of incendiaries lying on the bomb doors under my seat!! I told Jack to let it go when over the North Sea. Then I remembered a briefing warning of some change in the structure of the incendiary crate. I asked Jack if he remembered and he said he'd check. Then he called back, 'Jesus, you're right. There's a 30 pound charge and its set to go off at 4000 feet!!' Whew — someone was looking after us that night. If I had gone on to 4000 feet we would have been history. The 30 pound charge would have been enough, let alone the 150 four pound incendiaries, sticking through us like prickles on a porcupine. To be doubly sure I grabbed another thousand feet and later we dropped the case over the North Sea.

This raid of 6/7 December saw the final sortie by Terry Ford and his crew:

We had a wonderful ground crew servicing our aircraft — 'Y' Yoke. They were intensely loyal and on our return from our last operation on 6th December, our rigger who was off duty, cycled six miles from his billet in Ely in freezing conditions to greet us at 3 o'clock in the morning and to congratulate us on completing our tour.

As one crew finished, another was about to begin. Ken Moore was a mid-upper gunner, who arrived with his pilot, Ronnie Flamank, a New Zealander from Dunedin. Ken came from Portsmouth, England:

We arrived at Mepal on 6th December and lunch-time in the Sergeant's Mess next day found us feeling very much the new boys. We rubbed shoulders with the rest of the lads whose topic of conversation was last night's Op, as one crew had originally been reported as missing, but had turned up later in a shaken condition. [Flying Officer D. Atkin and crew.] It appears that the pilot had been forced to come down in the drink.

To his credit he had made a successful ditching and all the crew had got into the dinghy without further mishap. One can only imagine their thoughts as they sat out the night with water all round them, weighing up their chances of survival, etc. Then, one of them suddenly said, 'I heard a cow moo!' It probably brought moments of light relief but then the other men thought he was being affected by the situation and so his remarks were ignored. As a misty dawn broke, their spirits must have raised a few degrees at least, for someone might spot them when daylight finally arrived.

As they peered out across the water and things became discernible, they were amazed to see not miles of water but the shores of England. They hadn't ditched in the North Sea, but in the estuary of the River Orwell. In short time they were ashore, gingerly making their way across a field which had its share of cow pats — and cows! This then was our introduction to 75 Squadron.

Sixteen aircraft went for the Ruhrstahl steelworks at Witten on 12 December, another daylight Op by 3 Group using G-H. For once enemy fighters intercepted the Lancasters and eight did not return. No. 75 Squadron did not lose any, but Flight Lieutenant L. Hannan did collide with another aircraft, damaging the starboard aileron. However, he got his aircraft home safely. There was also another collision, witnessed by Alex Simpson:

After 'bombs gone' we maintained our easterly heading when another Lancaster overtook us on our port side, descending through our flight level, and took up a position dead ahead of us at about 200 yards.

A second Lanc also passed on our port side and took up a position on the port side of the Lanc immediately in front. Then, to our horror, the second Lanc commenced his turn to starboard — a fairly steep turn — and went straight into the Lanc in front of us.

In the collision the starboard wing came off the turning Lanc, the fuselage rolled over and on top of the other Lanc which at that moment blew up. In the next instant — and it is clearly imprinted on my mind — a completely cowled Merlin engine, with windmilling prop, was coming straight for our windscreen. I made a panic dive and do not know to this day how we missed it. I expected to feel the impact along the top of the fuselage at any second, but it missed us, yet feel certain if we'd been flying a Stirling, we would have lost our fin and rudder.

On the 16th December, we had another close call on a daylight Op on Siegen, where we dropped the squadron's second 12,000 pound bomb. The first had been dropped a couple of days previously, from my aircraft, by the CO.

On the run up to the target, the stream was very concentrated and we were on the starboard side. Suddenly, I had a premonition of danger and turned to look at my Engineer, Jack Johnstone, standing next to me, to see Jack looking directly overhead with his face as white as a sheet. Following his gaze I could see part of the bomb load of another Lancaster which was so close that I could clearly read the stencil writing on the bombs. The aircraft's nose was slightly ahead of us and slightly to starboard, but right on top of us, with a separation of no more than 15 feet!

I could not turn to port due to other aircraft. In fact, I could not apply bank to turn as we were so close I would have put my wing into him. Starboard of us was clear so the only escape route was to apply full starboard rudder, cross aileron controls and slide out from underneath him. As we straightened up, his bomb doors were closing!

Where his bombs went I do not know, for we were still sufficiently short of the target to continue our bomb run and, in fact, we were credited with an aiming point with our 12,000 pounder. Another interesting fact of this operation was that our bomb was painted yellow and two of my crew were able to watch it right to the point of impact, from 21,000 feet.

Arthur Long was the Navigator in Harry Tweed's crew and by this date they were nearing the end of their tour, which they started in September 1944. They flew minelaying sorties on 14 and 19 December as Arthur recalls:

We laid mines in the Kattegat and in the Baltic on these nights, and during our final run-ups, used radar. At the moment of release, the radar screen was photographed to provide a record of the mine locations.

Minelaying operations began with a sea-level run at zero altitude over the North Sea to keep below enemy scanners. Then up to 10,000 feet over Sweden and finally down again to 6000 feet for the actual minelaying. The pattern was repeated for the return trip.

Navigators usually had their heads down, working hard. However, on one bombing raid I was looking up front and saw an aircraft ahead blown out of the sky. I remember its Australian crew well.

Returning from another raid, a light bomb was discovered rolling around in the bomb bay. It had apparently frozen to the hooks during our bomb run over the target and later fallen away when descending to a lower altitude. We jettisoned it over the sea.

After a raid-free Christmas for the squadron, a maximum effort for a raid on Cologne was switched to an attack on Rheydt on 27 December. Inexperienced crews and those with special equipment on board were stood down, while the rest bombed the railway yards. One of the 200 Lancasters despatched failed to return — a 75 Squadron aircraft flown by Flying Officer H. Miles. Only his bomb aimer survived, as a prisoner of war. The Lancaster was seen to be hit by falling bombs and spiral earthwards. That was the final loss of the year of 1944.

Flying Officer Stan Davies had a lucky escape when he and his crew, having had their starboard outer catch fire on the way out, were unable to climb above 11,000 feet, after feathering it. They flew on, however, bombed last after cutting corners off the route, but then saw a FW190 looking them over. They fired off a Verey flare and the 190 was chased off by an American P.38 Lightning fighter. Stan says:

*W*e were just about to try a corkscrew when the other fighters turned up, but then we saw them drop their wheels and we recognised them as Lightnings. They escorted us back over France before leaving us.

However, it was an inexperienced crew which took part in a raid on Coblenz two days later. Flying Officer Dick Egglestone and his crew were on only their second operation, but they very quickly became veterans that day. Gordon Mitchell was the crew's navigator:

> **O**ur Lancaster AA-U had fallen behind the wave of bombers after one of the engines cut out over the North Sea. Instead of turning for home, our pilot and myself decided to carry on to the target, with the agreement of the rest of the crew.
>
> Unable to reach proper height and way behind the rest, we ran straight into the force of enemy AA fire. Our Lancaster was peppered by flak but somehow we managed to drop our load and limp home. We were so late back that we found we had been assumed missing.
>
> A count of the holes in the Lanc was made and 92 were discovered, yet miraculously no one in the crew had been injured. Our flight commander asked us what had possessed us to carry on with a partially crippled aircraft! At the time we were young, keen and stupid, but he was pleased to see us back. We did not take those sort of risks again.

On the night of 30/31 December four aircraft dropped mines in Heligoland Bight. One of these, captained by Flight Sergeant R. Pearson, saw a night fighter which dropped flares just half a mile from his Lancaster. His mid upper and rear gunners shot them out, and then Pearson corkscrewed his bomber into the safety of some clouds.

The New Year of 1945 dawned bright and clear. For the past few days, bad weather on the Continent had kept 2nd Tactical Air Force (TAF) aircraft on the ground, unable to help and support the hard-pressed American troops fending off Hitler's Ardennes offensive. The Luftwaffe, too, had been kept on the ground, delaying their massive air strike on 2nd TAF airfields, planned for late December. But the weather promised to clear before first light on January 1, so scores of FW190s, Me109s, Ju88s and Me262s, hit Allied airfields at dawn.

The Lancasters of 75 Squadron had hit marshalling yards after Christmas and, on the last day of 1944, had bombed the railway yards at Vohwinkel — a 3 Group raid. Strong winds had carried many of the bombs south of the aiming point, so the raid had to be repeated. Wing Commander Newton led 21 aircraft from 75 Squadron back there on 1 January, part of a force of 146 Lancasters from 3 Group. This time the raid was a success, but Wing Commander Newton's aircraft failed to return. All eight men on board were killed.

Newton had said something in the Mess the previous evening that had been recorded in the squadron's Line Book: 'If you want to do a good bombing run you don't look out, you put your head in the cockpit. And if you want a photograph, you count to 20 and then go round again and take some more. And that was in the days when flak defences were comparatively good!' That had been at 10.50pm — 24 hours later he was dead.

Over 500 bombers blasted Nuremburg on 2/3 January, which left much of the city devastated. No. 75 Squadron put up only nine aircraft, of which eight bombed. However, a couple of days later, the squadron put up 21 aircraft against Ludwigshaven — another 3 Group daylight effort against the town's rail yards. Stan Davies, a cousin of Newton, recalls that it was the heaviest flak — barrage flak — he had ever seen. His Lancaster returned with over 40 holes in it and one wing had to be changed. Flying Officer D. Sadgrove's Lancaster was hit in the starboard outer engine, and the oil feed and pneumatics were also severed. As they dropped below the formation, they were bracketed by flak and, fearing they might attract enemy

Flight Lieutenant C. M. Stevens and some of his crew. Back row, left to right: George Giles (AG), Les Hofert (FE), Les Hall (Nav); Front row, left to right: Jim Saunders (Nav), Chas Stevens.
(C. M. STEVENS)

Another long serving Lancaster was HK576, photographed here after her 63rd Op. Notice how the shape of the 'bombs' have changed after the 26th sortie.
(S. GITTINGS)

The ground crew of 'M' — Mike (NE181) 'The Captain's Fancy'. The craft completed its 101st mission on 5 January 1945. Jack Bailey, in foreground, who usually flew 'Mike', flew it on its 100th sortie but Alex Simpson flew the 101st. Left to right: Sgt Grantham, LAC F. Woolterton, LAC Taylor, LAC Thompson, SL Bailey, unknown. (RNZAF)

fighters, fired off 'reds' to call in RAF fighters to help them. But none seemed to notice their plight. Nevertheless, they got home safely.

Alex Simpson recalls an important event at this time:

> **S**quadron Leader Jack Bailey, 'C' Flight Commander, usually flew Lanc NE181 'M' for Mike — named 'The Captain's Fancy', which was a dog of an aircraft and I guess understandably so, as it was approaching its 100th operation. When the time came, Jack asked me if I would take 'Mike' to Ludwigshaven on the 5th — the day after my 21st birthday. I protested for I had a very good aircraft of my own, and I had flown 'Mike' previously — in December.
>
> It became apparent that Jack was superstitious about flying 'Mike' on its 100th, so in the end I agreed. After the operation, we did an in-depth study of the aircraft's log book and associated paper work and found to Jack's geat surprise that he had already done the 100th — I had in fact done the 101st!
>
> Jack and I tried very hard through Bill Jordan, the NZ High Commissioner in the UK, to get permission to fly JN-M out of New Zealand on a flag-waving War Bonds tour, as it was then the first NZ aircraft to reach 100 operations, but we never got approval. I delivered 'Mike' to Waterbeach on 17th February, and it was later struck off charge on 30th September 1947.
>
> My usual aircraft was HK600 'K', in which we did 21 operations. I recall this was due for a service and on the day prior to this, I spotted a semi-articulated low-loader trailer arrive, with eight brand new, beautiful, Rotol propellers. That evening I made a beeline for Flight Lieutenant Rose, the Engineering Officer, whom I knew reasonably well and proceeded to state my need for a set of these props. Well, after a lot of beer, 48 hours later 'K' King rolled out of the hangar — 10th January — with four new paddle blade props. And did it perform! It immediately became the best aircraft on the squadron.

◇ ◇ ◇

Following the death in action of Wing Commander Newton, the new CO arrived a few days later. Newly promoted Wing Commander Cyril Henry Baigent DFC and bar arrived just days before his 22nd birthday. Known to everyone as 'Mac' (or 'Baige'), Cyril Baigent came from Ashburton, having joined the RNZAF in March 1941. His first operational squadron had been No. 15, which he joined in 1942. He had completed his first tour of 32 Ops by November. A year later he went to 115 Squadron, beginning his second tour with six straight trips to Berlin, followed by two more to the Big City after raids to Brunswick and Magdeburg. He completed his second tour in November 1944, having now completed 55 Ops, and with the DFC and bar, was posted to 3 Group HQ. Then came the command of 75 New Zealand Squadron.

Mac Baigent's first Op with his new command came on 13 January — a daylight show by 3 Group to the railway yards of Saarbrucken. Baigent kept a diary of his sorties, and he recorded:

> **M**y first operation as Wing Commander and also a follower on a G-H led daylight attack. Formed up on S/L Rodgers and kept pretty good formation right to the target. Really bang-on sight, all the Lancasters in formation. We bombed the snow covered marshalling yards and saw a few cookies hit the lines. Flak was nil apart from one burst reported by the rear gunner! The crew were very scratch, including the new signals leader. Our bombs hung up and W/T was u/s. We called up Bob and followed him over rolling clouds to Portreath. Made a poor landing but a good one at base next day.

Seventeen Lancs bombed Wanne-Eickel's benzol plant on 16/17 January, yet another

3 Group effort. Flight Lieutenant T. Blewett crashed at Wood Ditton, Suffolk, on his return and was killed. His bomb aimer also died while the navigator succumbed to his injuries two days later. There was nearly a week of inactivity because of weather, but finally on the 22/23 January 1, 3 and 8 Groups sent 286 Lancasters and 16 Mosquitoes to Duisburg. The target was another benzol plant in the Bruckhausen district.

Cologne and Krefeld were bombed at the end of the month, then Munchen-Gladbach on 1 February. Bad weather reduced flying for several days in early February, but then came the night of 13/14 February and the attack on Dresden. A good deal has been written about the Dresden Raid, but this is not the place to discuss its pros and cons. Suffice it to say that 75 Squadron put up 20 of the 796 Lancasters and nine Mossies that set out to make the attack.

The raid was part of 'Operation Thunderclap', an operation designed to cause confusion to the hard-pressed German war-machine at an appropriate moment. By this mid-February date, with the Russians pressing hard from the east, and the Allied armies doggedly advancing from the west, this seemed the moment. Berlin, Leipzig, Chemnitz and Dresden were all likely targets, being close to the Russian advance, with masses of troops and refugees making their way through these towns. The US 8th Air Force had been due to hit Dresden in daylight during 13 February, but the weather prevented it, so the RAF made the attack that night. At the time, and before any controversy about such a raid being carried out arose, Cyril Baigent noted in his diary:

> Rather a long trip, so thought I had better go! Flew F/L Banks and crew on their first Op which probably rather shook them. Set course no trouble and apart from a little flak in the Frankfurt area, the trip to the target was fairly quiet. From some distance we could see the glow from earlier attacks on Dresden and Leipzig. A steady run in, in formation with another Lanc, and dropped right in the middle of large fires, on top of a red TI. After leaving the target, we looked back and saw clouds of smoke billowing up to 16–17,000 feet. A spot of flak at Chemnitz and Brux but we had a fairly quiet trip home. Banks flew from Strasbourg. I took over and made a reasonable landing.

Tiny Humphries was also on the Dresden raid:

> Probably our most spectacular trip. The fires were tremendous. We were not the first ones over, the place being well alight by the time we got there. Fred Chambers, our WOP, had finished his tour by that time and we had a spare WOP flying with us. You could actually see the fires from the burning city over 160 miles away. I remember the skipper saying he could see it and I said he couldn't as it was so far, but he could. Later we were flying in smoke over the city when at 17,000 feet and we could actually smell the smoke! It was probably the most awe-inspriing sight I'd ever seen.

Gordon Mitchell:

> I remember Dresden, where one of the most devastating raids in the war took place, for two reasons. First, our main navigation aid packed up when crossing the English coast, and while navigating on dead reckoning, flew over one of the heavily defended areas of Germany. Sharp evasive action resulted, and equipment in the aircraft became dislodged, but it gave us a reliable ground fix to carry on to the target.
>
> Secondly, the raid, as we now realise, was one of the most horrifying incidents of WW2, when something like 50,000 people may have died.

No. 5 Group had led the raid, and marked and bombed accurately, setting the town on fire. Something like 1500 tons of bombs and 1200 tons of incendiaries fell on Dresden that night. Then the Americans attacked the next day, their Mustang escort also strafing anything they saw on the surrounding roads.

Chemnitz was attacked the next night, 75 Squadron putting up 21 of its aircraft and losing one — Flight Lieutenant G. S. Davies. He remembers:

> We suddenly had a fire in the wing, probably an oil line. I couldn't feather the engine so it was time to go before the wing burnt through. The routine was that everyone should go out through the front hatch so I could count them out. One went out the back and I had to send Tommy White (WOP) back to check. Later in our POW camp — we all got out — I 'mentioned' this to the chap concerned! Only my bomb aimer, Jack Chalmers, didn't make it home. He was killed when the train in which we were travelling was strafed by RAF fighters.

With the Allied armies in the west fast approaching the Rhine — Germany's natural border — Bomber Command switched some of its effort to bombing areas close to the front-line in preparation for the eventual Rhine crossing. No. 75 Squadron attacked Wesel on 16, 18 and 19 February, and Dortmund on 20/21 February. Then came Gelsenkirchen, Kamen, Dortmund again, and back to Gelsenkirchen. Time was fast running out for the Third Reich.

19

Victory in Europe

FEBRUARY — MAY 1945

A daylight raid on Osterfeld by 21 of the squadron's aircraft took place on 22 February, flak trying desperately to inflict hurt and injury. Flight Sergeant T. Cox had his starboard inner hit by flak, but the flames were put out by cutting the petrol and using the extinguisher. Flying Officer H. Russell's bomber was also hit, the prop on the port inner and damage to the leading edge of the wing between his two starboard engines giving some moments of concern. Flight Lieutenant Doug Sadgrove had his port outer hit on the bomb run but he continued on, while Warrant Officer E. Ohlson also had an engine knocked out. Flight Lieutenant K. Jones lost an engine on the way out and had to abort.

On 25 February, 18 Lancasters of 75 went to Kamen, losing Flight Sergeant L. Klitscher, who was seen heading away from the stream with his port inner engine feathered after being hit by flak northwest of Wesel. They became POWs.

Flight Lieutenant Sadgrove wasn't having too much success of late, and it didn't improve on 27 February following take-off for Gelsenkirchen. The pipe into the undercarriage selector blew out after becoming airborne, rendering all hydraulics u/s. The bomb doors could not be opened to jettison the load so he had to land with them aboard. He succeeded.

March 1945 began with another daylight on the oil plant at Kamen by 3 Group, followed the next day by a daylight raid on Cologne. This was hit in two waves, 75 being part of the second, although few of the second wave bombed because the G-H station in England was not working properly.

Norman Waite was a qualified pilot but, due to a shortage of Flight Engineers at Advanced Flying Unit (AFU) he had been given a six-week engineers' course then crewed up with men who had completed their Operational Training Unit (OTU). So on 75 he was able to double as second pilot and engineer. He remembers:

> For 17 of our operations we flew JN-Z. The first, when it was new, was a trip to Cologne when it only had 4½ hours delivery time logged. However, we returned with two of our outboard motors u/s due to flak and its fuselage and wings looking like a pepper-pot!
>
> Flak was usually heavy over the Ruhr. I also remember one night raid when a FW190 crossed above us. If it had been three feet lower it would have been curtains for us.
>
> Wing Commander Baigent was our CO during our tour and he always chose to fly on the 'dicey' trips. I expect he, like us, was always happy to see Ely Cathedral, which was just a few minutes flying time from our base.

In the first ten days of March, the squadron participated in nine raids. Then on 11 March it went to Essen, as Duncan Stevenson remembers:

> **O**n this day 75 Squadron led a force of over 1000 four-engined bombers, each carrying 10,000 to 12,000 pounds of bombs on this daylight raid. No. 3 Group, of approximately 600 aircraft, flew in formation — No. 5 Group flew in a gaggle! All the aircraft passed through the target area in 40 minutes. The next day 75 led a daylight raid on Dortmund — 1108 aircraft, one of the biggest force of bombers ever, by any air force.

Richard Woodhouse, a navigator from Auckland, recalls the daylights:

> **S**eventy-five flew, not in a loose gaggle but in good formation, vics [V-shaped formations] of three with the fourth aircraft behind and slightly lower. Building up to 16 or more it took quite a lot of concentration to stay together. It usually took the best part of an hour for the whole squadron to form up, flying a triangular course over East Anglia before heading out. We knew we had fighter escort but being able to clearly see what went on around us, after our night Ops, was not always the best option. For sitting in the Lanc at 20,000 feet, blue sky and bright winter sunshine, the Lanc to starboard and slightly ahead, gently rising and falling as though on a sea, wisps of cloud below and just ahead the Rhine twisting its way through the land like a silver snake; then looking towards the Ruhr and the barrage of flak and thinking: 'God, do we have to fly through that!'

The squadron's first loss for some time occurred on 14 March when 20 aircraft went for Heinrich-Hutte, a benzol plant near Bochum. Flight Lieutenant E. G. Parsons and his crew were seen to be hit in the port inner engine on the run-in, then the whole wing caught fire. Before anyone could bale out, the wing broke off and the Lanc went spinning in.

Targets were still mainly oil plants and railway centres, two more benzol installations being attacked on 17 and 18 March. Then came Hamm marshalling yards on the 20th, followed the next day by an attack on the Munster Viaduct. No. 3 Group put up 160 Lancasters to hit the railway yards and nearby railway viaduct, but three Lancasters — all from 75 Squadron — failed to return. Norman Waite:

> **D**ue to bad planning, two streams of bombers arrived over Munster simultaneously, at different heights and courses. Several aircraft in our stream were struck by bombs from above.

Tiny Humphries was in one of the aircraft hit:

> **T**his would probably have been our last raid. We had already completed our allotted 30, but at that stage of the war the recognised tour seemed to vary a bit from week to week — 30 to 35 — but we were looking forward to finishing our tour.
>
> On this daylight raid to Munster things went reasonably well until we were almost coming up to the target, flying in formation. But something went wrong with the leading aircraft and we overshot the turning point and flew on for quite some distance. Then we turned onto the target but now on the wrong heading and, in fact, under-flew another squadron bombing from above. At that stage the flak was very, very heavy. We didn't get hit from falling bombs, although there were bombs falling all around us. We were hit by flak, in one engine, which went on fire and another engine got hit on the other side, so things weren't too good at this stage!
>
> The aircraft was now burning and we were given the order to bale out. Unfortunately, the bomb aimer couldn't open the escape hatch in the nose, so we had a problem

there. I think our mid-upper was hit badly because we could hear him screaming with pain. Nobody, except possibly the rear gunner, actually baled out.

I learned after I returned from Germany that we went into a spin and a wing came off, then 'chutes appeared. This would fit in with my own recollections. I had managed to get my 'chute on and was standing, waiting to go down out of the front of the aircraft, when we went into the spin. The last thing I remember was my feet leaving the floor. I blacked out and when I came to I was falling free and didn't need to be told twice to pull the ripcord!

I was captured almost immediately by some school kids who were waiting to receive us. I made a poor landing, twisting an ankle, so I couldn't have gone far anyway. I was taken into an army barracks and held there overnight. There was another raid that night and we were pushed into an air-raid shelter and got severely abused by some civilians, and remember my backside being well-kicked by one of them.

Later I was taken to see Mac, our rear gunner. He was lying on a bunk and had been rather severely burnt around the face and hands. I made myself understood by the Germans to send him to hospital, which they did, where his burns were treated. The hospital was over-run by the Allies within about a week. Maurice Fell, our engineer, came out too but he had a very severe jagged cut on his face, running almost from one ear to the point of his chin. I was to meet up with him later in a camp in Munster.

The pilot, Jack Plummer DFC, on his 29th Op, was killed, as were the bomb aimer and mid-upper. Tiny Humphries was in fact on his 32nd Op. He was awarded the DFM. The crew of Flying Officer D. Barr's aircraft were all killed, while Flying Officer A. E. Brown and his bomb aimer were killed, the rest of the crew taken prisoner. Whether the latter two Lancasters were hit by bombs is uncertain, but it seems likely. As it turned out, these were to be the last operational losses sustained by 75 Squadron in the war, although not the last operational casualties.

The Rhine was now about to be crossed, the operation finally taking place on 24 March. One of the towns just across the river — Wessel — had been bombed by 75 a couple of weeks earlier, and the town was bombed yet again prior to the crossings. Duncan Stevenson remembers:

> Just before Field Marshall Montgomery crossed the Rhine, 3 Group — with 75 Squadron leading! — was called to G-H bomb Wesel from low level in daylight. This was so devastating and effective that British troops were unable to pass through the town and had to outskirt it. The AOC of 3 Group noticed that our crew was not on this raid. Wing Commander Baigent was called down to Group HQ to explain, as by now, we were the Master Bomber Crew of the Group, having dropped eight practice bombs on G-H, from 20,000 feet with an average error of 28 yards! We had also been the Master Bomber Crew on Wellington OTU with an average error of 52 yards and again on HCU [Homing Comparator Unit] on Lancasters.

◇ ◇ ◇

April opened slowly for 75, but they attacked the Leuna Works at Merseburg on the 4th, the first sortie since the Rhine. The Lancaster flown by Flying Officer J. Wood was hit by flak and set on fire. Both Wood and his bomb aimer, Flight Sergeant N. Hooper, were burned putting out the fire, and the engineer, fell out through the under turret gun hatch, but he had on his parachute and later returned to the squadron.

At this time, Brian Waugh, second pilot to Flying Officer Trevethen, had just become operational. Brian had been an RAF Halton Apprentice in 1938, but like so many of these 'Trenchard Brats' he eventually became aircrew and pilot. He flew his first raid with Trevethen, with the CO, on 4 April and then Trevethen took them to Kiel on 9 April to bomb the Howaldt Works. Brian was injured in a plane crash in 1967, in New Zealand, and his injuries prevented him flying again. Before he died, he had begun to write his story. His son, the Reverend Richard Waugh, sent the following extract for this history:

> We flew a few Operations before the war ended. Sorties over Bremen in a rare daylight raid; night raids on Leipzig, to the Leuna Oil refinery, and a memorable night attack along with 1000 Lancaster and Halifax bombers to Kiel, where we learned later the German pocket battleship *Admiral Scheer* had been sunk. This was on the night of 9th April, 1945, and I like to think that it was one of our block busters that turned the battleship upside down as later reconniassance photos proved.
>
> 'Watch that bloody searchlight to port!', the rear gunner shouted. Then it swung towards us, searching all the time and three more got us in their beams. Absolutely blinded — 'Dive the bastard!' Two hundred and fifty miles an hour indicated air speed. It is a wonder the wings did not come off! Thousands of feet lost, from 19,000 to 12,000 feet, and tremendous G-forces as we pulled out of that dive. Our thermos flasks floated in mid-air — out of that blinding light to dear, dark safety.
>
> The flak and flaming onions that appeared so slowly, mesmerised one and you stared in complete astonishment as the shell went screaming by, to explode in orange brilliance; better than a Brocks display.

The *Admiral Scheer* had indeed been sunk in this attack, and two other capital ships, the *Admiral Hipper* and the *Emden* were both badly damaged. The U-boat pens, too, had been badly hit.

Brian had heard so much of New Zealand from the New Zealanders on 75 that after the war he took his young bride and emigrated. He became one of New Zealand's most experienced air charter pilots, and had amassed over 7000 flying hours before his final crash.

Another period of non-Ops followed, but 21 aircraft attacked Kiel on 13/14 April. Warrant Officer Neville Staples, a navigator, remembers Kiel:

> Upon our return to Mepal, our Lancaster, AA-R, skippered by Flight Sergeant Evenden, had its undercarriage collapse. The date was Friday the 13th April!! I had a tooth knocked out!

The next day 75 went to Potsdam, the first time Bomber Command had flown their four-engined bomber to the Berlin area since March 1944. Most of the route was now over Allied-occupied territory, which cut the losses to just one Lancaster out of the 500 which took part. It was lost to a night fighter, while a 75 Lancaster was also attacked by two night fighters. Flying Officer A. Baynes' machine was damaged and his Flight Engineer killed. Four days later, 21 aircraft took off for a daylight raid on Heligoland.

Regensburg was the target for 20 March, 100 3 Group Lancasters going for this distant target's oil installations. Twenty-eight of these came from 75, but this was the last raid against German oil, since the major effort to hit German's oil production had begun shortly after D-Day. Then two days later, 21 Lancasters went for Bremen, in preparation for Montgomery's 300 Corps assault on the town. In all, 767 Lancasters were supposed to bomb but cloud and smoke hampered the attack, so the Master Bomber was forced to call off the raid after 195 aircraft had bombed. None of 1 or 5 Group's aircraft dropped a bomb. Baigent went, his diary noting that it was his 69th operation, but actually it was his 70th.

Several Lancasters were hit by flak, with 19 of the squadrons 21 being damaged. One of the damaged Lancasters brought back the body of its dead Flight Engineer, Sergeant R. Clarke — 75's last fatal casualty of the war.

The squadron's last operational war sorties were flown on 24 April, when 21 aircraft joined 89 other RAF Lancasters to attack the railway yards at Bad Oldesloe, midway between Hamburg and Lubeck. None of the Lancasters were lost.

◇ ◇ ◇

Everyone had the feeling that the war would soon be over, but none guessed that the raid on the 24th had been their last. Although no Ops were flown for the next four days, there then came a series of flights which, while not warlike, were important. And as far as 75 were concerned, it was just another job to do, before getting back to Germany.

A large area of western Holland was still in German hands, but with few supplies of food getting through, the population was in danger of starving. To help out, a truce was organised with the local German commander to allow the RAF to fly over and drop food stuffs for the Dutch civilians. It was called 'Operation Manna'.

Over the following weeks prior to the final surrender of the Germans, nearly 3000 RAF sorties were flown, with 75 flying its share. Occasionally the aircraft came under fire from hostile batteries or small arms fire from enemy troops, but in the main the flights went unmolested. However, they were not allowed as operations in the normal way, counting only as one-third of a sortie. So a crew had to fly three to qualify for one Op on their tour total, as Wing Commander Baigent wrote in his diary:

> **A**n Aerodrome near the Hague. My last three trips were all on food dropping missions to the Dutch. Quite a change from bombing but the reception we got from the people really made it worth while. On the first one a few aircraft were hit by small arms fire but none on the following Ops. Jerry chose the route and we went at 1500 feet, dropping down to 500 feet to release bags of choc, flour, meat, salt, etc. We dropped on a white cross on the aerodrome. The Dutch waved at us with flags, sheets and anything they could lay hands on. It was jolly good fun, low flying over the Hague and the sea! The trips only counted as a third, so did three.

The squadron's first supply trip was flown by nine Lancasters on 29 April to the Delft area. The next day, 21 went to Rotterdam, and 21 back to Delft on 1 and 2 May. Drops to the Hague and to Delft came on 3 and 4 May. Neville Staples flew on some of them:

> **S**ome two years later I was talking of this Operation to a group of workmates over a morning tea break when I was intercepted by a young man who had recently joined the firm's employ. He clasped my hands and shook them vigorously and, with tears in his eyes, told me that he and his family had helped to retrieve the food from the golf course where we had dropped it. His family had emigrated to New Zealand a few months earlier and by coincidence we were both working together. Quite a moving experience which I still remember with pride and humility.

Then it was VE Day. Mepal staged a Station parade to celebrate the victory and all personnel not required for specific duties were allowed to stand down. However, eight aircraft flew over to Rotterdam to drop further supplies, and the following day came the first landing in France by a 75 Squadron aircraft. Ten Lancasters flew to

Juvincourt to evacuate ex-prisoners of war. This most pleasant duty was carried out a number of times during the month, and a figure of 2219 former guests of the Germans has been recorded as being flown home by the squadron by 24 May.

Another event in this momentous month was 'Operation Baedeker', in which ground personnel, including men and women from the Station and Group HQ, were flown to Germany so they could view from the air the damage inflicted upon towns and cities. Ralph Jeffrey was a wireless operator with 75 during the last months of the war, in Flying Officer Bob Elliott's crew. He recalls these activities at the war's end:

> On Manna sorties we aircrew loaded up the bomb racks with sacks, boxes, etc. We then added personally bars of chocolate, bags of sweets, and so on. The route was prescribed by the German High Command in Holland and no deviations or 'second attempts' were allowed. The drop zone was a field on the outskirts of the Hague and aircraft went in almost nose to tail. People could be seen running about in the field, retrieving packages, while other supplies were falling all around them.
>
> At the war's end, we flew press photographers, journalists, senior officers on very low level tours of the Ruhr Valley targets — Aachen, Munchen-Gladbach, Dortmund, Cologne, stand out as the highlights of one such trip. We also took in Hamburg and Berlin on subsequent trips, which we entitled 'Operation Cook's Tour' instead of Baedeker. Average flying heights were 200 to 300 feet!
>
> On VE Day aircrew were too busy with these operations to be involved in any celebrations. We also flew groups of civilians to Brussels, presumably Government-in-Exile personnel, returning loaded with ex-prisoners of war from Juvincourt.

Suddenly reaction set in. The war was finally over and several men recall the feeling of something of a vacuum created by the ending of operational activities which had dominated their lives for so long. At first it was a little depressing. The only light in the tunnel was the possibility that the squadron might go to the Far East, the war with Japan not yet won.

Then this possibility seemed remote when in June came the announcement that most of the New Zealand personnel were to be repatriated home. Ralph Jeffrey recalls what happened next:

> There was a great party in both Officer's and Sergeant's Messes as a prelude to embussing down to the nearby railway station at March, in Cambridge. When the special train pulled in, all the New Zealand lads got on board, leaving the UK chaps on the platform, eventually to be re-directed to other duties and stations, etc. During the long pause before the train pulled out, taking our New Zealand comrades out of our lives, emotions were at breaking point. A speech should have been made — perhaps no one could find the words. Suddenly a chant was started by a small group, which grew and grew to a roar which rattled the windows — 'not 71...not 72...Not 73...NOT 74...BUT 75!!!'

20

No. 75 Squadron RNZAF
JUNE 1945 — 1953

Number 75 (New Zealand) Squadron had certainly earned its place as one of Bomber Command's top squadrons during World War Two. Its operational performance was impressive in terms of raids carried out:

Aircraft	Bombing	Minelaying	Leaflet	Recce	
Wellington	291	24	4	1	
Stirling	103	107	—	—	
Lancaster	190	18	1	—	
Totals	584	149	5	1	(739)

As far as sorties and losses were concerned, both (unfortunately) were also impressive:

Aircraft	Sorties	Losses	Percentage
Wellingtons	2540	74	2.9
Stirlings	1736	72	4.1
Lancasters	3741	47	1.3
Totals	8017	193	2.4

The squadron had carried out the fourth highest number of bombing raids in Bomber Command, had flown the most sorties of any 3 Group squadron, and of any (heavy) squadron in Bomber Command! Tonnage dropped was the third largest in the Command — some 21,600 tons — and it had in addition layed 2344 sea mines, the second highest in the Command. With 193 aircraft lost in action, the squadron suffered the second highest casualty rate. (115 Squadron suffered the heaviest with 208 losses.)

No. 75 Squadron had been the only 'New Zealand' heavy bomber squadron in the RAF during the war, with many New Zealanders among its air and ground crews. Other New Zealanders had flown just as gallantly with other RAF units. In addressing them all, Sir Arthur Harris wrote, to the Air Officer Commanding RNZAF, London, at the war's end:

> Please convey to all the New Zealand personnel who have served or are serving in Bomber Command my great appreciation of their loyal co-operation and gallant and

determined contribution to the defeat of Germany and the freedom of mankind. To all New Zealand aircrews and to all ground staff personnel, their British cousins give heart felt thanks. We in Bomber Command are proud indeed of the great record of service of the New Zealand crews, who were second to none in courage and efficiency.

◇ ◇ ◇

The war with Germany may have been over, but Japan had still to be defeated. By mid-1945, the Americans and their Pacific Allies were closing in on Japan and the RAF were beginning to prepare to support them. Bomber Command was already organising 'Tiger Force' with which to bomb the Japanese mainland, and 75 Squadron was scheduled to be part of this force. In the meantime, new aircraft were being assigned to the squadron — the Avro Lincoln.

To this end, the squadron at last left RAF Mepal, moving to RAF Spilsby, Lincolnshire, in July 1945, and coming under the command of No. 5 Group. The squadron was to have an establishment of 24 Lincoln IIs in two Flights. The letters 'AA' were to remain, but the former 'C' Flight's JN was dropped. Individual aircraft letters would be 'A' to 'Z', omitting 'I' and 'O'. Duncan Stevenson was still on the squadron and remembers:

The majority of aircrew arrived from RAF Mepal by coach on Saturday 21st July. The squadron was now 100 per cent New Zealand aircrew, regretfully all the very experienced and professional English aircrew were left at Mepal, where No. 44 Rhodesian Squadron were moving in from Spilsby, as 44 was not going to the Far East and were about to be disbanded.

No. 75 Squadron took over 24 'very tired' and not very well maintained Lancasters from 44 Squadron and the other resident squadron at Spilsby. A few of the aircraft had flown less than 2000 hours while the majority had flown nearly 1000; two had already flown 1200 and one nearly 1400 hours! This age of aircraft was to show up in the serviceability which was a problem on the intensive 'Tiger Force' training. The aircraft 75 had left behind, nearly all were below 400 hours, with many less than 200.

Our task now was to have 30 crews fully trained, both flying and ground subjects, fully kitted out for the tropics and converted onto Avro Lincoln IIs with Merlin 68 engines, within 12 weeks. The squadron was very lucky in that most of the crews had pilots, navigators, bomb aimers and wireless operators who had only recently come off war-time opertions. It was decided to concentrate on the less experienced crews.

On Monday 23rd July, everyone was busy completing arrival procedures and as much as possible en-bloc. Flying training began on the 24th with the usual local familiarisation, fighter affiliation, cross-country navigation and bombing exercises. Later, dual take-offs (ie, two aircraft abreast, rolling down the runway) and stream landings were practised at the few opportunities when there were sufficient aircraft available for rapid take-offs and which returned together for a stream landing. Frequently we had 20 aircraft on the runway after such a landing.

We were told that in the Far East we were to operate mainly at night from a three-mile strip on Okinawa. The RAF squadrons were all to be dispersed along one side of the runway and the USAAF B29 Super Fortresses, which would be operating by day, were to be dispersed along the other side. Both aircraft types were to carry 20,000 pounds of bombs and, in the case of the Lincolns, operate between 25 and 30,000 feet while the B29s were expected to be from 30 to 35,000.

All flying ceased after VJ-Day — 14th August — and for a fortnight we waited until the 'powers that be' decided that we could be usefully employed on the squadron until shipping became available for the squadron to be repatriated to New Zealand and demobbed.

The Avro Lincoln with which the squadron was equipped at the end of the war. (RNZAF)

Wing Commander C. H. Baigent DSO DFC and bar, the last wartime CO of 75 Squadron who commanded again 1947–50. With him is the adjutant in 1944–45, F/L Paul Bewsher. (RNZAF)

Mosquito aircraft of 75 Squadron taxi through 14 Squadron's hard stand at Ohakea on their way to the 1952 exercise 'Hardtack'. Note 75 Squadron flag on the leading Mossie. On the last aircraft flies the upside-down flag of 14 Sqn! (RNZAF)

In early September the squadron was used on 'Exercise Exodus' — ie, flying British troops back from Italy on leave and repatriation. The main pick up points were Bari, Foggia and Naples. Our commitment was 20 Lancasters by the international route, flying at a height of 7 to 8000 feet for the seven to eight-hour trip. There were normally about 500 aircraft on the operation, each picking up 20 men and their kit. This meant that the aircraft flew out one day and returned the next, after a night stop. Frequently there were not enough troops for all the aircraft, which meant another night stop over.

The first Lincoln — 'AA-N' — arrived on 12th September; 'AA-U' on the 18th and 'AA-A' on the 20th. Although Lincoln bombers in various forms had been around for 12 months, we did not receive any pilot's or handling notes; only one typed sheet with a few basic facts, such as wing span, length, weight, quantity of fuel, boost and recommended cruising RPM. Nothing on take-off speeds with various loadings, stalling speeds, approach speeds or landing speeds, all of which had to be tried tested, compared and compiled for the conversion of other crews.

Allan Candish was also on the squadron when it converted to Lincolns:

Seventy-five moved to Spilsby in July and all RAF squadrons were canvassed for serving New Zealand volunteers to go on 75, as it had been promised by the RAF for service in the Far East. The New Zealanders in my crew, of which I was the navigator, applied for the transfer. We set about doing navigational exercises without the use of the usual radar which we were told was not available where we would be going.

We had six-man crews, one air gunner having been dropped and all crew personnel were New Zealanders. Flight engineers generally were New Zealand pilots who had arrived in Britain with no job to do and they spent time on Air Traffic Control duties before being posted to where there were openings, such as those provided by 75 Squadron.

Cyril Baigent was our CO and I recall the Wednesday afternoon cross-country runs he made us go on. As a good number of the men showed up in shorts with some reluctance, he reminded us the fitter we were, the more beer we could drink!

There was also the occasion when the station ran out of beer — a serious business. Mac Baigent got on the phone to some pal in Whitehall and as a result, a Lancaster took off for London about 10am with some ground staff aboard and returned about 2pm with enough kegs of beer to keep the station going until rations arrived.

We were not allowed to use Gee for any navigation as we were told it could not be used where we were going, and we also had a rest camp at Ingoldmels on the Lincolnshire coast, where we lived under canvas. We had been issued khaki shorts, socks and shirts, and we regarded the camp as a bit of a joke (except when it rained) but it provided an opportunity to don our khaki.

Duncan Stevenson also remembers the beer and that, after further enquiries, an aircraft was despatched to Mepal, when it was discovered they had at least three kilderkins (an 18-gallon barrel) more than their weekly needs. A weekly liaison flight was quickly authorised!

With the ending of war with Japan, Tiger Force and then 75 Squadron were disbanded. This occurred on 15 October 1945 at Spilsby, but not before the squadron flew one sortie — a farewell fly past and escort to the Royal Mail Line ship *Andes*, which sailed from Southampton in September. On board the ship were 1500 RNZAF officers and men, mostly aircrew, who were going home. Its last CO, Mac Baigent, had been awarded the DSO in July and was at the disbandment ceremony. He had no way of knowing that it would not be long before he was in command of 75 once again.

164

◇ ◇ ◇

In 1946, New Zealand was still a part of the British Empire and there was no reason to believe things would not continue as before. With peacetime aims, it was unclear how any of the air forces would proceed but in New Zealand it was decided to acquire, certainly as an interim measure, a force of 80 DeHavilland Mosquito fighter bombers — the famed 'Wooden Wonder'. Initially, it was planned to have three squadrons of 'Mossies' but in the event only one was formed.

At this early stage of the post-war period, the exploits of 75 Squadron were beginning to be even better known than they had been during the war. Its record was impressive, and being the only heavy bomber squadron the New Zealanders had, even though officially it was an RAF squadron, counted for much. The RAF, too, had been impressed by the squadron's fine achievements; so much so, that on 11 October 1946, it was announced that the British Air Ministry had consented to 75 Squadron RAF being given to the RNZAF to commemorate its remarkable work during the war. Thus the number was passed to the RNZAF. No longer was it possible for there to be a 75 Squadron within the Royal Air Force. This was a unique gesture and one greatly appreciated by the RNZAF.

To accommodate the number, No.2 (Bomber Reconnaissance) Squadron, based at Ohakea, New Zealand, became No. 75 Squadron RNZAF. Its first commanding officer was Wing Commander J. E. Watts AFC, his first task being to convert pilots and navigators to Mosquito aircraft and then to arrange the ferrying of the new aircraft to New Zealand.

The first four machines, however, were surplus Australian aircraft, with dual controls, delivered in November. The first four RAF Mosquitos were flown out from England by RAF crews in January 1947, and in the same month, the first 75 crews departed to England to collect the first of the next batch. The first New Zealand crew left on the return trip on 12 March, the pilot being none other than Squadron Leader C. H. Baigent DSO DFC and bar, in TE739, with Flight Lieutenant D. B. Sisley as navigator. Baige had dropped a rank since the end of the war, which was normal practice. With Warrant Officer P. F. Prichard and Master Navigator F. Hazel in the other aircraft (TE765) the trip, which went via Singapore and Sydney, took them 17 days. By the end of the year, 54 Mosquitos had been ferried out while four more dual-controlled machines had arrived from Australia. It took until December 1948 for all the aircraft to arrive, the last being RF595 flown by Flying Officer Connors.

Unfortunately, these flights were not made without casualties. One was lost in March 1947 during a tropical storm in the Gulf of Carpentaria; another crashed at Darwin in August, although the RAF pilot and New Zealand navigator survived. Also in August, another went missing between Mauipur and Santa Cruz in bad weather, while in November another aircraft was destroyed in an accident at Rangoon, although again the crew survived. In all, 76 of the original 80 Mosquitoes arrived, Baigent having made three trips in all.

The 'new' squadron settled down to conversion and training routines, the unit now having seven Mark VI fighter-bomber Mossies and two Mark 43 dual control models. The rest of the aeroplanes went into storage.

Baigent had taken over command in April 1947 and proved just as great a CO as he had been at Mepal. In the New Year's Honours List for 1948 he received the AFC, another going to Flight Lieutenant T. A. M. Morgan. Commendations for Valuable Service in the Air went to Flying Officer J. D. Garnett and Warrant Officer Hazel. Jack Garnett had been Baigent's navigator on his second trip, Morgan his navigator on the third, which was also Morgan's third trip.

Over the next couple of years the squadron, now fully operational, extended its area of operations to the Chatham Islands and the Kermadec Group, and to Fiji with deployments in 1950. There was one fatal crash — Flight Lieutenant G. R. Simich DFC, the 'B' Flight Commander, who had been with 75 Squadron back in 1941, and his navigator Flight Sergeant V. H. Baird, crashed in NZ2330 one mile south of Himatangi Beach on 27 August 1948. Nelson Bright was on the squadron and recalls:

> *A*bout a week after I arrived Ron Simich was working up a summer aerobatic display for a show and crashed. Our Station Commander was the famous A. E. Clouston DSO DFC AFC, and when he heard of the crash came racing down to the airfield, saying: 'Give me an aeroplane'. He didn't know how to start it up but somebody got it going for him, took off, turned and flew back across the airfield doing slow rolls at about 800 feet. On landing, he got out and told someone to shut the thing down, then stalked back to his office!
>
> Our OC [Officer Commanding] Flying at the time was Aubrey Breckon, a former pilot with 75 in World War Two. He hadn't flown for some time and decided he ought to be converted to the Mosquito. We used to insist on about 10 hours dual before going solo. I got him pretty well through and we were doing a final practice of single-engined circuits and landings. In those days, we'd feather one engine down completely and we were halfway down the down-wind leg with one motor feathered, wheels and flaps down, when the good engine blew a con-rod! There was sudden silence. I got pretty busy there for a while but eventually got things back on an even keel and climbed back up to 500 feet or so and did a circuit. I chatted away, telling Aubrey what I was doing and then I looked across and all I got was a glazed look, his eyeballs sticking out on stalks, and sweat dripping from the bottom of his oxygen mask! Anyway, he eventually soloed.

Baigent handed over temporary command to Nelson Bright in February 1950, Squadron Leader E. C. Gartrell OBE DFC then taking over in May. Ernie Gartrell had been a fighter pilot during the war, seeing action at Singapore, Java and Sumatra. It is certain the Mac Baigent was destined for high rank within the RNZAF but fate was against him. It was a great shock to those who had known him in 75, when news came in 1953 that he had died of cancer, at the age of 30.

By that time, 75 had changed its aircraft — and entered the jet age. In April 1952, Mosquito training ceased and word came that DeHavilland Vampire jet fighters would soon arrive. During that month the Mosquito aircraft were flown to Woodbourne and the squadron personnel attached to 14 Squadron. The Vampire was the first jet aircraft to go into service with the RNZAF, with 14 Squadron.

Vampire flight training took place at Ohakea, which 75 shared with 42 Squadron with its Dakotas and Devon aircraft. The new CO was Squadron Leader A. F. Tucker DFC, who commanded until June 1953 when Squadron Leader N. H. Bright returned to take over. Fred Tucker had also been a figher pilot in World War Two, flying Corsairs in the Pacific, and remembers:

> *I* arrived at Ohakea following a Naval Air Weapons Course with the FAA [Fleet Air Arm] in England. Fourteen Squadron had been flying Vampires and were now preparing to go to Cyprus. They left their aircraft for 75 and I arrived to take them over. So that was really the start of the 75 jet fighter squadron in NZ, 14 having really been doing the conversion onto jets.
>
> Alan Staples was my flight commander, a former wartime Mosquito intruder pilot, so we started off 'red raw'. We worked very hard with our very young pilots and as we had no dual Vampires as yet, we sent them off in Harvards to do flapless tail-high landings to prepare them for a tricycle undercarriage!
>
> We developed ranges at Ohakea and basic weaponry; we had no sights other than the

gyro — it was all 'eye-ball' stuff. We had British armament; rockets — HVARs — eight being the maximum. Drogues were being towed by Mustangs until we finally gained four T11 Vampires, which came with an RAF chap, Mike Beavis, who was to retire from the RAF as an Air Chief Marshal.

Finally, we got some of the experienced 14 Squadron pilots coming back from Cyprus posted onto the squadron. Our Wingco Flying was the famous New Zealand fighter pilot Johnny Checketts, and his press-on flying approach to fighter aviation was certainly infectious and one of the driving forces.

For Nelson Bright it was a return to 75, having flown a bomber tour with it in 1944–45. He left the airforce for a time, rejoining in 1947 and being with 75 for brief time on Mosquitoes before going to 14 Squadron. Then it was back to 75 as a flight commander, being acting CO when Baigent finally left. Now he was back as the real 'Boss'. He recalls:

*M*ost of our time was spent training but one highlight was when the Queen came out in 1953 and we provided a fly-past for the opening of Parliament.

21

Vampires and Canberras
1954 — 1969

The Vampires of 75 became increasingly associated with aerobatic displays in the latter 1950s. The first 75 Squadron formation team was formed in 1954 when a three-man flight flew for the National Aero Club Pageant at Masterton.

There are always the ever-present dangers in any form of flying and on 18 October 1954 Pilot Officer K. Milne, flying Vampire NZ5735, had his moment of drama. During a night flying exercise the aeroplane had a booster pump fail at 25,000 feet when 60 kilometres north of base, resulting in flame extinction. Milne was given the choice of baling out by the WingCo Flying, but chose to attempt a landing. With excellent Ground Control Instructions (GCI) instructions given by Flight Lieutenant Jeffs, Milne glided down, crossing the boundary fence at 130 knots to make a superb landing. He later received a commendation from the Chief of Air Staff.

Then on 17 January 1955 Flying Officer Gordon Tanner experienced an explosive decompression when the canopy of NZ5733 disintegrated during high level Battle Fours at 30,000 feet. Tanner felt a sharp blow in the chest and lost consciousness. Coming round, he turned his oxygen to 'emergency' and made a rapid descent, landing with no ill after-effects. Bits of the canopy had struck and damaged the tail otherwise the Vampire was still airworthy.

During 1955, the four-man display team and a solo display aircraft flew a show for Air Force Day. In 1958, during the RNZAF's 21st Anniversary at Ohakea on 29 March, the team really made a name for itself, using smoke for the first time. Again a solo display, flown by Flying Officer M. Turnbull, almost stole the show. (One of the many high ranking officers watching the display that day was the RNZAF's 8th Chief of Air Staff, Air Vice Marshal C. E. Kay.) No. 75 Squadron now became a display team recognised internationally. One of the best known teams consisted of Flight Lieutenant C. W. Rudd, Flying Officer T. E. Enright, Flying Officer P. M. Rhodes and Flying Officer R. D. Banks.

Two Vampires were lost and a pilot killed on 22 November 1955 during an afternoon practice interception at 20,000 feet. In the first pass, Pilot Officer H. H. V. 'Hal' Paine's aircraft (NZ5723) and Pilot Officer F. B. Brown's (NZ5756) collided. Brown parachuted safely but Paine was killed.

Then came a change of aircraft, the Vampire being replaced by the Engligh Electric Canberra bomber. Once again 75 was a bomber squadron and, as with the Mosquito, had to increase its crew to two — pilot and navigator. Now began a period of deployment to the Far East. The Commanding Officer from July 1958 was Squadron

Leader G. R. B. Highet DFC AFC, who had been a fighter pilot in World War Two, flying against the Japanese. Flying P40s in the South Pacific with 17 RNZAF Squadron, he had shot down at least three Japanese aircraft.

The decision to acquire Canberra jet bombers was made by the RNZAF and the Mark B12 went into service with 14 Squadron at Ohakea in 1958. No. 75 Squadron were to be assigned B2s and T4s, converting onto them after collection from RAF Stations Bassingbourn and Marham in England.

The change was heralded when New Zealand navigators were sent to England in November 1957 for a bombing course. Then in January 1958 pilots went to the United Kingdom and, together with the navigators, completed the 231 Operational Conversion Unit Bomber Course. Meantime, 75's CO and Navigation Leader trained in Australia before flying on to England to meet up with the crews at RAF Coningsby. On 9 July 1958, the crews flew their new aircraft — four B2s and one T4 — to Singapore. Geoff Highet remembers:

*F*ollowing Staff College in Australia, followed by a Canberra conversion course with the RAAF, I was CO designate for the first New Zealand Canberra squadron. Meantime all the other squadron aircrew were being trained in the UK; but for me, Aussie training was expedient to allow me to take my wife and children with me when I was posted to Australia.

After Canberra conversion, I moved with family to Singapore to work with 45 Squadron RAF, already operating there. Then off to the UK with my navigator, Colin Hanson. The trip was marred by a series of engine failures in RAF Hastings aircraft, but eventually we got there and set up the Squadron Base at Coningsby to await our crews and aircraft.

75's Aerobatic Team, February 1955. Left to right: F/O Dyer, F/L Beavis RAF, F/O Stew McIntyre, Sgt Shaw. Beavis later became RAF Chief of Air Staff and McIntyre, New Zealand Director of Civil Aviation. (RNZAF)

Squadron Vampires flying near Wellington in early 1955. (RNZAF)

Squadron Leader Nelson Bright, CO 1953–54, during an inspection at Ohakea by the Governor-General of New Zealand, Sir William Norrie in 1954.
(RNZAF)

Wing Commander E. C. Gartrell OBE DFC commanded the squadron between 1950–52, when a Squadron Leader.
(RNZAF)

Geoff Highet letting his bombs go on the first raid flown by the squadron during the Malayan crisis, 30 September 1959. (RNZAF)

Squadron Leader G. R. B. Highet DFC AFC, OC 75 July 1958–January 1961. (G. R. B. HIGHET)

Squadron Canberras at Tengah during operation 'Josstick', with a USAAF Canberra (B57) in the foreground. Note variety of tail colours, while the second Canberra is camouflaged. (RNZAF)

The squadron's Canberras peel-off over Tengah, 1959. Note tail marking in foreground; the Kiwi is red, New Zealand is blue. (RNZAF)

We had all sorts of problems — aircraft not up to the contracted standard, inevitable crew delays, etc. Finally, Air Marshal Willie Merton, who had been Chief of Air Staff RNZAF, was contacted (illegally) and after a few signals we really got the VIP treatment. The hired B2 Canberras were put right and we were given a tremendous send off by Gus Walker RAF, and Group Captain Dim Strong, the Station Commander. We met some tremendous people in the UK, although the squadron nearly lost its CO when the ailerons jammed on my Instrument Flight check. But the squadron, I think, acquitted itself well.

Then off we went! Over France, Idris, Cyprus, Karachi, Ceylon to Singapore. A great welcome at Singapore — quite embarrassing really as we all had dysentry picked up in Karachi! We had no incidents on the trip out, all the aircraft were in good shape and we soon got the squadron operating.

We took part in anti-terrorist activities and I think we worked in very well with the RAF and RAAF squadrons at Butterworth. I loved the command and was very sad when they promoted me to Wing Commander (and gave me a bar to my AFC), and packed me off to attend another Staff College. In the three years I commanded 75, we never broke an aircraft or lost a crew member. It was the best job of my life. I was replaced by Squadron Leader 'Mo' Moss and while he was in command, the RNZAF withdrew the Squadron to New Zealand, by which time the RNZAF had purchased its own B12 Canberras from the UK.

The squadron at Singapore was based at RAF Tengah. Soon the squadron was committed during the 'Malayan Emergency', operating alongside other Commonwealth Forces against the Communist terrorists. The squadron made its first operational strike on 30 September, when three of its aircraft dropped 18×1000 pound bombs from 12,000 feet, direct hits being claimed. The three crews — each aircraft carrying a third man for this sortie — were:

1 Squadron Leader G. R. B. Highet DFC AFC	Flight Lieutenant C. M. Hanson	Flight Lieutenant Russell	WH739
2 Flight Lieutenant I. M. Gillard	Flight Lieutenant P. Neville	Flying Officer P. Pennel	WF915
3 Flight Lieutenant D. M. Crooks	Flying Officer N. Richardson	Flying Officer D. McMahon	WJ988

The squadron's second 'Op' came on 14 November when four Canberras, each carrying six 1000 pound bombs, attacked and then 'beat-up' the village of Raya — in part to show the terrorists' supporters the air strength against them. Sortie number three was flown on 8 December, again three aircraft bombing with Target Director Post, northwest of Kuala Lumpur. It was some months before Ops 4 and 5 occurred, on 13 and 17 August 1959. The first was a full-blooded operation in company with aircraft from 45 RAF Squadron, 2 RAAF Squadron, plus RAAF Sabres with rockets. The target was in the Korahi area, in the State of Penang, and the army later confirmed the destruction of the living and cultivated areas of the target village. On the 17th, three Canberras bombed a target in the Selangor jungle.

Ian Gillard, a future CO of the squadron, flew on these Ops but recalls another incident at Tengah:

I was in the circuit and was just lowering the undercarriage when there was an enormous bloody bang. I remembered back at RAF Coningsby a chap there had lost his nose wheel oleo, too. My instructor told me how this chap had got away with it by burning all his fuel from the front and keeping his rear tank full, then making a flap-less landing, dropping her down on the tail. So I did the same, coming down on Tengah with that long runway — 6000 feet — and everything was going well except the tail wasn't going down, so I just gave the stick a bit of a nudge, not a big one, when the . . . . aeroplane shot into the air! It immediately stalled. I cut the throttles and we just took off across the airfield with the squadron buildings in the distance. Eventually it all came to a halt, having crossed a couple of taxi ways. Webster, our Staff Navigation Officer, had come along for the ride. He'd sat in the right-hand seat and had jettisoned the top hatch as per instructions but had hurt his hand a bit.

Pat Neville, a future Air Vice Marshal and Chief of Air Staff recalls this period at Singapore:

*W*e were part of the Light Bomber Force [LBF]. Our percentages were 70 per cent night and 30 per cent day, so in this period of 75's history we flew a hell of a lot at night. The 'Emergency' was still on so we were committed to supporting land forces against the terrorists. The Canberras were very limited in that roll, for we had 500 and 1000 pound bombs and the techniques involved were what you'd expect in a limited war. TDP — Target Director Post — which was radar directing 'a-la' Vietnam; the Vietnam technique followed our Emergency techniques. We also had Flare Data, Flare Marking, FAC [Forward Air Controllers] — a whole variety but were all based on a safe air environment — there was nobody shooting at you!

We would fly at 48,000 feet indicated and the B2 was a good aeroplane so we could get up there despite few aids. We had an ADF [Air Direction Finder] — a 'Rebecca' — but that was all. As part of LBF, our visual bombing was from 10,000 feet, so that when we got somewhere near the target, the leader had to make a decision as to whether you could or could not see the target. Later we operated 70 per cent low level, 30 per cent high, and we did it all 'down in the weeds' but that was because of our collective experience.

Between times the squadron won the annual bombing competition in 1959. It also found time to show the flag at a fly-past during the Queen's Birthday Parade, 14 June 1959, for the RNZ Aero Club Pageant at Timaru, as well as at the International Aviation Show at Manila, in the Philippines, in November.

After the Malayan Crisis ceased in mid-1960, the Canberras continued operating from Tengah, now under the command of Squadron Leader Harold 'Mo' Moss. One incident of note occurred on 4 February 1961, when Flight Lieutenant J. A. Scrimshaw and his navigator Flying Officer Tunley were on an air test in WK102. 'Scrim' noticed that a main wheel had failed to retract as the D-door had malfunctioned. They had to circle for some time to burn off the fuel then make a wheels-up landing. An unwelcome feature of the navigator's hatch was that it didn't jettison cleanly but entangled itself in his ejection seat.

Harold Moss recalls the squadron at this stage; also the loss of one of his crews:

> At one stage we had a total of eight B2s and one T-bird, and there were several times when we got the whole lot up into the air, which made 45 Squadron (RAF) our sister squadron, hopping mad! The most they seemed to get up was five. Mind you, it took a bit of fiddling to get all eight up. It was usually the ground staff who came to me to say they'd have all eight serviceable the next day, and that the boys would like us to fly them all, so it was also a morale thing for the lads.
>
> At Singapore we had 'Josstick' exercises with the Australians with their B20s and the Americans with their B57s. They'd come down and operate with us for a week or two and we'd go up and operate at Okinawa or Clark Field in the Philippines. The other things we'd do were called 'Lone Rangers' where we'd go up to Hong Kong or even to Australia.
>
> Then in October 1961 [26th] Flying Lieutenant P. G. Bevan and Flying Officer D. L. Finn were flying a night exercise and got into some cu-nim cloud and lost control. Peter told David to eject, but he didn't go; by then they were in a flat spin.

Vampire NZ5753 'blasts off' at Rangitaiki airstrip, during 'Reflex II' Exercise. The engine thrust kicked up huge clouds of pumice dust which went everywhere, including the engine intakes.
(RNZAF)

Flight Lieutenants J. A. Scrimshaw and Tunley stand self-consciously in front of WK102 after their wheels-up landing at Tengah on 3 February, 1961. Scrimshaw was to command the squadron during 1967–68 and 1969–70. (RNZAF)

Squadron Leader Brian Stanley-Hunt AFC, OC 1962–65, in the cockpit of a Vampire FB5. (RNZAF)

Pat Neville continues:

> When Finn's body was found he was still strapped into his seat but he was jack-knifed over the belt buckle. What he had done was taken off the shoulder straps so he could lean forward to work and the 'bang' seat was too far back from his table. Unlike the RAF, who had three-man crews, we only had two, one man doing both the bomb aimer and nav's jobs. For David to reach his seat he had to undo his straps, so when they got into difficulties, Bevan ejected but David couldn't because the G-forces pinned him over his belt so he just went in on his seat.

One of the hard-working ground crew at Tengah was LAC B. R. 'Andy' Anderson, who was later destined to have a long association with the squadron in New Zealand. He says:

> A specific personal achievement with 75 at Tengah was in designing and building a one-operator test set for the bombing system. Leftover armament equipment included release units from light series bomb carriers and electrical indicators. After studying the bombing circuit diagrams, I proposed to our Armament Staff that we could build a test set that would serve both as a one-operator item and be useful in training staff to understand the Canberra system.
>
> The result was a box using scrapped release units to simulate the Canberra release units and indicators to show the fusing system operation. With the test set in the cabin, one person could fully check the aircraft bombing system. The test proved very good value in solving a problem with one aircraft that inadvertently released more than the selected bombs. The problem was shown to be with the adjustment of the bomb door microswitches and readily traced due to the test set.

The Canberras finally had to be returned to the RAF in England, as 'Mo' Moss recalls:

> As our Canberras were all hired, and because a lot on my chaps hadn't seen England, we volunteered to fly them back to the UK. When it came time to go, 45 Squadron found that some of our aircraft were so much better maintained that we finished up flying back with four of their aircraft, and they kept ours!

Back at Ohakea, the squadron became an Operational Conversion Unit (RNZAF BOCU), effective 1 April 1962, with B12s and T13 Canberras, then Vampire FB5s and T11s. At Ohakea, however, there was very little change and many of the base staff didn't even appreciate that a change had taken place. (It remained the BOCU until 75 was reactivated as an operational unit in October 1963.) The CO during this phase was Squadron Leader B. Stanley-Hunt AFC, and its new operational role was that of day-fighter/ground attack, again with Vampires. It was also able to return to its pre-Canberra display team role. Brian Stanley-Hunt gives the background to these events:

> I was one of those pilots who joined 75 after returning from Cyprus. I'd gone through the Canberra period at Singapore with 14 Squadron, then reformed 14 onto Vampires at Ohakea; so what happened was that the Air Staff had taken the 75 B2 Squadron, which had folded at Singapore, and reformed it from whatever was left in New Zealand, which was the two conversion units — jet coversion and bomber conversion. I was only too pleased to get it as a squadron of course.
> Fourteen Squadron had a bit of a dilemma as they didn't have priority because we were doing the training so maintained we had priority to get the B12 conversion aircraft;

and if aircraft were a bit short, we tended to get them. So 14 Squadron were a bit sore about things. Eventually, the conversion unit went to them which disappointed me a bit but we got a consolation prize in that it was decided to have re-equipment with fighter/ground attack type aircraft and a whole lot of Vampires came out of storage to set us up — thus 75 Squadron was re-borne.

It was a fascinating challenge with a lot of young 'Gung-Ho' keen pilots who'd just done their Wings course and were looking for something meaningful to do. I was also able to fire-up the lads with our squadron history and they soon felt they were part of something that went back a long way. It also helped in that we began to have contact with some of the former old boys from the wartime 75 and we became part of their Reunions etc.

Meantime, the Vampire Squadron flourished and we flew various exercises in New Zealand, including one to the pumis strip at Taupo; although the aircraft had the habit of devastating the concrete, so taking them onto the actual pumis proved quite interesting. The army engineers could spend all day trying to level it off, for if we had a ground run with the Vampires on their brakes, we could tear a hole about 30 feet long, 12 feet wide and eight feet deep!

We also reformed the aerobatic team and flew some displays, but didn't have a specific fancy name. We were only allowed to display in fours, but we eventually had two 'fours' which from a squadron of twelve pilots wasn't bad!

The team participated in a wide variety of airshows on civilian airfields around New Zealand and at all major events. The squadron largely had ex-RAF Vampires, ordered to replace the original aircraft ot the 1951-53 era. It was in this mid-1960s period that the squadron's image as both fighters and aerobatic flyers was firmly established in the public eye. This image continues to the present day.

Brian's flight commanders were Barry Flavell, Peter Rhodes and then Ken Brooking. The first Jet Conversion Unit course for the reactivated squadron comprised Pilot Officers Ross Ewing, Roger Henstock, Richard Histed, Graham Lloyd, Murray Crawford and Bryan Lockie. These were joined by Peter Waller, Graeme Jackson, John Woolford, Richard Metcalfe, John Denton and Trevor Bland.

The squadron was designated a DFGA unit — Day Fighter Ground Attack — the Vampires carrying four 20 mm cannon and rockets. At the end of the exercise to Taupo — Reflex II — the main memory, apart from the pumis destruction, was the flying display put on by the CO when a cloud of dust was kicked up from the runway by his jet exhaust as he pulled out of a vertical manoeuvre in front of the crowd!

In 1964, 75 put on a display for the RNZAF's 25th Anniversary air show. The following year Larry Olsen led another team, comprising Angus Kingsmill, Ross Ewing and Barry Mitchell, with Peter Rhodes flying 'solo'.

Squadron Leader Dougall 'Kiwi' Dallinson, who had flown Vampire in Cyprus, became the next CO; followed in 1965 by Colin Rudd, a former jetobatic pilot. It was during Rudd's term that another pilot died — on 8 August 1967. Flying Officer Murray Whinnery crashed in NZ5754 when landing as number three in the stream after an aerobatic team fly-past. The occasion was to mark the handing over of No. 485 RNZAF crest to Strike Wing, Ohakea, the crash happening in front of the spectators. One of the squadron ground crew who saw the crash was Steve Williams:

*W*e watched the echelon of aeroplanes on the downwind leg and saw that the number three possibly wasn't where he should have been. The bank near the end of the runway then — has been cut away now — but on this day I believe his left wing actually

The 1966 'Jetabatics' Team. Left to right: F/L Larry Olsen, F/L John Denton, S/L Colin Rudd (CO), F/O Gus Kingsmill. (RNZAF)

Yellowhammers Aerobatic Team in February 1969. Left to right: Squadron Leader Ross Donaldson (CO), F/O Dave Bevan, F/L Ken Gayfer, F/O Mike Callinan, F/O Pete Waller. (RNZAF)

Three of the squadron pilots soon after 75 received the Skyhawk: Flight Lieutenants Woolford, Ross Ewing and Trevor Bland. Both Ewing and Bland became flight commanders on 75. (R. EWING)

clipped the banking and he went in. I do remember that all the pilots soon went off for another flight.

In those days, the routine at Ohakea was for us to get the aircraft out in the morning and prepare them for flight. As the day progressed and the aeroplanes went off to do their tasks, we supported the activities in the squadron hangar. The aircraft would then come back to be refuelled and have minor adjustments made, then sent off on another sortie.

Once every four to six weeks we would get a week where our activities would be transferred to nights for the purpose of night flying. We also had deployments to Gisborne and one to Taupo, where the routine would be similar to base. I recall one occasion when the efficiency of the self-sealing fuel tanks was proved when a bullet ricochetted off a range, back into the leading edge of the Vampire's wing and hit the tank!

When the Vampires were starting to get near to the end of their time, getting heavy on fuel and so on, screws started to come loose. We used various tricks to keep the screws in — but that's all I'm saying!

Squadron Leader John Scrimshaw took command late in 1967, with Flight Lieutenants Henstock and Ewing as his flight commanders. Yet another aerobatic team was activated — Scrimshaw, Callanan, Henstock, Thompson — with Ewing flying as solo pilot. Tented camps were held at Kerikeri, Tauranga and Gisborne. Ross Ewing remembers:

At Kerikeri I authorised my first eight ship sortie as a newly fledged flight commander, but thought I was about to see the end of my career when only two aircraft returned to base. The other six had been caught out by sudden and unexpected bad sub-tropical weather and diverted to Whangarei [four] and Whenaupai [two] — the latter diversion involving the award of a Green Endorsement to Pilot Officer Callanan, who was quite junior but who hung on to Flight Lieutenant Henstock's wing through a thunderstorm before landing in atrocious weather with minimal fuel.

The Gisborne detachment was planned to coincide with the Captain Cook Bicentenniary Celebrations and a fly-past over the city was part of the function. Scrimshaw was required at a function in the city so the formation was led by our American Exchange Pilot, Fred Myers, a Vietnam war veteran. He lined the formation up at the required time and began his run-in. He claimed later that 'everything was under control at all times' but the eight pilots who followed him 'down the main street' that day, still swear that they were glancing up at buildings and flag poles as they flashed by! All returned safely although it was nearly not the case for me.

I was authorised to fly a solo low-level display in the T11 over Gisborne airfield, when I 'fell out' of a low-level Derry Turn and recovered literally feet from the ground, causing Pilot Officer Barclay, who was broadcasting live over the local radio station, to instinctively say, 'Oh, shit!'

The display was witnessed by the OC [Officer Commanding] Strike, Group Captain 'Mo' Moss (a former CO who called everyone 'horse') who reprimanded me with, 'You were a bit low "horse"!'

During 1968, Squadron Leader Scrimshaw and Ross Ewing were posted to Active Service as FAC — Forward Air Controllers — with the 7th US Air Force in Vietnam. They spent six months flying Cessna O2As on these duties and were the first of a total of 12 RNZAF strike pilots to see active war flying in Vietnam. Two of these — Flight Lieutenant Bruce Donnelly and Flying Officer Callanan — received DFCs.

Once again a new CO had taken over; this time it was Squadron Leader Ross Donaldson, who formed yet another aerobatic team. This he named the 'Yellow Hammers.' But then he was posted to the US Navy to convert onto Douglas A4 Skyhawks, which as events were to prove, were to be the next generation of fighters for the RNZAF and for 75 Squadron.

22

Skyhawks
1969 — 1990

In 1969 came the re-emergence of 75 Squadron as an RNZAF operational Attack Squadron, when it re-equipped with American McDonnell Douglas A4 Skyhawk jet fighters. The A4, in US Navy parlance, is an attack aircraft and this is in effect exactly how the RNZAF use and support it, although now it is called the strike role. Of course, in NATO's book this implies nuclear armed, which is not and never has been the case in New Zealand.

Squadron Leader W. R. Donaldson had taken command of 75 in December 1968. Almost immediately he activated a display team — 'Yellow Hammers' — comprising himself, Flying Officer D. M. Bevan, Flight Lieutenant K. A. Gayfer, Flying Officer M. R. Callanan and Flying Officer P. T. Walker, the solo pilot. However, Donaldson was then sent on a two-year period of exchange duty with the US Navy in Florida to train on and then to set up a training programme for the RNZAF pilots who would follow him out.

In December, Donaldson was flying a TA-4 at low level when a mallard duck came through the aircraft's canopy — he heard the bang but, with a sudden loss of vision, saw nothing. A student had been flying the machine, but when Donaldson could not raise the student on the intercom and not being able to see, he assumed that the worst had happened and that he was now in sole control of the Skyhawk.

He knew they had been flying at 200 feet at more than 400 knots, so Donaldson began to climb and, as the speed reduced, he ejected, landing in a field, bleeding and quite blind. As it happened, the student was still in the Skyhawk, but he regained control and made an emergency landing. In hospital, Donaldson was told that one eye was beyond repair and had to be removed but the other recovered sufficiently for him to remain in the service. The Americans requested that he be allowed to complete his attachment and, although his operational days were over, he did in fact set up and complete the training programme for the RNZAF pilots.

Fourteen Skyhawks arrived in New Zealand early in 1970 on an American aircraft carrier, cocooned against the elements. After being landed at Auckland, they were towed along the city's northwest motorway to Whenuapai, where they were prepared for flight. No. 75 Squadron's 'new' Commanding Officer, Squadron Leader J. A. Scrimshaw, back from Vietnam, flew the first on 21 May. The aircraft were officially handed over at Ohakea on 10 June. The New Zealand Skyhawks were the A-4K and TA-4K (K for Kiwi) versions, with straight refuelling probes and Southeast Asia camouflage schemes. At about the same time the Royal Australian Navy purchased A-4G and TA-4G aircraft for HMAS *Melbourne*, so the RNZAF and RAN squadrons were able to exchange officers to gain experience of each other's duties.

Ross Ewing was also back on the squadron, having converted to the A4 in Florida. He recalls:

> *T*he sturdy A4 was a 'quantum leap' from the 'stick and throttle' wooden fuselaged Vampires and had its own forward looking radar, a radar altimeter, a 'ground position' navigation computer as well as improved navigation aids. The little jet — its cockpit was actually smaller than the Vampire's although the A4 stood a lot taller and was several times heavier — could be flown supersonic in a steep dive without underwing stores, and this was also a new experience for Kiwi 'Knucks'. (The term Knuck is short for 'Knucklehead' which is believed to derive from the belief that anyone who is silly enough to repeatedly dive his aeroplane at high speed towards the ground, pulling out at the last moment, must be comprised of solid knuckle/bone — at least from the neck upwards!)

Over the 1970s 75 Squadron became established as the RNZAF's front line 'sharp end', the Canberras of 14 Squadron reaching retirement and 75's Vampires transferring to them. They later equipped with the BAe 167 Strikemasters. John Scrimshaw was made an MBE for his work with the new Skyhawks and so, too, was the Engineering Officer, Squadron Leader Sean Robinson. Meantime, Ross Ewing had become the Operational Flight Commander.

Squadron Leader F. M. Kinvig took over command in April 1971 and, once the pilots were familiar with their new fighter, routine detachments became a familiar pattern, with trips to Singapore. The squadron also began exercising regularly with the RAAF and the Republic of Singapore Air Force (RSAF) squadrons, and occasionally with the Malaysian and Indonesian Air Forces as well as the USAF and the Philippino Air Force in Manila.

One of the most memorable exercises was with the British naval aircraft carrier HMS *Eagle* during her final cruise. As the *Eagle* approached New Zealand waters across the Tasman Sea, some 800 kilometres west of Ohakea, four Skyhawks, using three underwing fuel tanks for maximum range and literally 'sitting on the water', snuck beneath the carrier's obsolescent radar. The first the navy knew of the 'attack' was a visual sighting from one of its escort ships.

The Skyhawk initially had little more than a general capability for close air support and limited interdiction work, which, for the period, was just adequate. By the early 1980s, however, and especially after the Government's Defence Review in 1983, there was a need to expand the range of all air combat tasks to defend New Zealand's interests — in maritime strike, counter-air, sea and land interdiction as well as close support. It was therefore decided to upgrade the A-4 type. Eight Royal Australian Navy A-4Gs and two TA-4Gs Skyhawks were purchased and ferried to New Zealand by RNZAF pilots in July 1984.

While operating the Skyhawks, the squadron has maintained a very good safety record. By 1990, it had lost only three aeroplanes in 20 years, which has to be something of a record for a figher in the strike role. The first — NZ6207 — flown by Wing Commander Fred Kinvig, was lost on 18 October 1974. The Skyhawk suffered a catastrophic engine failure at 1300 feet while commencing the down-wind leg for Runway 09 at Ohakea. Kinvig had to eject in a hurry, the fighter crashing three kilometres from the centre of the nearby town of Bulls. Kinvig broke a leg on landing, while the only fatality, strangely considering the name of the town, was a

1981 — Graeme Goldsmith's Aerobatic Team, RNZAF Day at Ohakea. (RNZAF)

In-flight refuelling, circa 1970. Ross Ewing gets the juice! (R. EWING)

Squadron Leader J. A. Scrimshaw AFC, with former CO and now Ohakea Station Commander, Group Captain H. G. Moss AFC. (RNZAF)

bull as the wreckage slid through a paddock! The cause of the engine failure was due to an incorrect assembly of an oil pump.

By this date, Wing Commander J. S. Boys was the 'Boss'. He had been with 75 previously, having commanded for a few months in 1970 before commanding 14 Squadron. Stu Boys says of the A4:

> Although the A4 is not a nice pilot's aeroplane, it is much more capable in the operational role than what we had been used to. It takes up to 200 operational hours — one year — for a pilot to become capable on it. It is a very busy aeroplane from the pilot's point of view, with a steep learning curve. An A4 can practically carry the same bomb load as a Lancaster in about one third of the time from London to Berlin, using not seven men but one.

The squadron's activities continued through the 1970s and the 1977–78 Commanding Officer was C. C. McAllister. One story about McAllister goes back to his early days when he was serving in England. 'Mo' Moss remembers landing at RAF Bassingbourne where a wing commander wanted to ask 'Mo' about this 'young buck McAllister'. It appears that, while giving McAllister a check out, the Wing Co had deliberately closed a throttle on take-off. He then said, 'Come on McAllister, what are you going to do about it?' 'I'm not going to do anything about it,' replied McAllister, 'You got us into this, you can get us out!' Thus are legends made.

Graeme Goldsmith took temporary command of 75 in 1978, having previously been with it under Brian Stanley-Hunt in the Vampire days. Now he was back as the Operational Flight Commander and acting CO:

> At the end of that tour we had the one and only flight to Hawaii. In-flight refuelling was essential and we used three US Marine KC130 tankers. We began with a flight to Fiji, which we'd done before without tanker assistance, then on to Kwajalein. The way they supported us was to put a tanker about 300 miles north of Fiji so we all had a good top-up there, then flew on to Kwaj. On the third leg, which was really the big one from Kwaj to Hawaii, they put on a single tanker about 300 miles out, from which everyone took a brief suck.
>
> We were flying in two four-man flights, despite our usual pattern of flights of two, but we had a critical distance where everyone had to have fuel and the only way to do it was to fly in fours. Short of Johnson Island there were two tankers orbiting. We found them and cycled everyone through. If we failed to fill up everyone, they still had time to get back to Kwaj and the tanker which was orbiting there, but we had no difficulties.
>
> I'd planned the trip as Operational Flight Commander but was not due to fly, but, as Wing Commander McAllister then left us, I was put in charge.

Wing Commander J. S. Hosie took over in June 1978, and then Graeme Goldsmith finally had full command in December 1979. During 'Goldie's' term of office, the squadron began to fly 'Cope Thunder' exercises but, sadly, they also lost a pilot and the second Skyhawk. Graeme recalls:

> We did the first Cope Thunder exercise out of Clark Field in the Philippines, although it was a very limited one. It was like 'Red Flag' — a two-week exercise. During the first week we managed to show the Americans we weren't totally incompetant and that they could trust us to be fully part of the deal. We did well despite fixed sights which also impressed the Americans.
>
> We lost [Flight Lieutenant] John Dick in the T-bird (NZ6253). He was part of a pair on a low-level bounce on a four-ship formation that was coming through on the low level

area. Basically he went into the ground and we never really discovered how or why he had crashed.

This accident occurred on 25 March 1981 over the Ruahine Range. It was thought he may have struck a spur of land and in fact had ejected just before the Skyhawk hit the ground, but he was too low for his parachute to deploy.

One memorable event in February 1980 was when 75 Squadron received the freedom of nearby Wanganui. To some extent, credit for this must go to 'Andy' Anderson, whom it will be remembered had been an armourer with 75 some years earlier. While the squadron was away on Exercise Vanguard, the Station Commander at Ohakea received a letter from the Wanganui City Council proposing the freedom be bestowed on Ohakea. Andy was now a commissioned navigator and 75's adjutant. When the letter was shown to him, he suggested it was more appropriate to bestow the freedom on a squadron:

> *T*his was suggested to the Council who quickly suggested 14 Squadron. But my advice was that 75 Squadron, with the close tie to Wanganui through Jimmy Ward VC, was more appropriate, Ward having attended Wanganui Technical College. When 75 returned to base they found they were to accept the 'Freedom of Wanganui.' Befittingly, also, was that Graeme Goldsmith was an old boy of the same Wanganui Technical College

After Goldsmith left in December 1981, John Lanham took charge for his two year tour as 'Boss'. He had previously commanded 14 Squadron and flown with 75 under Stanley-Hunt. So he had done his time on Vampires, supporting the Canberras, just as now the Strikemasters were supporting the Skyhawks. He had gone through the

Wing Commander G. J. W. Goldsmith (OC 1979–81) receiving the Freedom of Wanganui on behalf of the squadron in 1980 from the Mayor of the City, Allan Millward.
(RNZAF)

Aerobatic Team, 1983, which flew the world's first 'Plugged' Barrel Roll sequence. Left to right: F/L Steve Pilkington, F/O 'Herb' Keightley, Wg Cdr John Lanham (CO 1981–83), F/O Glen Stuart, F/L Frank Sharp (OC 1985–89). (RNZAF)

Arrival of the first ex-Royal Australian Navy Skyhawks in July 1984, before being renumbered and repainted. (RNZAF)

Wing Commander Jim Barclay, CO December 1983 to November 1985, with Bill Scollay DFC, former Navigation Leader with 75 Squadron during World War Two, and later founder and chairman of the 75 Squadron Association. (RNZAF)

period where squadron pilots had progressed from wingmen to pairs leader to four leader, and helped to make the RNZAF fighter wing the success it had become. With the squadron Lanham had a five-aircraft display team which featured the first display, at Whenuapai in 1983, of a low-level 'plugged' barrel roll with two Skyhawks connected via the air refuelling hose! It was a world first for an aerobatic team. John Lanham recalls:

> The skills we developed by hand and feet flying, and having learnt well the basic skills in bombing, rocketing and gunnery — all very 'eye-ball' stuff — was the reason the NZ Squadrons did so well in exercises — and totally amazed our Allies sometimes too! They would ask: 'How do you guys get so consistently good bombing results?' We would reply, 'Oh, we have a thing called the T-LAR system.' 'Oh, really — is that like the F16's computer guidence stuff?' We'd say, 'No, it stands for "That Looks About Right"!' Yet is was true!
>
> The reasons our scores were so good was that we'd had this progression through a supporting aeroplane, with lots of good training and the RNZAF managed to stay relatively generous in terms of flying hours for fighter pilots. We also flew in 40–50 knot winds on some of our ranges, so if you can bomb accurately in those conditions, then hitting a target can't be difficult in a breeze. In the Cope Thunder scenario in the tropics it was generally calm or very light winds.
>
> During my term as CO, we were just getting into the Cope Thunder programme, following Graeme Goldsmith's abbreviated routine — just a look-see and establish confidence with our Allies. But I had the first full-fledged Cope Thunder where the squadron went through the whole two-week programme. That was the highlight of my tour, and was one of the best things that had happened to 75 Squadron in a long time.
>
> It was the first time we were in amongst a very capable and modern ally, evaluating

our techniques and tactics against the very latest things the Americans were doing. Having sort this opportunity for so long, we were just getting into it, with Jim Barclay following, when the handle was pulled on the whole scheme, losing us this invaluable opportunity to train and evaluate our training, against our Allies.

The 'handle', of course, was politics and government changes in policy which began to hinder the RNZAF's continued development and operational status. It started during Wing Commander J. S. Barclay's term as CO, which began in December 1983. He, too, had been a pilot with 75 in his younger days, rising to command 14 Squadron in 1982–83. When the Skyhawk arrived in New Zealand, he was among the first fighter pilots to convert onto them. He had recently returned from the United States where he had flown F-4 Phantoms. He remembers:

> We began to address flying the aeroplane as a fighter-bomber rather than pure bomber as the Canberras had, or a bit of fighter as the Vampires had. When later I returned to the squadron as CO, we were able to approach our tasks in a better manner, especially air to air, so we got quality from the missions; the guys began to achieve something, rather than just stooging around.
>
> Our deployments were always the highlights — Singapore, including Cope Thunder, the results of which reflected the sort of chaps we had on 75 at that time. We worked up for the deployment through Exercise Pitchblack at Darwin, where the Americans came in with their Phantoms and the Aussies with their Mirages. We then went into Triad-84, which was the last of the exercises we were involved with. Our people have lost a lot of valuable things from not going on these exercises, although we train hard and work to tight standards, it is always nice to compare ourselves to others.
>
> Of incidents, I recall when we bought the ex-Australian Navy Skyhawks, we did roll one over the end of the runway at Townsville. One of them didn't have a drag 'chute like our own aircraft had, so the braking technique is exactly as it says in the book which was something we hadn't worried about before, because the drag 'chute cures everything! But this particular fellow got down onto the runway and at first locked the brake, burst both tyres and tipped over, upside-down. He was very lucky to get out of that, but the aircraft was rebuilt and is flying again.
>
> We could claim to have set up the embryo A-4 Display Team when we put together a team for Air Force Day 1981. We learned then that the reasons we'd been reluctant to get the A-4 into an aerobatic roll was that we thought we'd have a problem with the slats. The Blue Angels, for instance, had their slats welded in. We tried it without this and it really didn't give us a problem, so we formed a team, calling ourselves 'The Red and Gold nothing special but quite good Aerobatic team'. It was only a one-off display, but I like to think it was something others were able to build on and develop.

It was certainly something which the next CO, Wing Commander F. S. Sharp was able to build on when he took over in November 1985. Frank Sharp continued to develop the display team as well as co-ordinate the Skyhawks in their operational combat role. In 1986, he led the team in a display at the Royal Australian Navy's 75th Anniversary at the NAS, Nowra, and at RMAF Kuantan, Malaysia. The team also flew displays at Rarotonga during the New Zealand joint Services Exercise in the Cook Islands. The team consisted of Flying Officer Peter King (Red 2), Flying Officer Donald Laming (Red 3), Flight Lieutenant Craig Tanner (Red 4), Squadron Leader Gavin Howse (Red 5), and Flying Officer Nigel Milne (Red 6).

Then, in January 1987, the squadron formed a six-aircraft team for the RNZAF 50th Anniversary celebrations in April. It performed with distinction at the 50th Anniversary of Christchurch International at Harewood while, later in the year, it flew two displays at Ohakea and two more over RNZAF Base Auckland. When the

Echelon Port — 75's Skyhawks in formation. Note the first and last machines are T-bird two-seat training versions. (RNZAF)

Aerobatic Team, 1988. Centre is the CO, Frank Sharp; the others (left to right) are: Nigel Milne, Peter King, Craig Tanner, Don Laming, Gavin Howse. (RNZAF)

The 1988 'Kiwi Red' Team looping above Lake Taupo. (RNZAF)

75 Squadron pilots in 1989. Standing, left to right: Peter 'Patch' Nelson, Huggy Hugham, Chris Calvert (Maintenance F/Cdr), Wg Cdr John Bates (CO), Bruce Keightley, Hutchinson, Graham Carter; Front, left to right: Robby Nicholls, Graeme 'Dobbo' Dobson, Robert 'Jug' Jackson, Craig Mitchell. Graham Carter was killed in a flying accident, 24 October 1989. (RNZAF)

1988 Australian BiCentennial Airshow was staged at RAAF Richmond, 75's team — now named 'Kiwi Red' — stole the show with its exciting routine.

Frank Sharp left 75 early in 1989, the new 'Boss' being yet another former squadron pilot, Wing Commander J. S. Bates. He had flown Vampires with 75 back in the early 1970s and a few years later returned as its Executive Officer before taking command of 2 Squadron. He came with a vast number of acrobatic flying hours, having flown a solo Harvard and Airtrainer displays between 1980 and 1982, and having been the solo Skyhawk pilot between 1983 and 1985. He has another 75 association — he married the daughter of a former wartime air gunner, Ham Hamerton DFC, who had been in the Trott/Scollay crew in 1943–44.

John Bates led 'Kiwi Red' during 1989–90, flying displays during the year. A special highlight was the display to celebrate the opening of the Commonwealth Games in Auckland in January 1990. His pilots at this stage were Flight Lieutenant Barry Nelson (Red 2), Flying Officer Graeme Dobson (Red 3), Flying Officer Craig Mitchell (Red 4), Flight Lieutenant Bruce Keightley (Red 5) and Flight Lieutenant Peter King (Red 6).

Unfortunately, 75 Squadron lost a pilot during the working up period for these displays. On 24 October 1989, 24-year-old Flying Officer Graham Carter crashed and died instantly. His place was taken by Craig Mitchell.

A long awaited plan was for the Skyhawks to be taken away for upgrading — 'Project Kahu'. As well as re-skinning the aircraft's delta wing, the project involves a complete rewiring of the airframe and the introduction of 'new generation' navigation, radar and weapons systems. The radar is now a full 'attack' radar, including a modern air-to-air mode, while the navigator system is fully electronic with no moving parts and replaces the clockwork computer. This means that the pilot can program all the relevant information into a 'PC' and plug this into the aircraft's computer before take-off. During flight all he has to do is push a button to display the information on two central TV screens on the instrument panel.

Another major Kahu feature is the Head-Up Display (HUD), so that the pilot need to longer look down into the cockpit while flying low and at high speed. He also has the ability, with extra swiches on the stick and throttle, to select all major systems without taking his hands off either — the so-called 'Hands on Throttle and Stick' (HOTAS) system.

It is fitting that the last words of this history should come from the 1989–1990 commander, John Bates AFC:

I had returned to 75 expecting to find a squadron of Kahu aeroplanes with advanced avionics but this didn't happen. In fact, by March 1990, we only had two Kahu Skyhawks on the squadron. Our AOC decided, in conjunction with the coming Sesqui Celebrations, and as a form of being available for the Commonwealth Games, that a display team would be a good thing. He also realised that the last team, developed for the Richmond Air Show in 1988, wasn't seen in New Zealand, just doing one display over Wellington before being disbanded. So we were the first team put together and used to tour the country.

We started aerobatic training in mid-August with a plan for being ready for the Games in late January 1990, realising we'd have to take a couple of months off to convert to the Kahu aeroplanes. However, that kept slipping so much that we never did and in the end we gave three guys a very quick conversion so they could just fly the aeroplane in formation and the rest of us survived over that period, keeping small formations going.

Finally, we reduced our strength down to just six people. We flew the aircraft once a day, usually in the mornings, so the ground crews could work on them in the afternoons. In the aerobatic role — being a full combat aircraft — it is slightly disadvantaged in that it takes about 7500 feet to loop, so straight away, the weather becomes more of a factor than it would for the RAF Hawk (Red Arrows), which can do its show under 4500 feet. I think we managed to overcome that in keeping the display tight anyway and keep right in front of the crowds, with something going on the whole time.

When we lost Graham Carter, we were landing back at Ohakea and we used to do a roll-under break. We'd be in echelon towards the break and we'd all just roll under. When you half roll you have to descend as well to get under the other guys. Graham just didn't do that and he ended up, being No. 4, behind No. 5, and crashed. It was quite a set-back to the team and we took it pretty hard. Suddenly the reality of it all was a bit different.

However, by mid-November we did a show at Manfield and two weeks later we were at the Nissan/Mobile 500 at Wellington. After Christmas we worked up for the Games and a very concentrated period of air displays. Our last public show was at Wellington on 24 March.

Following a break at the beginning of April, we shall be straight into our Kahu conversions and that will mean a complete conversion onto the aeroplane and then building up the squadron in not only numbers but onto tactics. We shall be getting the new AIM-9L air to air missiles tied into our new radar and developing our laser guided bomb (LGB). With the AIM-9L, instead of having to point the aeroplane to get a heat source, we can tie it into our radar. Also our 'new' Skyhawks will have indications to tell us that we are being interrogated by a (enemy) radar picture. Its going to be a busy but exciting time. Another new era for 75 Squadron.

John Bates and his 'Kiwi Red' display team did, however, fly one last display for a very special audience at Ohakea on Saturday 31 March 1990 — almost 50 years to the day that the New Zealand Flight became 75 (New Zealand) Squadron. At Ohakea was a gathering of former members (and their wives) of 75 Squadron, most wartime veterans not only from New Zealand but also from Britain and Australia. They were celebrating the squadron's 50th Anniversary that weekend at Wanganui and had come to visit the present-day squadron this fine, sunny late summer day.

They watched as John Bates and his men put on perhaps their most spectacular show. Certainly their audience was impressed, the old flyers among them being up their with them in more than just spirit. The final fly-past was made in the 'Missing Man' formation, in tribute on this last display to Graham Carter, who had been taken from them just five months earlier. He was the latest man to die for his country and his squadron, and the men who watched new only too well that feeling when a friend and comrade is taken from them. 'Nobody said it would be easy' were the words written by 'Kiwi Red' in their own tribute to Graham. Those words were true for all those who had ever served with 75, in peace and in war.

The next morning, the wartime veterans gave thanks for being allowed to survive for so long during a service at the Wanganui Technical College, where Jimmy Ward VC had received his schooling. And they remembered with pride, their friends and comrades who had not been so fortunate.

As I stood with them — proud to have been invited — I recalled that story of the chant at the railway station in 1945 when the New Zealanders started their journey home ... 'not 71 ... not 72 ... Not 73 ... NOT 74 ... BUT 75!!!'

McDonnell-Douglas A4 Skyhawk with original straight probe, 1970–75. (RNZAF)

Squadron Standard bearing the Battle Honours: Home Defence 1916–18, Norway 1940, Dunkirk 1940, Invasion Ports 1940, Fortress Europe 1940–44, Normandy 1944, Walcheren 1944, France and Germany 1944–45. (RNZAF)

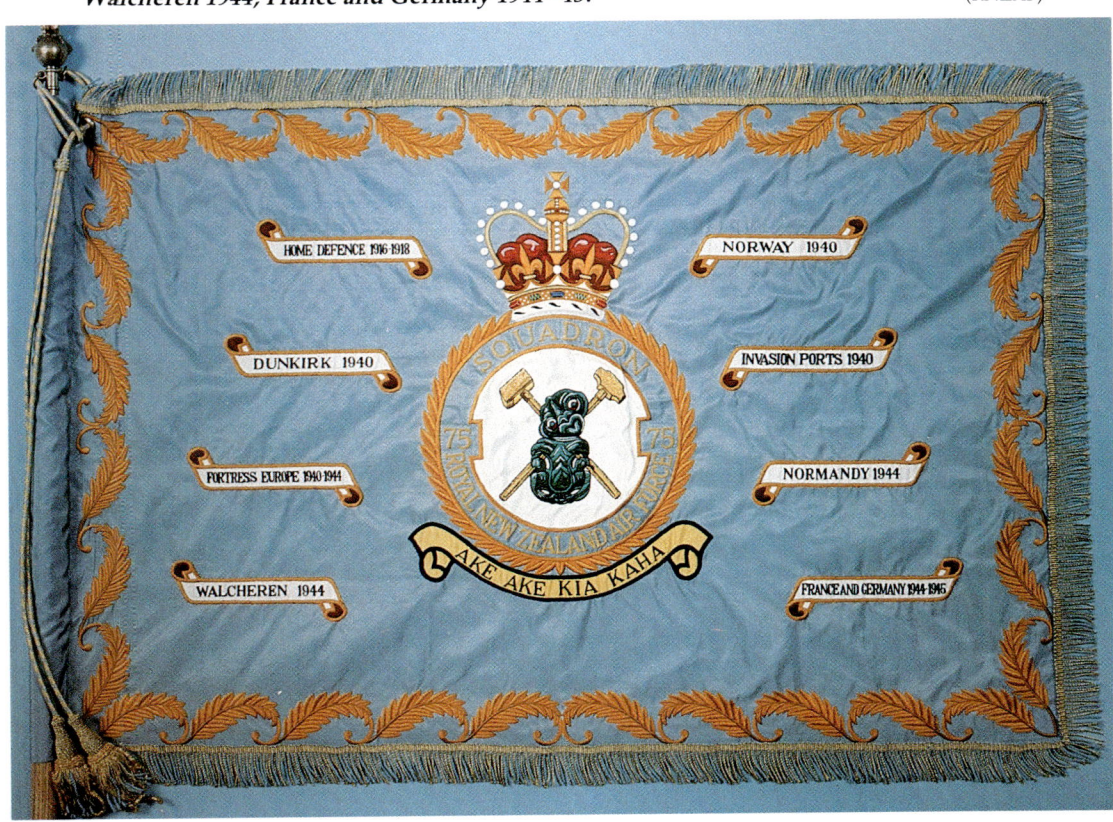

Skyhawks over the Kaimanawa Ranges, the central volcanic plateau of the North Island. In the background is Mount Ruapehu (2997 m), an active volcano and the highest peak of the North Island. (RNZAF)

Skyhawk NZ6203 over Lake Waikaremoana. (RNZAF)

Craig Tanner (Red 4) refuelling from Frank Sharp's A4 above Ohakea in 1988. (RNZAF)

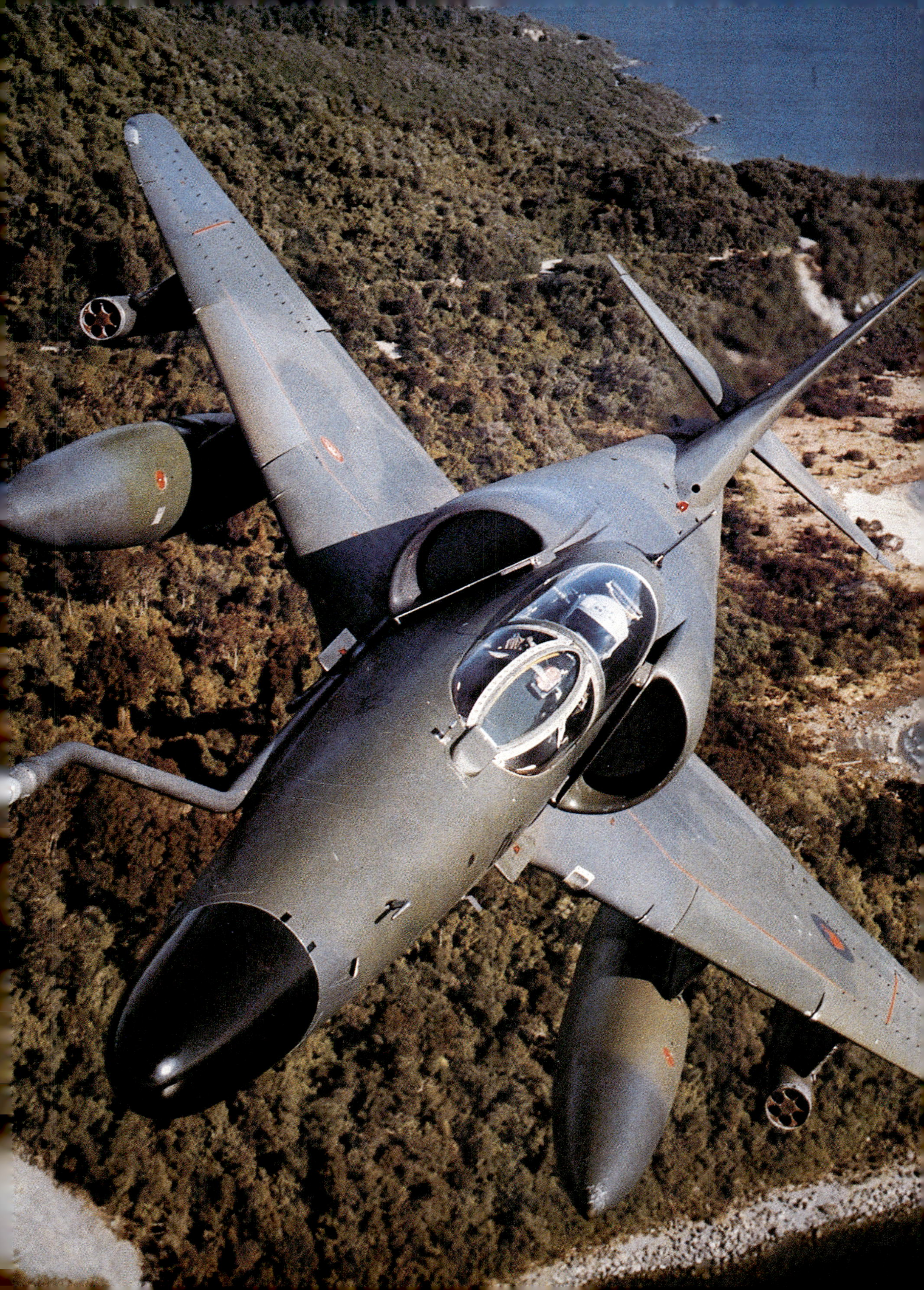

75 Squadron Maintenance Flight, commanded by Flight Lieutenant Chris Calvert, with his deputy, Warrant Officer Zap Harding.
(RNZAF)

Kiwi Red Leader Wg Cdr John Bates AFC, immediately after the final Aerobatic Display for the veterans of 75 Squadron on the occasion of the 50th Anniversary Reunion at Ohakea, 31 March 1990.
(N. FRANKS)

Appendix A
COMMANDING OFFICERS 1916–1990

Major H. A. Petre DSO MC	Oct 1916 — Jul 1917
Major T. O'B. Hubbard	Jul 1917 — Jul 1917
Major T. F. Rutledge MC	Jul 1917 — Oct 1917
Major C. S. Ross	Oct 1917 — Nov 1918
Major C. A. Ridley	Nov 1918 — Jun 1919
Squadron Leader H. L. Rough DFC	Mar 1937 — Oct 1937
Wing Commander K. E. Ward	Oct 1937 — Sep 1938
Wing Commander E. S. Goodwin AFC	Sep 1938 — Nov 1938
Wing Commander D. D'A. A. Greig DFC AFC	Nov 1938 —
Wing Commander M. W. Buckley MBE	Apl 1940 — Nov 1940
Wing Commander C. E. Kay OBE DFC	Nov 1940 — Sep 1941
Wing Commander R. Sawrey-Cookson DSO DFC	Sep 1941 — Apl 1942
Wing Commander E. G. Olson	Apl 1942 — Jul 1942
Wing Commander V. Mitchell DFC	Jul 1942 — Jan 1943
Wing Commander G. A. Lane DFC	Jan 1943 — May 1943
Wing Commander M. Wyatt	May 1943 — Aug 1943
Wing Commander R. D. Max DSO DFC	Aug 1943 — May 1944
Wing Commander R. J. A. Leslie DSO AFC	May 1944 — Dec 1944
Wing Commander R. J. Newton DFC	Dec 1944 — Jan 1945
Wing Commander C. H. Baigent DSO DFO and bar	Jan 1945 — Oct 1945
Wing Commander J. E. Watts AFC	Oct 1946 — Apl 1947
Wing Commander A. A. N. Breckon DFC	Apl 1947 — Apl 1947
Wing Commander C. H. Baigent DSO DFC and bar	Apl 1947 — May 1947
Squadron Leader R. F. Watson AFC (acting)	May 1947 — Sep 1947
Wing Commander C. H. Baigent DSO DFC & bar AFC	Sep 1947 — Feb 1950
Squadron Leader N. H. Bright (acting)	Feb 1950 — May 1950
Squadron Leader E. C. Gartrell OBE DFC	May 1950 — May 1952
Squadron Leader A. F. Tucker DFC	May 1952 — May 1953
Squadron Leader N. H. Bright	May 1953 — May 1954
Wing Commander D. F. St George DFC	May 1954 — Aug 1954
Squadron Leader N. F. Curtis	Aug 1954 — Aug 1956
Squadron Leader G. Amor	Aug 1956 — Jul 1958
Squadron Leader G. R. B. Highet DFC AFC and bar	Jul 1958 — Jan 1961
Squadron Leader H. G. Moss AFC	Jan 1961 — Apl 1962
Squadron Leader I. M. Gillard AFC	Apl 1962 — Apl 1962
Squadron Leader B. Stanley-Hunt AFC	Apl 1962 — Jun 1965
Squadron Leader D. M. Dallison	Jun 1965 — Dec 1965
Squadron Leader C. W. Rudd	Dec 1965 — Dec 1967
Squadron Leader J. A. Scrimshaw AFC	Dec 1967 — Dec 1968
Squadron Leader W. R. Donaldson	Dec 1968 — Jun 1969
Squadron Leader J. A. Scrimshaw AFC	Jun 1969 — Jan 1970
Squadron Leader J. S. Boys AFC	Jan 1970 — May 1970
Squadron Leader J. A. Scrimshaw AFC MBE	May 1970 — Apl 1971
Wing Commander F. M. Kinvig AFC	Apl 1971 — May 1973
Wing Commander J. S. Boys AFC	May 1973 — Feb 1975
Wing Commander R. F. Lawry AFC	Feb 1975 — Feb 1977
Wing Commander C. C. McAllister	Feb 1977 — Mar 1978
Squadron Leader G. J. W. Goldsmith (acting)	Mar 1978 — Jun 1978
Wing Commander J. S. Hosie	Jun 1978 — Dec 1979

Wing Commander G. J. W. Goldsmith AFC	Dec 1979 — Dec 1981
Wing Commander J. W. Lanham	Dec 1981 — Dec 1983
Wing Commander J. S. Barclay AFC	Dec 1983 — Nov 1985
Wing Commander F. S. Sharp AFC	Nov 1985 — Feb 1989
Wing Commander J. S. Bates AFC	Feb 1989 — Jan 1991
Squadron Leader I. Gore	Jan 1991 —

Appendix B

AWARDS TO 75 SQUADRON IN WORLD WAR TWO

Victoria Cross

Sergeant James Allen Ward RNZAF   5 Aug 1941* Plt†

Distinguished Service Order
Flying Officer David Leatham Prichard RAF   25 Jul 1941 Plt
Flying Officer Thomas Francis Gill RAF   23 Sep 1941 Plt
Squadron Leader Arthur Ashworth RAF   21 Aug 1942 Plt
Group Captain Edward George Olson RNZAF   20 Apl 1943 Plt
Pilot Officer Arthur William Burley RAFVR   31 Aug 1943 Plt
Wing Commander Roy Douglas Max DFC RNZAF   14 Jul 1944 Plt
Wing Commander John Alexander Leslie AFC RAF   15 Dec 1944 Plt
Wing Commander Cyril Henry Baigent DFC RNZAF   17 Jul 1945 Plt

Military Cross
Flight Lieutenant Eric Ernest Williams RAFVR   15 Sep 1944 AB

Conspicuous Gallantry Medal
Flight Sergeant Osric Hartnell White RNZAF   24 Sep 1943 Plt
Warrant Officer Alexander William Hurse RAAF   21 Jul 1944 AB
Flight Sergeant David John Moriarty RNZAF   15 Sep 1944 Plt

Bar to Distinguished Flying Cross
Squadron Leader Frederick John Lucas DFC RNZAF   14 Apl 1942 Plt
Flight Lieutenant William Edward McAlpine DFC RAFVR   13 Oct 1944 AG
Flight Lieutenant Alan Cheyne Baxter DFC RNZAF   16 Feb 1945 Plt
(DFC awarded in 1942 when a navigator with 88 Squadron (Dieppe))
Squadron Leader John Mathers Bailey DFC RNZAF   6 Apl 1945 Plt
Squadron Leader Jack Colin Parker DFC RNZAF   26 Oct 1945 Plt

Distinguished Flying Cross
Squadron Leader Cyril Eyton Kay OBE RNZAF   21 Jun 1940 Plt
Flying Officer Neville Williams RNZAF   30 Jul 1940 Plt
Flight Lieutenant Aubrey Arthur Ninnis Breckon RNZAF   13 Sep 1940 Plt
Pilot Officer Frank Henderson Denton RAF   1 Oct 1940 Plt
Flight Lieutenant John Adams RNZAF   22 Oct 1940 Plt
Flying Officer Trevor Owen Freeman RNZAF   22 Oct 1940 Plt
Flying Officer William Harcourt Coleman RNZAF   22 Oct 1940 Plt
Pilot Officer Duncan Harold McArthur RAF   1 Nov 1940 Plt
Pilot Officer Donald Joseph Harkness RAF   22 Nov 1940 Plt
Flight Lieutenant Frederick John Lucas RNZAF   22 Nov 1940 Plt
Flying Officer William Maurice Chalk Williams RNZAF   22 Nov 1940 Plt
Squadron Leader Norman Maxwell Boffee RAF   26 Nov 1940 Plt

---

* Dates shown are those of the *London Gazette* publishing the award.
† Abbreviations are:
    AB — Air Bomber   Plt — Pilot
    AG — Air Gunner   WAG — Wireless Operator/Air Gunner
    FE — Flight Engineer   WOP — Wireless Operator
    Nav — Navigator

Flying Officer Richard Melville Curtis RAF	11 Feb	1941	Plt
Flying Officer Gordie Keith Larney RAF	11 Feb	1941	Plt
Flying Officer Harry Albert Goodwin RAF	11 Feb	1941	Nav
Flying Officer Malcolm Hugh MacFarlane RAF	18 Feb	1941	Plt
Flying Officer Charles Aylmer Pownell RAF	18 Apl	1941	Plt
Flying Officer William Davenport Brown RNZAF	18 Apl	1941	AG
Pilot Officer George Eric Fowler RAFVR	18 Apl	1941	Nav
Pilot Officer Oliver Rayner Matheson RAFVR	18 Apl	1941	Plt
Pilot Officer Arthur Ashworth RAF	30 Jun	1941	Plt
Pilot Officer George Ronald Simich RNZAF	18 Jul	1941	Plt
Squadron Leader Reuben Pears Widdowson RAF	29 Jul	1941	Plt
Pilot Officer William Jeffrey Rees RAFVR	8 Aug	1941	Plt
Flying Officer Charles Stokes RAF	2 Sep	1941	AG
Pilot Officer George William Curry RAFVR	23 Sep	1941	Plt
Pilot Officer David Stewart Florence RCAF	23 Sep	1941	Nav
Pilot Officer Graham Wellesley Hamlin RNZAF	23 Sep	1941	Plt
Pilot Officer Alan Murray Hobbs RNZAF	23 Sep	1941	Plt
Pilot Officer James Williamson Thomson RNZAF	23 Sep	1941	Plt
Pilot Officer Timothy John Wilder Williams RNZAF	21 Nov	1941	Plt
Pilot Officer Robert Walter Bray RAFVR	14 Apl	1942	Plt
(Bar to DFC 19 Jan 1943)			
Pilot Officer Eric George Delancey Jarman RAAF	15 May	1942	Plt
Pilot Officer James Kenneth Climie RNZAF	26 Jun	1942	Plt
Squadron Leader Raymond John Newton RNZAF	11 Aug	1942	Plt
Flying Officer Francis John Chunn RNZAF	27 Oct	1942	AG
Pilot Officer John Leonard Wright RNZAF	29 Dec	1942	Plt
Pilot Officer Charles Wynne Brunsden Kelly RNZAF	12 Jan	1943	Nav
(DSO with 156 Squadron 30 Nov 1943)			
Flying Officer Robert Stanley Pearce RNZAF	12 Mar	1943	
Flight Lieutenant Leo George Trott RNZAF	14 May	1943	Plt
Flying Officer Dugald Louis Popperwell RNZAF	14 May	1943	AB
Flying Officer William John Scollay RNZAF	14 May	1943	Nav
Pilot Officer Harold Reginald Hamerton RNZAF	14 May	1943	AG
Pilot Officer Peter John Oswald Buck RNZAF	21 May	1943	Plt
Pilot Officer John Henry Symons RCAF	21 May	1943	WOP
Flight Lieutenant Guy Lionel Roy Heywood RNZAF	11 Jun	1943	AG
Flying Officer Alexander Fielding Minnis RAFVR	15 Jun	1943	Nav
Flying Officer Charles Fray Ormerod RNZAF	15 Jun	1943	Nav
Pilot Officer John Mathers Bailey RNZAF	15 Jun	1943	Plt
Squadron Leader Richard Broadbent RNZAF	9 Jul	1943	Plt
Flight Lieutenant Frank Albert Andrews RNZAF	9 Jul	1943	Plt
Flight Lieutenant Douglas Charles Lowe RAFVR	9 Jul	1943	Plt
Pilot Officer Richard Otway French RNZAF	13 Jul	1943	Plt
Squadron Leader Peter James Robert Kitchen RAF	27 Jul	1943	Plt
Flying Officer Geoffrey Turner RCAF	17 Aug	1943	Nav
Pilot Officer Francis Campbell Carswell RNZAF	17 Aug	1943	Nav
Squadron Leader Jack Joll DFM RNZAF	15 Oct	1943	Plt
Pilot Officer Hilton Clifford Williams RNZAF	19 Oct	1943	Plt
(Bar to DFC 10 Aug 1944)			
Warrant Officer John Lefevre Mitchell RAFVR	19 Oct	1943	Plt
Flying Officer Allan Mason Alexander RNZAF	22 Oct	1943	Plt
Flying Officer John Charles Kennedy Fabian RNZAF	2 Nov	1943	Nav
(Bar to DFC 18 May 1944)			
Flying Officer Thomas Cameron Graham RAFVR	7 Dec	1943	Nav
Pilot Officer John Gall RNZAF	10 Dec	1943	Nav
Pilot Officer Kenneth William Morgan RAFVR	23 May	1944	
Flight Lieutenant John David Grubb RNZAF	23 May	1944	Plt
Pilot Officer Colin Roy Baker RNZAF	6 Jun	1944	Plt
Pilot Officer Robert Albert Potts RAAF	7 Jul	1944	Plt
Flying Officer Thomas Balger Bradley RAAF	21 Jul	1944	AB
Flying Officer Albert Hart Robertson Zillwood RNZAF	21 Jul	1944	Nav

Flying Officer Stanley William Galloway RAFVR	15 Aug	1944	WOP
Flight Lieutenant Harry Leonard Burton RNZAF	15 Aug	1944	Plt
Flight Lieutenant Sidney Alfred Clark RNZAF	15 Aug	1944	Plt
Flying Officer Trevor James Nation RNZAF	18 Aug	1944	WOP
Flying Officer William Edward Anderson RNZAF	15 Sep	1944	AG
Pilot Officer Charles Mita Hikair Pinka RNZAF	19 Sep	1944	Nav
Pilot Officer Iwikau Tematauisa Teaika RNZAF	19 Sep	1944	AG
Warrant Officer Rex Tabor Andrews RNZAF	19 Sep	1944	FE
Flight Lieutenant Lyndon Oliver Sims RAFVR	13 Oct	1944	FE
Flying Officer Bryn McLane Melville-Smith RAFVR	13 Oct	1944	AG
Flying Officer Raoul John Wisker RNZAF	17 Oct	1944	Plt
Warrant Officer Cyril Aubrey Newark RAFVR	17 Oct	1944	WOP
Flying Officer Ronald Desmond Mayhill RNZAF	24 Oct	1944	AB
Flying Officer William David Topping RAFVR	3 Nov	1944	Nav
Flying Officer Stanley Pawson Walton RAFVR	14 Nov	1944	
Flying Officer John Dudley Perfrement RAAF	14 Nov	1944	Plt
Flying Officer Francis Charles Fox RNZAF	14 Nov	1944	Plt
Flying Officer Andrew David Mackenzie RAFVR	17 Nov	1944	Plt
Flying Officer Lawrence Michael O'Connor RNZAF	17 Nov	1944	Plt
Flight Lieutenant Ralph William Brumwell RAFVR	8 Dec	1944	Plt
Flight Lieutenant Charles Gordon Washer RNZAF	8 Dec	1944	Plt
Flying Officer John Kieller Aitken RNZAF	8 Dec	1944	Plt
Warrant Officer John Wright RAFVR	12 Dec	1944	Plt
Flying Officer Arnel Dean Hotorua Meyer RNZAF	12 Dec	1944	Plt
Squadron Leader Roy Campbell Earl RNZAF	16 Jan	1945	Plt
Flight Lieutenant Victor John Andrew RAF	16 Jan	1945	Plt
Pilot Officer Jeffrey Baines RNZAF	19 Jan	1945	Plt
Warrant Officer Leslie Howells RAFVR	26 Jan	1945	FE
Flight Lieutenant Jack Plummer RNZAF	2 Feb	1945	Plt
Flying Officer David Percy Leadley RNZAF	6 Feb	1945	Plt
Flying Officer William Henry Goodridge DFM RAF	16 Feb	1945	AG
Pilot Officer Reginald Rycroft Hartley RAFVR	27 Mar	1945	Nav
Warrant Officer Robert John Torbitt RAFVR	27 Mar	1945	AG
Flying Officer Raymond Alexander Ramsey RNZAF	27 Mar	1945	AB
Flight Lieutenant Alan Joseph Lyall Sedunary RAAF	3 Apl	1945	Plt
Flight Lieutenant Martin Adam Kilpatrick RNZAF	6 Apl	1945	Plt
Flight Lieutenant Henry Charles Yates RAFVR	13 Apl	1945	Plt
Flying Officer Thomas Christie Waugh RAFVR	13 Apl	1945	Plt
Flight Lieutenant Arthur Roy Bidwell Balton RNZAF	13 Apl	1945	
Flight Lieutenant Arthur Gethin Creagh RNZAF	13 Apl	1945	Nav
Flying Officer Harold Lowe RAFVR	24 Apl	1945	WOP
Pilot Officer Kenneth Howard Blincoe RNZAF	24 Apl	1945	Plt
Pilot Officer John McCullough RNZAF	24 Apl	1945	
Flying Officer Hubert Rees RAFVR	8 May	1945	Plt
Squadron Leader John Robert Rodgers DFM RNZAF	22 May	1945	Plt
Flight Lieutenant Wylie James Wakelin RNZAF	22 May	1945	Plt
Flight Lieutenant Kenneth William Roland McMillan RNZAF	22 May	1945	Plt
Pilot Officer Donald Rolston Wrigley Whittaker	25 May	1945	Nav
Pilot Officer Norman Frederick Wilson RAFVR	25 May	1945	Nav
Warrant Officer William Reavley RAFVR	25 May	1945	AG
Flying Officer William Lachlan Wilson RNZAF	25 May	1945	WOP
Pilot Officer William Robert Morris RNZAF	25 May	1945	
Flying Officer John Henry Thomas Wood RNZAF	5 Jun	1945	Plt
Flight Lieutenant Jack Geoffrey Brewster RAFVR	17 Jul	1945	Nav
Flight Lieutenant Ronald Henry Payne RAFVR	17 Jul	1945	Nav
Flight Lieutenant Jack Christopher Wall RAFVR	17 Jul	1945	AB
Flying Officer Norman Bartlett RAF	17 Jul	1945	FE
Flight Lieutenant Grant Alan Russell RNZAF	17 Jul	1945	AB
Flying Officer Thomas Douglas Gregory RAFVR	20 Jul	1945	AG
Flying Officer Thomas Munro RAFVR	20 Jul	1945	AG
Pilot Officer Enoch Charles Hughes RAFVR	20 Jul	1945	

Flying Officer Ivan John Williamson RNZAF	20 Jul 1945	WOP
Flying Officer Charles Frederick Green RAFVR	25 Sep 1945	AG
Flying Officer Harold George Howells RAFVR	25 Sep 1945	
Flying Officer David George William Hubert Jones RNZAF	25 Sep 1945	AB
Flying Officer Robert Douglas Sommerville RNZAF	25 Sep 1945	AB
Flying Officer Roy deWilmot Tully RAFVR	25 Sep 1945	AG
Warrant Officer Roderick Adrian Powell RAFVR	25 Sep 1945	AG
Warrant Officer Herbert Winn RAFVR	25 Sep 1945	AG
Flying Officer Alec Gordon Leech RNZAF	25 Sep 1945	AG
Flying Officer Gwyn Duglan RAFVR	26 Oct 1945	AG
Pilot Officer Stanley Graham Watson RAFVR	26 Oct 1945	WOP
Warrant Officer John Edward Britnell RAFVR	6 Nov 1945	AG
Flying Officer John Rees Layton RNZAF	6 Nov 1945	Plt
Flying Officer Maurice Edward Parker RNZAF	6 Nov 1945	AB
Flying Officer Douglas Ross Sadgrove RNZAF	6 Nov 1945	Plt
Flight Lieutenant Ernest Joseph Abraham RNZAF	16 Nov 1945	Plt
Flying Officer Alexander Dunbar Simpson RNZAF	16 Nov 1945	Plt
Flying Officer Raymond Sinclair Tait RNZAF	16 Nov 1945	Nav
Flight Lieutenant Nelson Hugh Bawden RNZAF	4 Dec 1945	Nav
Flying Officer Kenneth William John Tugwell DFM RAFVR	7 Dec 1945	AG
Flying Officer Herbert William Hooper RNZAF	7 Dec 1945	Plt
Pilot Officer Douglas William James Marvin RAFVR	18 Dec 1945	WOP
Flight Lieutenant George Stanley Davies RNZAF	12 Feb 1946	Plt

Distinguished Flying Medal

Sergeant John Whitelaw Carter	30 Jul 1940	Nav
Sergeant Edwin Peter Williams RNZAF	30 Jul 1940	WOP
Sergeant Lewis Alan White	6 Aug 1940	AG
Sergeant Norman Wilson Brown	13 Sep 1940	Nav
Sergeant Donald MacKay	13 Sep 1940	Nav
Sergeant Harold Smith	13 Sep 1940	WOP
Sergeant Walter Stanley Kitson	22 Oct 1940	WOP
Sergeant William Alfred Allinson	22 Oct 1940	Nav
Sergeant John James Joseph Mylod	1 Nov 1940	AG
Sergeant Robert John Ellis	22 Nov 1940	Nav
Sergeant Leonard Roy Gould	22 Nov 1940	WOP
Sergeant Robert Henry Hughes	22 Nov 1940	Nav
Sergeant Sidney Roy Garrard	17 Jan 1941	WOP
Sergeant Thomas Leonard Mumby	17 Jan 1941	WOP
Sergeant Eric Norman Albert	11 Feb 1941	WOP
Sergeant Val Burdett	11 Feb 1941	WOP
Sergeant Francis William Green	11 Feb 1941	WOP
Sergeant Ronald John Healey	11 Feb 1941	AG
Sergeant Richard Noel Stubbs RAFVR	11 Feb 1941	Plt
Sergeant Dennis Chadwick Barnett	18 Apl 1941	Nav
Flight Sergeant Robert Alexander Newton	18 Jul 1941	WOP
Sergeant George Gascoyne	18 Jul 1941	AG
Sergeant Fred Haigh	18 Jul 1941	WOP
Sergeant Malcolm George Harris RAFVR	18 Jul 1941	Nav
Sergeant Allen Robert James Box RNZAF	29 Jul 1941	AG
Sergeant Ivan William Lewis	8 Aug 1941	WOP
Sergeant Edward Callander	2 Sep 1941	AG
Sergeant Herrald Raymond Corrin RNZAF	2 Sep 1941	AG
Sergeant Gwyn Martin	2 Sep 1941	Nav
Sergeant David Alexander Abbot RNZAF	23 Sep 1941	AG
Sergeant James Sutton Blundell	23 Sep 1941	WOP
Sergeant Henry Cumberland Stapleton Cotton RNZAF	23 Sep 1941	WAG
Sergeant Jack Joll RNZAF (Awarded DFC 15 October 1943)	23 Sep 1941	Plt
Sergeant Ralph Norman Allen RNZAF	30 Jan 1942	Plt

Flight Sergeant Ivor John McLachlan RNZAF	15 May 1942	Plt
Sergeant Francis Lawrence Curr RAAF	2 Oct 1942	Plt
Sergeant Richard Stansfield Derek Kearns RNZAF	27 Oct 1942	Plt
Flight Sergeant Kenneth Atherton Crankshaw RNZAF	29 Dec 1942	AG
(Awarded DFC with 156 Squadron 19 October 1943)		
Sergeant Neville John Netscher Hockaday	29 Dec 1942	Plt
Sergeant Robert Ernest Tod RCAF	4 May 1943	WOP
Flight Sergeant Frank Arthur Stevens	14 May 1943	WOP
Sergeant Mikaere Tutahunga Tomika Manawaiti RNZAF	14 May 1943	WAG
Sergeant Herbert James Dalzell RNZAF	21 May 1943	Plt
Sergeant Alfred James Ames	30 Jul 1943	FE
Sergeant Alexander Brown RNZAF	13 Aug 1943	AG
Sergeant Cyril Alan Worledge	24 Sep 1943	FE
Sergeant Timothy James Collins RAFVR	24 Sep 1943	AG
Flight Sergeant Walter Donald Whitehead RNZAF	8 Oct 1943	Plt
Flight Sergeant Trevor Gordon Dill RNZAF	7 Dec 1943	Nav
Flight Sergeant Kenneth John Dunmall RAFVR	30 May 1944	Plt
Flight Sergeant Arthur Hill RAFVR	23 Jun 1944	Nav
Flight Sergeant Robert Carroll RAFVR	15 Aug 1944	WOP
Flight Sergeant Jack Manns RAFVR	15 Aug 1944	AG
Flight Sergeant Arthur James Zacariah CADEY	15 Sep 1944	
Flight Sergeant Clifford Billington RAFVR	15 Sep 1944	AG
Flight Sergeant James Henry Murphy	15 Sep 1944	AG
Sergeant Kenneth Gordon Hook RAFVR	19 Sep 1944	AG
Flight Sergeant Eldrid Duke O'Callaghan RNZAF	27 Oct 1944	Plt
Flight Sergeant Albert Kirkham RAFVR	14 Nov 1944	AB
Flight Sergeant Norman William Strathearn RAFVR	14 Nov 1944	AB
Sergeant Allan Gibb RAFVR	22 Apl 1945	FE
Flight Sergeant Arthur Leonard Humphries RNZAF	25 May 1945	Nav
Flight Sergeant John Austin White Pauling RNZAF	5 Jun 1945	Nav
Flight Sergeant Thomas Dewsbury RNZAF	21 Sep 1945	AG

Member of the Order of the British Empire
Warrant Officer E. Roberts
Flying Officer Charles Eddy   Plt

British Empire Medal
Sergeant T. R. Read
Flight Sergeant A. D. Gordon
Flight Sergeant W. J. Ashby
Flight Sergeant T. J. Murphy
(One name unknown)

French Croix de Guerre
Flying Officer A. M. Miller

Totals
VC	1
DSO	8
MC	1
Bar to DFC	5
CGM	3
DFC	153
DFM	64
MBE	2
BEM	5

Appendix C

RAIDS FLOWN BY 75 NZ SQUADRON 1940–1945

Date		Target	Number of squadron aircraft	Losses	Remarks
1940					
March	27/28	Nickels to N Germany	3		
April	6/7	Nickels to N Germany	4		
	10	Recce to Narvik	1		
	17	Stavanger	3		1 abort
	21	Aalborg	3		
May	3	Norge coast	1		
	10/11	Waalhaven	3		
	12/13	Krefeld-Verdingden	3		
	15/16	Bridges in France	6		
	17/18	Ruhr — various	6		
	19/20	France — various	7		1st injury
	21/22	Aachen and Dinant	8	1	1st loss
	23/24	France — various	5		
	25/26	France and Belgium — various	8		
	28/29	Roulers and Menin	7		
June	31/1	Nieuport	9*		
	3/4	Dusseldorf	8		
	5/6	Cambrai	7		
	7/8	France — various	8		
	9/10	France — various	7		
	11/12	Black Forest	6		
	11/12	Fumay	2		
	13/14	French coastal ports	7		
	14/15	Black Forest	1		
	17/18	Ruhr	7		
	19/20	Ruhr	8		
	24/25	Ruhr	8		
	26/27	Germany — various	8		
	28/29	Cologne	8		
July	30/1	Frankfurt (forest)	6		
	2/3	Ruhr	5		
	4/5	N. German Ports	5		
	6/7	Bremen (U-boat pens)	5		
	8/9	Mors (Benzine plant)	6		
	14/15	Germany — various	7		
	18/19	Germany — various	6		
	20/21	Holland and Gelsenkirchen	9	1	
	25/26	Kassel	9	1	
	28/29	Germany — various	9		

* Record Ops
** Casos = casualties

† Most Stirling air-borne

*** Most Lancasters on an Op
†† Most aircraft in one night

August	3/4	Horst, Ruhr	9	1	crash landing
	6/7	Holland — airfields	8		
	9/10	Holland — airfields	9		
	13/14	Baltic ports	9		
	15/16	Germany — various	10*		
	17/18	Soest	10		1 abort
	19/20	Kiel and Dutch airfields	10		
	24/25	Germany — various	11*		1 abort
	26/27	Germany and Holland	10		
	29/30	Holland — airfields	8		
	29/30	St Nazaire	3		
Sept	1/2	Germany — various	11	1	crash landing
	4/5	German forest dumps	8		
	4/5	Chartres airfield	1		intruder op
	7/8	Black Forest dumps	9		
	10/11	Ostend and Flushing	7		
	12/13	Emden and Flushing	9		
	14/15	Antwerp and Soest	10		
	18/19	Le Havre	9		
	20/21	Hamburg/Le Havre	10	1	over Ostend
	23/24	Berlin	9		
	26/27	Le Havre	8		
	29/30	Osnabruck	10	1	1 abandoned/crashed
Oct	2/3	Enemy airfields	10		
	5/6	Rotterdam and Flushing	2		
	8/9	Gremburg and Cologne	10		
	10/11	Eindhoven airfield	10		
	14/15	Hanover and Lingen rail yards	8		
	16/17	Kiel and Hamburg docks	9	1	abandoned/crashed
	21/22	Hamburg and Eindhoven	9	1	crash landing
	23/24	Berlin (Potsdam Stn)	5	1	
	25/26	Brussels airfield	9		
	28/29	Wilhelmshaven/Antwerp	10		
Nov	6/7	Germany	2		1 abort
	8/9	Lastrup airfield	8		
	10/11	Munster/Eindhoven/Flushing	8		
	12/13	Schipol/Soesterburg airfields	7		
	16/17	Schipol/Soesterburg airfields	9		
	23/24	Berlin/Cologne/Boulogne	11		
	26/27	Berlin/Cologne/Hanover	10		
	29/30	Cologne	6		
Dec	6/7	France — various	13*		3 didn't bomb
	9/10	Bremen	8		
	11/12	Mannheim/Dieppe/Boulogne	5		
	13/14	Bremen	8		
	15/16	Frankfurt/Berlin/Bremen	8		
	16/17	Mannheim	10		
	19/20	Ruhr	8		3 didn't bomb
	22/23	Flushing/Rheims/Mannheim	12	1	2 didn't bomb
	29/30	Frankfurt/Hamm/Wilhelmshaven	3	1	

1941
Jan	1/2	Bremen	7		1 abort
	4/5	Duisberg/Brest	10		2 didn't bomb
	8/9	Wilhelmshaven	7		
	11/12	Wilhelmshaven	6		
	11/12	Turin	2		1 abort
	15/16	Wilhelmshaven	7		1 abort
	22/23	Dusseldorf	5		

	26/27	Hanover	7		1 abort
Feb	1/2	Boulogne	2		1 didn't bomb
	4/5	Le Havre	2		1 didn't bomb
	10/12	Hanover	13		1 crash landed
	14/15	Gelsenkirchen	12		
	21/22	Wilhelmshaven/Boulogne	7	1	
	23/24	Boulogne	8		
	26/27	Cologne	9		
March	1/2	Cologne	6		
	3/4	Cologne	11		
	12/13	Hamburg	9		
	13/14	Hamburg	8		
	15/16	Lorient	5		
	18/19	Kiel/Rotterdam	11	1	abandoned/crashed
	21/22	Ostend/Lorient	3		
	23/24	Berlin	6		
	27/28	Cologne/Dunkirk	9		
	30/31	Calais	1		
April	31/1	Rotterdam	2		1 didn't bomb
	3/4	Brest	8		1 didin't bomb
	6/7	Brest	10		
	7/8	Kiel	11		
	9/10	Berlin	9		
	14/15	Brest	10		
	16/17	Bremen	10		1 didn't bomb
	17/18	Berlin	7	1	crash landing
	20/21	Rotterdam	2		1 didn't bomb
	24/25	Ostend/Kiel	9		3 didn't bomb
	29/30	Mannheim/Rotterdam	12		2 didn't bomb
May	2/3	Hamburg/Emden	13		
	4/5	Brest	13		
	6/7	Hamburg	10	1	hit balloon/crashed
	8/9	Hamburg	12		
	9/10	Mannheim	12		
	11/12	Hamburg	11		
	17/18	Cologne/Boulogne	14*		1 abort
	23/24	Cologne	10		
	27	Ship search	12		*Bismark*
June	2/3	Dusseldorf	3		
	10/11	Brest	12		
	11/12	Dussedof/Boulogne	5		
	12/13	Hamm	10		
	15/16	Cologne/Dunkirk	4		2 abort
	16/17	Dusseldorf	15*		
	18/19	Brest	17*		
	21/22	Cologne/Dunkirk	15		
	24/25	Kiel/Dusseldorf	18*		
	27/28	Bremen	16		
July	30/1	Cologne	11		1 abort
	3/4	Essen	16	1	
	5/6	Munster	12		
	7/8	Munster	10		Ward — VC
	8/9	Munster	7		
	13/14	Bremen	11	1	crash landing
	15/16	Duisberg	9	1	1 damaged/casos**
	21/22	Mannheim/Cherbourg	11		
	24	Brest — (daylight)	6	1	Battleships
	24/25	Kiel	5		

Month	Date	Target			Notes
August	3/4	Hanover	10		
	6/7	Mannheim/Calais	13	1	
	8/9	Hamburg	8		
	12/13	Hanover/Le Havre	9		1 force landed
	14/15	Hanover	8		
	17/18	Duisberg	5		
	18/19	Dunkirk docks	2		
	26/27	Cologne/Boulogne	14		2 didn't bomb
	28/29	Ostend	3		
	29/30	Mannheim	9		1 didn't bomb
Sept	2/3	Frankfurt	10		1 abort
	6/7	Huls	13	1	
	7/8	Boulogne	1		
	8/9	Kassel	10		
	11/12	Kiel	12	1	4 didn't bomb
	13/14	Brest	12		1 didn't bomb
	15/16	Hamburg	12	2	
	17/18	Karlsruhe	8	1	
	20/21	Berlin/Ostend	12		some recalled
	26/27	Emden	3		
	27/28	Genoa/Frankfurt	9		
Oct	30/1	Stettin/Hamburg	6		
	3/4	Dunkirk	3		
	10/11	Cologne	8	1	
	12/13	Bremen/Nuremburg	9	1	+ 1 cr/landed
	14/15	Dusseldorf	1		
	15/16	Cologne/Boulogne	10	2	
	16/17	Cologne	1		
	20/21	Bremen	6		1 crash landed
	21/22	Cologne	1		
	22/23	Mannheim	6	1	
	24/25	Emden	2		
	26/27	Hamburg/Cherbourg	5	1	
Nov	1/2	Kiel	11		
	4/5	Essen	9		
	6/7	Essen/Le Havre	5		
	7/8	Berlin/Ostend	14	2	1 abort
	8/9	Essen	11	3	
	23/24	Dunkirk	7		
	26/27	Emden/Ostend	17		few bombed
	30/1	Emden/Hamburg	12	1	
Dec	12/13	Brest	9		
	15/16	Brest	5		
	17/18	Brest/Le Havre	7		1 damaged/casos
	23/24	Brest	7	1	crash landing
	27/28	Brest/Dusseldorf	12	1	abandoned/crashed

1942

Month	Date	Target			Notes
Jan	2/3	Brest	5		
	15/16	Schipol	2		1 abort
Feb	12	Channel Dash — daylight	2		didn't bomb
	17/18	Le Havre	1		
March	3/4	Paris — Renault works	1		
	8/9	Essen	10		
	9/10	Essen	11		
	12/13	Kiel	8	3	
	13/14	Dunkirk	4		
	25/26	Essen/St Nazaire	12	2	
	28/29	Lubeck	10	1	
April	1/2	Hanau/Le Havre	11		
	5/6	Cologne	10	2	CO lost

	6/7	Essen	7		
	8/9	Hamburg	9		
	10/11	Essen	8		
	12/13	Essen/Le Havre	10		
	13/14	Boulogne	2		
	14/15	Dortmund/Le Havre	7		
	15/16	Dortmund/Le Havre	8		
	17/18	Hamburg	8		
	22/23	Cologne	10	1	2 damaged/casos
	23/24	Rostock	7		
	25/26	Rostock/Dunkirk	7		
	27/28	Cologne/Mine laying	8		
	29/30	Gennevilliers	8		
May	2/3	Minelaying — St Nazaire	9		
	4/5	Stuttgart	8		
	6/7	Stuttgart	8		
	7/8	Minelaying — Kiel Bay	9		
	9/10	Minelaying — Kiel Bay	11		
	13/14	Essen	1		
	15/16	Minelaying — Kiel Bay	8	1	
	17/18	Boulogne	1		crash landed
	19/20	Mannheim/St Nazaire	9		
	21/22	La Pallice/Lorient	7		
	29/30	Dieppe	4		
	30/31	Cologne (Thousand Raid)	23*	1	1 damaged
June	31/1	Cologne		1	
	1/2	Essen (Thousand Raid)	20		
	2/3	Essen	16	1	
	4/5	Dieppe	2		
	5/6	Essen	13		
	6/7	Emden	12		
	8/9	Essen	12	2	
	16/17	Essen	7		
	17/18	Minelaying — Frisians	8		
	19/20	Emden	11		
	20/21	Emden	12	1	
	22/23	Emden	13		
	23/24	St Nazaire	8		
	25/26	Bremen	20		
	28/29	Bremen/St Nazaire	4		
	29/30	Bremen	18	2	1 crashed on take-off
July	2/3	Bremen	12		
	3/4	Sea Search	1		
	7/8	Minelaying — Frisians	10		
	8/9	Wilhelmshaven	13	1	
	10	Dusseldorf	4	1	daylight raid
	13/14	Duisburg	9		
	14/15	Minelaying — Terschelling	3		
	20	Bremen	6		daylight raid
	21/22	Duisburg	13		
	23/24	Duisburg	14		
	25/26	Duisburg	13		
	26/27	Hamburg	15	2	
	27	Bremen	2		daylight
	28/29	Hamburg	17	6	
	29/30	Saarbrucken	10		
August	31/1	Dusseldorf	11		1 damaged/casos
	4/5	Essen	5		
	6/7	Duisburg	8		1 crash landed
	9/10	Osnabruck	7		

	11/12	Mainz	9	3	1 abort
	12/13	Mainz	5		
	17/18	Osnabruck	3		
	20/21	Minelaying — St Nazaire	5	1	
	24/25	Minelaying — Frisians	2		
	24/25	Frankfurt	8		
	27/28	Kassel	12	1	1 damaged/ crash landed
	28/29	Nuremburg	10	2	
Sept	1/2	Saarbrucken	11		
	2/3	Karlsruhe	6		
	3/4	Emden	6	2	
	4/5	Bremen	12		
	6/7	Duisburg	15	2	
	8/9	Frankfurt/Schweinfurt	9	1	
	10/11	Dusseldorf	13	3	
	13/14	Bremen	8		
	14/15	Wilhelmshaven	6		
	15/16	Minelaying — Frisians	4		
	16/17	Essen	8		1 crash landed
	18/19	Minelaying — St Nazaire	5		
	19/20	Saarbrucken	8		
	22	Sea search	3		
	24/25	Minelaying — Texel	5		
	26/27	Minelaying — Baltic	7		
	26/27	Minelaying — Frisians	4		
	28/29	Lingen	3		
Oct	30/1	Minelaying — Terschelling	4		
	2/3	Krefeld	13		
	5/6	Aachen	15		
	6/7	Osnabruck	14	1	
	8/9	Minelaying — Ostend	3		
	8/9	Minelaying — Ile de Grox	2		
	9/10	Minelaying — Frisians	7		
	11/12	Minelaying — Kattegat	9	1	
	13/14	Kiel	13	1	1 crash landed/ casos
	15/16	Cologne	7		
	22	Lingen	2		daylight
	22	Essen	3		daylight
	23/24	Milan	8	2	
	25/26	Minelaying — Frisians/Brest	4		
Nov	20/21	Turin	4		
	22/23	Stuttgart	2		
	28/29	Turin	4		1 crash landed
	29/30	Turin	2		2 abort
Dec	2/3	Frankfurt	2	1	
	4/5	Minelaying — Frisians	4		
	6/7	Mannheim	3		2 abort
	7/8	Minelaying — Frisians	2		
	8/9	Minelaying — Baltic	2		
	9/10	Turin	5		
	16/17	Minelaying — Bordeaux	9	1	crashed on take-off
	17/18	Fallersleben	5	4	CO missing
	20/21	Duisburg	1		
1943					
Jan	8/9	Minelaying — Denmark	3		
	9/10	Minelaying — Terschelling	2		
	12/13	Minelaying — Gironde	4		

	Date	Target	Sorties	Losses	Notes
	14/15	Lorient	3		
	15/16	Lorient	3		1 abort
	18/19	Minelaying — Gironde	2		1 abort
	23/24	Lorient	9	1	
	27/28	Minelaying — Terschelling	2		
Feb	3/4	Hamburg	9	2	
	4/5	Turin	7		2 bombed French target
	5/6	Minelaying — Frisians	4	1	
	7/8	Lorient	9		1 abort
	13/14	Lorient	11	1	1 abort
	14/15	Cologne	8		1 abort
	16/17	Lorient	7		
	16/17	Minelaying — Bordeaux	3		
	18/19	Minelaying — Gironde	7		
	19/20	Wilhelmshaven	7		1 abort
	25/26	Nuremburg	7		2 abort
	26/27	Cologne	7		2 abort
	26/27	Minelaying — Frisians	4		
	27/28	Minelaying — St Jean de Lux	2		1 abort
	27/28	Minelaying — Gironde	1		
	27/28	Minelaying — Frisians	4		
March	28/1	St Nazaire	6		
	1/2	Berlin	8		2 abort
	3/4	Hamburg	8		1 abort
	3/4	Minelaying — Frisians	3	1	
	5/6	Essen	9	1	crashed on take-off / 1 abort
	8/9	Nuremburg	9	1	1 abort
	9/10	Munich	5		1 abort
	9/10	Minelaying — Gironde	3		1 abort
	11/12	Stuttgart	8		
	12/13	Essen	7		1 abort
	23/24	Minelaying — Frisians	1		
	27/28	Berlin	11		1 abort
	28/29	St Nazaire	2		
	29/30	Berlin	8		3 abort
	29/30	Minelaying — Frisians	1		
April	4/5	Kiel	9		4 abort
	6/7	Minelaying — Gironde	2		
	8/9	Duisburg	9	1	crashed/4 abort
	8/9	Minelaying — Gironde	1		
	10/11	Frankfurt	12	2	3 abort/1 ditch
	10/11	Minelaying — Frisians	2		
	14/15	Stuttgart	11	1	1 abort
	15/16	Minelaying — Gironde	1		
	16/17	Ludwigshaven	11	2	1 abort
	20/21	Rostock	9	1	
	22/23	Minelaying — Gironde	8		
	26/27	Duisburg	7		1 crash landed
	27/28	Minelaying — Frisians	5		1 abort
	28/29	Minelaying — Kiel Bay	8	4	1 abort
May	1/2	Minelaying — Gironde	2		
	4/5	Dortmund	9		2 abort
	5/6	Minelaying — Frisians	5	1	
	9/10	Minelaying — Ile de Re	6		
	12/13	Duisburg	7	1	crashed on take-off
	13/14	Bochum	12		
	13/14	Minelaying — Frisians	1		
	16/17	Minelaying — Frisians	4		

	17/18	Minelaying — La Pallice	2		
	21/22	Minelaying — Frisians/Gironde	11		
	23/24	Dortmund	15†	1	
	27/28	Minelaying — Frisians	5		
	29/30	Wuppertal	20†	4	2 abort
June	1/2	Minelaying — Frisians	2		
	5/6	Minelaying — Frisians	5		
	11/12	Dusseldorf	16	1	2 abort
	14/15	Minelaying — Gironde	6	1	
	19/20	Le Cruesot	14		
	21/22	Krefeld	15		1 abort
	22/23	Mulheim	15	4	
	24/25	Wuppertal	13	1	1 abort
	25/26	Gelsenkirchen	11	1	
	25/26	Minelaying — Gironde	1		
July	3/4	Cologne	13		1 abort
	3/4	Minelaying — Frisians	4		
	4/5	Minelaying — Ile de Re	4		
	5/6	Minelaying — Frisians	4	1	
	8/9	Minelaying — Gironde	6		
	13/14	Aachen	9	1	crash landed
	24/25	Hamburg	23†	1	2 abort
	25/26	Essen	19	1	2 abort
	27/28	Hamburg	22		2 abort
	29/30	Hamburg	17		2 abort
	30/31	Remscheid	13	2	1 abort
	30/31	Minelaying — Frisians	1		
August	2/3	Hamburg	17	2	6 abort
	6/7	Minelaying — Gironde	5	1	1 abort
	9/10	Minelaying — Frisians	3		
	10/11	Nuremburg	19		
	12/13	Turin	18		
	15/16	Minelaying — Gironde	4	1	all diverted
	16/17	Turin	12		1 abort
	17/18	Peenemunde	12		2 abort
	21/22	Minelaying — Frisians	3		
	23/24	Berlin	23	3	5 abort/ 1 damaged
	24/25	Minelaying — Frisians	1		
	26/27	Minelaying — Gironde	1		
	27/28	Nuremburg	19	1	
	27/28	Minelaying — Frisians	2		
	30/31	Munchen-Gladbach	18	1	
	30/31	Minelaying — Frisians	2		
Sept	31/1	Berlin	16	4	
	2/3	Minelaying — Frisians	5		1 abort
	2/3	Minelaying — Ile de Re	2		
	5/6	Mannheim	19	1	1 abort
	8/9	Boulogne	17	1	crashed on take-off
	15/16	Montlucon	16		
	16/17	Modane	19		
	18/19	Minelaying — Gironde	3		
	21/22	Minelaying — Frisians	2		
	22/23	Hanover	20		
	23/24	Mannheim	18	3	
	24/25	Minelaying — Frisians	2		
	27/28	Hanover	16	2	1 abort
	27/28	Minelaying — Frisians	2		
Oct	2/3	Minelaying — Frisians/Baltic	9		
	3/4	Kassel	15		RG lost over tgt

207

		4/5	Frankfurt	13	1	3 abort
		4/5	Minelaying — Gironde	2		
		7/8	Minelaying — Frisians	6		
		8/9	Bremen	12		Spoof raid
		8/9	Minelaying — Gironde	2		
		17/18	Minelaying — Gironde/Frisians	3		
		20/21	Minelaying — Frisians	1		
		22/23	Minelaying — Frisians	3		
		24/25	Minelaying — Frisians	2	1	crashed
		25/26	Minelaying — Baltic	3		
	Nov	3/4	Minelaying — Frisians	3		
		4/5	Minelaying — Baltic	4	3	1 abort/1 dam'd
		7/8	Minelaying — Gironde	4		
		10/11	Minelaying — Gironde	2		
		11/12	Minelaying — Gironde	2		
		19/20	Leverkusen	16	1	
		22/23	Berlin	4	2	1 abort
		25/26	Minelaying — Biscay	5		
		25/26	Minelaying — Frisians	2		
		26/27	Minelaying — Frisians	4		
	Dec	30/1	Minelaying — Baltic	4		
		1/2	Minelaying — Danish coast	3	1	crashed
		16/17	V1 site — Abbeville	8	2	crashed
		16/17	Minelaying — Frisians/Biscay	4	1	crashed
		20/21	Minelaying — Frisians	3		
		22/23	V1 site — Abbeville	6		
		22/23	Minelaying — Le Havre	2		
		29/30	Minelaying — Gironde/Biscay	7		
		30/31	Minelaying — Gironde/Le Havre	3		
	1944					
	Jan	2/3	Minelaying — Frisians	3		
		4/5	Minelaying — North of Biarritz	6	1	crashed
		4/5	Minelaying — Gironde	4		
		6/7	Minelaying — Gironde	8		
		14/15	V1 site — Ailly	15		2 abort
		14/15	Minelaying — Frisians	2		1 abort
		20/21	Minelaying — Frisians	6		
		21/22	V1 site	20		
		25/26	V1 site — Pas de Calais	19		4 didn't bomb
		27/28	Minelaying — Heligoland	13		
		27/28	Minelaying — Danish coast	4		
		28/29	Minelaying — Kiel Bay	19		3 abort/1 crash landed
		30/31	Minelaying — Gironde	6		5 didn't drop
	Feb		Minelaying — various	108	1	(24 Feb — Kiel)
	March	2/3	Minelaying — Le Havre	4		1 abort
		2/3	Supply drops — France	10		
		3/4	Minelaying — Le Havre	8		
		4/5	Supply drops — France	15	1	
		6/7	Supply drops — France	1		
		7/8	Supply drops — France	10		
		10/11	Supply drops — France	19		1 abort
		11/12	Supply drops — France	7		6 didn't drop
		13/14	Minelaying — Biscay coast	16	1	1 abort
		15/16	Supply drops — France	15		
		16/17	Amiens — marshalling yards	12		1 abort
		18/19	Minelaying — Heligoland	7		
		19/20	Minelaying — River Adour	4		
		21/22	Minelaying — St Malo	4		
		22/23	Minelaying — Kiel Bay	6		

	23/24	Laon — marshalling yards	4		
	25/26	Aulnoye — railway yards	5		
	26/27	Courtrai — railway yards	7		
	30/31	Minelaying — Le Havre/Denmark	4		
April	5/6	Minelaying — La Rochelle	5		
	9/10	Lille — goods station	4		
	9/10	Villeneuve — railway yards	11		First Lanc Op
	10/11	Minelaying — La Rochelle	5		Stirlings
	10/11	Laon	8		Lancasters
	11/12	Minelaying — La Rochelle	1		Stirling
	11/12	Aachen	3		Lancasters
	18/19	Rouen — marshalling yards	9		Lancasters
	18/19	Minelaying — Kiel Bay	6	1	Stirlings
	20/21	Cologne	8		Lancasters
	20/21	Minelaying — Brest	4		Stirlings
	22/23	Dusseldorf	8		Lancasters
	22/23	Laon	5		Stirlings
	23/24	Minelaying — Kiel Bay	5	1	last Stirling
	24/25	Karlsruhe	16		Lancasters
	26/27	Essen	13		
	27/28	Friedrichshafen	16	1	1st Lanc loss
May	1/2	Chambly — marshalling yards	16	1	
	7/8	Bougon airfield	10		
	9/10	Cap Griz Nez — batteries	15		
	10/11	Courtrai — marshalling yards	23***		
	11/12	Louvain — marshalling yards	24***	1	
	19/20	Le Mans — marshalling yards	24		
	21/22	Duisburg	25***	1	1 abort
	22/23	Dortmund	23	2	3 abort
	24/25	Aachen	13		
	24/25	Boulogne — batteries	11		
	27/28	Aachen	18	2	1 abort
	27/28	Minelaying — La Rochelle	2		
	28/29	Angers — marshalling yards	16		2 abort
	30/31	Boulogne — batteries	10		
June	31/1	Trappes — marshalling yards	23		1 abort
	2/3	Wissant — batteries	15		13 didn't bomb
	3/4	Calais — batteries	10		
	4/5	Minelaying — North Sea	3		
	5/6	Quistreham — batteries	26***		pre D-Day
	6/7	Lisieux — landing support	24		D-Day
	7/8	Massy Palaiseau	6		1 abort
	8/9	Fourgeres	20		
	10/11	Dreux — marshalling yards	24	2	Conspicuous Gallantry Medal (CGM)
	11/12	Nantes	17		
	12/13	Gelsenkirchen	15		
	14/15	Le Havre	26		1 abort
	15/16	Valenciennes — marshalling yards	24	1	
	23/24	V1 site — Rimeux	25	1	
	27/28	V1 site — Biennais	15		
	30	Villers-Bocage — support	22		daylight
July	2/3	V1 site — Beauvoir	23		
	5/6	V1 site — Watton	24		
	7/8	Vaires — marshalling yards	21		3 abort
	9	V1 site — Linzieux	25		daylight
	10	V1 site — Nucourt	27***		daylight
	12	Vaires — marshalling yards	25		daylight
	15/16	Chalons-sur-Marne — marshalling yards	18 ⎤††		
	15/16	V1 site — Bois de Jardine	10 ⎦		

	18	Cagny — army support	28***		dawn/CGM
	18/19	Aulnoye — aircraft works	27	1	
	20/21	Homberg — oil refinery	26	7	record losses
	22/23	Minelaying — Kattegat	6		
	23/24	Kiel	20		
	24/25	Stuttgart	21	2	1 abort
	25/26	Stuttgart	14		4 didn't bomb
	28/29	Stuttgart	22	2	
	30	Amaye-sur-Seulles	17	1	dawn/low level
August	1	V1 site — Le Nieppe	16		6 didn't bomb
	3	V1 site — L'Isle Adam	20		daylight
	4	Bec D'Ambes — refinery	20		daylight
	5	V1 site — Bois de Cassan	18		
	7/8	Mare de Magne — support	17	1	
	8/9	Lucheux — petrol dump	20		
	9/10	Fort D'Anglos	17		
	11	Lens — marshalling yards	22		daylight
	12/13	Brunswick	6		
	12/13	Russelsheim	10	1	
	12/13	Falais	1		
	12/13	Minelaying — Gironde	6		
	14	Hamel	22		daylight
	15	St Trond — aerodrome	19		daylight
	16/17	Stettin	23		1 abort
	18/19	Bremen	25		1 abort
	25/26	Russelsheim	28	2	
	26/27	Kiel	20		
	29/30	Stettin	14	1	
	29/30	Minelaying — Danzig	6		
Sept	31/1	Pont Remy	18		
	3	Eindhoven airfield	10		daylight
	5	Le Havre	25		daylight
	6	Harquebec — German HQ	24		daylight
	8	Doudeneville — support	23		13 didn't bomb
	10	Montvilliers	27		daylight
	11	Kamen — refinery	15		daylight
	11/12	Minelaying — Baltic	8	1	
	12/13	Frankfurt	22		
	14	Waasenaar — ammo dump	10		daylight
	16/17	Moerdijk Bridge	12		
	17	Boulogne — support	14		1 crashed/casos
	17/18	Emmerich	10		
	20	Calais — support	27		
	23/24	Neuss — marshalling yards	26		
	26	Cap Gris Nez — support	18		daylight
	27	Calais — support	14		daylight
	28	Calais — support	12		11 didn't bomb
	29/30	Minelaying — Kattegat	5		
Oct	3	West Kappelle Dyke	21		daylight
	4/5	Minelaying — Kattegat	5		
	5/6	Saarbrucken	31***	1	17 didn't bomb
	6/7	Dortmund	29	1	
	7	Emmerich	26		daylight
	14	Duisburg	31		daylight
	14/15	Duisburg	29		
	15/16	Minelaying — Kattegat	5		
	18	Bonn	16		daylight
	19/20	Stuttgart	28		
	21	Flushing — gun battery	25	1	daylight
	22	Neuss	9		daylight
	23/24	Essen	27		

	25	Essen	26		daylight
	26	Leverkusen	10		daylight
	28	Flushing	13		daylight
	28	Cologne	7		daylight
	29	West Kappelle	14		daylight
	30	Wesseling	6		daylight
	30/31	Cologne	21		
	31	Bottrop — oil plant	6		daylight
Nov	31/1	Cologne	18		
	2	Homberg	20		daylight
	4	Solingen	21	1	daylight
	5	Solingen	18		daylight
	6/7	Coblenz	16		
	8	Homberg — refinery	12		daylight
	11	Castrop-Rauxel — refinery	6		daylight
	11/12	Minelaying — Oslo Fiord	4		
	15	Dortmund — oil refinery	25		daylight
	16	Heinsberg — support	25		daylight
	20	Homberg — refinery	28	3	daylight
	21	Homberg — refinery	21		daylight
	21/22	Minelaying — Oslo Fiord	3	1	
	23	Gelsenkirchen — refinery	25		daylight
	27	Cologne — marshalling yards	23		daylight
	28/29	Neuss	21		
	30	Osterfeld	18	1	daylight
Dec	2	Dortmund	17		daylight
	4	Oberhausen	20		daylight
	5	Hamm — marshalling yards	21		daylight
	6/7	Merseburg — oil refinery	12	1	ditched
	8	Duisburg	21		daylight
	11	Osterfeld	17		daylight
	12	Witten	16		daylight
	14/15	Minelaying — Kattegat	4		
	16	Siegen	18		3 abort
	19/20	Minelaying — Dornbusch	4		
	21	Trier	20		7 didn't bomb
	23	Trier	21		daylight
	27	Rheydt	20	1	daylight
	28	Grenburg — marshalling yards	21		2 abort
	29	Coblenz — marshalling yards	9		daylight
	30/31	Minelaying — Heligoland	4		
	31	Vohwinkel — marshalling yards	17		
1945					
Jan	1/2	Vohwinkel — marshalling yards	21	1	CO lost
	2/3	Nuremburg	9		1 abort
	3	Dortmund — oil refinery	14		daylight
	5	Ludwigshaven	21		daylight
	6/7	Neuss	15		4 didn't bomb
	6/7	Minelaying — Pilau	4		
	7/8	Munich	8		
	11	Krefeld	19		daylight
	13	Saarbrucken	19		daylight
	15	Langendreer	18		daylight
	16/17	Wanne Eickel	17	1	crashed
	22	Duisburg	15		daylight
	28	Cologne	20		daylight
	29	Krefeld — marshalling yards	19		daylight
Feb	1	Munchen-Gladbach	17		daylight
	2/3	Wiesbaden	18		
	3/4	Dortmund	16	1	crashed
	8/9	Hohenbudberg	21		

211

	13/14	Dresden	20		
	14/15	Chemnitz	21	1	1 abort
	16	Wesel	21		daylight
	18	Wesel	21		1 abort
	19	Wesel	21		daylight
	20/21	Dortmund	10		1 abort
	22	Osterfeld	21		1 abort
	23	Gelsenkirchen	16		
	24/25	Minelaying — Oslo Fiord	2		
	25	Kamen	18	1	daylight
	26	Dortmund	18	1	crashed
	27	Gelsenkirchen	18		2 abort
	28	Gelsenkirchen	15		daylight
March	1	Kamen	17		daylight
	2	Cologne	20		1 damaged/casos
	4	Wanne Eickel	18		daylight
	5	Gelsenkirchen	21		daylight
	6	Salzbergen — refinery	16		daylight
	6/7	Wesel	8		
	7/8	Minelaying — Kiel Bay	1		
	7/8	Dessau	13		
	9	Datteln — oil plant	21		daylight
	10	Gelsenkirchen	21		daylight
	11	Essen	21		daylight
	12	Dortmund	21		daylight
	14	Hattingen — oil plant	20	1	daylight
	17	Huls — oil plant	19		daylight
	18	Langendreer — oil plant	17		daylight
	20	Hamm	21		daylight
	21	Munster Viaduct	21	3	daylight
	23	Wesel	8		daylight
	27	Hamm	21		daylight
	25/26	Nickel — Hague	1		
	29	Salzgitter	21		daylight
April	4/5	Meresburg	21		1 damaged/casos
	9/10	Minelaying — Kiel Bay	7		
	9/10	Kiel	19		
	13/14	Kiel	21		
	13/14	Minelaying — Kiel Bay	5		
	14/15	Potsdam (Berlin)	25		1 damaged/casos
	18	Heligoland Naval Base	25		daylight
	20	Regensburg	20		daylight
	22	Bremen	21		1 damaged/casos
	24	Bad Oldesloe — rail yards	21		daylight
	29	Supply drop — Delft	9		daylight
	30	Supply drop — Rotterdam	21		daylight
May	1	Supply drop — Delft	21		daylight
	2	Supply drop — Delft	21		daylight
	3	Supply drop — Delft/Hague	10		daylight
	4	Supply drop — Delft/Hague	6		daylight
	5	Supply drop — Hague	4		daylight
	7	Supply drop — Delft	26		daylight
	8	Supply drop — Rotterdam	8		daylight

Appendix D

GERMAN AIRCRAFT CLAIMED BY SQUADRON AIR GUNNERS 1940–1945*

Date	Type	Claim	Gunner/s	Pilot	Aircraft	Target
1940						
July 20	Me109	Probable	Sgt L. A. White	FO N. Williams	L7797	Wessel
20	Me109	Probable	Sgt L. A. White	FO N. Williams	L7797	Wessel
20	Me109	Damaged	Sgt L. A. White	FO N. Williams	L7797	Wessel
Aug 27	Me109	In flames	Sgt J. Gibbs Sgt Anderson	PO J. Adams	L7784	Nivelles
Oct 10	Fighter	Destroyed	Sgt J. J. J. Mylod	PO D. McArthur	T2736	Eindhoven
1941						
Apl 4	Me110	Destroyed	FO W. D. Brown	FO D. Prichard	R1161	Brest
July 7	Me110	Damaged	Sgt A. J. R. Box	SL R. Widdowson	L7818	Munster
24	Me109	Probable	Sgt J. Callender	PO A. Saunders	R1457	Brest
Aug 12	Fighter	Damaged		PO H. A. Roberts	X9764	Hanover
Dec 28	Me110	Damaged			Z1077	Dusseldorf
1942						
Apl 28	Me110	Damaged	FS R. Newdick	PO R. Leggett	X3538	Bremen
June 3	Ju88	Destroyed	Sgt R. J. F. Hurst	FS F. Wilmshurst	X3720	Essen
21	Ju88	Damaged	Sgt B. Neal	Sgt J. Wright	X3646	Emden
26	Me109	Damaged	Sgt G. W. N. Archer	Sgt R. Bertram	Z1616	Oldenberg
30	Ju88	Destroyed	Sgt B. Philip	Sgt N. Hockaday	BJ837	Bremen
July 20	Me110	Damaged	Sgt T. Crearer	Sgt C. Croall	X3452	Bremen
Aug 25	FW190	Damaged	Sgt H. Price	Sgt R. Kearns	X3396	Frankfurt
28	Ju88	Probable	Sgt R. Gorman	Sgt F. Burrill	BJ584	Kassel
29	Me110	Damaged	Sgt H. Hamerton	FL L. G. Trott	X3936	Nurnberg
Sep 17	Ju88	Destroyed	FS R. C. Reynolds	FS J. Wright	BJ772	Essen
Dec 18	Me109	Probable	PO D. S-White	PO J. McCulloch	R9250	Fallersleben
18	Me109	Damaged	Sgt K. Kimberley	PO J. McCulloch	R9250	Fallersleben
1943						
Mar 2	Ju88	Destroyed	Sgt J. Negus Sgt J. Howat	FL G. Rothwell	BF451	Berlin
30	(unident)	Shot down	Sgt H. E. Moss Sgt M. J. Moran	PO R. O. French	BK602	Berlin
May 5	Ju88	Probable	Sgt J. Gratton	Sgt A. Sedunary	BK776	Dortmund
14	Me110	Destroyed	Sgt V. Newman	Sgt J. Mitchell	BF561	Bochum
14			Sgt G. Shinn			
14	FW190	Probable	Sgt J. O'Farrell Sgt A. E. Parker	Sgt A. Thomas	BK614	Bochum

---

* This list is not claimed as complete, having been taken from surviving records and an incomplete file of Squadron Combat Reports. This list indicates the following tally: Destroyed — 26, Probables — 14, Damaged — 47, Uncertain — 4.

   The squadron is often shown as having 'destroyed' 45 enemy night fighters but this author is unable to find whether certain 'probable' or 'damaged' claims were subsequently upgraded, or how the figure of 45 was reached. It may be that the 'destroyed' and 'probable' claims have been added together. This list, therefore, is just a guide to the work of the valiant air gunners in defending their aircraft and fellow crew members.

	24	Ju88	Damaged	Sgt W. Hemsley	Sgt H. Williams	'T'	Dortmund
	24	Ju88	Damaged	Sgt I. Kaye	Sgt H. Williams	'T'	Dortmund
June	12	Ju88	Damaged	FS V. Jamieson	FS W. Whitehead	EH880	Dusseldorf
	12	(unident)	Damaged	Sgt G. Colyer Sgt H. Squire	FO W. Perrott	BK768	Dusseldorf
	22	Me109	Damaged	Sgt J. Hubbock Sgt A. Peters	Sgt A. Burley	BF434	Krefeld
	26	S/E ftr	Destroyed	Sgt S. Kurton Sgt H. Jones	SL R. Broadbent	BK778	Gelsenkirchen
July	14	Me210	Probable	FS Scott	PO A. Alexander	BK777	Aachen
	14	Ju88	Destroyed	Sgt J. Ogden	PO A. Rankin	BK646	Aachen
	14	T/E ftr	Damaged	FS B. L. Cooksley	Sgt H. Nicol	BF518	Aachen
	26	FW190	Destroyed	Sgt W. Hemsley FS I. Kaye	FS H. Williams	EH936	Essen
	28	Ju88	Damaged	PO J. Hayden Sgt D. Haub	FS E. Roberts	EE897	Hamburg
	31	T/E ftr	Damaged	FL W. McAlpine	FO G. Duncan	EE898	Hamburg
	31	T/E ftr	Destroyed	Sgt R. Poole	FO G. Duncan	EE898	Hamburg
Aug	13	S/E ftr	Damaged	Sgt A. Peters	PO A. Burley	BF434	Turin
	17	S/E ftr	Damaged	Sgt G. Dummett Sgt T. Grange	WC M. Wyatt	EH880	Turin
	24	Ju88	Damaged	Sgt E. Robson Sgt G. Wilkinson	FS E. Wilkinson	EH901	Berlin
	24	Me109	Destroyed	FS V. Jamieson	FS W. Whitehead	BF465	Berlin
	24	Me110	Destroyed	Sgt F. Crowther Sgt A. Knox	PO C. Logan	BK778	Berlin
	24	Me110	Probable	FS A. Lyon FS W. H. MacDonald	FO A. Alexander	BK777	Berlin
	31	Me110	Probable	Sgt F. Crowther Sgt A. Knox	PO C. Logan	EH935	Munchen-Gladbach
	31	Ftr	Probable	Sgt G. Dummett	FS H. Batger	EF491	Munchen-Gladbach
	31	Me110	Probable	Sgt T. Grange	FS K. McGregor	EF501	Munchen-Gladbach
Sept	1	Me109	Damaged	Sgt F. Crowther Sgt A. Knox	PO C. Logan	EH881	Berlin
	1	Ju88	Damaged	FS T. O'Sullivan FS W. Eaton	WO P. Hartstein	EF454	Berlin
	1	Ju88	Damaged	Sgt E. Robson FS G. Wilkinson	FS E. Wilkinson	EE893	Berlin
	1	Me109 Me109	Destroyed Damaged	FS A. Lyon FS W. MacDonald	FO A. Alexander	EH880	Berlin
	1	T/E ftr	Damaged	Sgt C. Middleton Sgt A. North	WO P. Moseley	EE958	Berlin
	6	Me109	Destroyed	Sgt C. Billington Sgt J. Manns	FS H. Batger	EF435	Mannheim
	6	Ftr	Destroyed	Sgt Chesson Sgt T. Waerea	FS R. Whitmore	EH877	Mannheim
	17	Ju88	Destroyed	FS F. McGregor PO A. Black Sgt R. Ingrey	PO G. Williams	BF461	Modane
	17	Ju88	Damaged	Sgt R. Ingrey	PO G. Williams	BF461	Modane
	24	FW190	Damaged	Sgt V. Newman	PO J. Mitchell	EF152	Mannheim
	24	S/E ftr	Destroyed	FO S. Strong	PO A. Burley	EF137	Mannheim
	24	T/E ftr	Damaged	FO S. Strong	PO A. Burley	EF137	Mannheim
	24	T/E ftr	Damaged	FO S. Strong	PO A. Burley	EF137	Mannheim
	24	Ju88	Damaged	Sgt A. North	WO P. Moseley	EE958	Mannheim
	28	Ju88	Destroyed	Sgt R. McGregor Sgt T. Anderson	FS F. Burton	KF465	Hanover
	28	Ju88	Destroyed	Sgt I. T. Teaika	FS D. Horgan	EF148	Hanover

Oct 5	Me109	Damaged	PO W. Reid	SL J. Joll	EH880	Frankfurt
9	Ju88	Damaged	Sgt J. Kenefick	FS H. Humphreys	EF462	Bremen
9	Ftr	Damaged	FS I. Kaye	PO H. Williams	EH936	Bremen
Nov 11	Ju88	Damaged	FO M. Eaves	FS C. McKenzie	EF514	mining
19	Me109	Damaged	FS J. Clift	FS R. Spiers	EF512	Ludwigshaven
20	Ju88	Damaged	Sgt Cooper FS I. T. Teaika	FS D. Horgan	LJ462	Leverkusen

1944

Jan 5	FW190	Damaged	Sgt A. Newnham	FS E. Burke	BK695	V1 site
7	Ju88	Damaged	Sgt G. Hopkins Sgt H. Pritchard	Sgt J. Carey	EF454	mining
Apl 26	Me210	Damaged	Sgt Griffin	FS A. Gray	R5692	Essen
May 12	Ju88	Destroyed	FS N. Trott	FL S. A. Clark	ND917	Louvain
24	Ftr	Destroyed	Sgt Bellis	FO R. Berney		Aachen
June 18	FW190	Probable	FS Fletcher	FS H. Whittington	ND756	Montdidier
July 19	(2 unident)	Shot down	Sgt T. Hopkins Sgt T. Farrow	FO G. Kennedy	ME751	Aulnoye
21	Me410	Damaged	FS G. Ellis FO W. Cotterall	SL L. Drummond	HK568	Homberg
26	FW190	Destroyed	Sgt B. Johnson	FS M. Smith	HK554	Stuttgart
26	JU88	Damaged	FO D. F. Archer	FO F. E. Stott	ND917	Stuttgart
29	(unident)	Destroyed	FO W. Cotterall	SL L. Drummond	LL921	Stuttgart
29	Ju88	Damaged	FO W. Cotterall	SL L. Drummond	LL921	Stuttgart
Aug 17	Ju88	Damaged	Sgt L. B. Moore	PO J. Layton	ND782	Stettin
26	S/E ftr	Damaged	Sgt S. Glendening FS B. Chatfield	FS G. Moore	HK953	Russelheim
30	Ju88	Probable	Sgt J. Beardmore Sgt J. Bayes	FO J. Scott	HK601	Stettin
Sept 12	(unident)	Destroyed	Sgt T. Farrow	FO J. Bateman	LM266	mining
Oct 7	(unident)	Destroyed	Sgt A. Ballard	FS W. Farr	NF935	Dortmund
Dec 30	(unident)	Damaged	Sgt J. Nicol	FO E. Parsons	LM544	mining

1945

Feb 4	Me110	Destroyed	WO T. Kemp FO R. Tully	SL J. Wright	ME751	Dortmund

Appendix E

SQUADRON OPERATIONAL LOSSES 1940–1945

(Compiled by Kevin King and John Tyler)

Abbreviations:

A/c — Aircraft	AB — Air Bomber	
POW — Prisoner of War	Capt — Captain	AC — Aircraftman
	FE — Flight Engineer	FL — Flight Lieutenant
	F/gnr — Front Gunner	FO — Flying Officer
	MU — Mid-upper Gunner	FS — Flight Sergeant
	Nav — Navigator	PO — Pilot Officer
Aus — Australia	2/Plt — Second Pilot	Sgt — Sergeant
Can — Canada	R/gnr — Rear Gunner	SL — Squadron Leader
NZ — New Zealand	WOP — Wireless Operator	WO — Warrant Officer

Date: 21 May 1940.
Target: Dinant.
A/c. Wellington Ic. R3157.
  Capt: FL Collins, J. N. (NZ) — Killed
  2/Pilot: PO De La
    Bouchere-Sparling,
    F.A.G.F.J. — Killed
  Nav: Sgt Thorpe, G. — POW
  WOP: AC Brooks, J. S. — POW
  R/gnr: PO Hockey, L. P. R. — POW

Date: 20 July 1940.
Target: Gelsenkirchen.
A/c. Wellington Ic. R3165.
  Capt: FO Watson, S. M. M. MID — Killed
  Nav: PO Cameron, E. C. J. — Killed
  WOP: Sgt Cumming, G. M. — Killed
  F/gnr: FS Anderson, R. A. J. (NZ) — Killed
  R/gnr: Sgt Owen, J. L. (NZ) — Killed

Date: 25 July 1940.
Target: Marshalling Yards, N.W. Germany.
A/c. Wellington Ic. R3235.
  Capt: FO Coleman, W. H. DFL
    (NZ) — Killed
  2/Pilot: PO Poole, F. T. — Killed
  Nav: Sgt Brown, N. W. DFC — Killed
  WOP: Sgt Nevill, W. E. — Killed
  F/gnr: Sgt Dowds, J. — Killed
  R/gnr: Sgt Annan, W. D. F. (NZ) — Killed

Date: 20 September 1940.
Target: Ostend.
A/c. Wellington Ic. T2463.
  Capt: PO Braun, M. R. — Killed
  2/Pilot: Sgt Green, A. J. — Killed
  Nav: Sgt McCormick, J. E. — Killed
  WOP: Sgt White, L. A. DFM — Killed
  F/gnr: Sgt McDonald, N. — Killed
  R/gnr: Sgt Anderson, L. D. (NZ) — Killed

Date: 23 October 1940.
Target: Industrial & Communications,
  Germany.
A/c. Wellington Ic. P9292.
  Capt: PO Sanderson, R. M. — Killed
  2/Pilot: PO Finlayson, W. J. (NZ) — Killed
  Nav: PO Cleak, F. B. — Killed
  WOP: Sgt White, R. W. B. — Killed
  F/gnr: Sgt Gibbs, J. — Killed
  R/gnr: Sgt Hitchmough, W. G. — Killed

Date: 22 December 1940.
Target: Mannheim.
A/c. Wellington Ic. T2474.
  Capt: Sgt Chuter, E. R. — POW
    (Seriously injured;
    repatriated March 1944)
  2/Pilot: Sgt Falcon-Scott, C. (NZ) — POW
    (Escaped 1941)
  Nav: Sgt English, H. M. (NZ) — POW
    (Repatriated July 1943)
  WOP: Sgt Donaldson, A. — POW
    (Repatriated February 1945)
  F/gnr: Sgt Willis, E. G. — POW
    (Escaped 1941)
  R/gnr: Sgt Ritchie, A. H. (NZ) — Killed

Date: 29 December 1940.
Target: Hamm.
A/c. Wellington Ic. R3211.
  Capt: PO Newman, H. D. — POW
  2/Pilot: Sgt Garrett, J. M. (NZ) — POW
  Nav: PO Stark, R. G. (NZ) — POW
  WOP: Sgt Spittle, S. L. — POW
  F/gnr: Sgt Fenn, M. C. — POW
  R/gnr: Sgt Protheroe, D. G. B. (NZ) — POW

Date: 21 February 1941.
Target: Wilhelmshaven.
A/c. Wellington Ic. T2503.
  Capt: PO Falconer, A. J. (NZ) — Killed
2/Pilot: SL Solbe, E. U. G. — Killed
  Nav: PO Muir, A. V. (NZ) — Killed
  WOP: Sgt Morrison, W. D. — Killed
  F/gnr: Sgt Hellier, H. T. — Killed
  R/gnr: Sgt Brodie, A. M. (NZ) — Killed

Date: 3 July 1941.
Target: Essen.
A/c. Wellington Ic. W5621.
  Capt: Sgt Reid, I. L. (NZ) — Killed
2/Pilot: PO Greening, J. W. (Aus) — Killed
  Nav: Sgt Nation, J. R. — Killed
  WOP: Sgt Jones, H. — Killed
  F/gnr: Sgt Haycock, R. E. — Killed
  R/gnr: Sgt Hartstone, R. H. (NZ) — Killed

Date: 15 July 1941.
Target: Duisburg.
A/c. Wellington Ic. R3171.
  Capt: Sgt Fotheringham, R. E. E. (NZ) — Killed
2/Pilot: Sgt Higgins, E. V. K (Aus) — Killed
  Nav: Sgt Roberts, J. H. C. (Can) — Killed
  WOP: Sgt Dyer, S. A. (NZ) — Killed
  F/gnr: Sgt Hare, P. E. (NZ) — Killed
  R/gnr: Sgt. McKinnion, D. M. (NZ) — Killed

Date: 24 July 1941.
Target: Daylight attack against battleship *Gneisenau* at Brest.
A/c. Wellington Ic. N2854.
  Capt: Sgt Streeter, D. F. (NZ) — Killed
2/Pilot: Sgt Owen, W. (Can) — Killed
  Nav: Sgt Carling, R. P. — Killed
  WOP: Sgt Turner, R. J. — Killed
  F/gnr: Sgt Walker, G. S. (NZ) — Killed
  R/gnr: Sgt Craig, R. S. C. — Killed

Date: 6 August 1941.
Target: Mannheim.
A/c. Wellington Ic. R1648.
  Capt: Sgt Millet, L. I. A. — POW
2/Pilot: Sgt Morgan, R. G. (NZ) — POW
  Nav: Sgt Polly, D. — POW
  WOP: Sgt Simpson, C. — POW
  F/gnr: Sgt Bottomley, J. W. — Killed
  R/gnr: Sgt Mellon, W. N. K. — Killed

Date: 6 September 1941.
Target: Huls.
A/c. Wellington III. X9767.
  Capt: PO Johnson, J. E. — Killed
2/Pilot: Sgt Johnson, P. S. D. — Killed
  Nav: Sgt Minchin, R. M. — Killed
  WOP: Sgt Bearne, W. — Killed
  F/gnr: Sgt Davies, R. — Killed
  R/gnr: Sgt Barker, W. J. — Killed

Date: 11 September 1941.
Target: Kiel.
A/c. Wellington Ic. R1038.
  Capt: Sgt Roe, K. V. D. — Killed
2/Pilot: Sgt Tomlinson, K. A. — Killed
  Nav: Sgt McVety, M. W. S. — Killed
  WOP: Sgt Dunlop, D. F. — Killed
  F/gnr: Sgt Tweedie, N. (Aus) — Killed
  R/gnr: FS Hopkins, T. B. (Can) — Killed

Date: 15 September 1941.
Target: Hamburg.
A/c. Wellington III. X3205.
  Capt: Sgt Ward, J. A. VC (NZ) — Killed
2/Pilot: Sgt Sloman, H. G. — Killed
  Nav: Sgt Toller, R. W. — Killed
  WOP: Sgt Watson, H. — POW
  F/gnr: Sgt Toothill, K. H. — Killed
  R/gnr: Sgt Peterson, L. E. (NZ) — POW

Date: 15 September 1941.
Target: Hamburg.
A/c. Wellington III. X9759.
  Capt: Sgt Hawkins, A. H. R. (NZ) — Killed
2/Pilot: Sgt Blakeway, R. B. (NZ) — POW
  Nav: Sgt Foulkes, J. G. — Killed
  WOP: Sgt Mullins, W. E. — POW
  F/gnr: Sgt Fawcett, D. P. — Killed
  R/gnr: PO Aitchison, H. MacL. (Can) — Killed

Date: 17 September 1941.
Target: Karlsruhe.
A/c. Wellington III. X9834.
  Capt: Sgt Smyth, W. B. H. — Killed
2/Pilot: PO Smith, W. J. S. — POW
  Nav: PO Savage, K. E. A. — Killed
  WOP: Sgt Reid, J. W. — POW
  (Shot dead by prison camp guards on the 29/12/1941)
  F/gnr: Sgt Haselden, H. C. McL. (NZ) — Killed
  R/gnr: Sgt Heard, A. H. — POW

Date: 10 October 1941.
Target: Cologne.
A/c. Wellington III. Z8909.
  Capt: Sgt Curlewis, R. F, (Aus) — Killed
2/Pilot: Sgt Thompson, C. M. (NZ) — Killed
  Nav: Sgt Edwards, A. C. — Killed
  WOP: Sgt Garde, F. — Killed
  F/gnr: Sgt Warburton, R. L. — Killed
  R/gnr: Sgt Murphy, T. R. (NZ) — Killed

Date: 12 October 1941.
Target: Bremen and Nuremburg.
A/c. Wellington III. X9981.
  Capt: SL Chamberlain, P. B. — Killed
  2/Pilot: Sgt Holley, D. C — Killed
  Nav: PO Robinson, J. A. (Can) — Killed
  WOP: Sgt Butt, R. G. — Killed
  F/gnr: Sgt Austin, F. E — Killed
  R/gnr: Sgt Ashley, J. R. — Killed

Date: 15 October 1941.
Target: Cologne.
A/c. Wellington III. Z8945.
  Capt: Sgt Barker, R. C. — Killed
  2/Pilot: PO Robertson, T. B. (NZ) — Killed
  Nav: Sgt Grimes, H. D. (Aus) — Killed
  WOP: Sgt Beney, D. L. — Killed
  F/gnr: Sgt Cole, G. F. — POW
  R/gnr: Sgt Stephenson, J. B. — POW

Date: 15 October 1941.
Target: Cologne.
A/c. Wellington Ic. W5663.
  Capt: Sgt Matetich, J. A. — Killed
  2/Pilot: Sgt Wood, F. L. R. (NZ) — Killed
  Nav: FS Welsh, N. H. (NZ) — Killed
  WOP: Sgt Worlledge, F. H. — Killed
  F/gnr: Sgt Service, A. — Killed
  R/gnr: Sgt Barkhouse, D. F. (Can) — Killed

Date: 22 October 1941.
Target: Mannheim.
A/c. Wellington III. X9914.
  Capt: Sgt Taylor, C. — Killed
  2/Pilot: Sgt Spark, F. A. (NZ) — Killed
  Nav: Sgt Levack, S. J. L. — Killed
  WOP: Sgt Roberts, J. (AUS) — Killed
  F/gnr: Sgt Steele, W. R. — Killed
  R/gnr: Sgt Tasker, R. H. — Killed

Date: 26 October 1941.
Target: Hamburg.
A/c. Wellington III. Z1168.
  Capt: Sgt Isherwood, S. J. G. — POW
  2/Pilot: Sgt Pyman, D. J. (NZ) — POW
  Nav: PO Sangster, E. M (Can) — POW
  WOP: Sgt Stanley, H. A. D. — POW
  F/gnr: Sgt Shelnutt, B. W. (Can) — Killed
  R/gnr: Sgt Bell, H. — POW

Date: 7 November 1941.
Target: Berlin.
A/c. Wellington III. X9951.
  Capt: PO Methven, W. R. — POW
    (Repatriated)
  2/Pilot: Sgt Gibson, J. C. Mc. (NZ) — Killed
  Nav: PO Webster, D. A. (Can) — POW
  WOP: Sgt Frisby, A. B. — POW
  F/gnr: Sgt Duffy, T. P. (NZ) — POW
  R/gnr: Sgt Pattinson, R. — POW

Date: 7 November 1941.
Target: Berlin.
A/c. Wellington III. X9976.
  Capt: FS Black, J. W. (NZ) — Killed
  2/Pilot: Sgt Gray, T. H. (NZ) — Killed
  Nav: PO Lloyd, E. (NZ) — Killed
  WOP: FS Green, L. C. — Killed
  F/gnr: Sgt Thompson, J. D. — Killed
  R/gnr: Sgt Black, C. T. — Killed

Date: 8 November 1941.
Target: Essen.
A/c. Wellington III. X9628.
  Capt: Sgt Smith, K. M. — POW
  2/Pilot: Sgt French, W. F. — POW
  Nav: Sgt Howe, L. C. — POW
  WOP: Sgt Rugg, R. J. — POW
    (Seriously wounded; died 15/11/1941)
  F/gnr: Sgt Eggar, L. G. — POW
  R/gnr: Sgt Thain, G. M. — Killed

Date: 8 November 1941.
Target: Essen.
A/c. Wellington III. Z8942.
  Capt: Sgt Wilson, J. S. (NZ) — Killed
  2/Pilot: PO Foster, R. O. (NZ) — Killed
  Nav: PO Ryder, R. L. O. (Aus) — Killed
  WOP: Sgt Reid, J. H. — Killed
  F/gnr: Sgt Mappin, Sir C. T. H. 4th Bt. — Killed
  R/gnr: Sgt Hope, L. B. H. (NZ) — POW
    (died 19/4/1945)

Date: 8 November 1941.
Target: Essen.
A/c. Wellington III. X9977.
  Capt: Sgt Nunn, G. S. — Killed
  2/Pilot: Sgt Wyllie, T. Y. (NZ) — Killed
  Nav: Sgt Dundas, R. — Killed
  WOP: FS Harrison, A. H. (NZ) — Killed
  F/gnr: FS Elliott, T. E. (Can) — Killed
  R/gnr: Sgt Massey, W. — Killed

Date: 30 November 1941.
Target: Emden and Hamburg.
A/c. Wellington III. Z1099.
  Capt: FS Harrison-Smith, F. C. (NZ) — Killed
  2/Pilot: Sgt Sizmur, D. V. — Killed
  Nav: Sgt McCready, D. — Killed
  WOP: Sgt Meagher, B. N. — Killed
  F/gnr: Sgt Painter, E. H. J. — Killed
  R/gnr: Sgt Buckby, P. — Killed

Date: 12 March 1942.
Target: Kiel.
A/c. Wellington III. X3585.
  Capt: FO Sandys, J. F. K. (Can)   Killed
  2/Pilot: Sgt Woodcock, R. J. D. (NZ)   Killed
  Nav: PO Earle, J. (NZ)   Killed
  WOP: FS Price, H. J. (NZ)   Killed
  F/gnr: Sgt Dunn, L. J.   Killed
  R/gnr: FL Baber, T. J. D. MID (NZ)   Killed

Date: 12 March 1942.
Target: Kiel.
A/c. Wellington III. X3282.
  Capt: Sgt Parnham, J. F. M.   Killed
  2/Pilot: FS Brown, J. L. (NZ)   Killed
  Nav: Sgt McGibbon, R.   Killed
  WOP: Sgt McDonald, M. A. (Aus)   Killed
  F/gnr: FS Aitcheson, C. E. J. (NZ)   Killed
  R/gnr: FS Godfrey, R. E. (Can)   Killed

Date: 12 March 1942.
Target: Kiel.
A/c. Wellington III. X3588.
  Capt: SL Kitchen, P. J. R. DFC   Killed
  2/Pilot: PO Parton, W. J. (NZ)   Killed
  Nav: Sgt Cullen, H. S. G.   Killed
  WOP: Sgt Clezy, W.   Killed
  F/gnr: Sgt Carter, T. K.   Killed
  R/gnr: FS Chamberlain, L. M. (NZ)   Killed

Date: 25 March 1942.
Target: Essen.
A/c. Wellington III. X3652. 'O'
  Capt: PO Slater, A. R. (Aus)   POW
  2/Pilot: Sgt Addis, J. H.   Killed
  Nav: FS Fletcher, J. (NZ)   POW
  WOP: Sgt Wainwright, A. E.   POW
  F/gnr: Sgt Orr, A. G. (NZ)   POW
  R/gnr: Sgt Burridge, P. L.   POW

Date: 28 March 1942.
Target: Lubeck.
A/c. Wellington III. X3462. 'N'
  Capt: PO Bell, M. P. (NZ)   Killed
  2/Pilot: Sgt Cran, F. B. (NZ)   Killed
  Nav: Sgt Harris, C. J. (NZ)   Killed
  WOP: Sgt Allen, R. G.   Killed
  F/gnr: Sgt Cross, T. R.   Killed
  R/gnr: Sgt Hinton, J. W.   Killed

Date: 5 April 1942.
Target: Cologne.
A/c. Wellington III. X3661.
  Capt: FS Thomas, G. J. E. (NZ)   POW
  2/Pilot: FS Robertson, S. MacI. (NZ)   POW
  Nav: Sgt Reay, W. G. (NZ)   POW
  WOP: Sgt Harris, W. H. (NZ)   POW
  F/gnr: Sgt Roynon, S. W.   POW
  R/gnr: Sgt Dorrell, P. G.   POW

Date: 5 April 1942.
Target: Cologne.
A/c. Wellington III. X3489.
  Capt: WC Sawrey-Cookson, R.
    DSO, DFC   Killed
  2/Pilot: PO Budge, W. F. (NZ)   Killed
  Nav: Sgt Emery, R. H.   Killed
  WOP: Sgt Hainsworth, E.   Killed
  F/gnr: Sgt Stock, D. P.   Killed
  R/gnr: FO Mitchell, G. E.
    DFM (Can)   Killed

Date: 22 April 1942
Target: Cologne.
A/c. Wellington III. X3667.
  Capt: FS Mahood, T. S. (NZ)   Killed
  2/Pilot: Sgt Wrightson, C. C. (NZ)   Killed
  Nav: FS Dromgoole, S. H. (NZ)   Killed
  WOP: Sgt Kelly, R. J. S. (NZ)   Killed
  F/gnr: Sgt McMahon, H. T. O. (NZ)   Killed
  R/gnr: Sgt McLinden, J. F.   Killed

Date: 15 May 1942.
Target: Mining — Kiel Bay.
A/c. Wellington III. X3482. 'J'
  Capt: FS Fraser, M. F. G. (NZ)   Killed
  Nav: FS Smith, A. I. (NZ)   Killed
  WOP: Sgt Nichols, J. O. H.   Killed
  F/gnr: Sgt Shaw, S. A. G.   Killed
  R/gnr: Sgt Whiting, N. E. (NZ)   Killed

Date: 30 May 1942.
Target: Cologne.
A/c. Wellington Ia. N2894. (Attached from Central Gunnery School (CGS) Sutton Bridge)
  Capt: PO Johnson, D. M.   Killed
  2/Pilot: WO Jambor, O.   Killed
  Nav: FL Batten, H. A. C.   Killed
  WOP: FS Connor, J. R.   Killed
  F/gnr: FS McLean, J. M.   Killed
  R/gnr: FS Waddington-Allwright,
    G. J.   POW

Date: 2 June 1942.
Target: Essen.
A/c. Wellington III. X3408.
  Capt: PO Carter, C. W. P.   POW
  Nav: Sgt Ives, H.   POW
  WOP: Sgt Mayall, J. R.   POW
  F/gnr: Sgt Coy, J. L.   POW
  R/gnr: FS Howard, P. N.   POW

Date: 8 June 1942.
Target: Essen.
A/c. Wellington III. Z1573.
  Capt: PO Murdoch, G. E.   Killed
  Nav: Sgt O'Dowd, A. W.   Killed
  WOP: PO Weston, R.   Killed
  F/gnr: Sgt Knight, L. G.   Killed
  R/gnr: Sgt Morris, J. W.   Killed

Date: 8 June 1942.
Target: Essen.
A/c. Wellington III. X3587.
  Capt: PO Smith, R. J. — Killed
  Nav: Sgt Clark, W. G. — Killed
  WOP: Sgt Coulter, B. H. — Killed
  F/gnr: Sgt Ramsey, W. R. — Killed
  R/gnr: Sgt Jones, H. E. — Killed

Date: 20 June 1942.
Target: Emden.
A/c. Wellington III. X3760.
  Capt: FO Fraser, A. A. (NZ) — Killed
  Nav: PO Buckley, W. E. (NZ) — Killed
  WOP: FS Christie, A. S. (NZ) — Killed
  F/gnr: Sgt Brailey, C. R. (NZ) — Killed
  R/gnr: PO Trengrove, R. W. J. (NZ) — Killed

Date: 29 June 1942.
Target: Bremen.
A/c. Wellington III. X3539.
  Capt: PO Monk, W. J. (NZ) — Killed
  Nav: Sgt Randall, D. H. (NZ) — Killed
  WOP: Sgt Moncrieff, E. F. S. (NZ) — Killed
  F/gnr: Sgt Hegan, J. G. G. (NZ) — Killed
  R/gnr: Sgt McGregor, M. G. (NZ) — Killed

Date: 8 July 1942.
Target: Wilhelmshaven.
A/c. Wellington III. X3557.
  Capt: PO Smith, T. H. (NZ) — Killed
  2/Pilot: PO Potts, D. N. (NZ) — Killed
  Nav: PO Broun, A. S. (NZ) — Killed
  WOP: Sgt McKenzie, F. E. (NZ) — Killed
  F/gnr: Sgt Young, G. A. (NZ) — Killed
  R/gnr: PO Gavegan, J. R. (NZ) — Killed

Date: 10 July 1942.
Target: Dusseldorf.
A/c. Wellington III. X3720.
  Capt: Sgt Wilmshurst, S. C. (NZ) — Killed
  Nav: Sgt Gould, J. D. (NZ) — Killed
  WOP: Sgt Sharp, R. E. (NZ) — Killed
  F/gnr: FS Lowther, P. D. (NZ) — Killed
  R/gnr: Sgt Hirst, R. J. (NZ) — Killed

Date: 26 July 1942.
Target: Hamburg.
A/c. Wellington III. Z1596.
  Capt: PO Shepherd, I. J. (NZ) — Killed
  Nav: PO Lees, R. S. (NZ) — Killed
  WOP: PO Robertson, N. B. (NZ) — Killed
  F/gnr: Sgt Winstanley, J. F. (NZ) — Killed
  R/gnr: Sgt Dixon, J. — POW

Date: 26 July 1942.
Target: Hamburg.
A/c. Wellington III. X3714.
  Capt: FS McPherson, C. V. (NZ) — Killed
  2/Pilot: FS Ross, S. D. (NZ) — Killed
  Nav: PO Spittal, P. C. (NZ) — Killed
  WOP: Sgt Coppersmith, R. P. (NZ) — Killed
  F/gnr: FS Cairns, L. T. (NZ) — Killed
  R/gnr: FS Bryson, N. A. (NZ) — Killed

Date: 28 July 1942.
Target: Hamburg.
A/c. Wellington III. X3558.
  Capt: FS Sutherland, A. G. (NZ) — Killed
  Nav: WO Shone, G. E. — Killed
  WOP: Sgt Tabor, A. O. (NZ) — Killed
  F/gnr: PO Harkness, C. — Killed
  R/gnr: Sgt Stewart, I. G. (NZ) — Killed

Date: 28 July 1942.
Target: Hamburg.
A/c. Wellington III. X3452.
  Capt: Sgt Croall, C. (NZ) — POW
  Nav: FS Harvey, R. S. (NZ) — POW
  (Repatriated)
  WOP: FS Gratton, J. R. (NZ) — POW
  F/gnr: Sgt Bright, W. H. (NZ) — POW
  R/gnr: Sgt Crarer, T. E. (NZ) — Killed

Date: 28 July 1942.
Target: Hamburg.
A/c. Wellington III. Z1570. 'B'
  Capt: FS Johns, A. G. (NZ) — Killed
  Nav: Sgt Kraljevich, M. (NZ) — Killed
  WOP: Sgt Ellis, R. — Killed
  F/gnr: Sgt Frampton, L. A. (NZ) — Killed
  R/gnr: Sgt Stewart, L. I. (NZ) — Killed

Date: 28 July 1942.
Target: Hamburg.
A/c. Wellington III. X3664.
  Capt: FL Wilson, P. J. (NZ) — Killed
  2/Pilot: FS Westerman, V. K. (NZ) — Killed
  Nav: Sgt Brisco, R. H. (NZ) — Killed
  WOP: FS Davis, R. F. (NZ) — Killed
  F/gnr: FS Campbell, A. (NZ) — Killed
  R/gnr: Sgt Caitcheon, G. E. (NZ) — Killed

Date: 28 July 1942.
Target: Hamburg.
A/c. Wellington III. BJ661.
  Capt: FS Gilbertson, J. E. (NZ) — Killed
  Nav: FS Byrne, M. J. (NZ) — Killed
  WOP: Sgt Callaghan, R. P. (NZ) — POW
  F/gnr: Sgt Rutherford, A. W. (NZ) — POW
  R/gnr: Sgt Titcomb, W. A. — Killed

Date: 28 July 1942.
Target: Hamburg.
A/c. Wellington III. BJ599.
  Capt: FS Hutt, G. A. (NZ) — Killed
  Nav: PO Carncross, M. E. (NZ) — Killed
  WOP: Sgt McMurchy, J. G. (NZ) — Killed
  F/gnr: Sgt O'Shea, W. C. (NZ) — Killed
  R/gnr: Sgt Savage, J. H. (NZ) — Killed

Date: 11 August 1942.
Target: Mainz.
A/c. Wellington III. X3646.
  Capt: PO Bradey, G. E. F. (NZ) — Killed
  2/Pilot: FO Baker, T. H. W. — Killed
  Nav: SL Kimber, R. E. — Killed
  WOP: FS Ellis, A. I. (Can) — Killed
  F/gnr: FS Green, C. V. (NZ) — Killed
  R/gnr: Sgt London, J. E. — POW

Date: 11 August 1942.
Target: Mainz.
A/c. Wellington III. BJ625.
  Capt: FS Barclay, T. S. (NZ) — Killed
  Nav: FS Hodges, R. G. R. (Can) — Killed
  WOP: Sgt Warring, R. J. (NZ) — Killed
  F/gnr: Sgt Inglis, W. G. L. (NZ) — Killed
  R/gnr: Sgt Atkin, J. (NZ) (Wounded) — POW

Date: 11 August 1942.
Target: Mainz.
A/c. Wellington III. BJ767.
  Capt: FS Dobbin, L. StG. (NZ) — Killed
  Nav: Sgt Braddock, W. E. — POW
  WOP: Sgt McQueen, J. (NZ) — POW
  F/gnr: Sgt Jury, J. L. (NZ) — Killed
  R/gnr: Sgt Elson, A. — POW

Date: 20 August 1942.
Target: Mining — St. Nazaire.
A/c. Wellington III. BJ774.
  Capt: WO Anderson, E. K. A — Killed
  Nav: Sgt Stead, G. — Killed
  WOP: FS Stuart, R. C. (Can) — Killed
  F/gnr: FS McDonogh, A. I. (Can) — Killed
  R/gnr: FS Robitaille, A. H. (Can) — Killed

Date: 27 August 1942.
Target: Kassel.
A/c. Wellington III. BJ708.
  Capt: FL Osborn, A. F. A. DFC — Killed
  Nav: PO Dalzell, E. T. P. (NZ) — Killed
  WOP: Sgt Hogan, D. P. — Killed
  F/gnr: Sgt McGregor, R. — Killed
  R/gnr: Sgt Turnbridge, V. A. (NZ) — Killed

Date: 28 August 1942.
Target: Nuremberg.
A/c. Wellington III. DF673.
  Capt: FS Davis, S. B. T. — Killed
  Nav: FS Baittle, H. D. (Can) — Killed
  WOP: FS McKay, D. A. (Can) — Killed
  F/gnr: FS Vickers, C. H. — Killed
  R/gnr: FS Hiltz, L. D. (Can) — Killed

Date: 28 August 1942.
Target: Nuremberg.
A/c. Wellington III. X3389.
  Capt: FS Perks, E. (NZ) — Killed
  Nav: Sgt Lee, R. G. A. — Killed
  WOP: FS Irvine, W. H. (Can) — Killed
  F/gnr: Sgt McGillivray, J. D. R. — Killed
  R/gnr: Sgt Oaten, P. — Killed

Date: 3 September 1942.
Target: Emden.
A/c. Wellington III. X3396.
  Capt: Sgt Law, J. — Killed
  Nav: Sgt Grant, H. L. (NZ) — Killed
  WOP: Sgt Renton, R. E. (NZ) — Killed
  F/gnr: Sgt Newman, R. A. W. (NZ) — Killed
  R/gnr: Sgt Gill, J. T. V. (NZ) — Killed

Date: 3 September 1942.
Target: Emden.
A/c. Wellington III. X3794.
  Capt: FS Hunting, E. R. — Killed
  Nav: Sgt Beyer, E. H. — Killed
  WOP: Sgt Goldie, H. E. — Killed
  F/gnr: FS McArter, G. (Can) — Killed
  R/gnr: Sgt Anderson, W. — Killed

Date: 6 September 1942.
Target: Duisburg.
A/c. Wellington III. BJ765.
  Capt: Sgt Sharman, G. W. (NZ) — Killed
  Nav: Sgt Saul, N. P. (NZ) — Killed
  WOP: Sgt Jarvis, C. J. F. (NZ) — Killed
  F/gnr: PO Mills, G. W. A. (NZ) — Killed
  R/gnr: Sgt Coles, T. E. (NZ) — Killed

Date: 6 September 1942.
Target: Duisburg.
A/c. Wellington III. X3867.
  Capt: FS Parkes, W. R. (NZ) — Killed
  Nav: Sgt Crawford, H. V. G. (NZ) — Killed
  WOP: Sgt Rose, G. H. (NZ) — Killed
  F/gnr: FS Groves, A. L. (NZ) — Killed
  R/gnr: FS Wilson, E. G. (NZ) — Killed

Date: 8 September 1942.
Target: Schweinfurt.
A/c. Wellington III. BJ596.
  Capt: Sgt Johnson, E. W. P. (NZ) — POW
  Nav: Sgt Nicolson, U. (NZ) — POW
  WOP: Sgt Devine, T. W. (NZ) — POW
  F/gnr: Sgt O'Byrne, W. K. C. (NZ) — POW
  R/gnr: Sgt Bevan, L. S. (NZ) — POW

Date: 10 September 1942.
Target: Dusseldorf.
A/c. Wellington III. BJ828.
  Capt: Sgt Lees, E. — Killed
  Nav: Sgt Judd, D. H. (NZ) — Killed
  WOP: Sgt Young, P. A. — Killed
  F/gnr: Sgt Anderson, C. N. — Killed
  R/gnr: Sgt Guppy, F. R. — Killed

Date: 10 September 1942.
Target: Dusseldorf.
A/c. Wellington III. BJ968. 'W'
  Capt: FS Burrill, F. (Can) — Killed
  Nav: PO Smart, R. C. (NZ) — Killed
  WOP: FS St. Louis, M. B. (Can) — Killed
  F/gnr: Sgt Lavers, W. W. H. (Can) — Killed
  R/gnr: FS Gorman, R. E. (Can) — Killed

Date: 10 September 1942.
Target: Dusseldorf.
A/c. Wellington III. BJ974.
  Capt: Sgt Metcalfe, T. O. (NZ) — Killed
  Nav: PO Devlin, K. J. (NZ) — Killed
  WOP: Sgt Walsh, D. J. (NZ) — Killed
  F/gnr: Sgt Kelcher, W. F. (NZ) — Killed
  R/gnr: Sgt Lock, A. J. — Killed

Date: 6 October 1942.
Target: Osnabruck.
A/c. Wellington III. DF639.
  Capt: Sgt Rhodes, G. W. — Killed
  Nav: Sgt Howes, W. J. — Killed
  WOP: FS Forman, J. (Can) — Killed
  F/gnr: Sgt Slater, G. — Killed
  R/gnr: Sgt Forbes, J. — Killed

Date: 11 October 1942.
Target: Mining — Aalbsoly.
A/c. Wellington III. BK341.
  Capt: Sgt Shalfoon, C. J. (NZ) — Killed
  Nav: Sgt Wolfenden, H. — Killed
  WOP: Sgt Parsons, A. — Killed
  F/gnr: Sgt Posner, S. — Killed
  R/gnr: Sgt Scott, R. H. (Can) — Killed

Date: 13 October 1942.
Target: Kiel.
A/c. Wellington III. X3954.
  Capt: Sgt Watters, V. — Killed
  Nav: Sgt Parkinson, L. H. — Killed
  WOP: Sgt Firth, E. G. — Killed
  F/gnr: Sgt Orr, A. C. — Killed
  R/gnr: Sgt Goldsack, H. E. — Killed

Date: 24 October 1942.
Target: Milan.
A/c. Wellington III. Z1652.
  Capt: Sgt Hughill, H. J. (NZ) — Killed
  Nav: Sgt Pete, E. J. — Killed
  WOP: Sgt Worsdale, E. (NZ) — Evaded
  F/gnr: Sgt Barnes, J. G. (NZ) — POW
  R/gnr: Sgt Newbold, L. — Evaded

Date: 24 October 1942.
Target: Milan.
A/c. Wellington III. BJ725.
  Capt: Sgt McConnel (NZ) — Killed
  Nav: Sgt Smith, S. C. (NZ) — Killed
  WOP: Sgt Tonkin, D. N. (NZ) — Killed
  F/gnr: Sgt Quinn, A. — Killed
  R/gnr: Sgt Dimock, V. A. O. (NZ) — Killed

Date: 2 December 1942.
Target: Frankfurt.
A/c. Stirling I. BK618. 'Q'
  Capt: Sgt Scott, A. (NZ) — Killed
  2/Pilot: Sgt Sharpe, R. W. — POW
  Nav: Sgt Rey, A. E. (Can) — POW
  FE: Sgt Baker, D. — POW
  WOP: Sgt Smith, J. R. (NZ) — POW
  AB: Sgt Wright, W. K. (NZ) — POW
  MU: Sgt McMorrine, A. W. — Killed
  R/gnr: Sgt Preston, R. E. — POW
    (died 10/4/1945)

Date: 17 December 1942.
Target: Fallersleben.
A/c. Stirling I. BF396.
  Capt: WC Mitchell, V. DFC — Killed
  2/Pilot: WO Bagnell, T. H. (NZ) — Killed
  FE: Sgt Hart, R. — Killed
  Nav: WO Pearson, R. W. — Killed
  WOP: Sgt Goff, S. J. — Killed
  AB: Sgt Padden, G. T. — Killed
  MU: Sgt Rider, A. H. — Killed
  R/gnr: FS Parker, A. C. W. — Killed

Date: 17 December 1942.
Target: Fallersleben.
A/c. Stirling I. BF400.
- Capt: FO Jacobson, G. H. (NZ) — Killed
- Nav: PO McAlpine, W. D. (NZ) — Killed
- FE: Sgt Roff, L. A. — Killed
- WOP: Sgt Stokes, W. F. (NZ) — Killed
- AB: Sgt Ashwin, E. L. D. (NZ) — Killed
- MU: Sgt Lucas, C. — Killed
- R/gnr: Sgt White, W. G. H. (NZ) — Killed

Date: 17 December 1942.
Target: Fallersleben.
A/c. Stirling I. R9247. 'W'
- Capt: FS Rousseau, H. E. — Killed
- Nav: PO Clark, M. O. (NZ) — Killed
- FE: Sgt Morton, W. W. — Killed
- WOP: Sgt Kendal, C. J. (NZ) — Killed
- AB: Sgt Mocock, R. C. — Killed
- MU: FS Fellows, J. (Can) — Killed
- R/gnr: Sgt Pullar, H. W. (NZ) — Killed

Date: 17 December 1942.
Target: Fallersleben.
A/c. Stirling I. BK620.
- Pilot: FS Dunmall, K. J. — POW
- Nav: Sgt Glen, K. D. (Can) — POW
- FE: Sgt Magnus, A. L. (Can) — POW
- WOP: Sgt Atwell, K. J. (Can) — POW
- Capt & AB: PO Williams, E. E. — POW
  (Escaped from Stalag Luft 3 via 'The Wooden Horse' and was awarded the MC on his return to the squadron)
- MU: Sgt Ritchie, J. — POW
- R/gnr: Sgt Voice, W. J. S. (NZ) — POW

Date: 23 January 1943.
Target: Lorient.
A/c. Stirling I. R9248. 'H'
- Capt: Sgt Kidd, R. M. (NZ) — Evaded
- Nav: Sgt Schofield, J. W. — Killed
- FE: Sgt Mitchell, G. F. — Killed
- WOP: Sgt Berry, E. — Killed
- AB: Sgt Torrance, B. — Killed
- MU: Sgt Brewster, J. E. — Killed
- R/gnr: Sgt Fowler, P. D. — Killed

Date: 3 February 1943.
Target: Hamburg.
A/c. Stirling I. R9250. 'W'
- Capt: PO Blincoe, K. H. DFC (NZ) — Killed
- 2/Pilot: PO Scott, A. J. N. (NZ) — Killed
- Nav: Sgt Boese, F. A. — Killed
- FE: Sgt Hayward, D. D. — Killed
- WOP: FO Lowe, H. DFC — Killed
- AB: Sgt Cook, G. W. (NZ) — Killed
- MU: FS McDermott, E. (Can) — Killed
- R/gnr: Sgt Clearwater, D. (NZ) — Killed

Date: 3 February 1943.
Target: Hamburg.
A/c. Stirling I. BK604. 'S'
- Capt: PO McCullough, J. DFC (NZ) — Killed
- 2/Pilot: PO Henderson, R. W. (NZ) — POW
- Nav: FS Gibbes, W. E. (NZ) — POW
- FE: Sgt Allen, F. F. — Killed
- WOP: Sgt Smith, K. J. S. (NZ) (Wounded) — POW
- AB: Sgt Murphy, T. A. (NZ) — Killed
- MU: Sgt Kimberley, K. E. — POW
- R/gnr: Sgt Trevayne, P. R. — Killed

Date: 5 February 1943.
Target: Mining — Frisian Islands.
A/c. Stirling I. BK617. 'D'
- Capt: Sgt Redding, R. E. (NZ) — Killed
- Nav: FS Barton, A. J. (NZ) — Killed
- AB: Sgt Legge, R. C. (Can) — Killed
- WOP: Sgt Phillips, C. G. — Killed
- FE: Sgt Dennis, H. — Killed
- MU: FS Wilson, W. W. (Can) — Killed
- R/gnr: Sgt Freeman, P. P. D. (NZ) — Killed

Date: 13 February 1943.
Target: Lorient.
A/c. Stirling I. R9316. 'K'
- Capt: PO Williams, R. A. — Killed
- Nav: PO Browne, D. E. (Can) — POW
- FE: Sgt Gudmunsen, K. — POW
- AB: Sgt Sawyer, H. — POW
- WOP: Sgt Smith, T. H. — POW
- MU: Sgt Willis, L. (Can) — Evaded
- R/gnr: PO Harding-Smith, D. (NZ) — Killed

Date: 3 March 1943.
Target: Mining — Frisian Islands.
A/c. Stirling I. N6123. 'Q'
- Capt: Sgt Going, R. C. (NZ) — Killed
- Nav: PO Bridgman, A. M. (NZ) — Killed
- FE: Sgt Weaver, E. H. — Killed
- WOP: Sgt Eyre, K. C. — Killed
- AB: FS Willis, F. A. W. — Killed
- MU: Sgt Stewart, F. — Killed
- R/gnr: Sgt Burton, C. S. (NZ) — Killed

Date: 8 March 1943.
Target: Nuremberg.
A/c. Stirling I. BF437. 'L'
- Capt: Sgt Davey, C. R. (NZ) — Killed
- Nav: WO Arlen, A. (Can) — Killed
- FE: Sgt Howlett, A. E. — Killed
- WOP: Sgt Stone, L. M. — Killed
- AB: PO Brodie, I. J. D. — Killed
- MU: Sgt Feenan, A. J. — Killed
- R/gnr: Sgt Tarrant, A. B. — Killed

Date: 10 April 1943.
Target: Frankfurt.
A/c. Stirling III. BF456. 'J'
  Capt: Sgt Webb, J. — Killed
  Nav: Sgt Jones, D. V. — Killed
  AB: Sgt Anthony, D. T. — Killed
  WOP: Sgt Lowther, R. — Killed
  FE: Sgt Inglis, J. — Killed
  MU: Sgt Cunningham, L. — Killed
  R/gnr: Sgt Letherbarrow, E. J. — Killed

Date: 14 April 1943.
Target: Stuttgart.
A/c. Stirling III. BF513.
  Capt: PO McCaskill, D. G. (NZ) — Killed
  Nav: PO Grainger, J. K. (NZ) — Killed
  AB: Sgt Elwell, B. — Killed
  WOP: Sgt Green, R. T. C. — Killed
  FE: Sgt McVicar, A. — Killed
  MU: Sgt Cook, E. D. — Killed
  R/gnr: Sgt Smith, R. A. (NZ) — Killed

Date: 16 April 1943.
Target: Ludwigshafen.
A/c. Stirling I. W7469. 'T'
  Capt: PO Debenham, K. F. (NZ) — Killed
  Nav: WO Barnes, R. J. (Can) — Killed
  AB: Sgt Watts, M. T. — Killed
  WOP: Sgt Pearson, P. B. — Killed
  FE: Sgt Wainwright, D. — POW
  MU: Sgt Marlow, J. L. — Killed
  R/gnr: Sgt Davis, J. J. — Killed

Date: 16 April 1943.
Target: Ludwigshafen.
A/c. Stirling I. BF451. 'Z'
  Capt: PO Groves, K. H. G. (NZ) — Killed
  2/Pilot: WO Way, J. O. (Can) — Killed
  Nav: Sgt Shergold, T. — Killed
  AB: Sgt Wanstall, R. F. — Killed
  WOP: Sgt Pierson, R. L. — Killed
  FE: Sgt Cameron, L. C. — Killed
  MU: Sgt Stone, R. C. (NZ) — Killed
  R/gnr: Sgt Everden, L. L. — Killed

Date: 20 April 1943.
Target: Rostock.
A/c. Stirling III. BF506. 'P'
  Capt: PO Tolley, A. G. (NZ) — Killed
  Nav: FS Ellis, W. H. — Killed
  AB: FS Upton, F. W. (NZ) — Killed
  WOP: FS Cobb, C. T. (NZ) — Killed
  FE: Sgt Town, G. A. R. — Killed
  MU: Sgt Earle, F. J. — Killed
  R/gnr: FS Salt, I. C. — Killed

Date: 28 April 1943.
Target: Mining—Kiel Bay.
A/c. Stirling III. BK807. 'M'
  Capt: PO Hamer, D. V. — Killed
  Nav: Sgt Ross, D. R. (NZ) — Killed
  AB: FS Buckley, R. C. (NZ) — Killed
  WOP: FS Brian, W. L. F. (NZ) — Killed
  FE: Sgt Lennox, G. L. — Killed
  MU: Sgt Holme, H. P. — Killed
  R/gnr: Sgt Shogren, M. E. J. (NZ) — Killed

Date: 28 April 1943.
Target: Mining—Kiel Bay.
A/c. Stirling I. W7513. 'G'
  Capt: Sgt Halliburton, K. (NZ) — Killed
  Nav: Sgt Hunter, P. T. (NZ) — Killed
  AB: Sgt Scarfe, L. T. — Killed
  WOP: Sgt Church, D. — Killed
  FE: Sgt Sidhu, D. S. — Killed
  MU: Sgt Boxall, C. H. G. — Killed
  R/gnr: Sgt Howell, A. C. (NZ) — Killed

Date: 28 April 1943.
Target: Mining—Kiel Bay.
A/c. Stirling I. BF467. 'W'
  Capt: PO Thompson, D. L. (NZ) — Killed
  Nav: WO Ramsay, J. A. (Can) — Killed
  AB: FS Williams, J. M. (Aus) — Killed
  WOP: WO Jenkins, E. R. (NZ) — Killed
  FE: Sgt Abbot, C. — Killed
  MU: Sgt Phillips, G. — Killed
  R/gnr: Sgt Glendining, J. T. — Killed

Date: 28 April 1943.
Target: Mining—Kiel Bay.
A/c. Stirling I. R9290. 'X'
  Capt: FS Lewis, A. E. (Aus) — Killed
  Nav: Sgt Corin, H. G. (NZ) — Killed
  AB: FO Bickham, C. J. — Killed
  WOP: Sgt Moulton, F. A. — Killed
  FE: Sgt Graham, A. — Killed
  MU: Sgt Whitehart, J. H. — Killed
  R/gnr: Sgt Howes, V. C. (NZ) — Killed

Date: 5 May 1943.
Target: Mining—Frisian Islands.
A/c. Stirling I. EF340.
  Capt: PO Westwood, R. F. (Aus) — Killed
  Nav: PO Bentley, R. H. W. (NZ) — Killed
  AB: Sgt Lamb, E. H. R. (NZ) — Killed
  WOP: Sgt Harkness, W. — Killed
  FE: Sgt Bennetton, F. H. — Killed
  MU: Sgt Rogers, G. H. — Killed
  R/gnr: Sgt Boswell, J. McL. (NZ) — Killed

Date: 23 May 1943.
Target: Dortmund.
A/c. Stirling III. BK783. 'Q'
  Capt: Sgt Tietjens, S. M. (NZ) — Killed
  Nav: Sgt Turnbull, J. W. (NZ) — Killed
  AB: Sgt Joblin, F. J. L. (NZ) — Killed
  WOP: Sgt Bell, R. — Killed
  FE: Sgt Wayman, S. J. — Killed
  MU: Sgt Storey, D. G. A. — Killed
  R/gnr: Sgt Wale, L. R. — POW

Date: 25 May 1943.
Target: Dusseldorf.
A/c. Stirling I. BK602. 'R'
  Capt: FS Darton, T. W. (NZ) — Killed
  Nav: Sgt Coates, D. D. (NZ) — Killed
  AB: Sgt Riordan, J. M. P. (NZ) — Killed
  WOP: Sgt Whiteman, J. C. L. — Killed
  FE: Sgt McQuater, A. — Killed
  MU: Sgt Redpath, S. — Killed
  R/gnr: Sgt Wilsher, F. P. — Killed

Date: 29 May 1943.
Target: Wuppertal.
A/c. Stirling III. EH881.
  Capt: FS Carey, J. H. R. (NZ) — Killed
  Nav: Sgt Roberts, J. L. (NZ) — POW
  AB: Sgt Knight, P. G. (NZ) — POW
  WOP: FS Brady, M. (NZ) — POW
  FE: Sgt Beaver, T. — POW
  (Repatriated)
  MU: FS Owens, W. A. — Killed
  R/gnr: FS MacLeod, N. A. (NZ) — Killed

Date: 29 May 1943.
Target: Wuppertal.
A/c. Stirling III. BK776. 'B'
  Capt: PO Bennett, R. F. (NZ) — Killed
  2/Pilot: FS Norman, R. F. (NZ) — Killed
  Nav: FS Davidson, A. L. (NZ) — POW
  AB: FS Bandy, F. — Killed
  WOP: WO Kavanagh, S. L. (NZ) — Killed
  FE: Sgt Harrison, J. B. — POW
  (Wounded; repatriated)
  MU: FS Pirie, J. A. (Can) — Killed
  R/gnr: Sgt Middleton, C. P. F. (NZ) — POW

Date: 29 May 1943.
Target: Wuppertal.
A/c. Stirling III. BF561. 'O'
  Capt: FS Thornley, S. R. (NZ) — Killed
  Nav: Sgt McWilliam, A. (NZ) — Killed
  AB: Sgt McPhail, A. C. A. (NZ) — Killed
  WOP: Sgt Ruocco, D. — Killed
  FE: Sgt Larkin, C. W. — Killed
  MU: Sgt Dartnall, J. — Killed
  R/gnr: Sgt Hooper, F. — Killed

Date: 29 May 1943.
Target: Wuppertal.
A/c. Stirling I. EF398.
  Capt: FO Vernazoni, R. B. (NZ) — Killed
  Nav: Sgt Innes, O. A. (NZ) — Killed
  AB: FO Tong, H. (NZ) — Killed
  WOP: FO Riddle, C. H. (NZ) — Killed
  FE: Sgt Bramwell, W. — Killed
  MU: Sgt Cardoo, A. R. — Killed
  R/gnr: Sgt Chandler, J. — Killed

Date: 11 June 1943.
Target: Dusseldorf.
A/c. Stirling III. BK807. 'B'
  Capt: SL Laud, R. H. — Killed
  2/Pilot: Sgt Russell, J. H. — Killed
  Nav: Sgt McQuade, H. S. — Killed
  AB: Sgt Mulholland, H. S. — Killed
  WOP: FS Whatmough, T. — Killed
  FE: Sgt Waite, A. R. — Killed
  MU: Sgt Hawkins, F. J. — Killed
  R/gnr: Sgt Matthews, M. K. — POW

Date: 14 June 1943.
Target: Mining—Gironde Estuary.
A/c. Stirling I. BK646. 'N'
  Capt: FO Edwards, J. L. — Killed
  Nav: Sgt Dunnett, E. (NZ) — POW
  AB: PO Kirby, R. — Evaded
  WOP: Sgt Rawlinson, B. W. (NZ) — POW
  FE: Sgt Sansoucy, J. G. F. (Can) — Evaded
  MU: Sgt Jones, E. — POW
  (Wounded)
  R/gnr: Sgt Maxwell, T. — POW

Date: 22 June 1943.
Target: Mulheim.
A/c. Stirling III. BK810. 'G'
  Capt: PO McKenzie, F. M. (NZ) — Killed
  Nav: Sgt West, A. E. (NZ) — POW
  (Repatriated)
  AB: FS Blank, J. F. (NZ) — Killed
  WOP: Sgt Broadhead, B. H. (NZ) — POW
  FE: Sgt Triptree, R. A. — POW
  MU: Sgt Chrystal, R. G. — POW
  R/gnr: Sgt McGonigal, E. (NZ) — POW

Date: 22 June 1943.
Target: Mulheim.
A/c. Stirling III. EH889. 'Z'
  Capt: FL McCrorie, T. — Killed
  Nav: PO Stuckey, W. MID — Killed
  AB: Sgt Richards, J. L. (NZ) — Killed
  WOP: WO Tod, R. E. DFM (Can) — Killed
  FE: Sgt Grainger, E. — Killed
  MU: WO Tod, R. D. (Can) — Killed
  R/gnr: Sgt Kennedy, R. A. — Killed

Date: 22 June 1943.
Target: Mulheim
A/c. Stirling III. EF399. 'O'
  Capt: FS Burbidge, K. A. (NZ) — Killed
  Nav: FS Wilcockson, W. (NZ) — Killed
  AB: FS McEwin, A. J. (NZ) — Killed
  WOP: FS Martin, D. E. (NZ) — Killed
  FE: Sgt Lockey, G. — Killed
  MU: Sgt Cameron, G. — Killed
  R/gnr: Sgt Shaw, K. F. — Killed

Date: 22 June 1943.
Target: Mulheim.
A/c. Stirling III. EF408. 'P'
  Capt: FS Wood, B. B. — Killed
  Nav: FS Samson, G. K. (NZ) — Killed
  AB: FS Bisset, S. R. (NZ) — Killed
  WOP: Sgt Reader, E. H. — Killed
  FE: Sgt Webb, S. L. — Killed
  MU: Sgt Hobbs, F. J. — Killed
  R/gnr: Sgt Hemmings, C. B. — Killed

Date: 24 June 1943.
Target: Wuppertal.
A/c. Stirling III. EH902. 'K'
  Capt: PO Bluck, N. B. (NZ) — Killed
  Nav: FS Cooksey, J. B. (NZ) — Killed
  AB: FS Strong, G. W. (NZ) — Killed
  WOP: Sgt Kendlan, M. — Killed
  FE: Sgt Gillard, J. W. — Killed
  MU: Sgt Armitage, D. — Killed
  R/gnr: Sgt Cant, L. R. — Killed

Date: 25 June 1943.
Target: Gelsenkirchen.
A/c. Stirling III. BK768. 'L'
  Capt: FO Perrott, W. R. (NZ) — Killed
  Nav: FS Thomson, G. D. (NZ) — Killed
  AB: FS Whitelaw, C. J. (NZ) — Killed
  WOP: Sgt Mould, C. C. — Killed
  FE: Sgt Hilditch, W. W. — Killed
  MU: Sgt Colyer, G. W. — Killed
  R/gnr: Sgt Squire, H. — Killed

Date: 5 July 1943.
Target: Mining — Frisian Islands.
A/c. Stirling III. EF436. 'A'
  Capt: FS Thomas, R. (NZ) — Killed
  Nav: Sgt Stobbs, W. E. — Killed
  AB: Sgt Tayler, D. A. A. — Killed
  WOP: Sgt McLoughlin, J. B. — Killed
  FE: Sgt Lackenby, A. — Killed
  MU: Sgt Moore, C. J. (Aus) — Killed
  R/gnr: Sgt Lewington, L. O. — Killed

Date: 24 July 1943.
Target: Hamburg.
A/c. Stirling III. EE890. 'L'
  Capt: WO Nicol, H. — Killed
  Nav: FS Robinson, A. J. (NZ) — POW
  AB: PO Mansell, E. J. — POW
  WOP: Sgt Garvin, W. H. — Killed
  FE: Sgt Radford, C. E. — Killed
  MU: Sgt Norrington, H. S. F. — Killed
  R/gnr: FS Cooksley, B. L. (NZ) — POW

Date: 25 July 1943.
Target: Essen.
A/c. Stirling III. EE892. 'F'
  Capt: Sgt Ashdown, M. H. C. — Killed
  Nav: Sgt Harrold, R. K. — Killed
  AB: Sgt Threadgold, R. W. — Killed
  WOP: Sgt Denyer, E. C. — Killed
  FE: Sgt Broadley, R. — Killed
  MU: WO Cleveland, A. (Can) — Killed
  R/gnr: Sgt Dawson, H. C. (Can) — Killed

Date: 30 July 1943.
Target: Remscheid.
A/c. Stirling III. BF458.
  Capt: PO Thomas, A. J. — Killed
  Nav: Sgt Stewart, H. — POW
  AB: PO Cumpsty, F. W. R. (NZ) — Killed
  WOP: Sgt Boxell, R. H. — POW
  FE: Sgt Gale, J. W. — Killed
  MU: Sgt O'Farrell, J. H. — Killed
  R/gnr: WO Henry, E. F. (Can) — Killed

Date: 30 July 1943.
Target: Remscheid.
A/c. Stirling III. EE915. 'X'
  Capt: FS Darney, J. N. (NZ) — Killed
  Nav: FS Stone, R. J. (NZ) — Killed
  AB: Sgt Evens, R. C. G. — Killed
  WOP: Sgt Davies, G. C. — Killed
  FE: FL Dive-Robinson, L. C. — Killed
  MU: FO St. Ledger, P. S. A. (Aus) — Killed
  R/gnr: Sgt Vercoe, T. J. (NZ) — Killed

Date: 2 August 1943.
Target: Hamburg.
A/c. Stirling III. EH928. 'M'
  Capt: PO Bailie, C. P. — Killed
  2/Pilot: FS Thomson, J. (NZ) — Killed
  Nav: FO Turner, W. (NZ) — Killed
  AB: Sgt Isherwood, J. — Killed
  WOP: Sgt Millward, E. — Killed
  FE: Sgt Thompson, W. H. — Killed
  MU: Sgt Purdie, T. — Killed
  R/gnr: Sgt Hunting, E. F. — Killed

Date: 2 August 1943.
Target: Hamburg.
A/c. Stirling III. BF577.
   Capt: FS Couper, J. A. (NZ) — Killed
   Nav: Sgt Walker, G. A. — Killed
   AB: FS Corlett, G. (NZ) — Killed
   WOP: FS Reeves, S. C. O. (NZ) — Killed
   FE: Sgt Sneddon, J. W. — Killed
   MU: Sgt Wadeson, T. E. — Killed
   R/gnr: Sgt Ashworth, A. — Killed

Date: 7 August 1943.
Target: Mining — Gironde Estuary.
A/c. Stirling I. BK614.
   Capt: FS Mayo, J. R. (NZ) — Killed
   Nav: Sgt Turner, A. E. — Killed
   AB: FS Rothstein, I. S. (Can) — Killed
   WOP: FS Gittins, T. H. — Killed
   FE: Sgt Booth, R. — Killed
   MU: Sgt Kitching, S. T. — Killed
   R/gnr: Sgt Amstel, R. H. — Killed

Date: 15 August 1943.
Target: Mining — Gironde Estuary.
A/c. Stirling III. EE891. 'Q'
   Capt: FS Whitta, N. B. (NZ) — Killed
   Nav: FO Turnbull, J. G. (NZ) — Killed
   AB: FS Costello, M. (CAN) — Killed
   WOP: Sgt Andrews, R. F. — Killed
   FE: Sgt Mason, F. D. — Killed
   MU: Sgt Crisp, B. G. — Killed
   R/gnr: Sgt Lovewell, J. E. — Killed

Date: 23 August 1943.
Target: Berlin.
A/c. Stirling III. EE938. 'X'
   Capt: WO Fear, T. — Killed
   Nav: Sgt Ruddy, B. H. — Killed
   AB: Sgt Bain, A. — Killed
   WOP: Sgt Woolcott, D. G. — Killed
   FE: Sgt Munro, C. — Killed
   MU: Sgt Holmes, J. A. C. (Can) — Killed
   R/gnr: FS Davidson, A. (Can) — Killed

Date: 23 August 1943
Target: Berlin.
A/c. Stirling III. BF465.
   Capt: PO Rankin, A. — Killed
   Nav: PO Ericksen, M. A. (NZ) — Killed
   AB: PO Third, J. (NZ) — Killed
   WOP: FS Thorstenson, F. W. (NZ) — Killed
   FE: Sgt Freeman, F. M. — Killed
   MU: Sgt Catterick, D. — POW
     (Seriously wounded)
   R/gnr: Sgt Ogden, G. — Killed

Date: 23 August 1943.
Target: Berlin.
A/c. Stirling III. BF564.
   Capt: PO Sedunary, A. J. L. DFC. (NZ) — Killed
   2/Pilot: FS Lundon, F. D. (NZ) — Killed
   Nav: PO Lens, A. — Killed
   AB: Sgt Parish, C. R. — Killed
   WOP: PO Moss, D. H. (NZ) — Killed
   FE: Sgt Alcock, F. K. MID — Killed
   MU: Sgt Nicholson, J. E. — Killed
   R/gnr: Sgt Gratton, J. J. — Killed

Date: 27 August 1943.
Target: Nuremberg.
A/c. Stirling III. EE955.
   Capt: FS Higham, F. D. (NZ) — Killed
   Nav: Sgt Culshaw, J. R. — Killed
   AB: FS Bailey, M. (Can) — Killed
   WOP: FS Bridger, C. J. (NZ) — Killed
   FE: Sgt Renfrew, R. — Killed
   MU: Sgt Jennings, H. — Killed
   R/gnr: Sgt Clarke, A. — Killed

Date: 30 August 1943.
Target: Munchen-Gladbach.
A/c. Stirling III. EH938. 'F'
   Capt: FS Parkin, V. T. (NZ) — Killed
   Nav: FS Watters, T. (NZ) — Killed
   AB: Sgt Johnson, V. — Evaded
   WOP: Sgt Horrigan, W. — Killed
   FE: Sgt Silcock, T. — Killed
   MU: Sgt Grove, R. F. — Killed
   R/gnr: Sgt Saunders, A. F. — Killed

Date: 31 August 1943.
Target: Berlin.
A/c. Stirling III. EE918. 'D'
   Capt: FS Roberts, E. J. (NZ) — Killed
   Nav: FO Rainford, R. G. — Killed
   AB: PO Giles, J. C. — Killed
   WOP: FS Jackson, K. C. (NZ) — Killed
   FE: Sgt Saunders, E. — Killed
   MU: PO Haydon, J. (Aus) — POW
   R/gnr: FS Haub, D'A. L. C. (NZ) — Killed

Date: 31 August 1943.
Target: Berlin.
A/c. Stirling III. EF501. 'K'
   Capt: FS McGregor, K. A. (NZ) — Killed
   Nav: FO Lovelock, J. B. (NZ) — Killed
   AB: FS Kilby, W. A. (NZ) — Killed
   WOP: FS Baker, J. G. (NZ) — Killed
   FE: Sgt Bond, G. — POW
     (Wounded)
   MU: Sgt Dummett, G. — POW
   R/gnr: Sgt Grange, T. — Killed

Date: 31 August 1943.
Target: Berlin.
A/c. Stirling III. EH905. 'R'.
  Capt: PO Helm, G. V. (NZ) — Killed
  Nav: FS Stewart, D. M. (NZ) — Killed
  AB: FS Fisk, J. G. A. (NZ) — Killed
  WOP: Sgt Bishop, A. J. — Killed
  FE: Sgt McCoo, O. — Killed
  MU: Sgt Buglass, G. — POW
  R/gnr: Sgt Harries, F. — POW

Date: 31 August 1943.
Target: Berlin.
A/c. Stirling III. EE878. 'P'
  Capt: PO Henley, D. C. (NZ) — Killed
  Nav: FO Watson, C. A. (NZ) — Killed
  AB: FS Smith, I. H. R. (NZ) — Killed
  WOP: Sgt Quelch, R. N. — POW
  FE: Sgt Parsons, L. P. — POW
  MU: Sgt Box, D. C. — POW
  R/gnr: Sgt Grant, J. S. — POW
  (Wounded)

Date: 5 September 1943.
Target: Mannheim.
A/c. Stirling III. EE893.
  Capt: PO Wilkinson, E. S. (NZ) — Killed
  Nav: FS Simes, G. N. (NZ) — POW
  (Seriously wounded)
  AB: FS Treacher, N. G. R. (NZ) — POW
  WOP: Sgt Waterman, J. J. — Killed
  FE: Sgt Whatley, T. — Killed
  MU: Sgt Robson, E. S. — POW
  R/gnr: FS Wilkinson, G. S. — Killed

Date: 23 September 1943.
Target: Mannhiem.
A/c. Stirling III. EH935.
  Capt: FO Kirkpatrick, L. J. (NZ) — Killed
  Nav: FO Sands, H. P. (NZ) — Killed
  AB: FO Mason, W. (NZ) — POW
  WOP: Sgt Hoey, J. E. — Killed
  FE: Sgt Ellins, C. P. — Killed
  MU: Sgt Elliott, J. — POW
  (Repatriated 6/2/1945)
  R/gnr: FS Jarvis, W. L. (Aus) — Killed

Date: 23 September 1943.
Target: Mannheim.
A/c. Stirling III. EH936.
  Capt: FL Turner, G. DFC (Can) — Killed
  2/Pilot: FO Albiston, K. — Killed
  Nav: Sgt Cleghorn, A. H. — Killed
  AB: FO Howlett, A. D. (NZ) — Killed
  WOP: Sgt Bloxham, M. V. — Killed
  FE: Sgt Thomson, J. S. — Killed
  MU: Sgt Wilks, R. — Killed
  R/gnr: FS McRae, C. F. (Can) — Killed

Date: 23 September 1943.
Target: Mannheim.
A/c. Stirling III. BF459.
  Capt: FO Logan, C. C. P. (Aus) — Killed
  Nav: FS Sawerby, G. P. (NZ) — Killed
  AB: FO Ingham, J. P. — Killed
  WOP: Sgt Hegarty, T. J. — Killed
  FE: Sgt Stewart, T. — Killed
  MU: Sgt Crowther, F. E. W. — POW
  (Seriously wounded; died 3/10/1943)
  R/gnr: FS Knox, A. (NZ) — POW

Date: 27 September 1943.
Target: Hanover.
A/c. Stirling III. EF515.
  Capt: Sgt Martin, R. E. (NZ) — POW
  Nav: Sgt Dwight, H. G. (NZ) — POW
  AB: Sgt McKay, E. (NZ) — POW
  (Repatriated 6/2/1945)
  WOP: Sgt Harries, W. V. — POW
  FE: Sgt Smith, C. A. — POW
  (died 8/4/1944)
  MU: Sgt Bangs, A. R. — Killed
  R/gnr: Sgt Summerhayes, R. (NZ) — POW
  (Repatriated 6/2/1945)

Date: 27 September 1943.
Target: Hanover
A/c. Stirling III. EH877.
  Capt: PO Whitmore, R. C. (NZ) — Killed
  Nav: FO Adamson, D. M. (NZ) — Killed
  AB: Sgt Munn, H. — Killed
  WOP: Sgt Cowan, F. — POW
  FE: Sgt Beresford, J. B. — Killed
  MU: Sgt Chesson, F. J. C. — Killed
  R/gnr: PO Waerea, T. H. (NZ) — Killed

Date: 4 October 1943.
Target: Frankfurt.
A/c. Stirling III. EF130.
  Capt: Sgt Middleton, H. J. — Killed
  Nav: Sgt Massie, C. J. — Killed
  AB: FS Pennycook, C. (Can) — Killed
  WOP: Sgt Pow. L. — Killed
  FE: Sgt Hudson, E. F. — Killed
  MU: Sgt Thorpe, E. — Killed
  R/gnr: Sgt Lackenby, T. — Killed

Date: 4 November 1943.
Target: Mining — Baltic Sea.
A/c. Stirling III. BF461.
  Capt: PO Williams, G. K. (NZ) — POW
  Nav: FS Morice, W. J. (NZ) — Evaded
  AB: Sgt McGregor, F. E. (NZ) — POW
  WOP: Sgt Champion, W. — Killed
  FE: Sgt Moffat, H. N. — POW
  MU: FO Black, J. A. (Aus) — POW
  R/gnr: Sgt Ingrey, R. — POW

Date: 4 November 1943.
Target: Mining — Baltic Sea.
A/c. Stirling III. EE897.
  Capt: FO Wilson, N. C. B. (NZ) — Killed
  Nav: FO Lodge, T. (NZ) — Killed
  AB: FO Dance, A. T. (NZ) — Killed
  WOP: FS Charlton, R. — Killed
  FE: Sgt Stratton R. W. J. — Killed
  MU: Sgt Gaskins, L. C. — Killed
  R/gnr: FS Fawcett, A. G. (NZ) — Killed

Date: 4 November 1943.
Target: Mining — Baltic Sea.
A/c. Stirling III. BK778.
  Capt: PO Masters, W. S. (NZ) — Killed
  Nav: FS Imrie, G. B. (NZ) — Killed
  AB: FS James, C. (NZ) — Killed
  WOP: Sgt Thomas, R. J. — Killed
  FE: Sgt Copeland, A. A. — Killed
  MU: Sgt Grimwood, L. — Killed
  R/gnr: FS Crawford-Watson, L. S. (NZ) — Killed

Date: 19 November 1943.
Target: Leverkusen.
A/c. Stirling III. LJ442. 'F'
  Capt: FS Parker, N. N. (Aus) — Evaded
  Nav: Sgt Griffiths, R. — Evaded
  AB: FS Hyde, J. E. (NZ) — POW (Seriously wounded)
  WOP: PO Kell, W. R. (NZ) — Killed
  FE: Sgt Watkins, S. — Killed
  MU: Sgt Gilfillan, W. — Killed
  R/gnr: Sgt Day, M. I. R. — Killed

Date: 22 November 1943.
Target: Berlin.
A/c. Stirling III. LJ453.
  Capt: FS Single, A. R. (Aus) — Killed
  Nav: FO Brothwell, J. — Killed
  AB: FS Margetts, J. E. S. (NZ) — Killed
  WOP: FS Whittington, E. R. (NZ) — Killed
  FE: Sgt Holbrook, I. G. — Killed
  MU: Sgt Hughes, V. S. — Killed
  R/gnr: FS Bernard, A. G. (NZ) — Killed

Date: 22 November 1943.
Target: Berlin
A/c. Stirling III. EF148.
  Capt: FS Turner, J. C. (NZ) — Killed
  Nav: FO McKenzie, S. H. (NZ) — Killed
  AB: FO Pagett, W. G. S. — Killed
  WOP: FS Cowie, J. L. (NZ) — Killed
  FE: Sgt Blackman, G. J. — Killed
  MU: Sgt More, R. McL. — Killed
  R/gnr: Sgt McGloin, T. — Killed

Date: 24 February 1944.
Target: Mining — Kiel Bay.
A/c. Stirling III. EH948.
  Capt: PO Bruhns, H. H. (NZ) — Killed
  Nav: Sgt Wilkes, E. A. — Killed
  AB: FS Butler, L. L. (NZ) — Killed
  WOP: Sgt Summers, W. J. — Killed
  FE: Sgt Harry, J. W. — Killed
  MU: FS Sawtell, A. H. (Aus) — Killed
  R/gnr: Sgt Hall, R. E. — Killed

Date: 4 March 1944.
Target: Special operation trainer 124.
A/c. Stirling III. EF215.
  Capt: SL Watson, R. J. DFC (NZ) — Killed
  Nav: FO Henderson, H. W. (NZ) — Killed
  AB: FS Woods, R. M. — Killed
  WOP: FS. Jones, A. S. — Killed
  FE: Sgt Beech, C. — Killed
  MU: Sgt Armstrong, C. — POW
  R/gnr: FS Melville, R. J. I. (NZ) — Killed

Date: 13 March 1944.
Target: Mining — St. Nazaire.
A/c. Stirling III. LJ462. 'O'
  Capt: PO Rowberry, G. W. (NZ) — Killed
  Nav: FS Hadfield, G. S. (NZ) — Killed
  AB: Sgt Simnett, B. — Killed
  WOP: Sgt Bishop, S. T. — Killed
  FE: Sgt Horner, A. W. — Killed
  MU: Sgt Davies, R. D. — Killed
  R/gnr: Sgt Newnham, A. — Killed

Date: 18 April 1944
Target: Mining — Kiel Bay.
A/c. Stirling III. EH955. 'K'
  Capt: FO Murray, H. J. (NZ) — Killed
  Nav: Sgt McFarland, J. — POW
  AB: FS Hill, D. (NZ) — POW
  WOP: FS Irwin, G. J. (NZ) — POW
  FE: Sgt Kahler, H. C. M. — Killed
  MU: Sgt Mulligan, J. (Can) — Killed
  R/gnr: Sgt Woollam, P. — Killed

Date: 23 April 1944.
Target: Mining — Kiel Bay.
A/c. Stirling III. EF137. 'E'
  Capt: PO Lammas, M. (NZ) — Killed
  Nav: FS Vaughan, D. M. (NZ) — Killed
  AB: FS Bailey, R. (NZ) — Kiiled
  WOP: Sgt Harrison, W. F. — Killed
  FE: Sgt Thomas, E. H. — Killed
  MU: Sgt Butler, P. F. — Killed
  R/gnr: Sgt Larson, I. — Killed

Date: 27 April 1944.
Target: Friedrichshafen.
A/c. Lancaster III. ND796. 'J'
   Capt: FO Herron, R. W. (NZ) — Killed
   Nav: FS Henderson, M. R. (NZ) — Killed
   AB: Sgt Percival, W. R. — Killed
   WOP: FO McLachlan, E. W. (NZ) — Killed
   FE: Sgt Germing, J. W. — Killed
   MU: WO Smith, K. A. — Killed
   R/gnr: FO Chilman, P. E. — Killed

Date: 1 May 1944.
Target: Chambly.
A/c. Lancaster III. ME689. 'Y'
   Capt: SL Sachtler, E. W. (NZ) — Killed
   Nav: FO Heron, A. G. — Killed
   AB: PO Lombard, M. F. — Killed
   WOP: FS McKenzie, D. J. (Aus) — Killed
   FE: Sgt Stevens, P. T. — Killed
   MU: Sgt Peevers, T. A. (NZ) — Killed
   R/gnr: Sgt Pettifer, J. G. — Killed

Date: 11 May 1944.
Target: Louvain.
A/c. Lancaster III. ND919. 'D'
   Capt: FL Warren, D. — Killed
   Nav: FO Irving, A. E. (Can) — Killed
   AB: PO Gage, D. I. (Can) — Killed
   WOP: F/S Clough, D. — Killed
   FE: Sgt Riley, F. C. — Killed
   MU: Sgt Dewhurst, H. — Killed
   R/gnr: FS Hewett, H. M. (Aus) — Killed

Date: 21 May 1944.
Target: Duisburg.
A/c. Lancaster III. ND804. 'K'
   Capt: PO Willis, W. J. (NZ) — Killed
   Nav: FS Brown, R. H. (NZ) — Killed
   AB: FS Kay, A. L. (NZ) — Killed
   WOP: FS Hancock, S. A. — Killed
   FE: Sgt Rimmer, D. — Killed
   MU: FS Ferguson, A. A. (NZ) — Killed
   R/gnr: PO Reid, W. F. (Can) — Killed

Date: 22 May 1944
Target: Dortmund.
A/c. Lancaster III. ND768. 'F'
   Capt: PO Armstrong, C. E. (NZ) — Killed
   Nav: FS Payne, D. B. (NZ) — Killed
   AB: FS Marshall, E. W. E. (NZ) — Killed
   WOP: Sgt Warburton, C. A. — Killed
   FE: Sgt Sleightholm, D. — Killed
   MU: Sgt Davies, R. J. — Killed
   R/gnr: FS Pepper, J. — Killed

Date: 22 May 1944.
Target: Dortmund.
A/c. Lancaster III. ME690. 'Z'
   Capt: PO Burke, E. L. (NZ) — Killed
   Nav: FO Downing, J. W. — Killed
   AB: WO Page, F. (Aus) — Killed
   WOP: FS Bromley, A. S. — Killed
   FE: Sgt Pickering, W. — Killed
   MU: Sgt Cooper, J. H. — Killed
   R/gnr: Sgt Grant, D. C. K. — Killed

Date: 27 May 1944.
Target: Aachen.
A/c. Lancaster III. ND908. 'M'
   Capt: FL Fauvel, S. F. (NZ) — Killed
   2/Pilot: FO Lukey, F. H. C. (NZ) — Killed
   Nav: FO Clare, F. W. — Killed
   AB: PO Fitzgerald, M. I. J. — Killed
   WOP: PO Marwin, D. W. J. DFC — Killed
   FE: Sgt Clinch, K. — Killed
   MU: FS Gower, K. W. (NZ) — Killed
   R/gnr: FS Mason, J. R. (NZ) — Killed

Date: 27 May 1944.
Target: Aachen.
A/c. Lancaster III. ND802. 'D'
   Capt: Sgt Scott, F. A. J. (NZ) — Killed
   2/Pilot: WO Clark, R. (NZ) — POW
   Nav: FS Hill, L. (NZ) — POW
   AB: FS Cook, S. A. (NZ) — Killed
   WOP: Sgt Howson, R. — Killed
   FE: Sgt Harris, F. M. — POW
   MU: Sgt Mantle, A. — POW
   R/gnr: Sgt Dale, R. — POW

Date: 10 June 1944.
Target: Dreux.
A/c. Lancaster I. ME702. 'Q'
   Capt: PO Bonisch, L. L. (NZ) — Killed
   Nav: FS McKenzie, J. M. T. (NZ) — Killed
   AB: FS Miller, J. S. (NZ) — Killed
   WOP: FO Marsh, H. H. — Killed
   FE: Sgt Reaveley, W. T. — Killed
   MU: Sgt Allen, B. — POW
   R/gnr: Sgt Cousins, F. W. — Killed

Date: 10 June 1944.
Target: Dreux.
A/c. Lancaster I. HK553. 'S'
   Capt: FS Donaghy, T. R. (NZ) — Killed
   Nav: Sgt Parkin, R. — Killed
   AB: Sgt Williams, W. I. — Killed
   WOP: Sgt Mitchell, H. G. — Killed
   FE: Sgt Lea, J. V. — Killed
   MU: Sgt Jackson, K. — Evaded
   R/gnr: Sgt Dew, H. N. — Killed

Date: 15 June 1944.
Target: Valenciennes.
A/c. Lancaster I. LL888. 'X'
  Capt: FS Betley, R. D. E. (NZ) — Killed
  Nav: Sgt Gilliatt, E. G. — Killed
  AB: FS Hale, L. E. (NZ) — Killed
  WOP: WO Toohey, E. W. (NZ) — Killed
  FE: Sgt Griffiths, B. — Killed
  MU: Sgt Howe, R. — Killed
  R/gnr: FS Cook. P. J. (NZ) — Killed

Date: 24 June 1944.
Target: Rimeux.
A/c. Lancaster III. ND920. 'P'
  Capt: FS Bateson, B. W. (NZ) — Killed
  Nav: Sgt Startin, G. L. — Killed
  AB: Sgt Morgan, M. F. — Killed
  WOP: Sgt McIntyre, F. C. — Killed
  FE: Sgt Slater, C. H. — Killed
  MU: Sgt Connett, E. L. — Killed
  R/gnr: FS Milne, B. (NZ) — Killed

Date: 19 July 1944.
Target: Aulnoye.
A/c. Lancaster I. LL921. 'E'
  Capt: FL Myers, J. W. A. (NZ) — Killed
  Nav: FO Cormack, W. (NZ) — POW
  AB: FO Cunningham, W. (Can) — Evaded
  WOP: FS Murphy, J. W. (NZ) — Evaded
  FE: Sgt Andrews, D. E. — POW
  MU: Sgt Burn, A. E. — POW
  R/gnr: Sgt Mason, W. — Evaded

Date: 20 July 1944.
Target: Homberg.
A/c. Lancaster III. PA967.
  Capt: PO Howell, E. (NZ) — Killed
  Nav: FS Wilkinson, R. J. — Killed
  AB: FO McGeorge, J. R. — Killed
  WOP: FS Redwood, G. H. (NZ) — Killed
  FE: Sgt Blundell, J. J. — Killed
  MU: Sgt McAdam, R. D. — Killed
  F/gnr: FS Hickford, L. L. (NZ) — Killed

Date: 20 July 1944.
Target: Homberg.
A/c. Lancaster III. ND800.
  Capt: PO MacKay, K. M. (NZ) — Killed
  Nav: FS Quinn, E. J. (NZ) — Killed
  AB: FO Jones, R. K. (NZ) — Killed
  WOP: WO Davies, W. J. — Killed
  FE: FS Knapton, R. — Killed
  MU: Sgt Dunn, W. J. — Killed
  R/gnr: FS Worth, J. (NZ) — Killed

Date: 20 July 1944.
Target: Homberg.
A/c. Lancaster I. HK569. 'Q'
  Capt: FS Davidson, N. D. (NZ) — Killed
  Nav: Sgt Goddard, A. E. J. — Killed
  AB: Sgt Little, T. G. — POW
  WOP: Sgt Corris, D. — Killed
  FE: Sgt Sloman, R. G. — Killed
  MU: Sgt Lang, R. S. — Killed
  R/gnr: FS Hiscox, H. J. — Killed

Date: 20 July 1944.
Target: Homberg.
A/c. Lancaster III. ND752. 'O'
  Capt: PO Burtt, H. J. (NZ) — Killed
  Nav: FS Connell, V. (Aus) — POW
  AB: WO Coedy, H. J. W. (Can) — POW
  WOP: WO Gillan, G. L. (NZ) — Killed
  FE: Sgt Cornish, V. C. — Killed
  MU: Sgt Carter, W. F. — Killed
  R/gnr: Sgt Levy, G. A. — Killed

Date: 20 July 1944.
Target: Homberg.
A/c. Lancaster III. ME691. 'R'
  Capt: PO Whittington, H. (NZ) — Killed
  Nav: FL Stevens, J. — Killed
  AB: Sgt Simpson, A. A. (NZ) — Killed
  WOP: FO Tompkins, P. E. — Killed
  FE: Sgt Gore, D. — POW
  MU: Sgt Batty, R. J. M. — Killed
  R/gnr: FS Fletcher, A. C. (NZ) — Killed

Date: 20 July 1944.
Target: Homberg
A/c. Lancaster III. ND915.
  Capt: WO Gilmour, H. E. (Aus) — Killed
  Nav: WO Woodward, L. (Aus) — POW
  AB: FS Mills, S. (Aus) — Killed
  WOP: FS Osborne, J. E. (Aus) — Killed
  FE: Sgt Buzza, R. E. — Killed
  MU: Sgt Ballard, W. — POW
  R/gnr: Sgt Stephenson, J. L. — Killed

Date: 20 July 1944.
Target: Homberg.
A/c. Lancaster I. ME752.
  Capt: FS Roche, G. B. (NZ) — Killed
  Nav: FO Callow, H. (NZ) — Killed
  AB: FS Burgess, J. (NZ) — POW
  WOP: Sgt Barson, J. F. Mac. — Killed
  FE: Sgt Armstrong, J. — Killed
  MU: FS McGee, W. (NZ) — Evaded
  R/gnr: FS Smith, K. E. (NZ) — Killed

Date: 24 July 1944.
Target: Stuttgart.
A/c. Lancaster I. HK575. 'O'
- Capt: FO McRae, J. K. (NZ) — Killed
- Nav: FO Lowe, W. — Killed
- AB: FS Potts, T. C. (NZ) — Killed
- WOP: Sgt Booth, C. — Killed
- FE: Sgt Patten, F. H. — Killed
- MU: Sgt Roffey, D. A. T. — Killed
- R/gnr: Sgt Cunningham, G. — Killed

Date: 24 July 1944.
Target: Stuttgart.
A/c. Lancaster I. HK568.
- Capt: FO Whitehouse, K. O. (NZ) — Killed
- Nav: PO Milliner, J. (Aus) — Killed
- AB: FS Horsford, R. S. — Killed
- WOP: WO Dudding, K. (NZ) — Killed
- FE: Sgt Leighton, B. — Killed
- MU: Sgt Baker, R. C. — Killed
- R/gnr: FS Taverner, G. A. B. (Aus) — Killed

Date: 28 July 1944.
Target: Stuttgart.
A/c. Lancaster I. NE148.
- Capt: FL Stokes, N. A. D. (NZ) — Killed
- 2/Pilot: FO Morris, J. (NZ) — Evaded
- Nav: FO Sanders, G. (NZ) — Evaded
- AB: FS Sampson, N. (NZ) — Evaded
- WOP: FS Raynel, W. (NZ) — Evaded
- FE: Sgt Meanley, R. — Evaded
- MU: FS Drummond, M. K. P. (NZ) (Injured) — Evaded
- R/gnr: Sgt Wilding, N. — Killed

Date: 28 July 1944.
Target: Stuttgart.
A/c. Lancaster III. ND657. 'M'
- Capt: PO Blance, I. E. (NZ) — Killed
- Nav: FS Greig, C. F. J. (NZ) (Wounded) — POW
- AB: WO Spencer, R. H. — Killed
- WOP: FS Climo, F. W. P. (NZ) — Killed
- FE: Sgt Hyde. W. J. — Evaded
- MU: FS Jenkins, F. F. A. (NZ) — Killed
- R/gnr: FS Kirk, A. C. (NZ) — Evaded

Date: 30 July 1944.
Target: Amaye-sur-Selles.
A/c. Lancaster I. HK558.
- Capt: PO Nairne, C. G. (NZ) — Killed
- Nav: PO Perry, L. C. (NZ) — Killed
- AB: WO Kidby, D. A. — Killed
- WOP: Sgt Stannard, A. R. — Killed
- FE: Sgt Smith, R. C. — Killed
- MU: Sgt Woodford, S. A. G. — Killed
- R/gnr: FS Falkiner, P. (NZ) — Killed

Date: 7 August 1944.
Target: Mare De Magne.
A/c. Lancaster I. HK567.
- Capt: FO Brunton, G. A. — Evaded
- Nav: FO Wilkinson, J. S. (NZ) — Evaded
- AB: FO Baker, B. C. (NZ) (Wounded) — POW
- WOP: FO Elliotte, J. M. (NZ) — Evaded
- FE: Sgt Board, K. B. — Evaded
- MU: Sgt Hall, T. J. — Killed
- R/gnr: Sgt Hayler, E. J. — Killed.

Date: 12 August 1944.
Target: Russelsheim.
A/c. Lancaster I. HK564. 'P'
- Capt: PO Mulcahy, C. D. (NZ) — Killed
- Nav: FO Hazard, W. F. (NZ) — Killed
- AB: FS Thomson, E. L. (NZ) — Killed
- WOP: PO Elvin, W. (NZ) — Killed
- FE: Sgt Parker, R. R. S. — Killed
- MU: FS Johnston, H. D. (NZ) — Killed
- R/gnr: FS Wright, J. H. (NZ) — Killed

Date: 25 August 1944.
Target: Russelsheim.
A/c. Lancaster I. LM593. 'N'
- Capt: FO Fleming, J. A. (NZ) — Killed
- Nav: FO Dale, J. A. (NZ) — Killed
- AB: FS Vincent, F. A. — Killed
- WOP: Sgt Garforth, E. — Killed
- FE: Sgt Croxon, K. E. — Killed
- MU: Sgt Slater, E. — Killed
- R/gnr: Sgt Stewart, A. R. B. — Killed

Date: 25 August 1944.
Target: Russelsheim.
A/c. Lancaster I. LL866. 'S'
- Capt: PO Barker, R. S. (NZ) — Killed
- Nav: FS Farnworth, J. — Killed
- AB: FS Norton, W. G. (NZ) — Killed
- WOP: WO Firth, R. (NZ) — Killed
- FE: Sgt Jones, G. — Killed
- MU: Sgt Baker, H. G. — Killed
- R/gnr: Sgt Nash, C. G. — Killed

Date: 29 August 1944.
Target: Stettin.
A/c. Lancaster I. HK594.
- Capt: FS King, D. A. S. — Evaded
- Nav: FS Watson, W. (NZ) — Killed
- AB: FS Fitzgerald, J. (NZ) — Killed
- WOP: Sgt Hill, C. B. — Killed
- FE: Sgt Callan, J. P. — Killed
- MU: Sgt Moon, D. L. — Killed
- R/gnr: Sgt Causley, H. W. — Killed

Date: 12 September 1944.
Target: Mining—Baltic Sea.
A/c. Lancaster I. LM268.
  Capt: FO Hadley, W. O. (NZ) — Killed
  Nav: FS Gudgeon, J. (NZ) — Killed
  AB: PO Wilcox, D. J. R. (NZ) — POW
  WOP: FS Giles, J. D. A. (NZ) — Killed
  FE: Sgt Fowler, G. — Evaded
  MU: FS Boyd, W. J. V. (NZ) — Killed
  R/gnr: Sgt Biggar, J. M. (NZ) — Killed

Date: 5 October 1944.
Target: Saarbrucken.
A/c. Lancaster III. ND904.
  Capt: PO Galletly, A. R. (NZ) — Killed
  Nav: FS Mosely, S. E. (NZ) — Killed
  AB: Sgt Wells, R. A. — Killed
  WOP: Sgt Hond, R. S. — Killed
  FE: Sgt Tuthill, P. — Killed
  MU: Sgt Sutton, A. K. — Killed
  R/gnr: Sgt Cooke, J. P. — Killed

Date: 6 October 1944.
Target: Dortmund.
A/c. Lancaster I. LM104.
  Capt: FO Southward, K. (NZ) — Killed
  Nav: FO Thompson, A. (NZ) — POW
  AB: FO Clare, B. G. (NZ) — POW
  WOP: Sgt Vero, E. W. — POW
  FE: Sgt Roberts, D. J. — POW
  MU: Sgt Cooper, L. — POW
  R/gnr: Sgt Burnett, T. — POW

Date: 21 October 1944.
Target: Flushing.
A/c. Lancaster I. HK596. 'O'
  Capt: FO Johnson, J. — Killed
  Nav: WO Murdoch, T. T. — Killed
  AB: FO Penman, A. M. (NZ) — Killed
  WOP: Sgt Smith, J. — Killed
  FE: Sgt Marfil, L. — Killed
  MU: Sgt Reid, A. — Killed
  R/gnr: WO O'Loughlin V. J. — Killed

Date: 4 November 1944.
Target: Solingen.
A/c. Lancaster III. ND917.
  Capt: FO Scott, J. H. (NZ) — Killed
  Nav: FS Scott, A. H. (NZ) — Killed
  AB: FS Andersen, K. P. C. (NZ) — Killed
  WOP: FS Howard, E. J. F. (NZ) — Killed
  FE: Sgt Thomas, H. M. — Killed
  MU: Sgt Beardmore, J. T. — Killed
  R/gnr: PO Bayes, J. T. — Killed

Date: 20 November 1944.
Target: Homberg.
A/c. Lancaster I. PB689.
  Capt: FO Gorden, R. — Killed
  Nav: FO Bell, J. R. — Killed
  AB: FS Weston, A. — Killed
  WOP: PO Sampson, L. — Killed
  FE: Sgt Freeman, C. — Killed
  MU: Sgt Hone, S. G. — Killed
  R/gnr: Sgt Forrester, J. — Killed

Date: 20 November 1944.
Target: Homberg.
A/c. Lancaster III. PB520.
  Capt: FO Rees, H. — POW
  Nav: FO Preston, R. C. — POW
  AB: FO Westwood, D. C. (NZ) — POW
  WOP: FL Naismith, W. F. M. — POW
  FE: Sgt Mulhall, J. E. — POW
  MU: FS Alderson, R. — POW
  R/gnr: Sgt Allen, C. — POW

Date: 20 November 1944.
Target: Homberg.
A/c. Lancaster I. ND911.
  Capt: FO McCartin, P. L. (Aus) — Killed
  Nav: PO Miles, J. — Killed
  AB: FO Martin, L. A. — Killed
  WOP: FS Smith, P. F. (Aus) — Killed
  FE: Sgt Warlow, W. J. — Killed
  MU: Sgt Bryer, D. G. A. — Killed
  R/gnr: Sgt Gray, J. N. — POW

Date: 21 November 1944.
Target: Mining—Oslo Fiord.
A/c. Lancaster I. NN745. 'A'
  Capt: FL Martyn, L. A. (NZ) — Killed
  Nav: FO Elliot, T. I. (NZ) — Killed
  AB: PO Dunkerley, A. R. F. (Aus) — Killed
  WOP: FS Crabtree, J. C. — Killed
  FE: Sgt Starkey, C. R. — Killed
  MU: Sgt Lindsay, G. — Killed
  R/gnr: PO Wright, A. R. (Can) — Killed

Date: 30 November 1944.
Target: Osterfeld.
A/c. Lancaster I. NF980. 'F'
  Capt: FO McIntosh, J. A. (NZ) — Killed
  Nav: FS Morgan, R. C. (NZ) — Killed
  AB: FS Newman, R. W. (NZ) — Killed
  WOP: FS Boag, R. J. (AUS) — Killed
  FE: Sgt Taylor, R. — Killed
  MU: Sgt Brewer, C. — Killed
  R/gnr: Sgt Cooper, E. R. — POW
    (Seriously wounded; died 28/12/1944)

Date: 27 December 1944.
Target: Rheydt.
A/c. Lancaster I. NN710. 'Q'
    Capt: FO Miles, H. S. (NZ) — Killed
    Nav: FO Dowding, M. McL. — Killed
    AB: FO Gunn, F. J. — POW
    WOP: FS Coombridge, T. W. (NZ) — Killed
    FE: Sgt Haslam G. F. — Killed
    MU: Sgt Left, E. — Killed
    R/gnr: Sgt Mepham, D. N. — Killed

Date: 1 January 1945.
Target: Vohwinkel.
A/c. Lancaster III. ME321. 'N'
    Capt: WC Newton, R. J. DFC MID (NZ) — Killed
    2/Pilot: PO Aitchison, R. J. (NZ) — Killed
    Nav: Sgt Sansome, H. — Killed
    AB: FS Lee, A. — Killed
    WOP: Sgt Clark, V. J. — Killed
    FE: FS Hoskins, J. S. — Killed
    MU: Sgt Brennan, M. — Killed
    R/gnr: Sgt Cooke, L. J. — Killed

Date: 14 February 1945.
Target: Chemnitz.
A/c. Lancaster III. NG113. 'D'
    Capt: FL Davies, G. S. (NZ) — POW
    Nav: FS Greenhough, C. C. (NZ) — POW
    AB: FS Chalmers, H. E. (died 2/3/1945) — POW
    WOP: FS White, T. M. — POW
    FE: Sgt Evans, I. R. H. — POW
    MU: FS Muir, R. — POW
    R/gnr: Sgt Maher, J. J. — POW

Date: 25 February 1945.
Target: Kamen.
A/c. Lancaster III. LM740. 'B'
    Capt: FS Klitscher, L. S. B. (NZ) — POW
    Nav: FO King, D. W. — POW
    AB: FS Pilkington, W. C. F. — POW
    WOP: FO Craven, J. — POW
    FE: FS Brewer, W. H. H. — POW
    MU: Sgt Blackbee, K. A. — POW
    R/gnr: Sgt Amps, D. W. S. — POW

Date: 14 March 1945.
Target: Heinrich-Hutte.
A/c. Lancaster I. PB741. 'E'
    Capt: FL Parsons, E. G. — Killed
    Nav: FS Phinn, W. — Killed
    AB: FS Ebbage, F. — Killed
    WOP: FS Ramsay, E. — Killed
    FE: Sgt Longstaff, C. A. — Killed
    MU: Sgt Beard, J. L. — Killed
    R/gnr: Sgt Nichol, J. — Killed

Date: 21 March 1945.
Target: Munster viaduct.
A/c. Lancaster III. LM733. 'R'
    Capt: FO Brown, A. E. (NZ) — Killed
    Nav: FS Baker, A. D. (NZ) — POW
    AB: FS Wood, J. H. (NZ) — Killed
    WOP: FS Robson, A. E. (NZ) — POW
    FE: FS Lawrence, R. H. — POW
    MU: Sgt Griveson, J. — POW
    R/gnr: Sgt Barraclough, H. — POW

Date: 21 March 1945.
Target: Munster viaduct.
A/c. Lancaster I. NG449. 'T'
    Capt: FL Plummer, J. DFC (NZ) — Killed
    Nav: PO Humphreys, A. L (NZ) — POW
    AB: FO Holloway, E. J. (NZ) — Killed
    WOP: FO Wakerley, J. J. — POW
    FE: Sgt Fell, M. (Wounded) — POW
    MU: FO Scott, R. J. (NZ) — Killed
    R/gnr: FS McDonald, J. (NZ) — Evaded

Date: 21 March 1945.
Target: Munster viaduct.
A/c. Lancaster I. RA564. 'P'
    Capt: FO Barr, D. S. — Killed
    Nav: FS Oakey, A. L. A. (NZ) — Killed
    AB: FS Stewart, D. — Killed
    WOP: PO West, R. W. MID — Killed
    FE: FS Stocker, C. I. — Killed
    MU: Sgt Nicholl, B. H. — Killed
    R/gnr: WO Amos, A. — Killed

Appendix F

NON-OPERATIONAL AIRCRAFT LOSSES WHERE CASUALTIES OCCURRED 1940–1945

(Compiled by Kevin King and John Tyler)

Date: 10 January 1941   Cross Country   Wellington Ic T2550
Crashed near Duxford on flight to Bassingbourne to pick up a pilot.
Capt:	PO McNamara, B. P.	Killed
2/Pilot:	PO Ryan, A. J. (NZ)	Killed
Nav:	Sgt Elliott, R. B.	Killed
WOP:	Sgt Olive, J.	Killed
F/gnr:	Sgt Ritchie, M. R.	Killed
R/gnr:	Ashby-Peckham (NZ)	Injured

Date: 22 September 1941   Training   Wellington Ic T2805
Capt:	PO Raphail	
2/Pilot:	Sgt Machin	
Nav:	Sgt Craig, R. G. (Can)	Killed
WOP:	Sgt MacDonald	
F/gnr:	Sgt Aichison	
R/gnr:	Sgt Godrey	

Date: 28 February 1942   Air Test   Wellington III X3355 'Y'
This aircraft took off captained by Sergeant Colville. The starboard engine cut out, followed by the port engine. The aircraft crashed at Lakenheath. Sergeant Colville and AC Godwin were injured, Corporal K. J. Howes and AC2 W. Pownall were killed, while Sergeant H. W. Woodham died of his injuries.

Date: 22 May 1942   Training   Wellington III Z1566
Flew into a hill in bad visibility.
Capt:	PO Smeaton, W. H. (NZ)	Killed
	Sgt Beaven, J. W. (NZ)	Killed
	Sgt Bode, J. W.	Killed
	Sgt Hayton, C.	Killed
	PO Mackay, A. D. (NZ)	Killed
	Sgt Chappel (NZ)	Injured

Date: 28 November 1942   Training   Stirling I BF399 'O'
Crashed on training flight from RAF Oakington.
Capt:	Sgt Broady, R. H. J.	Killed
	Sgt Jobson, G. T.	Killed
	FS McWilliam, R. J.	Killed
	Sgt Dibben, R. O.	Killed
	Sgt McIssaac, A.	Killed
	Sgt Robers, C. T.	Died of injuries 30 November

Date: 17 May 1943　　　　　　Training　　　　　　Stirling I BF398
Lost both outer engines and crew baled out, although one man died. The pilot, knowing he was over Stoke-on-Trent tried to crash land but was killed.
Capt:　　　Sgt Wright, L. C.　　　　　　Killed
2/Pilot:　　Sgt Carey, J. H. R. (NZ)
Nav:　　　Sgt Roberts, J. L. (NZ)
FE:　　　　Sgt Beaver, T.
WOP:　　 FS Brady, M. (NZ)
AB:　　　　Sgt Knight, P. G. (NZ)
MU:　　　Sgt Macleod, N. A. (NZ)
R/gnr:　　Sgt Francis, A. J.　　　　　　Killed
Passenger: AC2 Bailey, R. G.

Date: 14 January 1944　　　　　Hurricane IV KW792
Aircraft took off from Mepal at 1305 hrs and never seen again
Pilot:　　　Sgt Allen, W. M.　　　　　　Killed

Appendix G

OPERATIONAL AIRCRAFT WHICH EITHER CRASHED IN THE UNITED KINGDOM OR RETURNED WITH DEAD OR INJURED AIRCREW ABOARD 1940–1945

Compiled by Kevin King and John Tyler)

Date: 3 August 1940   Wellington Ic R3176
Target: Horst
Force landed at Marham
Capt: SL Collett, W. J. (NZ)   Died of injuries
2/Pilot: PO Humphries   Injured
Nav: Sgt Simpkin   Injured
WOP: FS Williams   Injured
F/gnr: Sgt Holford   Injured
R/gnr: PO Ferris   Injured

Date: 2 September 1940   Wellington Ic R3159
Target: Hanover
Crashed in bad visibility
Capt: PO Peel, R. N. and crew   Injured

Date: 29 September 1940   Wellington Ic R3168
Target: Osnabruck
Aircraft abandoned over Devon.
Capt: PO Denton, F.   Injured
2/Pilot: Sgt White
Nav: Sgt Orrack
WOP: Sgt Hayter L. A.
F/gnr: Sgt Farquhar
R/gnr: PO Jelley, E. A.   Killed

Date: 16 October 1940   Wellington Ic L7857
Target: Kiel
Abandoned after raid and crashed near Penrith. PO J. Martin and crew safe.

Date: 21 October 1940   Wellington Ic R3158
Target: Channel Ports
Crashed at Manston after hitting balloon cable near Dover. All crew safe.
Capt: FO Elliott, R. P.
2/Pilot: Musselwhite
Nav: Johnson-Barrett
WOP: Day, D. R.
F/gnr: McLaughlan
R/gnr: Sheppard

Date: 18 March 1941   Wellington Ic T2736
Target: Kiel
Abandoned near Doncaster after operation.
Capt: FO Collins
2/Pilot: Sgt Mee, A. C. (NZ)
Nav: PO Evans
WOP: Sgt Gilmore, D.   Killed
F/gnr: Sgt Cole
R/gnr: Sgt Peters

Date: 6th May 1941 Wellington Ic R3169
Target: Hamburg
Hit balloon cable at mouth of River Humber
Capt: Sgt Nola, D. A. (NZ)   Killed
2/Pilot: Sgt Mee, A. C. (NZ)   Killed
Nav: PO Page, C. F.   Killed
WOP: Sgt Hall, J.   Killed
F/gnr: Sgt Russell, W.   Killed
R/gnr: Sgt Craven   Safe

Date: 11 May 1941 Wellington
Target: Hamburg
Attacked by night fighter
Capt: SL Widdowson, R. P. (CAN)
2/Pilot: Sgt Saunders, A.
Nav: Sgt Lawton, L. A. (NZ)
WOP: Sgt Partridge
F/gnr: Sgt Pearne
R/gnr: Sgt Gannaway, E. F. (NZ)   Killed

Date: 3 July 1941 Wellington Ic L7818 'R'
Target: Essen
Capt: Sgt Fotheringham, R. E.
2/Pilot: Sgt Higgins, E. U. R.
Nav: Sgt Roberts, S. H. C.
WOP: Sgt Dyer, S. A.
F/gnr: Sgt Hingley, L. G. H.   Wounded
R/gnr: Sgt McKinnon, D. M.

Date: 7 July 1941 Wellington Ic L7818 'R'
Target: Munster
Returned badly damaged after night fighter attack. VC to Ward, DFC to pilot, DFM to AG Box
Capt: SL Widdowson, R. P. (CAN)
2/Pilot: Sgt Ward, J. A. (NZ)
Nav: Sgt Lawton, L. A. (NZ)
WOP: Sgt Mason, W.
F/gnr: Sgt Evans, T.
R/gnr: Sgt Box, A. J. R. (NZ)   Wounded

Date: 13 July 1941 Wellington III X9634
Target: Bremen
Crashed near beach off Corton, near Lowestoft
Capt: Sgt Minikin, F. T.
2/Pilot: Sgt Gilding
Nav: PO Leacock, J. T.   Killed
WOP: Sgt Fox, E.   Killed
F/gnr: Sgt Price, F. J. E.   Killed
R/gnr: Sgt Clarkson, H. P.   Killed

Date: 15 July 1941 Wellington I W5663
Target: Duisburg
Attacked by night fighter; Nav fell out
Capt: PO Rees, W. J.
2/Pilot: Sgt Joyce, D. C.   Killed
Nav: PO Hunter, R. C. A. (Can)   POW
WOP: Sgt Lewis, J. W.
F/gnr: Sgt Conibear, D. H.   Died of wounds 30 July
R/gnr: Sgt Gwyn-Williams   Wounded

Date: 4 August 1941　　　　　　　　　　Wellington Ic X9760
Target: Hanover
Capt:　　Sgt Matetich, J. A.
R/gnr:　Sgt Twisleton　　　　　　　　　Wounded

Date: 12 August 1941　　　　　　　　　Wellington III X9764 'V'
Target: Hanover
Pilot crash landed, crew baled out
Capt:　　PO Roberts, H. A. (Aus)
2/Pilot:　Sgt Smith
Nav:　　PO Bere
WOP:　Sgt Hill, H. C.　　　　　　　　　Injured
F/gnr:　Sgt Strickland
R/gnr:　Sgt Fagny, P. A. (Can)　　　　　Injured

Date: 20 September 1941　　　　　　　Wellington III X9757
Target: Berlin
Hit by flak
Capt:　　WC Sawrey-Cookson, R.
2/Pilot:　SL Chamberlain, P. B.
Nav:　　FL Fowler
WOP:　Sgt Roberts
F/gnr:　Sgt Hopkins, J. B.　　　　　　　Wounded
R/gnr:　FL Greenaway

Date: 20 September 1941　　　　　　　Wellington Ic R1518
Target: Berlin
Abandoned over UK, crew baled out and Sgt J. A. Matetich made crash landing

Date: 20 September 1941　　　　　　　Wellington Ic T2805
Target: Berlin
Some of crew abandoned over Norfolk in fog upon return, pilot crash landed
Capt:　　PO Raphael, A. S.
Nav:　　Sgt Craig, R. G.　　　　　　　　Died of injuries

Date: 12 October 1941　　　　　　　　Wellington Ic X9951
Target: Bremen
Attacked by night fighter; crash landed at RAF Stradishall
Capt:　　Sgt Barker, R. C.
2/Pilot:　Sgt McLauchlan I. J.　　　　　Wounded
Nav:　　Sgt Grimes
WOP:　Sgt Cole
F/gnr:　Sgt Benny
R/gnr:　Sgt Day, M. R.　　　　　　　　Killed

Date: 17 December 1941　　　　　　　Wellington III Z1083
Target: Brest
Hit by flak
Capt:　　Sgt Climie, J. K.
2/Pilot:　PO Gunning　　　　　　　　　Wounded

Date: 23 December 1941　　　　　　　Wellington III Z8834
Target: Brest
Crashed on return at Berners Heath, Norfolk
Capt:　　FS Bentley, L. L. (NZ)　　　　Killed
2/Pilot:　Sgt Burke, T. W.　　　　　　　Injured
Nav:　　Sgt Ives, H.　　　　　　　　　　Injured
WOP:　Sgt Wilkes, K. C.　　　　　　　　Injured
F/gnr:　Sgt Olrod, W. H.　　　　　　　　Injured
R/gnr:　Sgt Hardman, S. V.　　　　　　Injured

Date: 22 April 1942   Wellington III X3487
Target: Cologne
Attacked by Ju88 night fighter
Capt: PO Jarman, E. G. D.
2/Pilot: PO Nicol, T. Mc. (NZ)   Died of wounds
Nav: Sgt Taylor   Wounded
WOP: Sgt Fernie   Wounded
F/gnr: Sgt Davey
R/gnr: Sgt Harris, R. J. (NZ)   Killed

Date: 22 April 1942   Wellington X3705
Target: Cologne
Attacked by night fighter; crash landed at Feltwell
Capt: FS McLachlan, I. J. (NZ)
2/Pilot: PO Fountain, C. N. (NZ)   Killed
Nav: Sgt Hoare, P. F.
WOP: Sgt Walters, J. W. (NZ)
F/gnr: Sgt Pugh, A. G. E.
R/gnr: Sgt Tutty, D.   Wounded

Date: 29 June 1942   Wellington III Z1616
Target: Bremen
Crashed on take-off
Capt: PO Bertram, R.   Killed
Nav: Sgt Quinn, J. G.   Killed
WOP: Sgt Grenfell, R. J. (NZ)   Killed
F/gnr: Sgt Mitchell, N. (NZ)   Killed
R/gnr: Sgt Archer, G. W. N.   Killed

Date: 31 July 1942   Wellington III X3646
Target: Dusseldorf
Hit by falling four pound incendiary bomb
Crew of Sgt Bradley, G. E. F. all safe but R/gnr FS Lewis, A. G. injured

Date: 27 August 1942   Wellington III BJ584
Target: Kassel
Damaged by night fighter; crash landed at RAF Wattisham
Sgt Burril, F. and crew safe

Date: 16 September 1942   Wellington III BJ760
Target: Essen
Attacked by night fighter
Sgt Blincoe, K. H. (NZ) and crew safe; WOP PO Lowe, H. wounded

Date: 13 October 1942   Wellington III BJ837
Target: Kiel
Crashed on landing at Lakenheath
Sgt Pilot Davey, C. R. (NZ) and crew safe, although four were injured and the F/gnr Sgt Redhead, J. B. died on 19 October

Date: 28 November 1942   Stirling I BK609 'T'
Target: Turin
Overshot after aborting sortie; crash landed at Bradwell Bay
Crew of Sgt McCullough, J. (NZ) all safe but AB Sgt Brodie, I. J. D. injured

Date: 16 December 1942 Stirling I R9245 'N'
Target: Mining — Bordeaux
Crashed on take-off and exploded
Capt: Sgt Franklin, B. A. (NZ)   Killed
Nav: Sgt Whitcombe, W. H. (NZ)   Killed
FE   Sgt Lawrence, W. J (NZ)   Killed
WOP: Sgt Welch, H. R. (NZ)   Killed
AB   Sgt Harvey, E. (NZ)   Killed
MU   Sgt Burridge, E. J.   Killed
R/gnr: Sgt Pascoe, T.   Killed

Date: 8 April 1943 Stirling I BK770 'L'
Target: Duisburg
Crashed on return at Bressingham, Norfolk
Capt: WO Walsh, I. A. E. (NZ)   Killed
Nav: FS Moffatt, B. (Can)   Killed
FE: Sgt Worthington, J.   Killed
WOP: Sgt Scudder, J.   Killed
AB: Sgt Reddicliffe, F. H.   Killed
MU: Sgt Curtis, S. A.   Killed
R/gnr: Sgt Stuart, P. G.   Killed

Date: 10 April 1943 Stirling III BF455 'Y'
Target: Frankfurt
Ditched on return; crew safe

Date: 16 April 1943 Stirling I BK664
Target: Mining — Gironde
Crashed on landing; crew safe but injured

Date: 26 April 1943 Stirling I BF517
Target: Duisburg
Attacked by night fighter; crash landed at base
Capt: PO Buck, P. J. (NZ)
2/Pilot: FL Appleton, E. R. M.
Nav: FO Minnis, A.
FE: Sgt Jones, J.
WOP: PO Symons, J.   Wounded
MU: Sgt Watson, J.   Wounded
R/gnr: Sgt Rogers, B. A.   Killed

Date: 13 May 1943 Stirling III BK721 'Z'
Target: Duisburg
Crashed on take-off
Capt: FL Appleton, E. R. M.   Injured (Killed in an American B17 on 31 August 1943)
2/Pilot: Sgt Harvey, R. (NZ)   Killed
Nav: FO Johnson, J. (NZ)   Killed
FE: Sgt Andrews, J.   Killed
WOP: FS Cocks, S. G. (NZ)   Injured
AB: PO Clubb, S. G, (NZ)   Killed
MU: Sgt Moore, B. A.   Killed
R/gnr: Sgt Wykes, J.   Killed

Date: 13 July 1943 Stirling III EE886
Target: Aachen
Crashed at Oakington on return
Capt: FO Eddy, C. (NZ)   Injured
2/Pilot: Sgt Hartstein, P.   Injured
Nav: PO Lane, A. W.   Injured
FE: Sgt Waring, H.   Injured
WOP: Sgt Burgeois, H.   Injured
AB: FS Hurt, H.   Injured
MU: Sgt Viccars, E. C.   Killed
R/gnr: FS Lucas, H.   Safe

Date: 23 August 1943 Stirling III EF435
Target: Berlin
Hit by flak and fighter; some of crew baled out; aircraft crash landed at base
Capt: FS White, O. H. (NZ)
Nav: FS Rogerson, J. (NZ)   POW
FE: Sgt Worledge, C.
WOP: Sgt Smith, A.
AB: PO Murray, J. (NZ)   POW
MU: Sgt Collins, T.   POW
R/gnr: Sgt Poole, J.   Killed

Date: 5 September 1943 Stirling
Target: Mannheim
Hit by flak; Flight Engineer lost an eye
Capt: FS Batger, A.
FE: Sgt Dalkins, R.   Wounded

Date: 8 September 1943 Stirling III BK809 'T'
Target: Boulogne
Crashed in house on take-off; two civilians and two service personnel killed on the ground
Capt: FO Menzies, I. R. (NZ)   Killed
Nav: PO Cordery, D.   Injured
FE: Sgt Mellor, A. L.   Died of injuries
WOP: Sgt Barker, R.   Injured
AB: FO Gale, N. H.   Killed
MU: Sgt Bullivant, G.
R/gnr: Sgt Muir, G.

Date: 3 October 1943 Stirling III LK378
Target: Kassel
Rear Gunner lost over target — turret shot away
Capt: FS Parker, N. N. (Aus)
R/gnr: Sgt Riddler, S. W. (NZ)   Killed

Date: 24 October 1943 Stirling III
Target: Mining — Frisians
Crashed on return, southwest of Mepal
Capt: FS Randle, J. R.   Killed
Nav: FS East, P. M.   Killed
FE: Sgt James, I. E.   Injured
WOP: WO Myhill, W. R.   Killed
AB: Sgt Purves, J. J.   Killed
MU:
R/gnr: Sgt Blissett, E. H.   Injured

Date: 4 November 1943 Stirling III EJ108
Target: Mining — Baltic
Attacked by night fighter
FO E. Witting's Rear Gunner, FS Hurdle, E. (NZ) killed

Date: 1 December 1943   Stirling III EH880
Target: Mining — Denmark
Crashed into house attempting to land at Acklington; five children killed
Capt: WO Kerr, G. J. S.   Killed
Nav: Sgt Wort, D. F.   Killed
FE: Sgt Copsey, L. G.   Killed
WOP: FS Holt, D. A.   Killed
AB: Sgt Smith, R.   Killed
MU: Sgt Hook, K.   Injured
R/gnr: Sgt Lucas, G. W. T.   Killed

Date: 16 December 1943   Stirling III EF163
Target: Mining — Frisians
Crashed on return at Bedinghams Farm, Cambridgeshire
Capt: PO Kinross, C.   Killed
Nav: FO Jenkins, R. F.   Killed
FE: Sgt Askew, R.   Killed
WOP: Sgt Savage, W.   Killed
AB: Sgt Emmerson, R.   Killed
MU: Sgt Newman, S.   Injured
R/gnr: Sgt Warner, J.   Killed

Date: 28 January 1944   Stirling III EF512
Target: Mining — Kiel Bay
Night fighter attack; crash landed at Coltishall
Capt: PO Baker, C. R. (NZ)
Nav: FS Gardner, C. (NZ)
FE: Sgt Watson, W. P.   Wounded
WOP: Sgt Marden, G.
AB: FS Jones, R. (Aus)
MU: Sgt Renwick, H. R.   Wounded
R/gnr: Sgt Schober, E. (Can)

Date: 11 June 1944   Lancaster 1 ME751
Target: Dreux
Hit by flak; AB flew aircraft back
Capt: PO McCardle, C.   Wounded
Nav: PO Zillwood, A. H. R. (NZ)
FE: Sgt Benfold, J.   Wounded
WOP: FS Hunt, E.
AB: WO Hurse, A. W. (Aus)
MU: Sgt Edwards, J.
R/gnr: Sgt Sparkes, D.

Date: 18 July 1944   Lancaster 1 HK568
Target: Cagny
Hit by flak
Capt: FS Moriarty, D. J. (NZ)   Wounded
Nav: FS Monoghan, T.
FE: Sgt Scott, A.
WOP: Sgt Teverson, A.
AB: FO Ward, I.
MU: Sgt Williams, A.
R/gnr: FS Fox, R.

Date: 26 August 1944   Lancaster 1 LM544
Target: Kiel
Hit by flak
Capt: FO Andrews, V. (NZ)
MU: Sgt Moloney, M.   Wounded

Date: 31 August 1944 Lancaster III PB427 'U'
Target: Pont Reay
Hit by flak
Capt: FO Aitken, J. K. (NZ)
AB: FO Mayhill, R. D. (NZ) Wounded

Date: 11 September 1944 Lancaster 1 HK574
Target: Kaman
Hit by flak; pilot wounded
Capt: FO Yates, H. Wounded

　　　　　　　　　　　　　　　　Lancaster 1 HK562
Hit by flak
Capt: FL Brown, D. (NZ)
Nav: FO Topping, W. Wounded

Date: 17 September 1944 Lancaster III PB430 'P'
Target: Boulogne
Crash landed at Hawkinge on return
Capt: SL Gunn, G. R. (NZ) Died of injuries 21 September
Nav: FO Smith, F. Injured
FE: Sgt Bruce, J. H. Killed
WOP: FL Naismith, W. F. M.
AB: FO Miller, A. M. (NZ) Injured
MU: FO Robinson, C. (NZ)
R/gnr: Sgt Johnstone, G. (NZ)

Date: 6 December 1944 Lancaster 1 HK574
Target: Merseburg
Ditched in the River Orwell; crew safe

Date: 16 January 1945 Lancaster 1 PB761
Target: Wanne-Eickel
Crashed on return at Wood Ditton, Suffolk
Capt: FL Blewett, T. D. (NZ) Killed
Nav: FS Cornell, B. T. Died of injuries 18 January
FE: Sgt Hunwicks, R. Injured
WOP: WO Smyrk, J. Injured
AB: FO Wilson, J. (NZ) Killed
MU: Sgt Pridmore, W. Injured
R/gnr: Sgt Hollins, K. Injured

Date: 3 February 1945 Lancaster III ND801
Target: Dortmund
Overshot on landing; crashed into a house
Capt: FO Crawford, R. B. (NZ) Injured
Nav: FS Boulton, F. Injured
FE: Sgt Allred
WOP: Sgt Scott, D. Injured
AB: Sgt Bullock, C. Injured
MU: Sgt Smith, A.
R/gnr: Sgt Tutty, J.

Date: 26 February 1945   Lancaster 1 ME450
Target: Dortmund
Crashed on return at Chatteris, Cambridgeshire
Capt: FO Thorpe, N. H. (NZ)   Killed
Nav: Sgt McManus, G. W.   Killed
FE: Sgt Duke, J. L.   Died of injuries 28 February
WOP: FS Francis, A. (NZ)
AB: FS Alfred, J. McK.   Killed
MU: Sgt Saffill, F.   Killed
R/gnr: Sgt Hark, H.

Date: 2 March 1945   Lancaster 1 HK600
Target: Cologne
Damaged by flak
Capt: FO Woodcock, A.   Wounded
FE: Sgt Gibbs, A.   Wounded

Date: 4 April 1945   Lancaster 1 HK601
Target: Meresburg
Hit by flak
Capt: FO Wood, J. (NZ)   Wounded
Nav: FS Pauling, J. (NZ)
FE: Sgt Williamson D.   Fell out (but returned to squadron)
WOP: FS Newey, C. (NZ)
AB: FS Hooper, N.   Injured (burnt putting out a fire)
MU: FS Cash, A. (Can)
R/gnr: FS Sparrow, R. (Can)

Date: 15 April 1945   Lancaster III PB132
Target: Potsdam
Attacked by night fighter
Capt: FO Baynes, A. (NZ)
FE: Sgt Sliman, A. M.   Killed

Date: 22 April 1945   Lancaster 1 NF935
Target: Bremen
Hit by flak
Capt: SL Parker, J. C. (NZ)
FE: Sgt Clark, R. S.   Killed

Index of Names

Adams FO J. 6, 9, 10, 11, 12, 23
Addis Sgt J. H. 51
Aitken FL J. K. 125, 126, 129
Alcock Sgt F. 91
Aldis LAC A. 145
Alexander PO A. 99, 213
Allcock SL G. M. 83
Ames FS A. 101
Amoganga 107
Anderson SL B. R. 176, 185
Anderson LAC R. A. J. 7, 8
Andrews SL F. A. 32, 36, 83, 84, 90, 98, 101, 103
Andrews FL V. 128
Anthony FL. 144
Armstrong PO C. 116
Ashdown Sgt M. H. C. 100
Ashworth WC A. 26, 28, 29, 31, 38, 43, 46, 61
Atkin FO D. 147

Bachard LAC. 144
Bagnell WO T. H. 73
Baigent WC C. H. 152, 153, 155, 158, 159, 164, 165, 166, 167
Bailey SL J. M. 135, 152
Bain SL G. C. 25, 28
Baird FS V. H. 166
Baker PO C. 111
Baker Phil 107
Baldwin AM Sir J. 37, 58
Ball F. 91–2
Ball Sgt C. 56
Banks FL 153
Banks FO R. D. 168
Barclay GC J. S. 180, 188
Barker PO R. S. 128
Barron WC J. F. 116
Barr FO D. 157
Bartlett FO N. 70, 76, 78, 98, 99, 133, 135
Bates WC J. S. 191–2
Bawden FL N. H. 110, 116, 117
Baynes FO A. 158
Beardmore W. 50
Beavis ACM M. 167
Belford E. 66, 68, 70
Benfold Sgt J. 118
Bennett Sgt 74
Benson Ben 96
Bentley Sgt L. L. 49
Bertram Sgt R. 57
Best PO E. V. 22, 24
Betley FS R. 118
Bevan FO D. M. 181
Bevan FL P. G. 174
Birch LAC A. 145

Bird FL 144
Bland PO T. 177
Blewett FL T. 153
Blincoe Sgt K. 63, 74
Bluck PO N. B. 98
Blundell Sgt J. 31
Boffee SL N. M. 23
Bonk UntOff H. 59
Box Sgt A. J. R. 41-3, 213
Box Sgt D. C. 105
Boys A/Cdr J. S. 184
Bradley Sgt T. 110
Brady Sgt 60
Braun PO M. R. 22
Breckon WC A. A. N. 6, 11–12, 15, 22, 26, 166
Breckon Sgt 36
Brewster J. 99
Bright A/Cdr N. H. 133, 166, 167
Broadbent WC R. 79, 82–3, 84, 97, 98, 100, 101, 103, 215
Broady Sgt 72
Brook LAC E. A. 92
Brooking FL K. 177
Brooks WO J. S. 15–16
Brown FS A. 101
Brown FO A. E. 157
Brown PO F. B. 168
Brunton FO G. 126
Buck FO P. J. O. 83
Buckley GC M. W. 6, 7, 23, 30, 37
Buckley PO T. 114, 116
Burke PO E. L. 116, 214
Burley PO A. W. 101, 215
Burridge Sgt P. L. 49, 50
Burrill Sgt F. 63
Burton FS R. 107
Byrne FS M. J. 59–60

Callaghan Sgt R. P. 60
Callanan FO M. R. 179, 180, 181
Callander Sgt E. 36, 44, 46
Campbell GC A. P. 136
Campion WO P. 88, 91
Candish A. A. 164
Carling Sgt P. 34
Carter PO C. W. P. 54
Carter FO G. 191, 192
Carter Sgt J. W. 18
Carter FL M. A. 56, 64
Chalken FO G. 145
Chalmers FS H. E. 154
Chambers Sgt F. 153
Chapman LAC C. 144, 145
Chapman N. 138
Checketts WC J. M. 167

Chuter Sgt E. R. 25
Climie SL J. K. 49, 50
Clouston GC A. E. 166
Cochrane AVM R. A. 68
Cohen SL R. J. 7
Coleman FO W. H. 7, 11, 12, 14, 15, 18, 22
Collett SL W. J. 18
Collins FO J. N. 7, 9, 10, 12, 14, 15, 16
Colville Sgt 50
Conibear Sgt D. H. 43
Connors LAC T. 96
Connors FO 165
Cooke Capt C. B. 2
Cooksley FS B. L. 99, 214
Cookson FL 92
Corder PO G. I. L. 5
Corrin Sgt H. R. 46
Cottrell Sgt F. 215
Cowell FO J. 117
Cox FS T. 155
Cox LAC 144
Crankshaw FS K. A. 64
Craven Sgt 31
Crawford PO M. 177
Crompton SL 67
Crooks AM D. M. 173
Cross LAC L. 145
Crowther Sgt F. E. W. 106, 214
Cuming FO G. 130
Cunningham FO W. 121–2
Curr Sgt F. L. 66
Curry SL G. W. 30, 36, 37–8
Curtis FL R. M. 19, 23

Dallinson SL D. 177
Dalzell Sgt H. J. 82
Dance FO A. T. 95
Davenport-Brown FL W. 29, 213
Davey Sgt C. R. 67, 78
Davies LAC R. 144
Davies FO S. G. 148, 154
Daws Sgt D. 111
Day WO D. R. 8, 10–11, 12, 23
Debenham FS K. F. 82
DeLabouchere-Sparling PO F. 15–16
Demirs M. 144
Dennis SL J. M. 116
Denton WC F. H. 19, 20, 22, 51, 56
Denton PO J. 177
Dick FL J. N. 184
Dickinson FS C. 108
Dixon Sgt J. 59
Dobson FO G. 191
Dobson P. 105
Donaldson Sgt A. 25
Donaldson SL W. R. 180, 181
Drew A. 64
Donnelly FL B. 180
Drummond FS M. K. P. 124

Dunmall FS K. J. 73

Easton S/Off J. M. 105
Eddy FO C. 78, 97, 99
Edwards FO J. L. 97
Edwards Cpl L. 144, 145
Egglestone FO R. 149
Ehrle Maj W. 63
Eisenhower Gen D. D. 117
Elliott FO R. 160
English Sgt H. M. 25
Enright FO T. E. 168
Erlich Sgt 107
Evans Sgt T. 41
Evenden FS 158
Ewing SL R. L. 177, 179–180, 182

Fairfax WO 88
Falcon-Scott Sgt C. 25
Falconer PO A. J. 28
Farmer LAC W. 145
Farquahar Sgt J. 20, 22
Farr FS W. 132, 215
Fauvel FL S. F. 117
Fell Sgt M. 157
Finn FO D. L. 174, 176
Fitzwater Sgt H. 133
Flamank R. 147
Flavell FL B. 177
Fleming FO J. A. 126
Fletcher FL 34–35
Florence D. 32
Ford FO T. A. 133, 138, 146
Fotheringham Sgt R. E. 43
Fountain PO C. N. 51–2, 56
Fowler SL G. E. 74, 83
Franklin Sgt B. A. 73
Fraser FS M. F. G. 53
Freeman WC T. O. 7, 15, 18, 22, 43, 44, 62
French PO R. O. 76, 98, 101, 213

Gale Sgt J. W. 108
Galletly FS A. 132
Gannaway Sgt E. G. 31
Garnett FO J. D. 165
Garrett Sgt J. M. 25
Gartrell SL E. C. 166
Gayfer FL K. A. 181
Gibbs Sgt J. 11
Gibson PO 116
Gilbert FL 23
Gilbertson FS J. E. 59–60
Gill FO T. F. 28, 32
Gillard A/Cdr I. M. 173
Gilmour Sgt D. 28
Gittings Sgt S. 95
Goldsmith GC G. J. W. 184–5, 187
Gordon Sgt W. 64
Gordon FO R. 137
Gore Sgt L. J. 32, 36

247

Gorman Sgt R. 63
Gow PO 22
Graas J. D. M. 73
Grainger Sgt E. 79
Grant Sgt J. S. 104–5
Greenaway FO A. B. 7
Grey E. 107
Groves PO K. H. G. 82
Grubb WC J. D. 91, 114
Gunn SL G. 118–9, 131
Gunning PO 49, 56
Gwyn-Williams Sgt 43

Halsall LAC W. 145
Hamerton FO H. R. 67, 68, 191, 213
Hannan FL L. 147
Hanson FL C. M. 173
Harkness PO D. J. 10, 11, 18
Harris Sir A. T. 53, 76–7, 97, 99, 103, 110, 126, 133, 161
Harris A. J. 93–4
Harris Sgt F. M. 112, 116–7
Hayter Sgt L. A. 19, 22
Hazel WO F. 165
Healey FS T. 86
Hemingway J. 146
Hemsley Sgt W. A. C. 85, 100, 108, 214
Henley FS D. C. 104–5
Henstock FL R. 177, 179, 180
Heperi T. 107
Herron FO R. 115
Higgins S. 107
Highet WC G. R. B. 169, 173, 192
Hill FS L. 117
Histed PO R. 177
Hockaday FS N. J. N. 54, 57, 58, 62, 63, 66, 213
Hockey PO L. P. R. 16
Hodgson FO D. W. 129
Holdsworth Sgt K. 144
Holmes S. 142
Hooper FS N. 157
Horgan FL D. G. G. 106–7, 215
Hosie WC J. S. 184
Howell E. 121
Howell F. W. 42
Howie Cdr F. O. 11
Howse SL G. 188
Hubbard Maj T. O'B. 2
Hughes Sgt 11
Hugill Sgt H. J. 68
Humphries PO A. L. 128, 133, 137, 153, 156–7
Hunt FL R. 110–111
Hunter FL C. C. 6
Hunter PO R. C. A. 43
Hurse WO A. W. 118

Isett A/Cdr L. 62

Jackson PO G. 177
James SL A. 24
James FS A. G. 144, 145
Jarman SL E. G. D. 51, 56
Jeffrey Sgt R. 160
Jeffs FL 168
Jelly PO E. A. 22
Johnson PO D. M. 53
Johnson PO J. E. 46
Johnstone J. 148
Joll SL J. 84, 92, 98, 103, 215
Jones FL K. 155
Jordan W. 62, 152

Kay AVM C. E. 6, 7, 9, 10, 12, 15, 18, 22, 24, 42–3, 49, 168
Kaye FS I. 85, 100, 215
Kearns FL R. S. D. 53, 59, 60
Keightley FL H. B. 191
Kelly SL C. W. B. 56, 60–1, 64
Kempthorne Maj J. P. 112
Kennedy FO G. 121
Kereamo Sgt W. L. 107
Kerr FS G. J. 110
Kidd Sgt R. M. 74
King FL P. 188, 191
Kingsmill PO A. 177
Kinross FS C. J. 110
Kinvig WC F. M. 182
Kitchen SL P. J. R. 50
Klitscher FS L. 155
Knight Cpl C. B. G. 7
Knox FS A. 106, 204
Kuthe Ltn W. 59

Laming FO D. 188
Lammas FS M. 115
Lane WC G. A. 83
Langridge AC1 J. H. 7
Lanham WC J. W. 185, 187
Larney FL G. K. 10, 19, 22, 24
Lattelier Cpl J. 144, 145
Laud SL R. H. 83, 91, 97
Lawton Sgt L. A. 31, 41–3, 48, 87
Lax Sgt G. 90
Leck Cpl J. H. 86–7
Leslie WC R. J. A. 115, 133, 137, 138, 147
Lewis Sgt A. 60
Lewis FO J. 96
Lewis Sgt J. W. 43
Lloyd PO G. 177
Lockie PO B. 177
Logan PO C. C. P. 99, 101, 106, 214
Long A. 148
Lowe FO D. C. 78, 82, 101
Lowe PO H. 63
Lowe FO J. H. 5
Lucas SL F. J. 6, 22, 23, 24, 36
Ludlow-Hewitt ACM Sir E. 9

Mackay Capt C. W. 2
Macpherson Sgt C. V. 59
McAllister SL C. C. 184
McArthur PO D. H. 22, 23, 213
McCardle PO C. 118
McCartin FO P. L. 137
McCaskill PO D. G. 82
McConnel Sgt 69
McCullough PO J. 74, 213
McDevitt Sgt P. W. 118
McElligott FL D. P. 130–131, 132, 136, 138
McGlasham SL D. C. 7, 8
McIntosh FO J. A. 138
McIvor FS 97
McKee A/Cdr A. 79
McKenna AC1 H. 145
McKenzie FO C. A. G. 117–8
McLaughlan Sgt I. J. 50, 51, 52, 56, 60
McMahon FO D. 173
McNamara PO B. P. 26
McSherry Sgt E. 31
Maaka Sgt I. 107
Machin Sgt 49
Mahood FS T. S. 51
Manawaiti Sgt M. 67
Manns FS J. 111
Mansell AC1 R. 145
Martin PO G. 30, 34, 36, 37–8, 43–4, 46
Martyn FL L. 139
Mason Sgt W. 41
Mason Sgt W. 121–2
Matetich Sgt J. A. 48
Max WC R. D. 103, 113, 115
Mayhill FO R. D. 126, 128, 129
Megson SL C. A. 114–5, 122
Menzies FO I. R. 105
Meurer Hpt M. 126
Merton AM W. 172
Metcalf PO R. 177
Middleton Sgt H. J. 108
Miles FO H. 101
Millar FO A. M. 118–9, 131
Millett Sgt L. A. 45
Milne FO K. 168
Milne FO N. 188
Minchin Sgt M. 34
Minikin Sgt F. T. 43
Mitchell PO B. 177
Mitchell FO C. 191
Mitchell G. 149, 153
Mitchell Sgt 94
Mitchell WC V. 62, 64, 73
Modin GC C. O. F. 140
Monk Sgt H. 129
Monk Sgt W. 129
Monk PO W. J. 57
Moore LAC 144
Moore Sgt K. 147
Morgan FL T. A. M. 165
Moriarty FL D. J. 118, 119–121

Morris FL D. 90–1, 139–140, 142
Morrison FL I. G. 7
Morton PO 22, 25
Moseley WO P. 100, 214
Moss A/Cdr H. G. 172, 174, 176, 180, 184
Moss Sgt R. 78
Mumby Sgt T. L. 11
Murdoch PO G. E. 57
Murphy FS J. W. 117, 121–2
Murphy FS T. J. 86, 90
Myers Capt F. 180
Myers FL J. W. A. 121

Nairne FS C. 124
Nelson FL B. 191
Neville AVM P. 173–4, 176
Newbold Sgt L. 69
Newman PO H. D. 25
Newman LAC P. 96
Newton WC R. J. 51, 138, 149, 152
Nicol WO H. 99, 100, 214
Nicol PO T. Mc. 51, 56
Noden Sgt 22
Nola Sgt D. L. 31

O'Callaghan FS E. D. 126, 128
Ogden Sgt J. 99, 214
Ohlson WO E. 155
Olsen FO L. 177
Olson WC E. G. 51, 61, 62, 68
Old FS W. J. 111–2
Ongar LAC M. 96
Ormerod FL C. F. 112–3
Orrock Sgt A. 20, 22
Osborn FL A. F. A. 63
Osborne H. 95

Paine PO H. H. V. 168
Parata Sgt M. T. 107
Parker FS N. 71, 72
Parkes FS W. R. 63
Parnham Sgt J. F. M. 50
Parone FS J. 107
Parsons FL E. G. 156, 215
Parsons Sgt L. P. 104–5
Pawnell LAC W. 50
Pearson Cpl 94
Pearson FS R. 149
Peel PO R. N. 19
Pennel FO P. 173
Penrose LAC R. 145
Perkins ACW1 A. 145
Perrott FO W. R. 98
Peterson Sgt L. E. 48
Petre Maj H. A. 1, 2
Philip Sgt B. 57–8, 63, 213
Philips FS J. 144
Pinka PO C. M. H. 107
Plummer FL J. 133, 137, 157
Pomfret LAC F. 145

Poole Sgt J. 104
Popperwell FO D. L. 67
Powell GC J. A. 62, 63
Pownell FO C. A. 22
Preston Sgt R. E. 72
Prichard FO D. L. 28, 29, 32, 38, 46, 213
Prichard WO P. F. 165
Pugh WC A. G. E. 51–2, 60

Quelch Sgt R. N. 104–5

Rahui (Raharuhi) Sgt R. H. 71
Randle FS J. R. 108
Rankin PO A. 99, 214
Rangiuaia FS W. 107
Ravan FS R. L. 87–9
Read Sgt T. R. 7, 8
Rees FO H. 137
Rees PO W. J. 29, 43, 46
Reid Sgt I. L. 39
Renskers Lt 144
Reynolds LAC F. 145
Reynolds Capt F. G. B. 2
Reynolds FS R. C. 63, 64, 213
Rhodes Sgt G. W. 66
Rhodes FL P. M. 168, 177
Richardson FO N. 173
Richards LAC J. 94–5
Richards Sgt J. L. 79
Richmond FO S. H. 135–6, 137–8
Riddle PO M. 144
Riddler Sgt S. W. 107
Ridley Maj C. A. 2
Ritchie Sgt A. H. 25
Roberts FS E. J. 101, 214
Roberts PO H. A. 45, 213
Robertson FO E. 135–6
Robertson LAC 144, 145
Robinson SL S. 182
Rodgers SL J. R. 152
Roe Sgt K. 46
Rose FL 152
Ross Maj C. S. 2
Rothschild FS C. 79
Rothwell FL G. M. 74–5, 78–9, 213
Rough SL H. L. 5
Rousseau FS H. E. 91
Rovira LAC P. 144, 145
Rowberry FS C. 113
Ruane FS M. 124
Rudd SL C. W. 168, 177
Russell FO H. 155
Russell FL 173
Rutherford Sgt A. W. 60
Rutledge Maj T. F. 2
Ryder Cpl 8

Sadgrove FO D. 149, 155
Sampson FS G. 79
Sanders FO G. 68, 70
Sanderson PO R. M. 19, 23
Sandys FO J. F. K. 50
Sansoucy Sgt J. G. F. 97–8
Saunders Sgt A. 31, 44, 213
Sawrey-Cookson WC R. 49, 51
Saxelby PO C. K. 24
Schnaufer Maj H-W. 126
Scollay FL W. J. R. 67, 84, 191
Scott WO A. 72, 119–121
Scott WC C. W. 28, 29, 35, 39
Scott WO F. 112, 116
Scott FO J. H. 128, 137
Scott AC1 W. 145
Scott Sgt 99
Scrimshaw SL J. A. 174, 179, 180, 181
Sedunary PO A. 98, 213
Selley Cpl S. 144, 145
Sewell FS S. 136
Shalfoon Sgt C. J. 66
Sharp WC F. S. 188, 191
Sharpe WO R. W. 72–3
Sharpe Sgt S. 91
Sharpe Sgt T. S. 2
Shepherd PO I. J. 59
Shepherd SL R. G. 24
Simich SL G. R. 29, 31, 166
Simpson FO A. D. 136–7, 146, 147–8, 152
Sims FL L. O. 113, 115, 126
Sisley FL D. B. 165
Skinner LAC A. 144, 145
Slater PO A. R. 50–1
Smith Sgt B. 36–7
Smith FS I. H. R. 105
Smith LAC R. 50
Smith PO R. J. 53, 57
Smith PO T. M. 58
Smyth Sgt W. M. 46
Solbe SL E. V. G. 28
Southward FO K. 133
Southwell SL J. M. 31
Spencer SWO 91
Spooner M. 107
Stanley-Hunt SL B. 176–7, 184
Staples FL A. 166
Staples WO N. 158, 159
Steven Sgt W. D. 7, 8
Stevenson FL D. M. 156, 157, 162–3, 164
Stokes PO C. 46
Stokes Sgt G. 105
Stokes FL N. A. D. 124
Stott FO F. E. 126, 215
Streeter Sgt D. F. 43, 44
Streib Col W. 126
Strong GC D. M. 172
Symons PO J. H. 83

Tanner FL C. 188
Tanner FO G. 168
Teaika PO I. T. 107, 214, 215
Thomas PO A. J. 108

Thomas Sgt R. 99
Thompson FL D. 90
Thompson J. 28
Thompson FO 179
Thompson PO 91
Thompson Sgt 38, 44
Thorne ACW1 J. 145
Thorpe Sgt G. 15
Tietjens Sgt S. M. 85
Titcomb Sgt W. A. 60
Tod WO R. D. 79
Tod WO R. E. 79
Tolley PO A. G. 82
Tomlins G. 107
Tompsett Sgt J. B. 36
Trent WC L. H.(VC) 103
Trevethen FO 157–8
Trott FL L. G. 67, 72, 191
Trott PO N. 117, 213
Tucker SL A. F. 166–7
Tunley FL 174
Turnbull Sgt J. W. 85
Turnbull FO M. 168
Turnbull Cpl 144
Turner FO G. 100
Tweed H. 148

Vale Sgt L. R. 85
Viccars Sgt E. C. 99
Voice Sgt J. S. 73

Waerea Sgt T. 107, 214
Wainwright Sgt A. E. 51
Waite FL N. E. 155, 156
Walker A/Cdr A. 172
Walker Sgt J. 111
Walker FO P. T. 181
Waller PO P. 177
Wallis Barnes 6
Walsh LAC J. 96
Walsh WO J. A. 79
Walters FO J. 116
Walters Sgt V. 67
Ward FO I. 121
Ward Sgt J. A.(VC) 41–3, 46, 48, 87, 192
Wasse GC M. 84
Watson Sgt H. 48
Watson SL R. 112

Watson FO S. S. M. 16
Watts WC H. 5–6
Watts WC J. E. 165
Waugh Sgt B. 157–8
Waugh Rev R. 157
Webb LAC L. 145
Webb Sgt J. 79
Weeks FS L. H. 92–3, 94
Wehi T. 107
Whinnery FO M. T. 177
White LAC J. T. 7, 8
White Sgt L. A. 18
White FS O. H. 101, 104
White FS T. M. 154
White Sgt 22
Whitehead FS W. D. 85, 105, 214
Widdowson SL R. P. 28, 31, 41–3, 46, 213
Wiffen Cpl W. 144, 145
Wilkins Cpl H. C. 95
Williams PO E. E. 73, 121
Williams Sgt E. P. 7, 8, 11, 18
Williams PO H. C. 85, 100, 108, 214
Williams LAC J. 144
Williams FO N. 7, 11, 12, 14, 18, 213
Williams Sgt R. A. 74
Williams WO S. 177, 179
Williams FO W. M. 7, 11, 12, 23
Williamson SL N. A. 118
Williamson LAC P. 145
Willis Sgt E. C. 25
Wilson J. 144
Wilson FO N. C. B. 95
Wilmshurst Sgt J. C. 56, 58
Wolley-Dod Lt C. F. 2
Wood FO J. 157
Wood Cpl R. 144, 145
Woodhouse FO R. 156
Woolford PO J. 177
Woolterton LAC F. 142–4
Worsdale Sgt E. 69
Wright SL J. L. 55, 63, 64, 213, 215
Wyatt GC M. 84–5, 97, 98–9, 101, 103
Wyman LAC C. 144

Young LAC W. 144

Zillwood PO A. H. R. 79
Zinzan FS V. J. 107